# ACTION TV

From re-runs of 'classics' like *The Avengers* or *Starsky and Hutch,* to current series influenced by the genre like *Buffy the Vampire Slayer,* the action series is enjoying a revival at the centre of prime-time TV. Yet relatively little attention has been paid to the specific history, nature and appeal of the action series, and its place in popular culture, past and present.

*Action TV* explores the historical development of this TV genre from its genesis in the 1950s, its place within the history of television institutions and systems of production, its relationship to other genres, and its position within broader social, cultural and political contexts. Articles include:

- Of leather suits and kinky boots: *The Avengers*, style and popular culture
- 'Who loves ya, baby?': *Kojak*, action and the great society
- 'A lone crusader in the dangerous world': heroics of science and technology in *Knight Rider*
- Angels in chains? Feminism, femininity and consumer culture in *Charlie's Angels*
- 'Who's the cat that won't cop out?': Black masculinity in American action shows of the sixties and seventies

Contributors: Paul Cobley, Anna Gough-Yates, Joke Hermes, Leon Hunt, Andy Medhurst, Nickianne Moody, Marc O'Day, Bill Osgerby, Elaine Pennicott, Martin Pumphrey, Roger Sabin, John Storey, Yvonne Tasker, Marianne Wells and Elizabeth Withey.

**Bill Osgerby** is Senior Lecturer in Cultural Studies at the University of North London. He is the author of *Youth in Britain Since 1945* (1998) and *Playboys in Paradise: Masculinity, Youth and the Rise of American Leisure-Style* (2001). **Anna Gough-Yates** lectures in the Sociology of Culture and Communication at Brunel University. She is the author of *Understanding Women's Magazines* (Routledge 2001).

# ACTION TV

## Tough-Guys,
## Smooth Operators
## and Foxy Chicks

*Edited by Bill Osgerby*
*and Anna Gough-Yates*

Routledge
London and New York

First published 2001
by Routledge
11 New Fetter Lane, London EC4P 4EE

Simultaneously published in the USA and Canada
by Routledge
29 West 35th Street, New York, NY 10001

*Routledge is an imprint of the Taylor & Francis Group*

Typeset in Garamond by Bookcraft Ltd, Stroud, Gloucestershire
Printed and bound in Great Britain by Biddles Ltd, Guildford
and King's Lynn

*British Library Cataloguing in Publication Data*
A catalogue record for this book is available from the British Library

*Library of Congress Cataloging in Publication Data*
Action TV: tough guys, smooth operators and foxy chicks /
edited by Bill Osgerby and Anna Gough-Yates.
p. cm
Includes bibiographical references and index.
1. Adventure television programs–History and criticsim.    I. Osgerby, Bill.
II. Gough-Yates, Anna, 1968–
PN1992.8.A317 A27 2001
791.45'6–DC21                                        2001031656

ISBN 0–415–22621–X
ISBN 0–415–22620–1 (hbk)

# CONTENTS

# FIGURES

# CONTRIBUTORS

**Paul Cobley** is Senior Lecturer in Communications at London Guildhall University and the author of a number of books, including *The American Thriller: Generic Innovation and Social Change in the 1970s*. After watching the pilot episode of Kojak he became a revolutionary socialist. For a while.

**Anna Gough-Yates** lectures in the Sociology of Culture and Communication at Brunel University and is the author of *Understanding Women's Magazines: Publishing, Markets and Readerships* (Routledge, 2001). Anna has never fulfilled her ambition to be Charlie's seventh Angel, but her love of shopping has helped her to become an accomplished lifestyle feminist.

**Joke Hermes** is still somewhat mystified at how her long-standing high regard for low culture earned her a degree in political science (with a study of cheap romance novels) and a doctorate in the social sciences (with a thesis on reading women's magazines). These days she is overjoyed to teach television studies at the University of Amsterdam.

**Leon Hunt** is a lecturer in Film and TV Studies at Brunel University. He is the author of *British Low Culture: From Safari Suits to Sexploitation* (Routledge, 1998), a study of 1970s popular culture. He has never driven a Ford Capri, but did in his youth experiment with recreational aftershaves.

**Andy Medhurst** teaches Media and Cultural Studies at the University of Sussex. He is the co-editor of *Lesbian and Gay Studies: A Critical Introduction* (Cassell, 1997), the author of *A National Joke: Popular Comedy and English Cultural Identities* (Routledge, 2001), and has published widely on issues of culture and identity. He has, at best, a semi-detached relationship to action TV.

**Nickianne Moody** is Principal Lecturer in Media and Cultural Studies at Liverpool John Moores University. She is convenor for the Association for Research in Popular Fictions, edits the ARPF journal *Diegesis*, and has edited a number of collections. Research interests include an oral history of the Boots Booklovers' Library, turn of the century British bestsellers and a cultural history of animal welfare in Britain.

**Marc O'Day** is Associate Dean of Social Studies at Suffolk College, Ipswich, where he teaches on the Media Studies programme. He has published essays on fiction, film and television. As a youngster he studied at a customized desk topped by an Emma Peel collage. His academic shortcomings may be due to this.

**Bill Osgerby** still harbours hopes of one day becoming a millionaire playboy and international trouble-shooter. In the meantime he teaches Cultural Studies at the University of North London and writes about British and American cultural history. His publications include *Youth in Britain Since 1945* (Blackwell, 1998) and *Playboys in Paradise: Masculinity, Youth and Leisure-Style in Modern America* (Berg, 2001).

**Elaine Pennicott** is currently working on her PhD dealing with constructions of black masculinity and popular literature. She has just slapped her husband for reminding her that she sported an afro and a stripy beige tanktop in the 1970s.

**Martin Pumphrey** is part-time Senior Lecturer at Cheltenham and Gloucester College of Higher Education and is presently working on a film audience project. Before Ché, Bobby and Jean-Luc, it was the luminous presence of Cheyenne that first taught him the possibility of resistance.

**Roger Sabin** is the author of several books, including *Comics, Comix and Graphic Novels* (Phaidon), and lectures at Central St Martins College of Art and Design, London. The main problem with 'Starsky cardies', he recalls, was that they had a belt, which could be used to tie the wearer to bus hand-rails, lamp-posts, moving trains, etc.

**John Storey** is Professor of Cultural Studies and Director of the Centre for Research in Media and Cultural Studies, University of Sunderland. His publications include *Cultural Studies and the Study of Popular Culture* (1996), *What is Cultural Studies: A Reader* (1996), *Cultural Theory and Popular Culture: A Reader* (1998), *Cultural Consumption and Everyday Life* (1999), *Cultural Theory and Popular Culture: An Introduction* (2000).

**Yvonne Tasker** is Senior Lecturer in Film Studies at the University of East Anglia. She is the author of *Working Girls* (1998) and *Spectacular Bodies* (1993) and is currently working on a collection of new essays on action and adventure cinema.

**Marianne Wells** is a Lecturer in Media Studies at the University of East London, where she is completing a doctorate on 1950s film and fan cultures. During the Decade of Big Hair she found Stefanie Powers' *Hart to Hart* coiffure particularly inspiring.

**Elizabeth Withey** writes about the confluence of music and television. Since her earliest memories blend, in equal parts, the theme to the original *Star Trek* series, Grieg's Piano Concerto, and the flashing black and white television images of John F. Kennedy's assassination, it is no great wonder that she has been led astray into the study of television music.

# ACKNOWLEDGEMENTS

The editors would like to thank the following for permission to use stills and illustrations: Pictorial Press Ltd for stills of *The Untouchables, Miami Vice, Knight Rider, Charlie's Angels, Shaft, Bonanza* and *The Avengers*; Tony Gale/Pictorial Press Ltd for stills of *The Persuaders!* and *Department 'S'*; Polygram/Pictorial Press Ltd for stills of *The Saint* and *Jason King*; Sunstills/Pictorial Press Ltd for the still of *Kojak*; Pan Macmillan for the *Call For The Saint* book cover; Paramount Pictures/BFI Films: Stills Posters and Designs for the still of *Mission: Impossible*; TV Times/BFI Films: Stills Posters and Designs for the illustration of *Kung Fu*; London Weekend Television/BFI Films: Stills Posters and Designs for the still of *The Professionals*; RCA Records for the cover of *More Music from 'Peter Gunn'*; Grafton's for their catalogue illustration; TV Publications for the cover of *TV Crimebusters Annual*; Polystyle Publications for images from *Target*; K.K. Publications for the comic covers of *The Avengers, Mission: Impossible* and *The Man From U.N.C.L.E.*; and Decca Records for the cover of *Themes for Secret Agents*. Every effort has been made to obtain permission to reproduce the photographs and illustrations. If any proper acknowledgement has not been made, we invite copyright holders to inform us of this oversight.

We would also like to thank: Rebecca Barden and Alistair Daniel at Routledge; the anonymous readers of the proposal for this book; colleagues, and former colleagues at the University of North London (especially Lyn Thomas) and the University of East London; Mike Richards and library staff at Southampton Institute; Charlotte Bush; Tony Gale; Veronica Hitchcock; and our friends and families.

# INTRODUCTION
## Getting into gear with the action TV series

*Bill Osgerby and Anna Gough-Yates*

### FAST CARS, BLAZING GUNS …
### AND A WELL-TAILORED WARDROBE

They were tough. They were resourceful. They never shrank from a challenge. And, to cap it all, they also had a finely-tuned sense of style and panache. They were the heroes and heroines of the profusion of television 'action' series that emerged as a staple ingredient in popular television schedules from the late 1950s through to the end of the 1970s. During the 1980s their numbers thinned, but in the 1990s they were back, firmly on top of the situation. The likes of *The Saint, The Avengers, Charlie's Angels* and *The Professionals* remained a force to be reckoned with. Wherever there was a hot-spot or a tight corner they were there, setting the world to rights and restoring order – but always with a particular élan and sharpness of attitude. Their blend of irrepressible resilience and keen-nerved *savoir-faire* proved a winning combination and, into a new century, audiences still enjoyed their world of fast-paced adventure and sexy flourish. Moreover, their ranks had been joined by a new generation of action TV champions. The times, the places and the motivations were certainly different – undoubtedly nuanced and re-configured – yet there was no doubting their 'action TV' lineage. They may have been vampire-slayers in suburban high-schools, FBI investigators on the trail of an extra-terrestrial conspiracy, or Amazonian warriors in a neo-classical fantasy world – but they were still the nieces and nephews of the original action TV line-up. The tell-tale trademarks were unmistakable. There was the same robust vigour, the same slick dynamism and the same stylish flair.

For some, the recent success of series such as *The X-Files* (1993–), *Xena: Warrior Princess* (1995–) and *Buffy the Vampire Slayer* (1997–) marks a new era of exchange and flow between popular television genres. Indeed, *The X-Files'* fusion of pulp science fiction, police procedural drama and suspense thriller, and *Buffy's* ironic blending of gothic horror and teen melodrama, seem to testify especially strongly to a new permeability of generic boundaries in popular TV.[1] At the same time, however, Mulder and Scully, Buffy and their ilk can be seen as the latest variants in a longer-established TV genre – the action series. The technical conventions, iconography and visual style of programmes such as *The X-Files* and *Buffy* can all be seen as indebted to a

1

heritage of action-oriented TV narratives that first took shape in the 1950s and 1960s. Even in its earliest incarnations, moreover, the action TV genre displayed traits of fluidity and malleability – informed by, and crossing-over with, close generic cousins such as the Western series and the police drama.

Popular genres are often difficult to define with exactitude and precision. The intertextuality and dynamism endemic to popular culture makes it hard to determine decisively where one genre ends and another begins. Yet cultural producers and consumers both tend to operate with notions of identifiable generic forms – textual typologies associated with particular narrative formulae, symbolic codes and technical conventions. In the field of television, for example, concepts of genre not only influence the strategies through which programmers compose their schedules, but also organize and marshal audience expectations, viewers relating to shows in terms of their existing experience of programme style and format. The roots of the action series as a recognizable television genre lie in the 1950s and developments in American TV programming. As the network giants competed for mass audiences, the imperatives of economic efficiency and profitability impelled a move away from live drama towards the filmed serial format. Initially, the existing popularity of the Western with cinema audiences ensured that Western-based TV series had a steel grip over 1950s prime-time. By the end of the decade, however, the declining popularity of the Western as a generic form made way for newcomers. *Dragnet* (1951–58) and *The Untouchables* (1959–63) led a growing battalion of crime and hard-boiled detective series, though also taking shape were shows that appropriated both the Western's spectacle of adventure and the crime show's narrative structure of enigma and resolution, combining these with an accentuated emphasis on style and image.

In America, *Peter Gunn* (1958–61) was an early precursor to the action series format, its central character's mixture of two-fisted machismo and suave cosmopolitanism being set off by the show's fast-paced visual style and slick jazz soundtrack. During the 1960s and 1970s the networks' attempts to capture lucrative 'niche' advertising markets laid the way for the heyday of the action series – a burgeoning number of prime-time shows featuring detectives, spies and trouble-shooters whose chic and exciting lifestyles were designed to appeal to audiences of young, affluent and style-conscious consumers. In Britain, too, the action series came of age in the 1960s. Shows such as *The Saint* (1962–69) and *The Avengers* (1961–69) were indicative of commercial programmers' attempts to develop products that could not only guarantee high domestic ratings, but would also deliver profitable returns in an increasingly trans-national television market.

In the past ten years the academic study of television has undergone considerable expansion, though the action-oriented series formula (using recurring protagonists in discrete episodes, as opposed to the 'soap opera' *serial* format of diverse characters in a continuing narrative) remains relatively uncharted. In one of the first of the few analyses of the development of the action TV series, David Buxton interprets the history of the genre in terms of three thematic strands – the human nature series, the pop series and the police series (Buxton, 1990). The golden age of the human nature series, Buxton argues, was the 1950s. Anthology drama series such as *Alfred Hitchcock*

*Presents* (1955–65), *The Twilight Zone* (1959–65) and *The Outer Limits* (1963–65), together with Westerns such as *Gunsmoke* (1955–75) and the early crime show *The Untouchables* (1959–63) represented, according to Buxton, attempts to explore and illustrate timeless truths about human nature in the context of a rapidly changing society. Buxton also includes 1960s series such as *The FBI* (1965–74), *Star Trek* (1966–69) and *The Invaders* (1967–68) within the 'human nature' category, but argues that their search for moral certitudes was increasingly anachronistic in an age of intensified consumerism. Instead, the pop series came into its own, Buxton citing *The Avengers* as the quintessential 'pop' show through its self-conscious modernism and integration within the world of design and consumer aesthetics. The pop show was attuned to the accelerating rhythms of the consumer society – socially mobile and sexually liberated, it side-stepped the 'yardstick of social reality' as it waged war against conservative traditionalism and trumpeted 'the victory of consumption and pleasure values over those of the moralistic stuffed shirts' (Buxton, 1990: 108). But by the mid-1970s, Buxton argues, the moment of pop had faded and the period's deepening political and ideological crisis found its corollary in a new breed of 'realistically' gritty police series.[2] The new police genre included shows with inflections of both conservatism (*Ironside* (1967–75), *Hawaii Five-O* (1968–80)) and liberalism (*The Mod Squad* (1968–73), *Starsky and Hutch* (1975–79)), but they shared a common theme of tough cops who worked within the system yet were individualistic and unorthodox in their fight against crime and social disorder.

Buxton's account is informed and insightful – indeed, his ideas are referenced and drawn upon by many of the contributors to this volume. Nevertheless, while providing an impressive semiotic analysis of his examples, Buxton gives only limited attention to their institutional and production backgrounds, while their place within wider social, economic and political contexts is also fairly underdeveloped. The three-fold thematic classification is also something of a blunt instrument, tending to under-state the elements of continuity and overlap between those series placed in the different categories. By implication, this analysis also presents a somewhat pessimistic history of the genre. While 1960s 'pop' series such as *The Avengers* are treated as the harbingers of an exciting, style-conscious modernism, these aesthetic sensibilities are seen as losing their meaningful edge as they became integrated into common-sense expectations of popular television, advertising, fashion and music in a 'postmodern' media universe dominated by image and surface. As Buxton ruefully puts it, it is 'impossible to recreate the excitement provoked by the emergence of a modern consumer society, the seduction exercised by pleasingly designed objects, the over-whelming presence of a greater aesthetic sensibility' (Buxton, 1990: 117). In contrast, many of the contributors to this volume insist on the enduring significance of the action series as a genre that is not only constituent in wider patterns of social, economic and political change, but which provides audiences with an avenue through which to articulate meaningful cultural responses to these patterns of change. Indeed, a theme which recurs through several of the chapters is that action series can be seen as a kind of 'lifestyle' television in the way they combine fantasies of thrilling adventure with mythologies of affluence and consumption. In these terms, programmes like *The*

*Saint*, *Charlie's Angels*, *The Professionals* and their more recent incarnations are understood as being embedded in a matrix of commodity relations in which spaces exist for a broad variety of differently gendered and 'racialized' identities.

While contemporary action TV series such as *The X-Files* and *Buffy the Vampire Slayer* are attracting growing interest from media and cultural theorists, their forebears remain relatively ignored by the academy.[3] Aside from Buxton's survey, the earlier action canon has been accorded scant critical attention.[4] The contributions to this volume attempt to address this omission. It is a timely intervention. The action TV series of the 1960s, 1970s and 1980s developed visual styles, narrative conventions and symbolic iconographies that continue to influence and inform the contemporary crop of action vehicles. Additionally, many of the earlier shows have, themselves, seen a new lease of life with a plethora of cable and satellite channel re-runs and a proliferation of video and DVD sales. Film-makers and TV producers, meanwhile, have plundered the vaults of 'action' television to develop new versions of 'classic' action shows for both the big and small screen. Indeed, the action TV series continues to register its popular appeal across a wide range of cultural forms and texts – from soundtrack CD compilations to toys, T-shirts and all manner of merchandise and ephemera.

This volume brings together a broad-ranging and inter-disciplinary range of specially commissioned chapters to analyse the nature and development of the action TV series from its genesis in the 1950s, through to its re-articulation in contemporary popular culture. In doing so, the collection aims to move beyond a simple focus on the formal properties of 'the text', instead contextualizing the action series within its economic and cultural conditions of production, circulation and consumption. Attention, therefore, is given both to the changing nature and organization of the television industry, and to the wider patterns of social, economic and political relations which provided the context for the rise, and subsequent development of, the action genre. Consideration is also given to issues of reception, several contributors exploring the experiences of different audience groups, understanding these issues within the wider field of debates regarding the relationship between popular culture, identity and consumption.

## TOUGH-GUYS, SMOOTH OPERATORS AND FOXY CHICKS

*Action TV* is divided into four sections, each considering a specific facet of the action genre. Many of the chapters in each section choose to focus on a specific television programme and the selection will inevitably disappoint some readers. The idiosyncrasies of *The Prisoner*, for example, are touched on by several authors, though the series is not considered in systematic depth. Nor are the camp hijinks of *Batman*, *The Man from U.N.C.L.E.* or *Get Smart* accorded detailed consideration. Other favourites may also have fallen through the net – for example *The Rockford Files*, *The Six Million Dollar Man* and even *David Cassidy: Man Under Cover* (we kid you not). Yet each author uses their subject as an avenue through which to explore a collection of themes and issues germane to the action genre as a whole, offering the reader perspectives through which to reflect critically on the action TV phenomenon in its entirety.

The book's first section, 'Situating the action TV series', deals with the emergence and development of the action series from the 1950s through to the 1980s, situating the genre within its wider institutional and historical context. As Tony Bennett (1990: 3–5) cogently argues, the analysis of popular texts always demands recognition of the nexus of economic, technological and institutional relationships that regulate their production. In the first chapter, therefore, the volume's editors, together with Marianne Wells, examine the changing face of the action series as a product of shifts within the American and British television industries since the 1950s. Yet the formal characteristics and narrative themes of the action genre are not solely the outcome of institutional and industrial contingencies. Action series have also condensed and articulated a wide range of contemporary cultural preoccupations and the subsequent chapters in Part I consider the ways that specific series functioned as sites for a many-faceted range of cultural transactions.

In '"So *you're* the famous Simon Templar"': *The Saint*, masculinity and consumption in the early 1960s', Bill Osgerby considers the action series as constituent in the broader transformation of constructions of masculinity during the 1960s, programmes such as *The Saint* serving as a forum in which a male consumerist personality was increasingly legitimized and eulogized in a masculine embrace of hedonistic consumption. In the 1970s it was the detective series *Kojak*, Paul Cobley argues, that was especially significant as a response to patterns of social and political change. In '"Who loves ya, baby?"': *Kojak*, action and the great society', Cobley shows how prevalent discourses around racism, economic inequality, criminal justice and civic corruption were fundamental influences on the development of *Kojak*, the programme appealing to audiences on the basis of its verisimilitude and uncompromising social realism. In '"A lone crusader in the dangerous world": Heroics of science and technology in *Knight Rider*', Nickianne Moody highlights *Knight Rider* as a programme which engaged with the cultural impact of the momentous technological developments of the 1980s, Moody positioning the series as a relatively ambivalent and open-ended response to the growing penetration of daily life by computer technology and its attendant discourses.

None of the chapters in Part I present action series as straightforward embodiments or 'reflections' of the historical context in which they were produced. Instead, the emphasis is on highlighting the ways these texts actively operated to explain and interpret the world, deploying particular textual codes and techniques to suggest particular ways of making sense of cultural relations and patterns of social change.

As Charlotte Brunsdon observes, the rise of new social movements which engage politically with the concepts of 'race', class, sexuality and gender has, since the mid-1970s, generated a body of work within television studies that asks questions about the representation of particular social groups within TV texts, analysing how these representations are configured and how they circulate within a variety of viewing contexts (1998: 108).[5] This volume's second section, 'Representation and cultural politics in the action TV series', contributes to that tradition, examining the various representations of gender and 'race' within popular action series of the 1970s and 1980s.

In 'Angels in chains? Feminism, femininity and consumer culture in *Charlie's*

*Angels*', Anna Gough-Yates relates the representations of femininity in *Charlie's Angels* to the wider cultural dialogue surrounding feminism in the United States during the 1970s. Though many contemporary critics deplored the show as intrinsically 'anti-feminist', Gough-Yates contends that the programme could successfully appeal to audiences of women through its codification of feminism as a pleasurable 'lifestyle' choice rather than a confrontational political programme. Elaine Pennicott's '"Who's the cat that won't cop out?": Black masculinity in American action series of the sixties and seventies' discusses the action show as an arena for the construction of black masculinity, arguing that the representations of black men in texts such as *Mission: Impossible*, *Shaft* and *The Mod Squad* can be situated in a long history of racist stereotypes that have functioned to regulate the social presence of African–American men in the United States. The focus on masculinity and issues of 'race' and representation is continued by Yvonne Tasker in her chapter '*Kung Fu*: re-orienting the television Western'. Tasker explores the action-Western hybrid *Kung Fu* and its attempts to combine the generic conventions of the Western with representations of Asian culture, philosophy and martial arts. During the 1970s, Tasker argues, the basis of the show's appeal lay in the way it engaged with American perceptions of the East, harnessing these to an emergent counter-cultural vision of a new, non-violent form of masculinity which carefully negotiated the fine line between pacifism and confrontation. The final chapter of Part II, Leon Hunt's '"Drop everything … including your pants!": *The Professionals* and "hard" action TV', explores a peculiarly British articulation of masculinity in the early 1980s. Hunt situates *The Professionals* within the context of the growth of Far Right politics in Britain, conservative discourses about 'law and order', 'the permissive society' and the 'British malaise' being played out through the programme's constructions of 'hard' masculinity. Yet Hunt argues that within the series these discourses often collided with other, more liberal, agendas of the early 1980s – making *The Professionals* a more 'open' text than previous commentators have implied.

The contributions in the third section of the book, 'Audiences reading and re-reading the action TV series' address viewers' consumption of action shows. The relationship between audiences and texts has long been a concern for media theorists, the 1980s seeing a move away from crude models of popular texts as a homogeneous stream of dominant ideological meanings (the audience being regarded, by implication, as passive and undiscriminating) towards a recognition of the polysemic potential of the text. In these terms, audiences were increasingly seen as actively engaging with television programmes, analysing and discussing texts and sometimes producing 'resistant' or 'oppositional' readings. This notion of the 'active' audience has informed a large amount of recent work on audiences within the realm of television studies, yet it is an approach that should be tempered by the recognition that texts often work to channel audience readings in particular directions, 'polysemy' always existing within a distinct set of boundaries and parameters.[6]

The authors in this section explore the audience/text dynamic with an emphasis on the diversity of interpretations made by audiences as they decode action series in the context of their everyday lives. In 'The games we play(ed): TV Westerns, memory and masculinity', Martin Pumphrey examines the experience of the action Western genre as it was used, and reused, by the boys (now mature men) who grew up with it. Pumphrey points to the enduring constructions of masculinity within this genre and investigates the ways in which these (now unfashionable) constructions of gender identity are negotiated by the programmes' former viewers. Tony Curtis and Roger Moore may seem an unlikely pair of feminist icons, but in '*The Persuaders!*: A girl's best friends' Joke Hermes argues that, despite the fiercely heterosexual and masculine assumptions characteristic of the action genre, it is possible to read programmes such as *The Persuaders!* in terms of a 'duplicitous masculinity' which (in some contexts) can serve rather than oppose the development of a feminist consciousness. Andy Medhurst concludes Part III with 'King and queen: Interpreting sexual identity in *Jason King*'. Exploring the ambiguous and contradictory constructions of masculinity within the series *Jason King*, Medhurst reads the 'foppery' of the central character as a paradoxical and polymorphous performance of gender that was capable of appealing to a wide range of contrasting audiences. Medhurst also considers the place of *Jason King* within the recent vogue for kitsch retro-culture, arguing that while practices of pastiche may open up space for critiques of outdated attitudes to sexuality, 'race' and gender, these same practices are often fuelled by misogyny and a smug class elitism.

The final section, 'The cultural circulation of the action TV series', continues Medhurst's interest in the way the codes, conventions and iconography of action TV series have cut across a range of different media forms, 'spilling out' beyond the parameters of the original texts. According to John Fiske (1987) television is situated within two separate, but related, economies – the financial and the cultural. In the financial field TV programmes initially circulate as a material commodity, bought by networks and distributors, subsequently producing an audience that can itself be sold as a commodity to advertisers and sponsors. From this point onwards, however, programmes move into the cultural economy where they become bearers of meaning and pleasure for their consumers. Fiske's account is contentious and can be challenged for the level of autonomy it accords to audiences' consumption of media forms.[7] Yet the notion of a cultural economy can be a useful concept and, in different ways, the contributions to Part IV of this volume all consider action TV series as symbolic forms that have circulated well beyond their original textual and temporal 'locations' of production.

The opening chapter, Elizabeth Withey's 'TV gets jazzed: The evolution of action TV theme music', examines the symbolic capacities of action series music scores and the way their intertextual references served to strengthen the profile of the action idiom as a distinct genre. Roger Sabin's 'The comics connection: Low culture meets even lower culture' also highlights the intertextual dimensions to action narratives. Sabin shows how the visual codes and conventions of action TV filtered into the world of children's comics, their adaptation of action shows offering young audiences a kind of 'portable TV' that provided access to an exciting, 'adult' television culture. In 'Of leather suits and kinky boots: *The Avengers*, style and popular culture', Marc O'Day explores the ways in which the imagery, style and symbolism developed in *The Avengers* has permeated the universe of fashion, pop and consumer culture since the 1960s. O'Day argues that the 'stylish' and 'stylized' aesthetic that originally established *The Avengers'* iconic status is also the basis for its longevity, allowing the show to circulate in (to use Fiske's terms) both the financial and the cultural economies of the postmodern era. The anthology's final chapter further explores the significatory meanings of the original action TV canon in contemporary culture. John Storey's 'The sixties in the nineties: Pastiche or hyperconsciousness?' discusses a range of critical work dealing with postmodern culture and its attempts to explain the recycling of action TV series from the 1960s and 1970s within contemporary culture. Storey argues that, whilst some theorists would explain this phenomenon in terms of a 'postmodern' collapse of traditional boundaries between high and low culture, commerce and art, such explanations fail to grasp the new meanings generated through the processes of cultural recycling. Rather than marking a random, and uniquely 'postmodern', cannibalization of the past, Storey suggests that the re-animation of 'the sixties in the nineties' was constituent in a longer tradition of appropriation, bricolage and intertextuality that has characterized the history of popular culture – practices in which media forms are commandeered and mobilized in meaningful ways throughout the different lived cultures of everyday life.

*Action TV*, therefore, draws together a collection of diverse and contrasting approaches to the study of the action TV formula. They all, however, share an interest in relating the historical and the particular to broader theories about the nature of television and its place within the wider social landscape. Collectively, they show that the emergence and development of a television genre can only be understood through reference to forces that operate both inside *and* outside the institutions of textual production. This book considers the complex relationships between these forces and the various ways they have worked to shape the form, content and audience interpretation of action TV series.

## NOTES

1  For discussion of *The X-Files'* fusion of genres see Vitaris (1995). Analysis of *Buffy the Vampire Slayer* as a postmodern text can be found in Owen (1999).
2  In a British context, a similar relationship between discourses around escalating crime and the emergence of 'tough cop' series such as *The Sweeney* (1975–82) was highlighted by both Buscombe (1976) and Dennington and Tulloch (1976).
3  Braun (2000), Lavery, Hague and Cartwright (eds) (1996) and Owen (1999) all exemplify the growing critical interest in the contemporary action TV series.
4  Though there exist several thorough-going studies of individual programmes. Especially noteworthy, for example, are Miller's analysis of *The Avengers* (1997) and Vahimagi's volume dealing with *The Untouchables* (1998).
5  See, for example, D'Acci (1994), Feuer (1995) and Jhally and Lewis (1992).
6  Adept critiques of 'active' audience theory are elaborated by Cobley (1994), Curran (1990) and Seaman (1992).
7  For critiques of notions of the 'creativity' of consumer practice, see McGuigan (1992) and Silverstone (1994).

## REFERENCES

Bennett, T. (ed.) (1990) *Popular Fiction: Technology, Ideology, Production, Reading*, London: Routledge.

Braun, B. (2000) '*The X-Files* and *Buffy the Vampire Slayer*: The Ambiguity of Evil in Supernatural Representations', *Journal of Popular Film and Television*, Vol. 28, No. 2.

Brunsdon, C. (1998) 'What is the "Television" of Television Studies?', in C. Geraghty and D. Lusted (eds), *The Television Studies Book*, London: Arnold.

Buscombe, E. (1976) 'The Sweeney – Better Than Nothing', *Screen Education*, 20: 66–69.

Buxton, D. (1990) *From The Avengers to Miami Vice: Form and Ideology in Television Series*, Manchester: Manchester University Press.

Cobley, P. (1994) 'Throwing Out the Baby: Populism and Active Audience Theory', *Media, Culture and Society*, Vol. 16, No. 4: 677–88.

Curran, J. (1990) 'The New Revisionism in Mass Communication', *European Journal of Communication*, Vol. 4, Nos. 2/3: 135–64.

D'Acci, J. (1994) *Defining Women: Television and the Case of Cagney and Lacey*, Chapel Hill: University of North Carolina Press.

Dennington, J. and Tulloch, J. (1976) 'Cops, Consensus and Ideology', *Screen Education*, 20: 37–46.

Feuer, J. (1995) *Seeing Through the Eighties: Television and Reaganism*, London: BFI.

Fiske, J. (1987) *Television Culture*, London: Methuen.

Jhally, S. and Lewis, Justin (1992) *Enlightened Racism: The Cosby Show, Audiences, and the Myth of the American Dream*, Boulder, CO: Westview Press.

Lavery, D., Hague, A. and Cartwright, M. (eds) (1996) *Deny All Knowledge: Reading the X-Files*, London: Faber and Faber.

McGuigan, J. (1992) *Cultural Populism*, London: Routledge.

Miller, T. (1997) *The Avengers*, London: BFI.

Owen, A. S. (1999) 'Vampires, Postmodernity, and Postfeminism: *Buffy the Vampire Slayer*', *Journal of Popular Film and Television*, Vol. 27, No. 2.

Seaman, W.R. (1992) 'Active Audience Theory: Pointless Populism', *Media, Culture and Society*, Vol. 14, No. 2: 301–11.

Silverstone, R. (1994) *Television and Everyday Life*, London: Routledge.

Vahimagi, T. (1998) *The Untouchables*, London: BFI.

Vitaris, P. (1995) 'The X-Files', special issue of *Cinefantastique*, October.

# PART I

# SITUATING THE ACTION TV SERIES

# 1

# THE BUSINESS OF ACTION

## Television history and the development of the action TV series

*Bill Osgerby, Anna Gough-Yates and Marianne Wells*

### 'MONEY TALKS – BULLSHIT WALKS': THE COMMERCIAL IMPERATIVES OF TV PRODUCTION

Whether we're watching re-runs of the stylish, fashion-forward classic *The Avengers*, marvelling at the precise choreography of car chases on *Starsky and Hutch*, or tuning in for the latest (re-)incarnation of *Randall and Hopkirk (Deceased)*, the presence of the action series in prime-time TV programming is something we now take for granted. To date, most analyses of action series have tended to focus on their roles in social reproduction, viewing them as part of a larger '(unconscious) ideological project' promoted through the media industries (Buxton, 1990: 14). This chapter, however, seeks to understand the emergence of the action series in relation to the shifting political economy of television industries in post-war Britain and North America. Though attention to industry organization and business imperatives are often side-lined in analyses of popular television in favour of textual deconstruction and audience-based research, attention to the dynamics of political economy is essential if we are to fully engage with the ways that the moment of production inscribes itself into the meanings of cultural products (see McGuigan, 1992). Thus, as Douglas Kellner observes (1997: 18), analyses of specific historical, political and economic contexts and relations can illuminate our understanding of texts, enabling us to consider not only the sign value and audience responses to cultural products, but also the role of cultural producers in determining their form and content.

Whilst the organizational forms of British and American television broadcasting possess their own, quite distinct, histories of development, interesting parallels can be drawn between the ways in which pressures for commercial success have affected the types of programming developed in both countries. The American 'network' structure has, from the outset, placed advertising and profit at its core. And in Britain too, despite the (increasingly precarious) survival of a public service ethos, since the mid-1950s television organizations have had to compete with one another for audiences and market share. On both sides of the Atlantic, therefore, competitive pressures have resulted in a more or less constant drive to improve productivity whilst simultaneously reducing capital outlay – this leading to an emphasis on styles of programming that are both cost-effective and easily reproducible. The drive for cost-efficiency has often entailed trends towards standardization with, for example, the repeated use of teams of production and technical personnel (see Abercrombie, 1996: 121–27). The search for reproducibility, meanwhile, has meant that television, like all modern commercial industries, has tended towards industrialized methods of production in which more expensive 'craft' and 'artisanal' modes of authorship have been marginalized in favour of the economies of the production line. In TV programming this has been exemplified, above all, by the rise of the serial format. Whilst the serial was not necessarily the most 'natural' vehicle for the presentation of fiction narratives (indeed, the single play was the prevalent televisual story-telling device until the mid-1950s), economic contingencies ensured the place of the series format as an enduring mainstay of modern TV schedules.

Nevertheless, while the television industry has strived to develop increasingly efficient modes of production, the TV audience represents a market notable for its variability. As Todd Gitlin has observed in relation to American prime-time programming, whilst television executives may use audience research as a 'guide' to the market for their products, in reality the 'audience' remains an abstraction that defies attempts at scientific predictability. As a consequence, the TV industry 'tries to develop ways to control both supply and demand – supply in order to smooth its workings, demand so that it remains of a sort the networks are set up to satisfy' (Gitlin, 1983: 14). In order to manage market volatility, therefore, television executives prioritize the hunt for shows that will attract significant audiences on a regular basis – and thus generate substantial revenues from advertisers. Hence failure to deliver a solid audience share invariably spells a programme's demise. Indeed, in America it is not unknown for a 'failing' series to be axed mid-season to make way for a show with potential to pull higher ratings. In business parlance, therefore, 'money talks' – and failing TV shows 'walk'.

The commercial imperatives of television production can also militate against innovation in styles of TV programming. Unconventional shows are often considered risky ventures – even if they feature well-known actors or established scriptwriters. More often, the television industry attempts to duplicate successful output through a variety of means. The simplest and cheapest is to show repeats of popular shows (or 'classic re-runs', to use a hackneyed TV euphemism). Alternatively, producers may attempt to imitate the formula of an already successful programme on another channel or network, or produce a 'spin-off' of a popular series – using established characters, performers and producers in a new variant of a show with a proven track-record. All of these strategies have impacted upon the production of television fictions since the 1950s and – as we shall see – action and adventure series have been key players in the television industry's search for audiences and profitability.

## 'SAME TIME, SAME CHANNEL … ': AMERICAN TV NETWORKS AND THE RISE OF THE SERIES FORMAT

The origins of the TV serial format – recurring characters in discrete episodes – lie in 1950s America.[1] During the early 1950s American TV fiction was largely the preserve of 'one-off' plays and dramas, as many as thirteen 'playhouse' slots appearing on American TV by 1955, sponsored by large corporations (including household names like Philco, Revlon, Goodyear and Motorola) who hoped to gain prestige from linking themselves to 'quality' plays transmitted live, week after week, on network TV. The unpredictability of live production, however, could prove troublesome, while sponsors were sometimes unhappy with dramas like Paddy Chayefsky's *Marty* (1953) and J.P. Miller's *Days of Wine and Roses* (1958) – whose depictions of the turbulence and tragedy of human emotions seemed to jar disconcertingly with sponsors' cheery advertising slogans. Increasingly, therefore, sponsors sought more attractive modes of promotion and looked to Hollywood film companies for more up-beat alternatives.

Unsure of their new rival, film companies initially stood aloof from the developing television industry. By the mid-1950s, however, Hollywood had been forced to acknowledge the decline of traditional cinema audiences and began to see television not as a competitor but as a propitious new market. In 1955 Warner Brothers led the way, recycling their film sets and old footage in three 'film series' – *Casablanca, King's Row* and *Cheyenne* – produced for the ABC network's 1955–56 season. Other film companies followed suit (MCA, for example, developed a similar alliance with NBC), David Buxton (1990: 22) observing how Hollywood increasingly eschewed 'B' film production in favour of the greater profitability of series geared to television. Hollywood's growing presence in TV schedules further accelerated the move away from live drama. Whereas 'one-off' plays required the construction of unique sets for each programme, film companies found series production much more economical – allowing the regular reuse of existing studio facilities, actors and locations. The rise of the episodic series was also galvanized by the collapse of the big money quiz show during the late 1950s. Amid embarrassing scandals about the widespread coaching of contestants, TV networks quickly dropped prime-time quizzes from their schedules and scrambled to find alternatives that would fill the empty slots.

Corporate sponsors initially wielded significant power in the production of TV series, able to ensure that a show adopted a 'mood' and 'style' they believed was appropriate to the promotion of their products. By the late 1950s, however, the networks' greater financial stability allowed them to wrestle greater control of their prime-time schedules. All three major networks – NBC, CBS and ABC – pulled away from traditional practices in which advertisers were licensed as the sole sponsor of a prime-time show, in favour of a network-licensing of programmes in which shows were sold to advertisers on a multiple-sponsorship basis. Greater control of their schedules also allowed the networks to win concessions from producers in the form of a greater share of profits from syndication and merchandising. Indeed, such revenues were increasing appreciably as off-network re-runs and international syndication began to open up profitable new markets. During the late 1950s and early 1960s, therefore, the American TV networks possessed both the power and the incentive to work with production companies in the development of continuous and repeatable prime-time shows. Such programmes could not only guarantee advertisers regular audiences for the same weekly slot, but also maximized profitability through their reuse of facilities and personnel and their saleability across a variety of expanding national and international markets. These commercial dynamics, therefore, sealed the fate of the live broadcast play and by the late 1950s nine out of the ten most popular network shows were episodic series (Wheen, 1985: 106–7).

It was the Western that first blazed a trail into the TV series format. Adapting the Western genre to television allowed film companies not only to capitalize on the existing cinematic popularity of Western themes, but also to exploit their existing sets, props and other production resources. During the early 1950s, Western series such as *The Gene Autry Show* (1950–56), *The Lone Ranger* (1949–57) and *The Roy Rogers Show* (1951–57) had already proved popular. These programmes, however, were pitched at a largely juvenile market and it was only in 1955 that producers and network executives introduced new 'adult' Westerns in a bid to attract valuable advertising from manufacturers of household products and cigarettes. CBS's *Gunsmoke* (1955–75) was a huge success, though ABC dominated the field with *The Life and Legend of Wyatt Earp* (1955–61) and *Cheyenne* (1955–63) – the action-based series coming to represent ABC's key weapon as it battled for ratings against its larger network rivals. By 1956 the number of networked Western series had grown to seven, increasing to twenty-eight in the 1958–59 TV season, by which time they accounted for 26 per cent of total network prime-time (Boddy, 1998: 119–20).

By the beginning of the 1960s, however, the sun was setting on the TV Western. By the 1962–63 season only ten Westerns were to be found in prime-time schedules and the genre never recovered its former glories. Public anxieties about the social impact of television violence may have played some part in this decline, though William Boddy (1998: 131) argues that this issue was of relatively marginal importance compared to audience exhaustion with a genre which had reached saturation point. In place of the Western the networks looked for new themes to re-invigorate audience interest. Anthology drama series such as *Alfred Hitchcock Presents* (1955–65), *The Twilight Zone* (1959–65) and *The Outer Limits* (1963–65) proved popular, as did a wave of medical dramas such as *Ben Casey* (1961–66) and *Dr Kildare* (1961–66). Above all, though, it was the contemporary crime and action series that stepped into the Western's boots – crime shows such as *Dragnet* (1951–58) and *The Untouchables* (1959–63) (see Figure 1.1) representing early overtures to the developing action genre in which the Western series' episodic format, narrative structure and adventure-oriented storylines were transplanted to a modern day context.

A key figure in the early development of the crime/action series was Quinn Martin. Initially a writer and producer for both Ziv Studios and Desilu, Martin worked on the original pilot of *The Untouchables* and subsequently steered the series to success with ABC. Leaving *The Untouchables* after the first two series, Martin formed his own production company, QM Productions. QM's first series, *The New Breed* (1961–62), was another popular police series for ABC and initiated a long and mutually beneficial relationship which saw QM furnish the network with numerous ratings-grabbing crime/action series, including *The Fugitive* (1963–67), *The F.B.I.* (1965–74) and *The Invaders* (1967–68). These series saw Martin develop a programme model that became an established convention of action TV. QM's segmented programme format began with a scene-setting teaser, followed by an explanatory introduction (often

*Figure 1.1*  Eliot Ness (Robert Stack), Gangbuster star of *The Untouchables* (1959–63).

delivered by a narrator), then a body broken into four acts and finally a concluding epilogue (again, often using an off-screen narrator) to explain or offer words of wisdom on the episode's action. Indeed, this format became such a familiar convention that it was parodied consummately in the 1982 sitcom, *Police Squad.*

QM Productions also developed a reputation for rugged realism. In a bid for authenticity, Martin moved his productions from the sound-stage to outdoor locations and filmed night-time scenes at night (rather than simply darkening film footage, as was then common). Along with their penchant for gritty realism, QM's police shows articulated avowedly conservative ideals of rectitude, conformity and tough policing. Indeed, Martin was quite candid in his esteem for authority and an uncompromising enforcement of the law (see Newcomb and Alley: 1983). By the early 1960s, however, Quinn Martin's cultural conservatism was beginning to look out of step with the climate of the times. Instead, American producers began to develop action shows whose trademarks were dynamic characters and a slick stylishness that drew influence from developments in television programming on the other side of the Atlantic.

## 'I AM NOT HERE TO EDUCATE THE PUBLIC. I AM HERE TO ENTERTAIN THEM': LEW GRADE, ITC AND THE RISE OF BRITISH ACTION TV

As in America, the development of British TV series production and programming was influenced by commercial pressures. The early years of British television were dominated by the BBC's mandarin traditions of 'public service' paternalism which construed education and information as broadcasting's prime functions – with entertainment coming a lowly second (see Scannell, 1990: 11–29). With a monopolistic control of TV broadcasting and funded by an annual licence fee, the BBC was insulated from market competition and so faced limited pressure towards the development of new programme formats to maintain audience appeal. In 1955, however, the BBC's TV monopoly was breached by a Conservative government aspiring to 'Set the People Free' (as their 1951 election slogan put it), dismantling many economic controls and emphasizing notions of 'consumer choice' in a free market. A token of this commitment was the launch of ITV – a second, commercially-based, television channel.[2] Financed through the sale of advertising, the economic survival of commercial television rested on its ability to attract large audiences, hence its schedules laid an accent more squarely (compared to the BBC) on entertainment and the development of more populist styles of programming capable of generating and maintaining high viewing figures.

In this new approach to programming Lew Grade stood as a figure of crucial importance. Flamboyant and charismatic, Grade emerged as one of the most powerful men in commercial television through his ownership of the Independent Television Corporation (ITC), a leading TV production company, and his major stake in Associated Television (ATV – one of the first commercial broadcasting franchises). Despite high start-up costs, ATV soon found its financial feet and by 1957 was turning a healthy profit. This success was due, in large part, to the style of programming initiated by Grade. Proclaiming 'I am not here to educate the public. I am here to entertain them' (Grade, cited in Archer and Nicholls, 1998: 48), Grade's schedules were weighted towards light entertainment, the media tycoon happily taking credit for changing 'the whole complexion of television' through his introduction of programmes traditionally disdained by the BBC – soap operas, game shows, comedies, adventure series and American serial imports such as *Dragnet* (Grade, 1988: 196).

A shrewd judge of public taste, Grade was willing to bankroll any project he felt had potential for popular appeal and he scored notable success in Britain with variety shows such as *Sunday Night at the London Palladium*. Yet Grade was not content with his dominant role in British television and nursed aspirations to a worldwide entertainment empire. Casting a particular eye to the potentially lucrative American market, Grade set up his own television distribution company (ITC Inc.) in the United States and, by 1959, was spending several days a month in New York negotiating with the major TV networks (Grade 1988: 203).

ITC's first international breakthrough was the 1955 series *The Adventures of Robin Hood.*[3] In an early instance of transatlantic economic co-operation, the series was made in conjunction with the American company, Sapphire Films, and purchased in America by the CBS network. Profits from *Robin Hood* paved the way for further historically-based adventure exports – *The Buccaneers* (1956) and *The Adventures of Sir Lancelot* (1957) being networked in America on CBS and NBC respectively. ITC also enjoyed international success with a succession of science fiction puppet (and then live action) shows produced by Gerry and Sylvia Anderson – 1961's *Super Car* being followed by *Fireball XL5, Stingray, Thunderbirds, Captain Scarlet, Joe 90* and, later, *UFO* and *Space 1999.*[4]

ITC's success both at home and abroad prompted an ATV takeover in 1958, ITC becoming a wholly-owned subsidiary. Its coffers boosted, three years later ITC was able to acquire and refurbish British National Studios to create the best-equipped television centre in Britain. Renamed Elstree, these studios provided the centre of production for ITC's most successful programmes throughout the 1960s and 1970s. And in the foreground of this success was a stable of action series. With its recipe of thrilling exploits and racy glamour, the action genre promised wide appeal and so spearheaded Grade's campaign to capture overseas TV markets. Beginning in 1960 with *Danger Man*, ITC embarked on a succession of fast-paced action and adventure series. The 1960s, for example, saw the launch of programmes such as *Man of the World* (1962), *The Saint* (1962–69), *The Baron* (1966), *Man in a Suitcase* (1967), *The Prisoner* (1967–68), *The Champions* (1968), *Department 'S'* (1969) and *Randall and Hopkirk (Deceased)* (1969). The early 1970s, meanwhile, saw the release of *The Persuaders!* and *Jason King* (both 1971), *The Protectors* (1972) and *The Zoo Gang* (1973).[5] Not all of these series, by any means, enjoyed huge international success, but overall Grade's sales tactics proved astute – the TV mogul becoming responsible for more than $100 million of television sales to the US, his export achievements winning him official recognition with the award of a knighthood in 1969, followed by his investiture as Lord Grade in Prime Minister Harold Wilson's resignation honours of 1976.[6]

The emergence of the action series as a recognizable TV genre, therefore, was at least partly indebted to changes in the structure and organization of the American and

British television industries. Moreover, the degree to which action series were geared to international sales was a benchmark of developing trends towards the globalization of the finance and marketing of popular cultural texts – trends which steadily came to dominate the economics of media production. This transnational dimension to the development of the action genre, moreover, problematizes crude notions of 'cultural imperialism' in the analysis of international media communication.

The thesis of 'cultural imperialism' originally took shape in Herbert Schiller's 1969 book, *Mass Communication and American Empire*, Schiller presenting American capitalism as achieving a position of global domination through its export of media texts – especially films and TV series – which helped generate markets for US businesses and advertisers. Notions of linear and unilateral processes of cultural 'domination', however, have now been challenged by audience-based research (for example, that produced by Liebes and Katz (1996)) which suggests a relative openness to the meanings of transnational cultural texts that allows for a range of divergent (in some respects even 'resistant') readings by indigenous audiences. Concepts of a one-way 'cultural imperialism', meanwhile, have been further undermined by changing patterns of media production and distribution which, since the 1970s, have seen developing nations emerge as major players in the media environment – Western control increasingly cross-cut by an elaborate syncopation of non-Western communication systems and business interests. Even in the late 1950s and early 1960s, however, media flows were more complex than allowed for by crude models of 'imperialism'. The international circulation of cultural texts such as Lew Grade's action TV series, for example, undermines a simple, linear construction of American domination of popular media. Admittedly, British action exports such as *The Saint* and *The Avengers* can be seen, in some respects, as by-products of Americanization – the British media remaking and remarketing genres that had initially been imported from the States. Yet, as Jeffrey Miller (2000) argues, within a British cultural milieu these genres had been appropriated, re-interpreted and synthesized with cultural elements drawn from both Britain and continental Europe – the end-products being recognizable as distinctly 'British' cultural artefacts. In these terms, then, Miller argues it is possible to see British cultural imports as 'coming to occupy a space in the United States during the Eisenhower and Kennedy years perhaps not as large but in some ways just as significant as that occupied by American exports in Britain' (Miller, 2000: 13).

## 'THE YOUNG REBELS': NICHE MARKETS, DEMOGRAPHIC PROGRAMMING AND THE 'HIP' ACTION SERIES

The 1960s marked a peak in the power of the American network trinity. Dominating nearly every facet of the television industry, ABC, CBS and NBC effectively pulled the strings of local and regional TV stations, where failure to comply with the demands of the network supplier could lead to economic ruin – the network simply switching affiliation to a neighbouring independent. The networks also had a firm grip on the programme market – to the frustration of both independent producers and the major Hollywood studios, who were at the mercy of the network's programming whims. By the start of the 1970s, however, public unease and industry resentment combined to challenge the networks' hegemony (see Brown, 1998: 155–59). In 1970, after a long series of enquiries, the Federal Communications Commission (FCC) introduced a series of regulations designed to curb network control of TV production and programming time. The restructuring of the television industry that followed was a particular boon to the Hollywood studios and the independent producers. Given greater control over their shows, and able to sell re-runs of series to local syndication while new episodes were screened on the networks, it became possible for producers to garner huge profits from their products.[7] Syndication also began to prosper, with small distributors and independent producers now able to create shows for the programming slots opened up by the FCC's limitation of the networks' claims to prime time. This revolution in American television was also marked by a new emphasis on advertising demographics – the mass market that had underpinned the growth of American TV during the 1950s and 1960s increasingly eclipsed by programming strategies with an onus on 'niche markets' and audience segmentation.

Somewhat ironically, it was ABC that was best placed to steal the lead in the scramble for the most highly-prized segments of the American TV audience. During the era of mass markets and 'blanket' broadcasting, ABC was cursed by its reputation as the network with a largely young audience. With the new emphasis on market demographics, however, the same reputation became a huge asset – advertisers willing to pay twice as much (or more) for access to audiences in the 18–34 age bracket, a market regarded as especially fertile soil for the promotion of consumer goods (Brown, 1998: 158). By the early 1970s, therefore, ABC's star was in the ascendant. Better positioned than its two rivals to exploit the shift towards demographics, the network pressed forward with new programmes targeted at 'both teens and the six million dollar market of professionals and college students' (d'Acci, 1997: 80).

In Aaron Spelling ABC found an independent producer whose talents were ideally suited to the development of demographic programming. Spelling had won his TV spurs as a scriptwriter for the glut of Westerns and drama anthologies of the 1950s (Spelling, 1996: 23). In the 1960s, however, he made his name as a producer with *Burke's Law* (1962–66), a ritzy detective series which complemented ABC's growing retinue of action programmes. The action idiom also provided Spelling with his first foray into the field of niche-programming in the form of *Honey West* (1965–66). Produced, again, for ABC, *Honey West* was based around the exploits of a glamorous, female private eye and was intended to capitalize on an emergent market of the 'new single woman'. Lacklustre ratings, however, ensured that a second series never materialized. But Spelling bounced back – this time with an action series tailored to the prized youth audience. Working with co-producer Danny Thomas, Spelling came up with *The Mod Squad* (1968–72), a show that revolved around the adventures of a trio of hip, young undercover cops who worked as mavericks – outside the system though still committed to the ideals of law and order.

A hit with audiences, the success of *The Mod Squad* won Spelling a four-year contract from ABC, Spelling working with Leonard Goldberg (a former ABC executive) to create and develop programmes for the network (Condon and Hofstede, 2000: 4).

The popularity of *The Mod Squad* also ensured a legion of imitators. The 1970/71 season saw ABC reinforce its assault on younger audiences with three more variations on *The Mod Squad* theme – *The Young Lawyers* (hip, young idealists in a 'Neighbourhood Law Office'); *Matt Lincoln* (hip, young idealists in a down-town psychiatric service) and *The Young Rebels* (hip, young idealists in … er … a guerrilla movement in eighteenth-century Pennsylvania). The same season also saw CBS imitate *The Mod Squad*'s proven avenue to healthy ratings and desirable demographics. Given its older audience base, CBS was especially jittery about losing its advertisers and hurriedly launched 'hip, young idealist' series of its own, with *The Interns* (set in a hospital) and *Storefront Lawyers* (set in a charitable legal practice).

The pitch for youth-angled social relevance, however, failed to deliver the kind of ratings that the networks had hoped for. With the exception of *The Mod Squad*, most of the 'hip' action shows of the early 1970s were flops and failed to survive their initial season. Les Brown (1971: 310) explained this failure as a consequence of audiences' growing disinterest in narratives underpinned by themes of earnest (albeit superficial) social concern. *The Mod Squad* was a hit with the desired audience segments, Brown argued, not because it had appropriated 'counter-cultural' idealism, but because it had combined hard-nosed law-enforcement with stylish non-conformity (Brown, 1971: 310). The same combination characterized a spate of charismatic but violent 'roguecop' movies of the early 1970s, and their success with young cinema-goers gave added impetus for the networks to develop TV equivalents. CBS were first on the scene with *Mannix* (1967–75), though NBC were also soon on the case with *Madigan* (1972–73), followed by *Serpico* (1976–77). Once again, however, it was the Spelling–ABC alliance that had the edge. In *Starsky and Hutch* (1975–79) Spelling came up with an action formula perfectly suited to the young, independently-minded audience segment – the show mixing up a heady cocktail of laid-back individualism and gritty realism in its premise of youthful, streetwise cops struggling against pimps, muggers and drug-dealers in a downbeat cityscape.

In Britain, the organization of the television industry did not allow for a pursuit of market demographics on anything approaching the same scale. The resilience of the BBC–ITV duopoly meant that British programmers were catering for a mass audience for a much longer period than their stateside peers. Nevertheless, a vogue for gritty realism and an appeal to younger audiences still gradually filtered into British TV. ITV, in particular, not only bought many American 'tough-action' imports, but also developed a home-grown version of the genre with *Special Branch* (1969–74), *The Sweeney* (1975–78) and *The Professionals* (1977–83). In contrast, while the BBC was happy to buy in *Starsky and Hutch* for its prime-time schedules, its public service credo meant it generally hung back from developing 'populist' action series of its own.[8] *Target* (1977–78) marked a relatively rare excursion by the BBC into the realm of squealing tyres and kicked-in doors – though complaints about the show's violence cut short its first season and ensured that the second was considerably diluted. Generally, the BBC felt more comfortable with staid, middle-aged and middle-brow detective fare such as *Shoestring* (1979–80) and *Bergerac* (1981–91).

## 'MTV COPS': POSTMODERNISM, POLITICAL ECONOMY AND THE ACTION SERIES

By the 1980s the 'realist' aesthetics that had prevailed in action TV programming were increasingly giving way to a renewed emphasis on image, style and surface. Partly, this can be interpreted as a response to the new cultural environment ushered in by shifts in the social, economic and political character of Western societies. Sweepingly labelled 'postmodernism', this new cultural milieu is usually seen as being characterized by pastiche, intertextuality and a blurring of traditional boundaries, together with a visual aesthetic that foregrounds 'look' and the self-conscious use of styling (see Ewen, 1988; Fiske, 1987; Kaplan, 1987). Along with the MTV cable channel and music videos, it was the 1980s variant of the action series that was most commonly highlighted as exemplifying the 'new' aesthetics of postmodernism.

*Hart to Hart* (1979–84) can be seen as an early prototype of the genus. Another Spelling production, *Hart to Hart* enthusiastically embraced a world of glamour and glitzy signifiers – its millionaire protagonists (who also dabbled as amateur detectives) basking in a world of luxurious mansions, corporate jets and exotic locations. Above all, however, it was *Miami Vice* (1984–89) that many theorists took as exemplifying postmodern cultural codes. Chronicling the adventures of two Florida drug-squad cops, *Miami Vice* eschewed elaborate storylines and complex characterizations in favour of 'constant visual and sound excitement … aggressive camera movements, "unnatural" colour schemes and mood music' (Buxton, 1990: 140). *Miami Vice* was 'all on the surface' (Grossberg, 1987: 29), its heroes designed to be 'MTV Cops' prowling (to) a beat of depthless signification (see Figure 1.2). For Kellner, *Miami Vice* virtually defined postmodern sensibilities with its 'aesthetic spectacles that are intense, fascinating, and seductive. … Image frequently takes over from narrative and the look and feel become primary, often relegating story-line to the background' (Kellner, 1992: 148–49). The series also seemed to be emblematic of the 'fluidity' of the postmodern self – the two detectives, Crockett and Tubbs, slipping seamlessly through various identities, suggesting that rather than being fixed and immutable, identity was a game of style.

In the wake of the success of *Miami Vice,* 'postmodern' traits also began to surface in other TV adventure series. *Moonlighting* (1985–89), for example, could be interpreted as quintessentially 'postmodern' in its use of quirky self-reflexivity and multiple narratives interwoven through fast-paced editing (Nelson, 1997: 74), while *Baywatch* (1989–) echoed *Miami Vice* in its use of lush visuals and deployment of stylized 'music video' segments. In Britain, too, series such as *Dempsey and Makepeace* (1985–86) could be interpreted as articulating a 'postmodern' aesthetic through a gift for 'depthlessness' and unstinting devotion to 'surface' qualities such as the foibles of mid-Atlantic fashion sense.

In the realm of action TV, however, the aesthetic styles hailed as dazzlingly 'postmodern' during the 1980s were hardly a startling departure from existing practice. As David Buxton argues, an effacement of traditional cultural categories and boundaries was already evident in the vogue for spy/action narratives during the

*Figure 1.2* 'MTV Cops' – Don Johnson and Philip Michael Thomas as Detectives
Crockett and Tubbs in *Miami Vice* (1984–89).

1960s – the spy's talent for masquerade and mobility representing an ideal vehicle for
the exploration of style, surface and 'look' (Buxton, 1990: 76). Indeed, a taste for disguise, mutability and a questioning of taken-for-granted assumptions was a marked
feature of many of the classic action series of the 1960s – most obviously, *The Prisoner*
(1967–68). An idiosyncratic blend of the esoteric and the stylish, *The Prisoner* was
Patrick McGoohan's personal *tour de force* – the actor not only conceiving, writing

and producing the series, but also directing some of the episodes and starring in the title role. Regarded by some as one of the most innovative TV series of the period, *The Prisoner* related the surreal adventures of an ex-spy – known only as 'Number Six' – abducted and marooned in a mysterious village where he struggles to outwit his captors. For McGoohan, *The Prisoner* was much more than a simple action series. It was intended to be an 'allegorical conundrum', an existentialist disquisition on the nature of individual freedom in an age of ever-increasing bureaucracy and social control ('I am not a number. I am a free man!').[9]

In its attempt to deal with intellectual themes in the context of a popular TV series, *The Prisoner* can be seen as anticipating the 'postmodern' erosion of traditional frontiers dividing 'high' and 'mass' culture. At the same time, however, the series was rooted in conservative assumptions. As Buxton observes, in its anxieties about growing media manipulation and cultural conformity, *The Prisoner* presents 'a gratifying world view for an educated middle class, enabling at once resistance to a commodified, mass-mediated society and a rejection of the mindless consumption habits of the "masses"' (1990: 96). In its format, then, *The Prisoner* may have effaced established polarities between 'high' and 'low' culture, yet its intellectual preoccupations were firmly grounded in conservative cultural pessimism. In contrast, a 1960s action series much closer to the playful spirit of 'postmodern' sensibilities was *The Avengers* (1961–69).

The original season of *The Avengers* was still rooted in the conventions of realist television. As Toby Miller (1997) has chronicled, it was the later (and more successful) seasons that took on the more rigorously 'pop' aesthetic style for which *The Avengers* became famous. Revelling in a taste for *à la mode* fashions and infatuated with a sense of the bizarre and the illusory, the series foregrounded design, surface and artifice (Buxton, 1990: 96). Yet whereas *The Prisoner* was underpinned by palpitations of cultural anxiety, *The Avengers'* impish exuberance, celebration of style and sense of camp irony, was much more in keeping with the aesthetic codes that critics would later label 'postmodern'.

Attempts to present 1980s action series as evidencing a uniquely 'postmodern' cultural complexion can also be challenged on other fronts. Critical discussion of 'postmodern television' has tended to see the aesthetics of these programmes as occupying 'a space beyond ideology, that of pure pleasure' (Buxton, 1990: 141). Yet, as Buxton points out, such a position is untenable since, for all their 'stylistic force', such programmes are 'no more or no less "ideological" than any other series ... [and] ... no more or no less "styled" than any other series' (1990: 142). Indeed, rather than seeing the 1980s TV fetish for image as stemming from a crisis in contemporary culture, some critics have interpreted the rise of 'postmodern' aesthetics in television as the consequence of shifts within the structure and organization of the industry.

According to John Caldwell (1995), the 'extreme self-consciousness of style' commonly attributed to 'postmodern' television is best explained not through reference to aesthetic or cultural influences, but through attention to the developing corporate crisis faced by American TV networks. In the 1979/80 season the three major networks still dominated prime-time viewing, accounting for a staggering 90 per cent share of the audience. As the 1980s progressed, however, the transformation of the TV industry took its toll on the networks' ratings. The advent of cable stations and the creation in 1986 of the first successful fourth network, Fox, steadily ate into the ratings of the 'big three' – their combined share of the prime-time audience slipping to less than 60 per cent by 1990 and slumping to as low as 50 per cent during the summer months. For Caldwell, the aesthetics of 'excessive style' were one way (along with downsizing and hostile takeovers) that the networks responded to this developing crisis – 'stylistic exhibitionism' representing a tactical device through which the networks sought to claw back their diminishing audience share.

Robin Nelson (1997) also reads 'postmodern' TV aesthetics as a symptom of shifts in industrial organization. Nelson highlights the combination of technological development and economic deregulation which, during the 1980s, laid the basis for a proliferation of television providers. The rise of cable and satellite stations, in particular, challenged the hegemony of traditional television broadcasters and intensified competition for an audience increasingly able to cruise through a multi-channel universe. According to Nelson a consequence of these transformations has been the decline of modernist narrative forms geared to a 'mass audience' and the rise of what he terms 'flexiad' dramas that 'play on differences between people in different microcultures' (Nelson, 1997: 96). With a narrative structure akin to those found in advertising, flexiad dramas offer viewers a range of 'new textual strategies' and a 'new affective order' (Nelson, 1997: 74). Their visual and aural imagery both intentionally constructs and reflects the perceived 'values and lifestyles' of discrete audience segments, while their loose narrative framework shapes these into a dramatic form that can simultaneously appeal to a wide and heterogeneous audience. These processes, moreover, have additionally seen 'serious' concerns with social issues increasingly displaced by 'a preference for the up-beat as an over-emphasis on style displaces content' (Nelson, 1997: 56–63). In Nelson's terms, then, 'postmodern' television's celebration of the sensual and surface style should be seen as a facet of broader political and economic tensions – 'postmodern' TV series such as *Miami Vice* and *Baywatch* being constituent in, and serving to legitimate, consumer capitalism's reverence for style and image.

## THE 'GLOBALIZED' ACTION SERIES

By the mid-1990s the future of the major American TV networks was looking decidedly less shaky. The FCC rulings that had tied the networks' hands in the realms of production and programming were repealed in 1993, allowing them a much freer rein in exploiting the new economic opportunities opened up by an expanding world media market. Throughout the 1990s communications industries increasingly operated on a global scale, processes of deregulation, technological development and industrial merger leading to a steady 'internationalization' of media ownership, production and distribution. According to Negrine and Papathanassopoulous (1990: 130), these shifts ushered in both an intensified commercial ethos within communications institutions and greater patterns of linkage between different media enterprises.

A striking feature of these developments has been the way that European, Japanese and other overseas business interests have bought into American media corporations (foreign investors, for example, acquiring American entertainment 'majors' such as Twentieth Century Fox, Columbia Pictures and CBS). The growth of international communications conglomerates, however, has not levelled the playing fields of global media production. As the hub of transnational media corporations, the United States still wields enormous power within the accelerated global flow of media texts. American dominance of international television is indicative – the United States being the world's largest exporter of TV programmes, a trade further augmented by the scale of its domestic TV market. Indeed, some American series producers find it relatively easy to cover their production costs from domestic sales and view export profits as extra 'gravy' on their staple income. The degree of economic stability that this affords also allows American TV producers to maintain high production values in their output, setting standards that producers in other countries often struggle to match. Many countries, therefore, find it more economical to import TV programmes from the United States than to produce them at home, while relatively few foreign imports find a home in American TV schedules.[10] In the 'integration' of 'transnational' media, therefore, inequalities of ownership, access and supply remain pronounced – as Vijay Menon rhetorically asks, 'how much a part of the global village is Asia?' (1993: 29).

Britain has been more successful than many countries in exporting television programmes to the United States. Even here, however, the cost differences between British television companies producing new programmes of their own and buying in American products are keenly felt. Indeed, an apparent decline in the number of British action shows since the 1980s may be partly a consequence of these economic circumstances – British producers finding it increasingly hard to compete against the high production values of American action series. Moreover, the final arrival of demographic programming in Britain has worked against, rather than in favour of, action–adventure genres. Rather than gearing itself to the tastes of brash, young consumers, the commercial drift in British terrestrial television has been towards courting the tastes of the comfortable middle class – a market especially attractive to many contemporary British advertisers. The tastes of such audiences are understood by television programmers to be suited not to fast-paced and stylish action packages, but to more prosaic 'aga saga' narratives set within reassuringly 'traditional' contexts. Hence the action series' proclivity for high-powered sports cars and racy nightclubs has given way to a world of Hush Puppies and tea rooms in nostalgic police/detective dramas such as *Inspector Morse* (1987–2000) and *Heartbeat* (1992–).

American action productions have survived much more visibly, though, even here, the action genre has developed into a range of nuanced permutations as programme-makers tailor their products to a variety of niche-audiences in an international media marketplace. Intensified trends towards textual hybridity (marked by the development of series that cross-fertilize elements of the action series with aspects drawn from horror, sci-fi or soap opera genres) can be seen partly as a consequence of the use of more sophisticated and finely-tuned market research within the television industry.

As Nelson suggests, increasingly guided by detailed audience data, programme-makers have adopted practices of production that attempt 'to establish what is attractive to a number of audience segments and aggregate them by including in the drama elements that will appeal to each' (Nelson, 1997: 74). *The X-Files* (1993–), *Xena: Warrior Princess* (1995–) and *Buffy the Vampire Slayer* (1997–) can all be seen as the successful progeny of the search for generic hybrids able to embrace a variety of different 'niche' markets. Yet many of the textual codes and conventions of the action series continue to survive because they are ideally suited to an increasingly 'global' media environment. Rather than elaborate plots, complex characters or sophisticated dialogue, the action series' stock-in-trade has been the more 'accessible' qualities of thrilling visuals and exciting spectacle – delivered in fast-paced narratives, ostentatious consumption, provocative sexuality, breathtaking stunts, stylized violence and (increasingly) sensational special effects. The high degree of cross-cultural translatability afforded by these attributes gives action and adventure series a kind of televisual *lingua franca* – a mutually familiar cultural grammar that can be easily recognized, understood and assimilated in a diversity of contexts and markets.

Highlighting the place of the action series in the international circulation of media texts, however, need not automatically lead us to notions of a 'homogenized' global culture or a newly invigorated era of 'cultural imperialism'. Late modernity may well have seen the rise of a 'global popular' – cultural texts and practices whose audiences transcend geographic and national boundaries. And action/adventure narratives may well have been a cornerstone within these processes – especially through their close association with booms both in international merchandising and internet-based media promotion. At the same time, however, this does not necessarily mark an irresistible drive towards a 'mono-cultural' world. Localized forms of cultural production remain important while, somewhat paradoxically, globalized cultural technologies and networks of production may actually have served to generate an expanding array of locally produced and consumed cultural forms. Those media texts that make up the 'global popular', moreover, may circulate across national boundaries, but we must still allow for the way these texts are appropriated, mobilized and made meaningful as they are inscribed into a plurality of local cultures and micro-cultures. Buffy, Xena, Mulder and Scully may be popular with audiences throughout the world, but they represent a diversity of meanings, values and orientations to the various fragments of their 'global' audience.

Accounting for the emergence and subsequent development of the television action series, therefore, requires attention to a matrix of economic, political and cultural factors. To fully understand the action series phenomenon, we cannot simply focus on the formal properties of 'the text'. Instead, these series must be contextualized within both the economic and cultural conditions of their production. As we have seen, this entails considering the political economy of the television industry and the ways in which action series were shaped by changes and developments in the realm of television finance, organization, production and distribution. From here we can also begin to consider the way various action series have condensed and articulated a wide range of contemporary cultural preoccupations – these texts functioning as sites at which a many-faceted range of cultural transactions have taken place.

## NOTES

1  Though 25 years old, Barnouw (1975) still represents one of the fullest accounts of the rise of the American television industry.
2  For concise and well-elaborated accounts of the development of commercial television in Britain and the responses it elicited, see Crisell (1997: 83–106), Seymour-Ure (1991: 85–106) and Williams (1998: 158–70).
3  An encyclopaedic catalogue of ITC's output of television series is provided in Rogers and Gillis (1997).
4  A history of the output of the Andersons' Century 21 sci-fi stable can be found in Archer and Nichols (1998), while Osgerby (2000) provides a historicized analysis.
5  Throughout the 1960s and 1970s ITC dominated the action genre in British television. The only significant challenger was Associated British Pictures Corporation, who scored a major success with their series *The Avengers* (1961–69).
6  Grade's business empire scored further TV hits with *Moses the Lawgiver* (1976), *Jesus of Nazareth* (1977) and *The Muppet Show* (1976). Spurred by his success, Grade sallied into the field of movie production, bank-rolling more than eighty feature films, including *Capricorn One* (1978) and Blake Edward's *Pink Panther* series. Grade's backing of *Raise the Titanic* (1980), however, ultimately sank his empire – the financial burden of this box-office turkey prompting a business takeover by the tycoon Robert Holms à Court. A full account can be found in Falk and Prince (1987).
7  Twentieth Century Fox, for example, struck gold with *M.A.S.H.* While the latest series of the show ran in a weekly spot on CBS, re-runs of earlier episodes were screened five times a week on local independent stations (Brown, 1998: 157).
8  Though some existing programmes were 'rebranded' as action vehicles. Tulloch and Alvarado, for example, show how the BBC's popular science fiction series, *Dr. Who*, was 'regenerated' as an 'adventure in style' narrative in the early 1970s (Tulloch and Alvarado, 1983: 99–100).
9  A complete account of the production of *The Prisoner*, which includes some pointers towards McGoohan's intellectual ambitions for the series, can be found in Rakoff (1998).
10  According to Abercrombie (1996: 97–98), the United States imports only about 2 per cent of its television programmes from abroad. One of the few not entirely American shows to enjoy network success is *La Femme Nikita* (1997–). A joint Franco-American production, the series is based on a French film of the same title and focuses on a sexy but ruthless female secret agent reluctantly pressed into the service of a covert, hi-tech anti-terrorist organization.

## REFERENCES

Abercrombie, Nicholas (1996) *Television and Society*, Cambridge: Polity.

Archer, Simon and Nicholls, Stan (1998) *Gerry Anderson: The Authorised Biography*, London: Orbit.

Barnouw, Erik (1975) *Tube of Plenty: The Evolution of American Television*, New York: Oxford University Press.

Boddy, William (1998) '"Sixty Million Viewers Can't Be Wrong": The Rise and Fall of the Television Western', in E. Buscombe and R. Pearson (eds), *Back in the Saddle Again: New Essays on the Western*, London: BFI.

Brown, Les (1971) *Televi$ion: The Business Behind the Box*, New York: Harcourt Brace Jovanovich.

—— (1998) 'The American Networks', in A. Smith (ed.), *Television: An International History*, Oxford: Oxford University Press.

Buxton, David (1990) *From The Avengers to Miami Vice: Form and Ideology in Television Series*, Manchester: Manchester University Press.

Caldwell, John (1995) *Televisuality: Style, Crisis and Authority in American Television*, New Brunswick, NJ: Rutgers University Press.

Condon, J. and Hofstede, D. (2000) *Charlie's Angels Casebook*, Beverly Hills, CA, and London: Pomegranate Press.

Crisell, Andrew (1997) *An Introductory History of British Broadcasting*, London: Routledge.

d'Acci, Julie (1997) 'Nobody's Woman?: *Honey West* and the New Sexuality', in L. Spigel and L.M. Curtin (eds), *The Revolution Wasn't Televised: Sixties Television and Social Conflict*, London: Routledge.

Ewen, Stuart (1988) *All Consuming Images*, New York: Basic Books.

Falk, Q. and Prince, D. (1987) *Last of a Kind: The Sinking of Lew Grade*, London: Quartet.

Fiske, John (1987) *Television Culture*, London: Methuen.

Gitlin, Todd (1983) *Inside Prime Time*, New York: Pantheon.

Grade, Lew (1988) *Still Dancing: My Story*, London: Fontana.

Grossberg, Lawrence (1987) 'The In-Difference of Television', *Journal of Communication Inquiry*, Vol. 10, No. 2: 28–42.

Kaplan, E.A. (1987) *Rocking Around the Clock: Music Television, Postmodernism, and Consumer Culture*, London: Methuen.

Kellner, Douglas (1992) 'Popular XCulture and the Construction of Postmodern Identities', in S. Lash and J. Freidman (eds), *Modernity and Identity*, Oxford: Blackwell.

—— (1997) 'Overcoming the Divide: Cultural Studies and Political Economy', in M. Ferguson and P. Golding (eds), *Cultural Studies in Question*, London: Sage.

Liebes, T. and Katz, E. (1996) *The Export of Meaning*, Oxford: Oxford University Press.

McGuigan, Jim (1992) *Cultural Populism*, London: Routledge.

Menon, Vijay (1993) 'Tradition Meets Modernity on the Path to the Global Village', *Intermedia*, Vol. 21, No. 1: 29–31.

Miller, Jeffrey S. (2000) *Something Completely Different: British Television and American Culture*, Minneapolis: University of Minnesota Press.

Miller, Toby (1997) *The Avengers*, London: BFI.

Negrine, R. and Papathanassopoulos, S. (1990) *The Internationalization of Television*, London: Pinter.

Nelson, R. (1997) *TV Drama in Transition: Forms, Values and Cultural Change*, London: Macmillan.

Newcomb, Horace and Alley, Robert S. (1983) *The Producer's Medium: Conversations with Creators of American TV*, New York: Oxford University Press.

Osgerby, Bill (2000) '"Stand-By For Action!": Gerry Anderson, Supermarionation and the "White Heat" of Sixties Modernity', in X. Mendik and G. Harper (eds), *Unruly Pleasures: The Cult Film and Its Critics*, Guildford: FAB Press.

Rakoff, Ian (1998) *Inside the Prisoner: Radical Television and Film in the 1960s*, London: Batsford.

Rogers, Dave and Gillis, S.J. (1997) *The Roger and Gillis Guide to ITC*, Shrewsbury: SJG Communications Services.

Scannell, Paddy (1990) 'Public Service Broadcasting: The History of a Concept', in A. Goodwin and G. Whannell (eds), *Understanding Television*, London: Routledge.

Schiller, Herbert (1969) *Mass Communication and American Empire*, New York: Beacon.

Seymour-Ure, Colin (1991) *The British Press and Broadcasting Since 1945*, Oxford: Blackwell.

Spelling, Aaron (with Jefferson, Graham) (1996) *Aaron Spelling: A Prime Time Life*, New York: St Martin's Press.

Tulloch, John and Alvarado, Manuel (1983) *Doctor Who: The Unfolding Text*, London: Macmillan.

Wheen, F. (1985) *Television: A History*, London: Century Publishing.

Williams, Kevin (1998) *Get Me A Murder a Day!: A History of Mass Communication in Britain*, London: Arnold.

# 2

# 'SO YOU'RE THE FAMOUS SIMON TEMPLAR'

## The Saint, masculinity and consumption in the early 1960s

### Bill Osgerby[1]

> Roger Moore made a big impact in the first of ITV's new *Saint* series last night. He isn't exactly my idea of the tough, hard-hitting adventurer created by Leslie Charteris – but all the same, he made a very likeable hero. He had the right touch of charm and devil-may-care approach. … This series should put him right at the top.
>
> (Clifford Davis, review of *The Saint*, *Daily Mirror*, 1 October 1962)

### AN 'INTERNATIONAL MAN OF MYSTERY'

Simon Templar – a daring swashbuckler whose flair for fisticuffs was complemented by a debonair sense of sartorial panache and an impeccable taste for the finer things in life. Originally created by British author Leslie Charteris in the 1920s, the character of Templar – or 'The Saint' as he was known to both his adversaries and erstwhile police confederates – was conceived as a romantic yet roguish hero, part pirate and part philanthropist. Templar was a popular figure in books, film, radio and comics throughout the inter- and post-war years, yet in the early 1960s he found a new lease of life. In 1962 Lew Grade, then deputy managing director of Associated Television (ATV), secured television rights to the Charteris stories and the following seven years saw the production of over one hundred episodes of *The Saint* TV series, with the rakishly handsome Roger Moore taking the part of Templar.

The first episode, 'The Talented Husband', set the tone for the series that followed. The plot itself was unremarkable – Templar foiling a murderous husband's scheme to poison his wife and lay his hands on a hefty insurance cheque. Rather than the pedestrian narrative, it was the character of Templar that stood out. We first meet him in the kind of scene-setting vignette that would become one of the programme's trademarks. Young and good-looking, Templar is elegantly dressed in dinner jacket and bow tie, suavely sipping a drink in a crowded theatre bar. At home in the glitzy night-life of London's West End, he shares a friendly observation with the viewer in a relaxed aside to camera – 'Me, I come to the theatre for fun, for laughs, for excitement'. And for Templar excitement is never far away, a beautiful blonde running up to greet him and effusively introducing him to her friend as 'the most fantastic' Simon Templar. And, with a wry smile to the audience, the urbane Templar cocks an eyebrow upwards to acknowledge the appearance of an incandescent halo above his head as Edwin Astley's racy theme music kicks in and the programme's credit sequence announces the start of a thrilling adventure for The Saint.

It was, then, Templar's stylish charisma that gave the show its allure. Each episode of *The Saint* elaborated a male fantasy of luxury and laid-back cool. Templar would invariably find himself either in the heart of the throbbing metropolis or (courtesy of a skilful back-projectionist) in some cosmopolitan, foreign locale – Monte Carlo, Venice, Istanbul or Nassau. Faultlessly dressed and immaculately coiffeured, Moore played Templar as a jet-setting man of leisure. Lounging around a world of bars and nightclubs, fast cars and beautiful women, he was the personification of sybaritic ease. Yet Templar's reputation as chivalrous buccaneer was far-reaching. An episode would invariably begin with the hero being recognized by a hapless damsel in distress (usually with an awe-struck phrase along the lines of 'So *you're* the famous Simon Templar'). The characteristic halo would then appear and The Saint would swing into action – thwarting devious blackmailers or cunning jewel thieves, and generally setting the world to rights. Fast-paced adventure in a world of hedonistic leisure and conspicuous consumption, then, were the defining qualities of *The Saint*. This was a combination, moreover, that proved to be a winning formula and the 1960s saw a host of imitators follow in Templar's wake as both Britain and the United States saw the launch of a plethora of action-oriented TV series that dealt with the same brand of high-living glamour.

Accounting for the success of *The Saint*, and the array of playboy–adventurer TV series that followed it, requires attention to a matrix of economic and cultural factors. Developments in the realm of television organization, production and finance during the 1960s go some way toward accounting for the textual properties of such programmes, though it is these series' cultural conditions of production that largely account for their distinctive oeuvre. Templar and his compatriots found cultural resonance in both Britain and America during the early 1960s by condensing and articulating a wide range of contemporary cultural preoccupations, most obviously through their elaboration of a new archetype of masculinity – a form of masculine identity that embraced a credo of affluent pleasure, narcissistic style and personal 'liberation' through consumption.

## THE MAKING OF A 'POPULAR HERO'

In the seventy years of his existence Simon Templar has undergone many changes. Indeed, it is his sheer malleability that has allowed The Saint to be an enduring figure of popular fiction. He has been, to use Tony Bennett and Janet Woollacott's term, a 'popular hero' – a figure who has moved beyond the original textual conditions of his

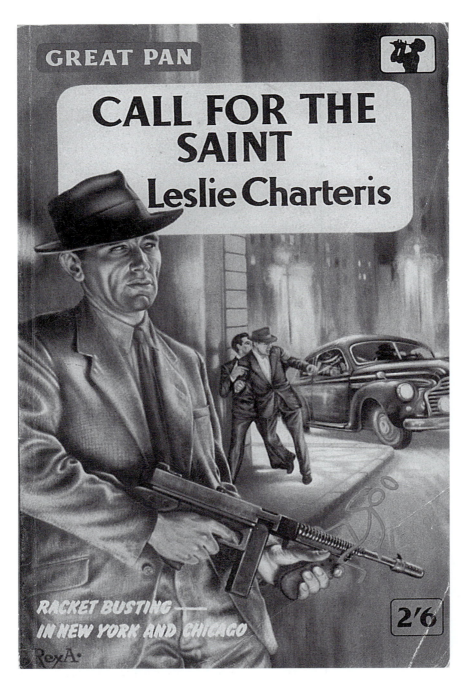

*Figure 2.1* The 'hard-boiled' Saint.

existence to condense and connect with a range of profound cultural and ideological concerns across an extended period of time (1987: 13–14).

After experimenting with a variety of prototypes, Leslie Charteris first introduced the figure of Simon Templar in his novel *Meet the Tiger*, published in 1928.[2] In the stories that followed (many published in the magazine *Thriller*) Charteris developed The Saint as a 'gentleman criminal' – a well-bred and winsome rogue whose more felonious activities were offset by his underlying valour and gallantry. Originally, therefore, The Saint bore some resemblance to the upper-class heroes of the 'imperialist spy thrillers' of the 1920s and 1930s. Like Cyril McNeile's Bulldog Drummond or John Buchan's Richard Hannay, Templar was a gentleman amateur who foiled the sinister machinations of foreign villains almost as a hobby or sport rather than a work-a-day profession.[3] In the 1930s, however, Charteris settled in New York, the move precipitating a significant shift in the character of Templar. The Saint retained the sophistication of his earlier incarnation as a gentleman adventurer, yet the move to America saw the emergence of a more gritty, hard-edged Templar who was more in keeping with the traditions of American hard-boiled detective fiction (see Figure 2.1). In the books, films and radio series of this period The Saint often worked in conjunction with crime-fighting agencies such as the FBI and was no stranger to the rough-and-tumble world of the tough-guy – as the character himself explained in *The Saint Sees It Through*:

> I ... am not a respectable citizen. I shoot people and I open safes. I'm not popular. People send me bombs through the mail, and policemen are always looking for an excuse to arrest me. There isn't any peace and stability when I'm around.
>
> (Charteris, 1961: 31, orig. pub. 1947)

Yet another variation of Templar emerged when the character appeared on the small screen in the 1960s. In the ATV series, The Saint's rough edges were smoothed down, Roger Moore playing him as a suave playboy. He was still wolfish and handy with his fists, yet Templar's tastes had become more hedonistic, his lifestyle more racy. Sporting exquisitely tailored suits and slicked-back hair, he had become a study in stylishness. In and out of fashionable night-spots, jetting to exotic locations and driving a high performance Volvo P1800 sports car, The Saint had become an exercise in swinging modernity (see Figure 2.2).[4]

As Tony Bennett argues, the analysis of popular texts always demands recognition of the nexus of economic, technological and institutional relationships that regulate their production (Bennett 1990: 3–5).[5] In these terms, the launch and subsequent success of *The Saint* TV series was intrinsically embedded in the wider reconfiguration of British television during the late 1950s and 1960s. With the launch of commercial television in 1955 market forces emerged as a determining factor in TV schedules, moguls like Lew Grade looking for programme formats that could guarantee the delivery of large audiences to advertisers. Along with soap operas, quizzes and variety shows, therefore, the 'action' series emerged as a key ingredient in commercial

*Figure 2.2*  Simon Templar as playboy–adventurer – Roger Moore as *The Saint* (1962–69).

broadcasting strategies – the cocktail of thrilling exploits and sparkling glamour deliberately appealing to popular tastes and ensuring that *The Saint* was climbing high in
British TV ratings by the beginning of 1963. Moreover, as a programme produced
with a specific view to international sales, *The Saint* (along with the many British
action series that followed) can be seen as constituent in incipient trends towards globalized flows in the finance, production and marketing of media texts.

British commercial broadcasters had already made initial forays into the American
TV market during the 1950s. Lew Grade led the way, financing the production of
historical adventure series such as *The Adventures of Robin Hood* (1955–59) and *The
Adventures of Sir Lancelot* (1957), picked up respectively by the CBS and NBC
networks. For American broadcasters and sponsors the savings offered by buying in
pre-produced programming from Britain were very attractive – and for British
producers the deal generated much-needed revenue for the finance of new ventures.
Profits from his early successes, for example, allowed Grade to follow up with *Danger
Man* (1960–66), a contemporary action series featuring Patrick McGoohan as
NATO special security operative John Drake. However, though CBS bought the first
season of *Danger Man* in 1961, ratings were disappointing and within six months the
series was dropped – only enjoying stateside popularity after being relaunched as
*Secret Agent* in 1965 amid the craze for spy adventures that followed the screen success
of James Bond. John Drake's initial failure in the American market, however, did not
deter Grade and he pressed ahead with the production of a new action series – *The
Saint*. Filmed in monochrome, the first two series of *The Saint* could be sold successfully in Britain (where colour broadcasting did not begin on the main channels until
1969) and to local American TV stations. A black-and-white series, however, was
unattractive to the more lucrative American networks and it was with this market in
mind that Grade ensured that the third (1966) season of *The Saint* was filmed in
colour. The strategy paid off and the series was not only snapped up by NBC (who ran
Templar for five years as the summer replacement for the *Dean Martin Show*), but was
ultimately sold to TV stations in no less than sixty-three different countries.

Changes in the structure and organization of the television industry, then, certainly
played a part in shaping *The Saint* TV series. Yet the success of the programme was not
indebted to economic contingencies alone. Also important was the way it constructed
a version of Templar very different from the character's earlier incarnations. As
Bennett and Woollacott (1987: 13–14) argue, the distinguishing trait of a 'popular
hero' is her or his ability to break free from their original textual context, serving as a
focal point to a variety of cultural meanings at different temporal moments. In these
terms, *The Saint* TV series of the 1960s can be seen as successfully re-articulating the
character of Templar, allowing him to condense and connect with contemporaneous
cultural and ideological concerns. In particular, the 1960s Saint achieved cultural
purchase by connecting with important changes taking place in consumption, lifestyle and (especially) dominant masculine identities in both Britain and America.

## 'THE SAINT' AS PLAYBOY OF THE WESTERN WORLD

Initially, at least, *The Saint* TV series stuck closely to the plots of the original stories. Templar's 1960s incarnation, however, was not quite the same as the hardy adventurer originally envisioned by Charteris. The TV series certainly captured the character's combination of raffish charm and square-jawed ruggedness, yet compared to his earlier incarnations, the 1960s Saint was decidedly more stylish and sybaritic. Since his original appearance in the late 1920s, the various manifestations of Templar had always been at ease in the chic world of opulence and high-living. Yet the 1960s TV series saw his affinity for hedonistic pleasure and conspicuous consumption heightened significantly. The episode 'The Gadget Lovers', for example, opens characteristically with The Saint relaxing in a plush Berlin niterie – the 'Kitten Club'. Scrupulously attired, Templar sits on a bar-stool, sipping a fine scotch and casting an approving eye (its brow raised suggestively) over an attractive waitress (dressed, of course, in a sexy 'kitten' outfit), before leaping into action to foil the assassination of a top British spy (see Figure 2.3). 'The Ex-King of Diamonds', meanwhile, finds our dapper hero unwinding on the exclusive Côte D'Azur. Stepping out of the airport into an idyllic setting, Templar's aside to the audience spells out his priorities – 'Golden sunshine, golden money, golden girls' – the character eyeing up a couple of bikini-clad belles as he produces a large wad of cash to hire a luxurious Rolls-Royce.

The 1960s inflection of The Saint, therefore, presented Templar as an exemplification of the lotus-eating (and martini-drinking) jet set: a shift in the presentation of the character which was informed by, and was itself constituent in, broader changes taking place in articulations of masculinity – away from what Paul Hoch terms the 'puritan' form of masculine identity ('hard-working, hard fighting' and adhering to 'a production ethic of duty before pleasure') and towards the ideal of the playboy 'who lives according to an ethic of leisure and sensual indulgence' (Hoch, 1979: 118).

Forms of masculine identity predicated on narcissism and conspicuous consumption were the focus of considerable academic scrutiny in Britain during the late 1980s and early 1990s. Attention focused on the concept of the 'New Man' – authors such as Rowena Chapman (1988), Frank Mort (1988; 1996) and Sean Nixon (1996) identifying a new brand of hedonistic and self-consciously stylish masculinity within 1980s advertising images and, especially, a new wave of glossy lifestyle magazines aimed at men.[6] The masculine foray into the world of commodity consumption, however, was hardly unique to 1980s Britain. The large body of research highlighting the pivotal role of women and constructions of femininity in the emergence of modern consumer culture has tended to obscure the historical presence of men in the fields of fashionable display and consumer practice.[7] Nevertheless, studies such as Christopher Breward's (1999) analysis of menswear retailing in Victorian London and Howard Chudacoff's (1999) survey of 'bachelor subcultures' in American cities at the turn of the century, have begun to suggest a degree of masculine involvement in the historical development of commodity culture much greater than has traditionally been recognized. However, while a relationship between masculinity, fashion and consumption can be identified even in the earliest manifestations of modern consumerism, this was

*Figure 2.3*  The Saint relaxes in the 'Kitten Club' ('The Gadget Lovers', 1966).

a relationship fraught with friction and contradiction. Masculine identities premised upon hedonism and conspicuous display have, for example, invariably conflicted with more conservative constructions of manhood rooted in ideals of hard work, thrift and moral self-discipline. Moreover, despite the history of a masculine presence in the realm of fashionable consumption, the arenas of stylistic pleasure and commodity consumerism have remained ones closely bound up with feminine connotations. The spheres of visual pleasure and consumer practice, therefore, have always been precarious waters for articulations of masculinity keen to avoid any suggestion of effeminacy or 'unmanliness' – thus care has had to be taken as men have increasingly stepped into the world of consumption and stylistic self-expression.

In America the embryonic style-oriented, male consumer of the late nineteenth century became more fully formed during the economic boom of the 1920s – and was an established figure by 1933, when *Esquire* magazine was launched as an up-market style-Bible for the fashion-conscious man about town. It was, though, amid the proliferating consumer culture of the late 1950s and early 1960s that hedonistic models of masculinity really came into their own.[8] For Barbara Ehrenreich, this period saw the traditional, middle-class, masculine 'breadwinner' ethos of sober thrift and family-based respectability steadily give way to a new 'playboy ethic' more in step with the demands of an economy increasingly predicated on commodity consumption (Ehrenreich, 1983: 170–71). Ehrenreich's 'playboy ethic' represented a new model of self-indulgent masculinity which refused to succumb to the fetters of domesticity and instead prioritized a quest for personal gratification in a sparkling world of endless leisure, luxury and lascivious indulgence (1983: 41). Especially indicative of this shift was the rise of Hugh Hefner's *Playboy* empire. Launched in late 1953, and virtually an instant hit, *Playboy* magazine was a eulogy to a masculine universe of stylistic pleasure and commodity consumption. Through combining this ethos of hedonistic consumerism with a swaggering image of boisterous heterosexuality, moreover, *Playboy* offered men an 'acceptable' avenue into the domain of self-conscious consumption. The inclusion of pornographic pin-ups and centrefolds served to mark out the magazine as avowedly masculine and heterosexual, allowing its male readers – secure in the knowledge that their heterosexual masculine identities would not be compromised – to cruise freely through its glossy features on furniture, interior decor, fashion and (sometimes quite sexualized) representations of men.

On the other side of the Atlantic, the economic toll of the war and the 'austerity years' that followed retarded British economic growth – but by the late 1950s and early 1960s Britain was enjoying a consumer boom of its own. As Frank Mort (1997) argues, however, the British transition into the age of commodity consumption was not identical to that of the United States. Like almost all West European democracies of the period, post-war Britain took the American economic model as a major point of reference, while American culture wielded significant influence as British popular culture entered into dialogue with the growing range of cultural imports from the US (especially in the form of films, fashion and popular music). But the slower, partial and more uneven development of British consumerism contrasted with the greater pace and impact of the American model. The emergence of a 'playboy ethic' in Britain, therefore, was slower, more hesitant and much less dramatic than in America. Nevertheless, such developments in forms of masculine identity *were* discernible – albeit with a markedly 'British' intonation – as men become more fully immersed and absorbed in the world of consumer experience.

The years when Britain had 'never had it so good' were, as Lynne Segal (1988; 1990: 20–21) shows, a period of profound disruption and transformation in the codes and identities of British masculinity. The greater visibility of working class youth subcultures (most obviously with the rise of the Teddy boys and the Mods, of the 1950s and early 1960s respectively) saw the appearance of models of masculinity in which style, leisure and consumption were deliberately – and spectacularly – evoked in the self-dramatization of identity. In the field of literature, meanwhile, the work of the Angry Young Men – most obviously Kingsley Amis, John Braine, John Osborne and Colin Wilson – saw the emergence of the 'intellectual tough': a brand of masculinity distinguished by a (decidedly misogynistic and homophobic) rebellious cynicism and a hostility to the conservative inertia of 'the Establishment'.

But change was also afoot in the world of more mainstream and middle-class masculinities.

During the late 1950s and early 1960s the dominant forms of middle-class masculinity – underpinned by a credo of respectability, reserve and sober decorum – gradually began to be eclipsed by masculine identities oriented around discourses of individuality, hedonism and consumer pleasure. Mort, for example, shows how Burton's, the empire of high-street men's clothes shops, underwent a set of profound transformations from the mid-1950s (1996: 134–45; 1997: 19–22). Since the 1930s the firm had cultivated an image of formal gentlemanly manhood, but during the late 1950s this ideal vanished as Burton's decor, advertising and products began to embrace a younger, more casual and leisure-oriented set of images. A glance through the Tailoring Style Guides produced during this period by Grafton, an up-market gentlemen's tailors, confirms a similar pattern of change – with an emphasis on formal suits and evening-wear increasingly giving way to sports jackets and 'Continental Styles for the Younger Man' (see Figure 2.4).

A similar set of changes also began to register in the world of British men's magazines. In 1951 *The Tailor and Cutter*, a long-established trade journal for men's tailors, introduced *Man About Town* – an up-market magazine for men. At first, *Man About Town* articulated a version of masculinity that was sophisticated and urbane (exemplified by its restaurant guides, fashion advice and travel features), yet was still securely anchored in the conservative and temperate ethos of the traditional upper-middle class. The featured fashions were all redolent of the smart city gent, while the short biographies of contributors revealed them to be mostly former public school-boys and ex-army 'rugger' enthusiasts. By the early 1960s, however, the magazine's content and mode of address had changed significantly. Its title abbreviated to *About Town* in 1961 (and then simply *Town* in 1962), the magazine became a beacon of the 'happening' world of hectic consumption in the nascent 'swinging sixties'. Undoubtedly taking its cues from *Playboy* (which, itself, was launched in a European edition in the mid-1960s), *About Town* was characterized by its swank fashion features and a fascination with sumptuous consumer goods – these mixed together with lavish travelogues, slick photo-journalism and regular 'glamour' photo-spreads. In 1964 *Town* was joined by *King* (another paean to masculine high-living and indulgent leisure), and the following year by *Penthouse* – a magazine marked out by its greater pornographic content, but which was also pitched to a market of hedonistic masculine consumers.[9] In British advertising, too, the codes and conventions of the playboy ethos began to surface with increasing regularity – campaigns, such as that for Double Diamond pale ale in 1963, picturing men in a world of 'affluence and jet-age leisure': surfing, parachuting, water-skiing and mountaineering (cited in Mort, 1997: 28).

The representation of The Saint in his 1960s TV series was constituent in this broad transformation of masculine identities. In both America and (less dramatically) Britain, the late 1950s and early 1960s saw the traditional virtues of middle-class masculinity – hard work, moderation and thrift – become an anachronism as newer, more indulgent and consumption-driven masculine identities began to come to the fore. In his high-class tastes, cosmopolitanism and laid-back insouciance, the sixties

Continental Styles
for the
Younger Man

217

When ordering these styles
please state whether turn-ups
or plain bottoms are required

*Figure 2.4* 'Continental Styles for the Younger Man' (*Grafton, Fashions for Men: Tailoring Style Guide, 1962*).

Saint personified this shift. With his proclivity for sharp Italian suits, razor-edge lapels and snappy 'slim-Jim' ties, The Saint also showed an affinity with style aesthetics similar to those conjured with by the (largely working-class) Mod youth subculture then taking shape in London's clubs and boutiques. But Simon Templar's sartorial flair enunciated him as a hip man of the moment rather than a semiotic terrorist. His (relative) maturity, (seemingly limitless) affluence and (consummately suave) demeanour firmly signposted him as a member of the British upper-middle class. As did some of his fashion statements – his predilection for the chic, smoothly-tailored lines of Italian style being held in check by an additional preference for that abiding signifier of the Home Counties gentry: the tweed jacket.[10]

The 1960s incarnation of The Saint, therefore, can be seen as emblematic of a new form of middle-class masculinity that was adapted to the emerging world of 'swing-ing' consumerism. This is not, however, to cast *The Saint* as documentary testimony to these wider changes. While historians such as Arthur Marwick (1984) have treated the cultural texts of this period virtually as historical artefacts in terms of the way they illuminate wider patterns of social transformation, Andy Medhurst correctly points out that such an approach is 'absurdly reductive, displaying a total disregard for textual complexity and contradiction' (Medhurst, 1984: 23). Rather than simply embodying or 'reflecting' social change, cultural texts actively construct a particular interpretation of the social world. It would, for example, be ludicrous to present *The Saint* as evidence that post-war Britain was populated by young men all living a life of lavish ease. Instead, the programme is better seen as a mythologized fantasy, a vehicle for aspirational fantasies and desires. Nevertheless, the programme's fantasies still connected with the material world in important respects.

As Graham Dawson perceptively argues, it is important to recognize the way repre-sentations of masculinity figure in the way consumers give meaning to their relation-ships with commodities and those around them. Dawson develops the concept of the 'imagined identity' to denote the way repertoires of cultural forms and images can be drawn upon in the imagining of lived identities. The 'imagined identity' may be '"made up" in the positive sense of active creation', but it also has 'real effects in the world of everyday relationships, which it invests with meaning and makes intelligible in specific ways' (Dawson, 1991:118). *The Saint* TV series can be seen as furnishing just such an 'imagined identity' – offering a mythologized ideal of masculinity which could be mobilized by men as they steered a course through an economic and social environment increasingly dominated by commodity consumption.

## 'WE'VE BEEN EXPECTING YOU, MR. BOND'

Simon Templar was not the first playboy–adventurer to emerge in British TV during the early 1960s. Two years before *The Saint, Danger Man* had already developed the formula – with its international outlook, exotic settings and John Drake's sleek, white sports car.[11] But Drake was always a dedicated professional. Keeping his eye on the job, Drake was more a skilled technician than a hedonistic man of leisure with a yen for excitement.[12] Indeed, rumours circulate that *Danger Man*'s star, Patrick McGoohan, actually declined an offer of the starring role in *The Saint* on the grounds that he objected to the philandering trysts planned for Templar.[13]

Leslie Charteris's own choice for the TV Templar was David Niven – an actor who would, perhaps, have captured the author's vision of a dauntless upper-class gentleman (or daredevil toff). But it was the younger, less gentrified, Roger Moore that the show's producers plumped for. Having spent some years working in America, Moore's relatively 'classless', mid-Atlantic persona was well-suited to the 1960s rebranding of The Saint. Played by Moore, Simon Templar still had the nuances of an affluent man of status, yet was less bound by the lofty sensibilities and conservativism traditionally associated with the British upper-class.

Roger Moore's experience in American television also suited Lew Grade's designs on the US market. Having starred in the Western series *Maverick* (1957–62), Moore was already familiar to American audiences and it was hoped that this would assist the success of *The Saint* in American TV schedules. Indeed, this was a strategy that Grade developed more rigorously in his subsequent action–adventure vehicles. Series such as *Man of the World* (1962), *The Baron* (1966), *Man in a Suitcase* (1967), *The Champions* (1968) and *Department 'S'* (1969) deployed the same playboy–adventurer concept, though were more manifestly tailored to the US market through their casting of American actors and use of American settings. The period's most famous hero configured as transatlantic playboy–adventurer, however, was James Bond.

Like Simon Templar, James Bond was re-articulated and up-dated during the early 1960s. The Bond of Ian Fleming's 1950s novels was a relatively conservative figure of the establishment – traditional and fairly reserved in his outlook and lifestyle. However, the release of the first Bond movie – *Dr. No* – in 1962 (the same year as The Saint's TV debut) saw 007 subtly modified and remodelled. Just as *The Saint* TV series revised and adjusted the character of Templar, making him more congruent with an ethos of masculine consumerism (and more appropriate to the American market), the Bond films of the early 1960s also transformed 007 into an Americanized playboy.[14] As Bennett and Woollacott observe of Bond's 1960s incarnation:

> His attitudes towards sex, gambling and pleasure in general are distinctly liberal and his tastes and lifestyle have a decidedly international and cosmopolitan flavour. In a word, Bond is not old fashioned ... Bond belongs not to the Breed but to a new elite – international rather than parochially English in its orientation – committed to new values (professionalism) and lifestyles (martini).
>
> (Bennett and Woollacott, 1987: 111)

The 1960s incarnations of both Bond and Templar, therefore, testify to a shift in dominant articulations of masculinity. In an age increasingly pervaded by consumption, advertising and style, 007 and The Saint both became agents for the upwardly-mobile jet-set – the two characters breaking with the constraints of traditional masculinity and moving into a mythologized world of hedonism, consumer pleasure and individual autonomy.[15] While these themes certainly resonated in 1960s Britain, however, it was in the United States that they found their spiritual home.

Film historian James Chapman insists that, despite being financed by American capital, James Bond movies have always been essentially *British* texts – largely produced using British studios and film crews, generically originating in British fiction and embodying an essentially British ideology of national identity (Chapman, 1999: 14). This is certainly true. But in their glossy materialism and stylishly hedonistic brand of 'modernized' masculinity, the early Bond films owed a heavy debt to developments in American culture and, indeed, were to a large part made with an eye to the American market. For example, whereas Fleming (like Charteris) had expressed a preference for David Niven to play his hero, this was over-ruled by film producers Albert Broccoli and Harry Saltzman. Instead, Sean Connery was selected as a Bond whose relative lack of class signifiers would make him more palatable to American audiences (Bennett and Woollacott, 1987: 55–56). As a consequence, the Bond films (like *The Saint* and other action TV series) successfully struck a chord in American culture. In the US, a narcissistic and leisure-oriented brand of masculinity was much more firmly established and fully-formed – and hence provided a ready market for cosmopolitan, playboy–adventurer narratives. America was ready for Bond.

In the US, the prevalence of models of masculinity based around (hetero-)sexual pleasure and hedonistic consumption ensured that Bond's celluloid incarnation was greeted with open arms on its arrival in the early 1960s. Indeed, even before the release of *Dr. No*, *Playboy* magazine had embraced 007 as one of its own. In an editorial of 1960, for example, *Playboy* proudly recounted a visit by Ian Fleming to its offices during which the author speculated that 'James Bond, if he were an actual person, would be a registered reader of *Playboy*' (*Playboy*, March 1960: 1). And, as Bond-mania set in, *Playboy* enlisted 007 in its crusade for materialistic and libertine masculine ideals – the magazine featuring numerous pin-up photo-spreads of the 'Bond girls' and serializing many of Fleming's novels and short stories. Not to be outdone *Esquire* (*Playboy's* main competitor) followed suit, the magazine producing a special Bond-themed issue in conjunction with the release of *Thunderball* in 1965 – a film which proved to be Bond's biggest triumph at the American box office.

Figures such as James Bond and Simon Templar, then, were especially successful in America because they arrived on the cusp of cultural changes that saw narcissistic and avowedly consumerist versions of masculine style increasingly validated, even celebrated.[16] And, in this context, it was their traits of 'Britishness' that gave characters such as Bond and Templar a special cachet. The 1960s incarnations of both heroes played down the class-rooted elements of their British identities – though, to American eyes, they were still recognizably British. During the 1950s American perceptions of British culture had been informed by notions of refinement and quality – but during the 1960s, Jeffrey Miller (2000: 17; 33) argues, the arrival of Beatlemania and the dazzling art and fashions of 'swinging London' saw British cultural imports accrue connotations of rebelliousness, 'difference' and exciting 'otherness'.[17] Indeed, writing in *Vogue* in 1965, American sociologist Herbert Gans identified a marked change in American perceptions of Britain as images of the British – especially British men –

became incorporated in domestic fantasies of sexual freedom and socially liberated lifestyles. Citing the American popularity of Richard Burton, Bond and the Beatles, Gans contended that an older image of the 'British gentleman' ('well-bred, sophisticated, reserved, public spirited') had been displaced by images of British men as 'potent sexual idols, armed with unusual energy and vitality, and given to public declarations of skepticism and satire' (Gans, 1965: 108). Their attributes of 'Britishness', then, made both Bond and Templar especially appealing in America during the early 1960s – their qualities of 'difference' serving to accentuate their connotations of cultural autonomy and thrilling modernity.

British playboy–adventurers were especially attractive to American audiences, but home-grown equivalents also made themselves felt. During the 1950s American serial TV drama had been dominated by representations of gritty machismo in tough cop shows such as *Dragnet* (1952–58) and *Highway Patrol* (1955–59), or Westerns such as *Cheyenne* (1955–63) and *Have Gun, Will Travel* (1957–63). But the end of the 1950s and early 1960s brought a new wave of hip and stylish adventure heroes. *Peter Gunn* (1958–61), for example, showcased a new brand of cool, laid-back and well-groomed detective hero – equally at home in bohemian jazz clubs and plush up-town restaurants. Above all, though, the field was led by Warner Brothers' set of creations. Beginning with *77 Sunset Strip* (1958–64), Warner developed a niche for adventure TV shows featuring young and glamorously debonair male heroes. *77 Sunset Strip* featured a pair of up-market and Ivy-League-educated private eyes. Fully equipped with modish wardrobe and slick hairstyles, the duo cracked cases in the world's ritziest glamour spots (helped out by a proto-beatnik car park attendant). Warner followed up its success with a range of spins on the formula, each with its own inspired gimmick. Lasting for four seasons, *Hawaiian Eye* (1959–63) featured private detectives based in a trendy, poolside office at the Hawaiian Village Hotel (inspired gimmick: duo live in Honolulu – and wear Hawaiian shirts). The least commercially successful of Warner's playboy–adventurer series, *Bourbon Street Beat* (1959–60) teamed up a Chandler-esque ex-cop with a young blade from one of New Orleans' most well-to-do families (inspired gimmick: funky allusions to the jazz underground). *Surfside Six* (1960–62), meanwhile, revolved around a pair of dashing Miami Beach private eyes (inspired gimmick: er … the heroes live on a houseboat).[18] Perhaps the most unlikely working of the playboy–adventurer formula, however, came in an Aaron Spelling production – *Burke's Law* (1963–66). Here, Los Angeles Chief of Detectives, Amos Burke, was also was a millionaire *bon vivant* – arriving at crime scenes in a chauffeur-driven Rolls-Royce.

In his third (1965) season Burke returned – but with a difference. Now he was *Amos Burke: Secret Agent*. The show retained its high-rolling glitz, but now Burke had quit the police to become a globe-trotting spy for the US secret service. Burke's transformation was indicative of the growing accent on espionage within the playboy–adventurer formula that followed the American success of James Bond. *The Man From U.N.C.L.E.* (1964–67), *I-Spy* (1965–68) and *Get Smart* (1965–70) explored the same discourses of male individualism, conspicuous consumption and sexual pleasure, though this was situated within (invariably tongue-in-cheek) spy narratives.[19]

## GLOBAL *FLÂNEURS* AND THE 'LICENCE TO LOOK'

While the playboy–adventurers of the early 1960s were constructed as living in a liberated world of breathless consumption and pleasure, it is important to recognize the dimensions of sexism and racism that underpinned this 'liberation'. Both Simon Templar and James Bond (and their legion of imitators) can be read as 'global *flâneurs*' – touring the world's fashionable resorts and nightspots in search of excitement and spectacle. These characters subject the world to their sovereign gaze, turning it into their own domain, their playground. This exemplifies what Michael Denning (1987) describes as James Bond's 'licence to look'. In his daring missions around the world Bond, Denning argues, constructs an imperialist and racist 'tourist gaze' in which unfamiliar and 'exotic' locations are represented as the object of 007's Western, metropolitan scrutiny (Denning, 1987: 103–7). Bond's 'licence to look', moreover, also extends to women. Just as 007's 'tourist gaze' constructs peripheral societies as objects of spectacle, so his 'male gaze' (sharing many of the narrative codes of pornography) constructs women as the objects of a voyeuristic look (Denning, 1987: 103–7). The same 'licence to look' was issued to The Saint and the other playboy–adventurers of British and American TV series during the 1960s. These programmes' narrative codes privileged the gaze of the playboy–globetrotter – cars, clothes, 'exotic' locations and women all existing as objects for their consumption.[20]

At the same time, however, it would be misleading to present series such as *The Saint* as monolithic texts – equating them unproblematically with dominant ideological discourses. Popular texts are always complex and ambiguous, shot through with contradictions and inconsistencies. For example, Bennett and Woollacott argue that, while women were certainly objectified and subordinated within the Bond-esque texts of the 1960s, these texts also broke with traditional constructions of passive and domestic femininity – though admittedly only through women becoming subject to the hero's gaze (and thereby the fantasy object of the male reader) (Bennett and Woollacott, 1987: 123).[21]

Perhaps more significant is the way in which the gaze of heroes such as Bond and The Saint was not one-way. They were also objects for the gaze of others – it is, after all, 'the famous Simon Templar' who is eminently recognizable, both to the audience and to the characters around him. The Saint does not simply consume, he is also the object of the audience's consumption.[22] Here, it may be possible to draw parallels with analyses of more recent archetypes of masculine consumption. Authors such as Mort (1988; 1996) and Nixon (1996) have, for example, argued that the visual codes of the narcissistic and self-conscious 'New Man' (together with the array of glossy lifestyle magazines with which he has been associated) have worked to 'rupture traditional icons of masculinity', thus making space for a plurality of more provisional masculine identities (Mort, 1988: 194). It could be argued that similar processes took place during the early 1960s in texts such as *The Saint* and the Bond films. In their hectic consumption and fastidious narcissism, both Simon Templar and James Bond broke with more conservative and traditional forms of masculine identity – elaborating instead a form of masculinity predicated on discourses of hedonism and consumer pleasure.

## 'THE LAST OF THE FAMOUS INTERNATIONAL PLAYBOYS':
## THE RETURN(S) OF THE SAINT

The golden age of the playboy was, however, ephemeral. While swinging bachelors such as Simon Templar may have pioneered a masculine credo of leisure and conspicuous consumption, by the late 1960s they were beginning to look increasingly dated. In 1971 Roger Moore was enticed to reprise his playboy role, this time as Lord Brett Sinclair in *The Persuaders!* But, despite its gloss and lavish locations, the series was discontinued after failing to draw American audiences.

By the late 1960s the playboy–adventurer's claims to urbane cool were steadily undercut by the pace of social change. Alongside the stylistic and libertine excesses of the counter-culture, figures such as Simon Templar and Brett Sinclair began to look terminally unhip. In the late 1970s ATV tried to revive Templar in a new series starring Ian Ogilvy. But *The Return of the Saint* (1978) fared no better than *The Persuaders!* In the age of disco's sexual exuberance and punk rock's cultural iconoclasm, Ogilvy's version of The Saint looked ridiculously outdated. Unsurprisingly, the series lasted only one season. Similarly, in 1997, Paramount's big screen production of *The Saint* (starring Val Kilmer) met an ignominious fate – losing considerable money at the box-office as it failed to connect with the wider cultural milieu (or a coherent plot).

If a 'popular hero' is to be an enduring cultural phenomenon he must be adaptable and 'socially mobile' – able to function as 'the bearer of different meanings at different points in time, in different contexts and for different audiences' (Bennett and Woollacott 1987: 18). During the 1970s James Bond managed this successfully. As Roger Moore left behind The Saint to assume the mantle of 007, Bond's adventures (in line with other spy narratives of the time) developed a more markedly comic inflection (Bennett and Woollacott, 1987: 38). Moore's Bond was a parody of the playboy mythology, playfully debunking the formula of the earlier 007 films. In a similar vein, ITC's *Jason King* series of 1972 was an ironic pastiche of the 'action' series. Peter Wyngarde played the part of King as an outrageously camp dandy, turning the series into 'patently a huge send-up of heterosexuality's ridiculous contortions' (Medhurst, 1994: 3).[23] By the mid-1970s, then, the sun had set on the world of Simon Templar. The 'playboy–adventurer' had become a cultural anachronism, living on only as *Austin Powers: International Man of Mystery* (1996) – an ironic, postmodern parody of his former self.[24]

## NOTES

1  Many thanks to Ian Van Eetvelt for allowing me access to his extensive action–adventure TV archive, and to Miguel Nachos and his colleagues for inspiration.
2  The origins and development of Charteris's character are extensively chronicled in Barer (1993).
3  Denning (1987: 37–49) offers an illuminating analysis of the work of these authors.
4  An entertaining account of ATV's television version of *The Saint* is provided by Simper (1997).

5   For further elaboration on the complex relation between cultural texts and their conditions of production see Bennett and Woollacott (1987: 16–20), Heath (1981: 226–27) and Mercer (1986: 183–84).

6   The field was led by the publication of *Arena* in 1986, its success prompting the launch of *For Him* (soon abbreviated to *FHM*) in 1987 and the arrival of British editions of the American magazines *GQ* (1988) and *Esquire* (1991).

7   For key studies highlighting the relationship between consumerism and female identity see Abelson (1989), Leach (1984), Nava (1996) and Walkowitz (1992).

8   For a more extended discussion of the development of consumption and leisure-oriented male identities in modern America, see Osgerby (2001, forthcoming).

9   In its style and mode of address, *Penthouse* magazine was originally conceived as a British counterpart to *Playboy* – *Penthouse's* publisher, Bob Guccioni, explaining that '[*Playboy*] was doing extremely well in those days – it was outselling *Punch*, which was one of the better news-stand magazines in the UK. So, it occurred to me … that if [*Playboy*] were selling that well – as a magazine aimed at primarily *American* readers and very much a part of *American* culture – I figured that if one were to adapt the formula to an English publication, then it would sell at least as well if not better' (interview with author, 3 December 1998).

10  As Medhurst (1985: 6) cogently observes, tweed (especially during the 1950s) stood as the 'sartorial correlative' to the stiff-upper-lip traditionalism of British middle-class masculinity.

11  Arguably, a similar brand of hedonistic masculinity had already been pioneered by the heroes of ATV's earlier, historically-based, adventure series – in particular *The Buccaneers* (1956), *The Count of Monte Cristo* (1956) and *The Scarlet Pimpernel* (1956).

12  Though, with some justification, Buxton includes *Danger Man* in his inventory of 1960s 'pop series' – TV programmes whose accent was squarely on the aesthetics of style, fashion and image (1990: 74; 76–78). After all, the show's closing credits revealed that Patrick McGoohan's clothes had been designed by 'The Fashion House Group of London'.

13  Interviewed in 1999, Robert Baker, co-producer of *The Saint*, contended that Lew Grade had been keen on McGoohan for the part of Templar but the production team turned him down, feeling the actor was too 'brittle' and humourless for the role (Wiseman, 1999: 18).

14  Elements of this transformation can, in fact, also be detected in Fleming's literary presentation of Bond. In the late 1950s and early 1960s elements of narcissism and hedonism increasingly crept into 007's lifestyle. In *Goldfinger* (1959), for example, Bond trades in his classic Bentley for a more racy Aston Martin DB III, while in *Thunderball* (1961) a whole chapter (Chapter 14) is dedicated to a controversy surrounding the correct way to mix a dry martini.

15  While the hedonistic playboy undoubtedly dominated the action, spy and thriller genres during the early 1960s, his hegemony did not go entirely uncontested. In Britain, for example, a more traditional and conservative brand of masculinity continued to be elaborated in detectives such as Francis Durbridge's Paul Temple. Appearing in a range of radio serials and books between 1938 and 1968, Temple was still alive and well in the 1960s – featuring in a BBC TV series in 1969. Temple, however, was no swinger. Unlike either Bond or Templar, Paul Temple remained a bastion of Home Counties' politeness and parochial conformity.

16  For an autobiographical account of the way Bond offered a beguilingly suave and consumption-literate (yet still unmistakably 'manly') model of masculinity to American men during the early 1960s, see McInerney (1996).

17  Frank (1997: 190–91) also highlights the flurry of media excitement that surrounded the arrival of 'Mod' attire on American shores in 1966 – the style of British men's fashion seen as expressing an excitingly heightened sense of individuality and flamboyance.

18  During the early 1960s Warner Brothers also applied the formula to non-private eye contexts, with *The Islanders* (an adventure series revolving around charter pilots in the tropics) and *The Roaring Twenties* (a series based around newspaper journalists).

19  See Worland (1994). The end to this particular spy-spoof cycle came with *Lancelot Link: Secret Chimp* (1970–72) – a series whose 'actors' were trained chimpanzees in the role of top secret agents from APE (Agency to Prevent Evil).

20  Like the 'action' and 'spy' TV and film genres of the period, *Playboy* magazine also elaborated a matrix of tourism, conspicuous consumption and sexual pleasure in the 'travelogue' features that were one of its staple ingredients during the 1950s and 1960s.

21  Representations of a more active and empowered femininity, however, can be identified in those action–adventure narratives that featured a central female protagonist. British shows such as *The Avengers* (from its second season, 1962–69) and American series such as *Honey West* (1965–66) and *The Girl From U.N.C.L.E.* (1966), for example, can all be seen as offering images of independent and sexually confident 'liberated' women – a model which resonated with the broader emergence of more autonomous and assertive models of femininity during the period. See D' Acci (1997), Miller (2000: 51–74) and Gough-Yates's contribution to this volume (Chapter 5).

22  For discussion of male sexuality as the object of the audience's gaze see Dyer (1982) and Medhurst (1985).

23  See also Medhurst's extended analysis of *Jason King* in this collection (Chapter 11).

24  In the action TV series of the 1970s, playboy–adventurer narratives were increasingly replaced by a combination of programmes based around the exploits of vaguely countercultural youngsters (most obviously *The Mod Squad* (1968–73) and by a new wave of 'tough cop' dramas (with *Mannix* (1967–75) and *Madigan* (1972–73) taking the lead). In the 1980s, however, it is possible to see the playboy–adventurer as making something of a comeback – albeit in a postmodern, semi-ironic form – the decade of the yuppie seeing the arrival of such series as *Magnum P.I.* (1980–88), *Matt Houston* (1982–85), *Miami Vice* (1984–89) and *Remington Steele* (1982–87).

## REFERENCES

Abelson, E. (1989) *When Ladies Go A-Thieving: Middle-Class Shoplifters in the Victorian Department Store*, Oxford: Oxford University Press.

Barer, B. (1993) *The Saint: A Complete History in Print, Radio, Film and Television of Leslie Charteris' Robin Hood of Modern Crime, Simon Templar, 1928-1992*, London: McFarland.

Bennett, T. (1990) *Popular Fiction: Technology, Ideology, Production, Reading*, London: Routledge.

Bennett, T. and Woollacott, J. (1987) *Bond and Beyond: The Political Career of a Popular Hero*, Basingstoke: Macmillan.

Breward, C. (1999) *The Hidden Consumer: Masculinities, Fashion and City Life, 1860-1914*, Manchester: Manchester University Press.

Buxton, D. (1990) *From the Avengers to Miami Vice: Form and Meaning in Television Series*, Manchester: Manchester University Press.

Chapman, J. (1999) *Licence to Thrill: A Cultural History of the James Bond Films*, London: I.B. Tauris.

Chapman, R. (1988) 'The Great Pretender: Variations on the New Man Theme', in R. Chapman and J. Rutherford (eds), *Male Order: Unwrapping Masculinity*, London: Lawrence and Wishart.

Charteris, L. (1961) *The Saint Sees It Through*, London: Pan (orig. publ. 1947).

Chudacoff, H. (1999) *The Age of the Bachelor: Creating an American Subculture*, Princeton: Princeton University Press.

D'Acci, J. (1997) 'Nobody's Woman? *Honey West* and the New Sexuality', in L. Spigel and M. Curtin (eds), *The Revolution Wasn't Televised: Sixties Television and Social Conflict*, London: Routledge.

Dawson, G. (1991) 'The Blond Bedouin', in M. Roper and J. Tosh (eds), *Manful Assertions: Masculinities in Britain Since 1800*, London: Routledge.

Denning, M. (1987) *Cover Stories: Narrative and Ideology in the British Spy Thriller*, London: Routledge.

Dyer, R. (1982), 'Don't Look Now – The Male Pin-Up', *Screen*, Vol. 23, No. 3–4.

Ehrenreich, B. (1983) *The Hearts of Men: American Dreams and the Flight From Commitment*, London: Pluto.

Frank, T. (1997) *The Conquest of Cool: Business Culture, Counterculture and the Rise of Hip Consumerism*, Chicago: University of Chicago Press.

Gans, H. (1965) 'Who's O-O-Oh in America', *Vogue*, 15 March.

Grafton (1962) *Fashions for Men: Tailoring Style Guide*, London: Grafton.

Heath, S. (1981) *Questions of Cinema*, London: Macmillan.

Hoch, P. (1979) *White Hero, Black Beast: Racism, Sexism and the Mask of Masculinity*, London: Pluto.

Leach, W. (1984) 'Transformations in a Culture of Consumption: Women and Department Stores, 1890–1925', *Journal of American History*, Vol. 7, No. 2.

McInerney, J. (1996) 'How Bond Saved America – And Me', in J. McInerney *et al.* (eds), *Dressed to Kill: James Bond, the Suited Hero*, New York: Flammarion.

Marwick, A. (1984) '*Room at the Top, Saturday Night and Sunday Morning* and the "Cultural Revolution" in Britain', *Journal of Contemporary History*, Vol. 19, No. 1.

Medhurst, A. (1984) '*Victim*: Text as Context', *Screen*, Vol. 25, Nos. 4–5.

—— (1985) 'Can Chaps Be Pin-Ups?: the British Male Film Star of the 1950s', *Ten/8*, Vol. 8, No. 17.

—— (1994) 'Home Amusement', in *Are We Having Fun Yet?: The Sight and Sound Comedy Supplement*, March.

Mercer, C. (1986) 'That's Entertainment: The Resilience of Popular Forms', in T. Bennett, C. Mercer and J. Woollacott (eds), *Popular Culture and Social Relations*, Milton Keynes: Open University Press.

Miller, J. (2000) *Something Completely Different: British Television and American Culture*, Minneapolis: University of Minnesota Press.

Mort, F. (1988) 'Boys Own? Masculinity, Style and Popular Culture', in R. Chapman and J. Rutherford (eds), *Male Order: Unwrapping Masculinity*, London: Lawrence and Wishart.

—— (1996) *Cultures of Consumption: Masculinities and Social Space in Late Twentieth-Century Britain*, London: Routledge.

—— (1997) 'Paths to Mass Consumption: Britain and the USA Since 1945', in M. Nava, A. Blake, I. MacRury and B. Richards (eds), *Buy This Book: Studies in Advertising and Consumption*, London: Routledge.

Nava, M. (1996) 'Modernity's Disavowal: Women, the City and the Department Store', in M. Nava and A. O'Shea (eds), *Modern Times: Reflections on a Century of English Modernity*, London: Routledge.

Nixon, S. (1996) *Hard Looks: Masculinities, Spectatorship and Contemporary Consumption*, London: UCL Press.

Osgerby, B. (2001 forthcoming) *Playboys in Paradise: Masculinity, Youth and Leisure-Style in Modern America*, Oxford: Berg.

Segal, L. (1988) 'Look Back in Anger: Men in the 50s', in R. Chapman and J. Rutherford (eds), *Male Order: Unwrapping Masculinity*, London: Lawrence and Wishart.

—— (1990) *SlowMotion: Changing Masculinities, Changing Men*, London: Virago.

Simper, P. (1997) *The Saint: From Big Screen to Small Screen and Back Again*, London: Chameleon.

Walkowitz, J. (1992) *City of Dreadful Delight*, London: Virago.

Wiseman, J. (1999) 'The Man Who Persuaded *The Persuaders!*: Interview with Robert S. Baker', *Action TV*, Vol. 1, No. 1, Winter.

Worland, R. (1994) 'The Cold War Mannerists: The Man From U.N.C.L.E. and TV Espionage in the 1960s', *Journal of Popular Film and Television*, Vol. 21, No. 4, Winter.

# 3

# 'WHO LOVES YA, BABY?'

## *Kojak*, action and the great society

### *Paul Cobley*

Between 1973 and 1978, Universal's *Kojak* was one of the most popular TV police shows ever aired. It was a major ratings hit in the United States (see *Variety*, 31 October 1973) and it went on to spark a heated battle over which TV channels would buy it in the United Kingdom (see *Evening Standard*, 10 December 1973). In the pantheon of the action TV series *Kojak* occupies a central place even though it appeared at a time when the television networks of the West were awash with police series (see Martindale, 1991). Popular discussion in the 1970s, in reviews and TV guides, circulated the idea that the cop show had simply *replaced* the Western as the foremost TV genre. Yet even after acknowledging that this is a gross oversimplification *Kojak* stands out from other police series: partly because of its depiction of action scenes but also because of the way in which it portrayed social problems and issues of identity which demanded action. Although it is long gone from our screens, *Kojak* arguably remains today as a credible example of the action TV series of the 1970s.

This essay attempts to assess *Kojak* as a historical artefact in its first moment of reception. It considers the resources available for such a task, specifically issues to do with *genre* – the thriller, the police sub-genre and the action TV series – and issues to do with *history*. However, it argues that these are not to be considered as separate problems – *Kojak* is not considered simply to 'reflect' social reality, nor is it suggested that the series was, by virtue of its generic paraphernalia, divorced from historical matters. On the contrary, it will be seen that demands of verisimilitude embedded in the genre necessitate a different approach to understanding contemporary receptions of *Kojak*. This entails a consideration not just of contemporary discourses regarding police work and crime, but also the social forces which impinge upon them.

### ALWAYS HISTORICISE

It is all too easy to laugh at texts from the recent past. The clothes worn by people in them have gone out of fashion; the hairstyles seem risible; and the social attitudes implicit in textual events and narratives seem archaic to our contemporary knowing sensibility. Texts from the recent past provide a 'shock of the familiar': they are not so remote that they exist as historical specimens but they embody positions whose proximate existence has been repressed by the unquestioned omnipotence of social mores.

Identifying texts as 'very much of their time' is not difficult in these circumstances. When there are clear textual indicators which provoke mirth, or even distaste, the task of placing a given artefact in its historical context is offered a head start.

But what about those texts which do not manifest these superficial historical characteristics? And what if these texts might actually be deemed in the present to be of 'quality', either by dint of production values or by virtue of the kinds of social consciousnesses implicated in them? The usual response is to suggest that somehow, such texts 'transcend their time', or worse, 'transcend their genre'. Somehow, these texts have something about them that makes them more forward-looking, more in tune with what will be the future – our present. As such, they are seen to be, in a way, not quite so subordinate to the historical forces which traverse those other texts which are quite clearly '*of* their time'.

Now, of course, this will not do. Simply because a past text has attributes that are found to be congenial to the contemporary mindset, this alone cannot exempt it from history. Consumers of entertainment texts can, nevertheless, be forgiven for adopting such a perspective or seemingly not adopting any strongly defended position at all on texts; their use of them does not necessarily foreground the difficult questions of historicality. But anybody concerned with a critical take on texts from the past – and this includes writers in journalism as well as academia – is duty-bound to meditate more seriously on historicality and textuality. The questions that need to be asked are: what were the key social forces when this text first appeared? What are the textual devices which inflect or refract social reality? And, above all, what might contemporary audiences have thought of this text?

All of these are formidable questions but all are undoubtedly crucial. Frequently, a 'historical' investigation of texts has involved cross-referencing with the historical record or historical writings in order to 'read off' the content of texts as representing historical changes. There is some mileage in this (see, for example, House, 1960) and it has smoothly passed into middle-brow and journalistic common-sense thinking about different kinds of cultural production. Similarly, investigations of textuality have charted changes which are specific to certain periods such as 'realism', 'modernism' and 'postmodernism', although it must also be said that such investigations are frequently selective and rely on a concept of the 'canon' even when the texts which are under discussion are popular rather than valorized (see Cobley, 2000: Chapter 1). It is when considerations of audience are introduced, though, that the cat is really put among the pigeons. How can we know what audiences in the past thought about the texts they consumed? Judicious use of qualitative methodologies might assist research into readings in the *present*; but as regards readers from the *past*, the moment is lost. Faced with this dilemma, the most useful expedient I have found involves revisiting some aspects of Marxist cultural theory and framing them within a semiotic perspective.

Reflecting on the different levels of a 'social formation' the Algerian-born French Marxist, Louis Althusser, famously invoked Lenin's (1916) analysis of Russia as 'unevenly developed' (Althusser, 1977: 94–97). For Lenin, Russia was a country marked not by a steady and equal progress in all spheres but characterized, instead, as consisting of some areas that were highly developed (the revolutionary elite, cultivated in exile in Europe, for example), some underdeveloped (heavy industry), and some positively antediluvian (religion). Althusser builds upon this insight into uneven relations in order to work through the links between features of the economy (and, by association, all brute facts of social existence) and features of the discursive world (including phenomena such as 'art'), each of which operates according to its own rules and circumstances.

The world of the economy, production and resources, however, is not subject to the same degree of human input as the discursive sphere; humans have to really be factored into this latter because they play such a significant role in making – or reading – discursive products such as 'literature' and 'art'. Bennett (1987; 1990) therefore extends the 'uneven' scenario by way of the concept of a 'reading formation'. He stresses the importance of a number of discursive practices that operate on readers before, and simultaneous with, the texts which make up the discursive sphere, ordering the relations between texts in a definite way 'such that their reading is always-already cued in specific directions that are not given by those "texts themselves" as entities separable from such relations' (Bennett and Woollacott, 1987: 64).

A reading formation will usually include, among other things, a certain kind of literacy training; a knowledge of authorship; a knowledge of how various institutions work – the film industry, publishing, broadcasting, advertising, publicity; popular, word-of-mouth, assessments of texts; and so on. One important multifaceted feature of the reading formation will be history, or the contemporary social world. But this is not to be understood, as is so frequently the case, as simply a set of ineluctable facts; it, too, may be implicated with the discursive. One fundamental semiotic tenet, derived from the work of Peirce, is that signs in history are not only determined by a relation to a real object but also by what the human being makes of them (Pencak, 1998: 105). Moreover, historical events which might be thought of as concrete and limited in their meaning, are more profitably to be conceived as messages which are decoded by addressees according to circumstances (Uspenskij, 1977). Humans, far from operating as completely free agents who pick and mix from the phenomena of the world, exist in an environment of signs (or an *umwelt* – see Sebeok, 1979). The text in history then is not just a text related to a series of easily ascertainable facts; instead, it is a text related to some facts and not others, and facts which mean particular things to contemporary audiences.

## *KOJAK* AND THE POLICE GENRE

This may seem like an unnecessarily heavy preamble to a popular TV series like *Kojak*. However, there is a need to be clear that *Kojak* is very much part of a specific historical period. True, it has not been subject to the 'cheesy' 1990s repackaging of a putative Zeitgeist that has been evident with such 1970s artefacts as *Starsky and Hutch* (from the United States), *The Persuaders!* (from Britain) and other texts discussed elsewhere in this volume.[1] But, such a repackaging would not be entirely out of the question because, after all, some of the same fashion statements appear in *Kojak* as these other texts. What is being stressed in this essay is the importance of recognizing the webs of relations in which highly popular artefacts from the past were suspended at their moment of first appearance, relations which might be much different from the ones experienced in our own, equally historically determined present, and whose configuration might actually reveal to us some insights about what we value.

The contemporary popularity of *Kojak* cannot be over-emphasized. Played by veteran actor, Telly Savalas, Kojak became a huge mainstream figure with his trademark lollipops, his distinctive bald head and features, and his signature enquiry to cops and villains, 'Who loves ya, baby?' (See Figure 3.1.) In spite of his lack of conventional musical talent Savalas went on to become a successful recording star, a cabaret artist and a transgenerational sex symbol. Audiences even began to conflate Savalas with Kojak, as 'Kojak' lollipops appeared in confectioners and 'Kojak' cuts were available at the barber's (Daly, 1975). In short, Kojak was very much a character who embodied a site of social investment for the reader; as Denning (1998: 46, 94, 139) would put it, Kojak was an ideological 'figure', like so many characters in the history of fiction – from Lovelace, through Sherlock Holmes, to James Bond – who, as a result of readers' demands, live on beyond the texts which initially embody them.

Yet the television production, *Kojak*, in spite of its many episodes, could not have built up such a complex site of investment – especially so quickly – without considerable work by readers. These readers would, of course, themselves, be caught up in the relations of history and the specific reading formation. One major constituent of this latter is the concept of genre and the fact that *Kojak* was part of the genre which concerns itself with the police. On its own, this fact is likely to produce certain expectations for readers. This is because the police genre or sub-genre is not, by any means, a new thing – police routine features as a major component in the very inception of the thriller genre (Knight, 1980; Panek, 1990). But *Kojak* was also part of the unprecedented explosion of police narratives onto the 1970s entertainment scene: in print, old hands like Ed McBain and Dorothy Uhnak continued to publish bestsellers, while newcomers such as Joseph Wambaugh and K. C. Constantine produced critically well-received books; in the cinema, the Dirty Harry series sustained a strong following while the narratives of no less than three films focused on the exploits of real-life detective, Eddie Egan – the commercially successful *The French Connection* (1971) and *The French Connection II* (1975) as well as the less lucrative *Badge 273* (1973); non-fiction narratives such as the books about the 'Super Cops' (Greenberg, 1977 and Whittlemore, 1974) and the film depicting their exploits (1974) presented details of police life which were viewed as 'strange but true'; and corruption was on the agenda in films like *McQ* (1974), *The Take* (1974) and, especially, *Serpico* (1973). By far the strongest evidence of the burgeoning of the police genre, however, was offered by television.

Television police series seemed to harbour a greater range of possibilities to deal with the unlimited breadth of police work. In terms of other genres within the broad category of 'thriller' (Harper, 1969; Merry, 1977; Palmer, 1978; Roth, 1995), the police genre has frequently been considered to possess a superior verisimilitude. This is largely because, in the real world, the sheer variety and danger of urban police work

*Figure 3.1* 'Who loves ya, baby?' – Telly Savalas as Lt. Theo Kojak.

outweighs the straightforward mundanity of, say, the security operations and surveillance which characterize real – as opposed to the heavily embellished fictional – private detection (see Ellroy, 1994 and Messent, 1997; cf. Cobley, 1997). Over the period of a season, a television police series might be able to touch on issues raised by different kinds of misdemeanour and the diverse determinants acting upon the interaction of police and public. This is not to say that all police series produced in the 1970s were characterized by narratives geared towards acute social investigation. One of the most popular, *Columbo* (1971), for example, traded exclusively in 'inverted whodunits' set in an upper-middle-class milieu, leaving little or no possibility of social comment or investment.

However, it seems to be the case that the police genre was, in a quite specific way, especially ripe for investments by audiences at this time. There was a convergence of forces in the social formation during the period which not only fostered degrees of cynicism about police operatives in a fashion which had not been encountered before, but also a set of discourses which served to heighten the complexity of public understanding of police work. A consideration of *Kojak* in its historical context needs to take these seriously.

## POLICING THE GREAT SOCIETY

The period leading up to the first appearance of *Kojak* had witnessed enormous change in the United States' organization of, and attitude to, policing. In 1967, the President's Commission on Law Enforcement and the Administration of Justice identified 420,000 people working for approximately 40,000 separate law enforcement agencies spending $2.5 billion a year (President's Commission, 1967: 91 ff). Since 1945, the police in America had become part of a large and unwieldy bureaucracy. In the face of mounting crime, departments repeatedly opted for specialization, transferring vice control, traffic regulation, crime prevention and a range of routine tasks from ordinary patrolmen to organized squads (Fogelson, 1977: 240 ff). At the same time, legal precedents made law enforcement and administration more difficult for police operatives. A series of landmark Supreme Court decisions, designed to protect against unsafe convictions, followed in quick succession during the 1960s. *Mapp* (1961) restricted previous guidelines on search and seizure, *Escobedo* (1964) re-drew the grounds for gaining confessions from suspects, while the cases of *Wade, Gilbert* and *Stoval* (all 1967) introduced new edicts on eye-witness identification and line-ups. One of the most momentous decisions, however, concerned *Miranda* (1966), which required police officers to read suspects their rights before placing them under arrest (Fogelson, 1977: 239). From the view of the police, as Jerry Wilson of the Washington DC force argues, none of the purposes of the new laws could be disputed; yet the 'commensurate increases in police personnel and court facilities' necessary to make the laws effective in most cities were never provided (1975: 30).

The changes in policing structures and in the law on suspects engendered, in retrospect, an unsurprising measure of conflict. As Fogelson puts it, police departments:

authorized uniformed officers to stop, question, and if they deemed it necessary, frisk anyone who aroused their suspicion. As a result of these changes,
the big-city police now intervened in all sorts of situations which in the
absence of a strong complaint they would have ignored a generation or two
before. By so doing – by arresting a taxpayer for gambling, citing a motorist
for speeding, and ordering a few teenagers to keep moving – they generated a
great deal of resentment.

(Fogelson, 1977: 241)

In addition – and in contrast to Britain – the American police lacked the weight of
custom or traditional respect of the public.[2] Among the police the widespread lack of
citizen deference manifested a socio-political dimension as well as a grass roots one.
Sociologists of the period repeatedly found that police–citizen encounters were potentially so fraught with communicative misunderstandings and the threat of hostility
and violence that police counter-assertions of authority were frequently liable to escalation.[3] Studies called for a renewal of citizens' understanding of the civic role of the
police (Livermore, 1980; Rubinstein, 1980; Wiley and Hudik, 1980; cf. Reiss, 1971:
179 ff).

Flashpoints arising from routine police–citizen encounters were almost always at
the root of disturbances with a palpable political or socio-economic bearing, instances
where resentment had built up over time. Thernstrom and Thernstrom (1997: 163)
suggest that the police were crucial catalysts in the racially-inflected riots in American
cities during the 1960s, not just because police actions were usually the precipitating
incidents in disorders but also because, for African–Americans especially, the police
represented a visible instrument of 'white' authority (cf. Wambaugh, 1970 and Richardson, 1974: 180). In a poll taken by the National Opinion Research Center, alongside the work of the President's Commission, it was found that 63 per cent of whites
thought the police to be 'almost all honest' while only 30 per cent of blacks believed
this to be the case (cited in Richardson, 1974: 183). The much-vaunted explosion of
crime rates in the 1960s – especially in respect to violent crime – did include a tripling
of rates of arrest of black men on homicide charges (Thernstrom and Thernstrom,
1997: 173). Yet whatever inference can be drawn from this it is also well-known that
over the next thirty years black men were to become murder *victims* at twice the rate
that they were in 1960 (ibid.: 262 ff).

The relation of 'race' and downgrading of authority was to solidify among the
police, especially when police complaints about the lack of respect for authority were
all too easily inflected along lines of ethnicity (Coles, 1971). In addition to conflict
with the growing 'ethnic minority' communities, the force – staffed overwhelmingly
by whites throughout the 1960s [4] – was also frequently loath to embrace the whole
package of liberal discourses which had given rise to the *Miranda* and *Escobedo* deci-
sions and which so regularly seemed to hamper them in doing their jobs. These
broader liberal discourses, which were to have a profound effect on attitudes toward
policing in the United States, had undoubtedly been the culmination of the civil
rights protests. As many have observed, one effect of the battle for civil rights in the

United States during the 1950s and 1960s was that American citizens in general became more acutely aware of *their* rights: as consumers, as citizens, as taxpayers and as police suspects (see, for example, Farber, 1994: 109). At the same time, President Johnson launched the Great Society programme to fulfil his campaign promise in the 1964 election. Passing a huge number of domestic bills in a period comparable only to that of the New Deal, the administration also announced a widespread 'War on Poverty' (Zarefsky, 1996). Central to the 'War on Poverty' was welfare provision in the form of AFDC (Aids to Families with Dependent Children) which was rapidly taken up by huge numbers.[5]

What all commentators would agree – even those who seek to explore a conservative/liberal consensus on welfare issues (Handler and Hasenfeld, 1991) – is that the 'War on Poverty' was largely responsible for a new public perspective on contemporary events which was more alert to the manifold implications of social determinants. It is true that the limited media coverage of the 'War on Poverty' as a major programme tends to infer that it was an issue that lacked newsworthiness, although there is evidence to suggest that when coverage did occur, it was positive towards the programme (Menzies, 1986; Green, 1986). Nevertheless, it can be argued that the social determinants of poverty and, by association, *crime* became cemented in the American consciousness in a fashion which had not been previously experienced, perhaps, since the 1930s.

Because the vision and the rhetoric of the 'War on Poverty' was not met by concomitant results, it was not surprising that disillusionment set in among the American public (Zarefsky, 1996: 205; Gelfand, 1987). In fact, it has been suggested that welfare, along with the extension in civil rights during the period, encouraged some Americans to view the Great Society as a 'nigger' society (O'Reilly, 1995: 245). Ethnicity, rights and poverty had become publicly foregrounded as a contemporary Gordian knot – where matters to do with one were raised, at least one of the others would invariably be entangled in it.

Police genres, perhaps, would seem an apposite place for the playing through of these matters as, indeed, in some cases, they were. As a result of the strong demands of verisimilitude entailed in the genre they could not help but touch on contemporary social dilemmas, even when they were at their most obtuse. Although it is easily forgotten, the issues of racism, criminal rights, corruption, reform and the social determinants of poverty were to be central to the police series developed around the character of Lieutenant Theo Kojak.

## 'WHEN THERE'S NO JUSTICE, THERE'S VIOLENCE'

The proliferation of various images of the police operative or private detective – the detective as disabled (*Ironside*, 1967–75), as urban cowboy *(McCloud,* 1970–77*),* as medical examiner (*Quincy*, 1976–83), as braless woman (*Charlie's Angels*, 1976–81), as black (*Tenafly,* 1973–74; *Shaft,* 1973–74) and even as ordinary and physically unattractive (*Cannon*) – is well known, especially on American TV in the 1970s. Yet, the social significance beyond the sometimes superficial exigencies of the image is usually crucial in sustaining widespread audience investment. This is certainly so with Kojak. The character first appeared in a feature-length pilot which set the tenor for the series that followed and provided the foundations for readings of the protagonist. *The Marcus–Nelson Murders* (March 1973) was a dramatization of a true-life drama, the case of the Wylie–Hoffert slayings which began to unfold in New York City in 1963.

The story dealt with the brutal murders of two young white middle-class women (Jo Ann Marcus and Kathy Nelson), career girls who shared a flat into which the murderer had gained entry. It goes on to detail the way that, eight months later, with pressure mounting on the police, a young Brooklyn man with learning difficulties, Lewis Humes (Gene Woodbury), is arrested on suspicion of a couple of attempted rapes and subsequently charged with the murders of the white women. The Manhattan detective leading the Marcus–Nelson case, Lieutenant Theo Kojack,[6] is suspicious about the arrest and the confession from the very outset. Further investigation by him reveals that the evidence, the confession and the arrest procedure in the case are all highly suspect. In league with a seasoned defence lawyer, Jake Weinhaus (Jose Ferrer), to whom he riskily leaks information, Kojack attempts to clear Humes' name.[7]

The film opens with a caption and a voice-over which states that the film is a dramatization of real events (with subsequent compressions, name changes, etc.) in a case which preceded the Supreme Court's *Miranda* decision of 1966. The opening shot shows a live televisation of Martin Luther King's speech from the steps of the Lincoln Memorial on 28 August 1963. The TV is being watched by Jo Ann Marcus (Elizabeth Berger), and so the event places the action in a specific year, before the *Miranda* decision. In addition, the momentous nature of the speech is of no small consequence to the plot, as it is later voiced in the case that the majority of black American adults would be likely to know where they were when the speech was made. Most crucially of all, though, the speech plays as the brutal killing takes place, with King's dream that 'my four little children will one day live in a nation where they will not be judged by the color of their skin but by the content of their character' echoing on the soundtrack as the prelude to a hideous miscarriage of justice.

As soon as the police are mobilized following the killings, it is Kojak's voice-over which is insistently heard. As well as this, the way in which the suspect is arrested and then questioned is obviously central to the case and the narrative. Humes is hauled in by patrolman Stabile (Paul Jenkins) the night after an attempted rape on Mrs Alvarez (Antonia Rey). He has been trying to keep warm in a derelict house but when questioned about the crime says that he thinks he saw the attacker – a man physically much different to himself, according to Rita Alvarez's description – and that he would be willing to help. That Humes becomes a suspect in this way despite the lack of 'clues' is not as removed from routine police work as it seems: as Reiss points out, most detective work depends on locating an individual who may be known in the community or a previous offender rather than following leads (1971: 108).[8] When taken to the station in Brooklyn an identification procedure involving Mrs Alvarez is set up. She looks through a peephole at Lewis Humes alone as he says, under police instructions, 'Lady, I'm gonna rape, you; lady, I'm gonna kill you'. Hearing the words that were used by her attacker, Mrs Alvarez becomes agitated and pronounces Lewis the criminal.

Humes is not read his rights; deprived of sleep and unaware of the crime that he is being interviewed about, he dictates a 61-page confession. Kojack is immediately suspicious when he drives down from Manhattan to read the document, but this is lost in the self-congratulation in the station. Later, as Kojack questions the suspect, flashbacks reveal the squeaky clean version of events offered by the detectives, preceded by Humes' version in which the confession was beaten out of him. In spite of the fact that the attacker in the Alvarez attempted rape case was described as black, the narrative makes clear at various points that Humes' implication in the Marcus–Nelson murders is very much tied up with common police racism. As Jake Weinhaus later adds in court, 'Law and order is being used in this country as a catchphrase for "stop the nigger"'.

Not all is black and white in the narrative, however. Kojack investigates a suspect whom he knows, a young white burglar and heroin addict, Teddy Hopper (Marjoe Gortner). Initially, Kojack is as insistent that Teddy is innocent as he has been about Lewis Humes. However, after a somewhat dubious entrapment procedure in which Teddy has all but implicated himself, Kojack loses his temper the night before Humes' trial and starts to beat a confession out of Teddy as he is in withdrawal. Fellow detectives pull Kojack back saying, 'You're doing exactly what you said the young guys from Brooklyn did'. If this does not give a sense of the way in which the narrative is by no means a neat portrayal of right and wrong as easy opposites, the rest of the narrative certainly does.

When Humes is acquitted the camera does not pull back from the courthouse to provide an Olympian view of the triumphant American judiciary. Instead, Kojack is back in his office and somewhat reluctantly accepts a telephone invitation to visit Lewis Humes and his family in celebration at the acquittal. He is then shown parking near a tenement which is mercilessly dilapidated even by the standards of iconography in this film. At the party, where one of Humes' male relatives shakes hands limply with Kojack, the only white man there, and treats him with contempt, Lewis presents Kojack with a painting of the detective holding back the legal wolves. Kojack accepts the picture but the film shows no signs of reaching a conclusion. As the family gather round the television with the detective to watch Lewis' release on the evening news, the bulletin concludes with the prosecutor in the case Mario Portello (Allen Garfield) saying that this is not the end.

The following scenes show Humes being retried on the same tired evidence for the attempted rape of Mrs Alvarez. This time he is convicted, and although he is a first-time offender and it is clear that his conviction is a political measure, he receives a five-to ten-year sentence. As the film ends, Kojack's voice-over dominates:

> I saw for the first time what Jake Weinhaus meant when he said 'When there's no justice, there's violence'.

> I remember the first time I walked the beat. I felt that we were doing the most wonderful job in the world. I thought of us as 'watchers of the city', protecting what was best in it.

Some people say the community gets the police force it deserves. I say the police force *is* the community.

That was the end of the Humes case. Except that it changed my life – and yours.

The Humes case was cited in the Miranda decision of the Supreme Court which demands that his constitutional rights be read to a man under arrest …

Kojack then goes on to list the fortunes of the players including himself – despite dreaming of handing in his badge, he says, 'The truth is, I still go on'.

If there is one feature which runs through the whole of the subsequent TV series, *Kojak*, it is this insistent weariness on the part of the protagonist. It is true that the character of Theo Kojak is also wryly humorous, streetwise and an admirer of the finer things in life. Likewise, it is the case that numerous other fictional police operatives have been marked by a special kind of occupational cynicism. Yet, set against the other semantic or iconographic elements of the series – the derelict buildings and slums in which many of the investigations take place; the dingy squad rooms; and the unwholesome or ordinary-looking colleagues such as Detective Stavros (George Savalas), Detective Rizzo (Vince Conti) and Captain McNeil (Dan Frazer) [9] – Kojak's weariness was meaningful and continuous. At the very least it signified the irresolute nature of social problems.

The final scenes of the pilot film, accompanied by the voice-over, show Kojack, driving his car onto the pavement, exiting it and chasing a petty criminal in a horribly rundown enclave in New York. This clearly sets up the series that is to follow; but even in the liberal reformist mood that the film can, perhaps, be accused of, it is quite a bleak ending. In fact, the chief part of the verisimilitude in the pilot and the series consisted of this bleakness. Universally, critics praised the unremitting ugliness of the city's slums as depicted in the film. This, of course, was helped by shooting entirely on location, especially in Spanish Harlem and the Brownsville section of Brooklyn.

It should be mentioned, though, that the authentic squalor of pre-urban-renewal New York was heightened for potential audience appreciation by the techniques of filming. There is constant background noise on the soundtrack, especially traffic sounds. In one scene where Humes is berated in the street by his brother for getting entangled with the police, the two characters move further and further away and their conversation diminishes over a long period, making it clear that just one microphone has been employed in the scene. Similarly, it appears that hand-held 16mm cameras were utilized on outdoor shots (and some indoor ones such as the courtroom) lending to the 'documentaristic' feel. Even the television series which, for reasons of profit opposed by its star (see Daly, 1975: 120) filmed many of its interior scenes at Universal's studios in Hollywood, was praised for 'an air of realism which permeates the show, giving it an almost "You Are There" aura' (*Variety*, 26 October 1973). For *Time* the series showed 'New York City in all its roach and racketeering misery' (26 October 1973).

In the pilot, the police stations had been as real as the outdoor locations and just as squalid. The series was to lose this a little but it compensated, perhaps, with realism elsewhere. When the series was first shown in the United States, in October 1973, there was controversy about the violence, particularly in the first episode, 'Siege of Terror', which starred Harvey Keitel as a mobster (see, especially, *Variety*, 26 October 1973 and *New York Times*, 25 October 1973). The characters' speech also was found to be candid: *The Daily News* said that 'There's no phony wasted dialogue in "Kojak" … [a] gripping, realistic production'. Arguably, this realism was the main cue for reading the film and the series even if the character of Kojak, the lollipops, the sharp suits and the catchphrases were soon to gain prominence.

Yet we must be clear that the phenomenon of realism in the series was based not so much on the 'facts' of reality, but on what audiences believed about the social formation. Obviously, the criticism to which the series is most susceptible is that it did not depict the out-and-out mundanity of police work (filing, report writing, etc.); but, notwithstanding this lament which could be lodged at any fictional representation, *Kojak* was found to be not dissimilar to other non-fictional discourses. Moreover, the idea that this was the case quickly entered circulation. In *The New Republic*, for example, Rosenblatt argued that 'The structure of *Kojak* takes its inspiration from the news … What are stories in the news are ideas and events on *Kojak*; rape, cops, citizen responsibility, vigilantes, guns, kids, ethnic groups …' (quoted in Daly, 1975: 122).

Even more frequently, the series was to be mentioned for its complex plotting and multi-causal view of events. Two examples taken virtually at random should suffice to suggest that *Kojak* was a little more sophisticated in this sphere than routine cops and robbers stories. In the third season, 'Money Back Guarantee' (December 1975) begins with the killing of an ageing patrol cop who has stopped an automobile repossession man; but this is not a revenge drama about bringing a cop killer to justice. Kojak visits the scene, which is surrounded by press and onlookers and demands that the 'circus' be cleared up and that the dead cop's partner, an injured victim in the incident, help with inquiries. Sergeant Crocker tells Kojak that the young partner has only been six months in the job; Kojak says it's an occupation where one becomes old very fast. With the young cop's help in identification, Kojak and his team eventually uncover the web of deceit which leads to the death of a policeman – an elaborate insurance scam involving grand theft auto, bogus repossession men, the complicity of a bank worker and, especially, over-stretched car owners.

Even if we take the penultimate episode of the fifth, and final, season, '60 Miles to Hell' (March 1978), the residue of Kojak's weary persona remains intact as does the complexity of the view of the criminal world. All this despite the fact that the episode stars Liberace as himself (!), features a 'topless twins magic act' and is set in Las Vegas. These elements are woven into a plot in which Crocker is delivering Vic Whitley (Gianni Russo), a racketeer who is being extradited to give evidence against his brother – and partner in crime – in New York. At Las Vegas International, though, after having his gun removed by flight security, Crocker, his prisoner, and some other passengers alighting from a plane are kidnapped by a group of men. Both Crocker and Whitley (as well as Kojak and McNeil in New York) believe that the kidnapping has been perpetrated by associates of the mobster brothers; it transpires, however, that this is not the case. Instead, it is one more highly elaborate scam in which the kidnappers –

some of whom are from the Sheriff's posse – wish to create a decoy so that the Sheriff and his men remain searching for their trail while they intercept a consignment of marijuana which is actually controlled (completely coincidentally) by none other than the Whitley brothers. Late in the episode, in a kind of reversal of 'Money Back Guarantee', it is revealed that the event that sets the following train in motion is that the Whitley brothers had previously shot a cop in New York when a marijuana consignment of theirs was stopped.

## 'WHO LOVES YA, BABY?'

The chief features of *Kojak* as a series and as a figure, then, revolve around 'realism' or verisimilitude. Weariness, complexity, squalor, and even 'documentaristic' techniques of filming, it might be argued, have not gone out of fashion in the intervening period. In fact, these features are so strong that a reading of *Kojak* in the present tends to over-ride the tendency of identifying the supposed 'naïveté' in texts from the recent past. But if we are to remain committed to a historical understanding of *Kojak* it is imperative that we do not rely on transcendent categories such as 'realism' or, even, 'political correctness'. The original audience for *Kojak* did not exist in a vacuum, untouched by other signs; the verisimilitude of the series operated within the new tangled co-ordinates of public knowledge about racism, criminal rights, civic corruption, reform and the social determinants of poverty. American police work was shown as one activity interacting with a huge set of formidable social forces including many which had come to prominence in contemporary discourses.

What were thought to be 'old' styles of depicting the police were, at the time, implicitly criticized in the praise heaped upon *Kojak*. Too often, though, police and, indeed, other action genres, have been analysed in terms of the ways in which they present imaginary resolutions to complex social problems, fictional conclusions that, it is frequently implied, amount to ideological palliatives. Yet it is in the very nature of the police genre that there is reference to the real world of social conditions and, in fact, the very seriality of a character like Kojak is, in a way, a guarantee of a certain level of verisimilitude. Apparent localized resolutions may occur in police narratives but, as Kojak says, he still goes on. He watches the city. He also asks 'Who loves ya, baby?' because he knows that a mass of social forces militate against loving relations, even in a Great Society. Far from being an ideological palliative, then, resolution in police genre texts like *Kojak* only reveals to an audience well apprised of the convoluted nature of social existence the infinite number of resolutions which must take place before there is absolute equilibrium.

## NOTES

1   Though, at the time of writing, early episodes of *Kojak* are about to be released on video.
2   The sociologist, Albert Reiss, suggests that 'The police in the United States have occupational prestige. They do not have status honor' (1971: 215). As Reiss and all other

researchers into American police work have found, the most common complaint among rank and file police operatives regards the failure of citizens to show respect for authority.

3  In their work for the President's Commission, Reiss and his researchers found that the citizen was described as 'agitated' or 'excited' in 48 per cent of all citizen–police encounters when an officer was deemed 'hostile', 35 per cent when he was 'brusque' or 'authoritarian', 42 per cent in which he openly ridiculed a citizen, and 57 per cent when the officer 'subtly ridiculed' or belittled a citizen (1971: 51).

4  A black recruitment drive during the early 1970s did meet with some success in several cities (Fogelson, 1977: 248), but the dominance of whites in the organization could lead to considerable difficulties for any young black people who had the temerity to join the force (see Alex, 1969).

5  The reasons for this sudden uptake revolve around the phenomena of increased single parenthood, migration from the South, discrimination, an increase in drug addiction and high rates of youth unemployment (Piven and Cloward, 1971). Nevertheless, welfare provision in the United States continued to provide an arena for heated public debate and it is worth pondering here in respect of attitudes towards policing and legal procedures which might tend to 'blame the victim'. The 'War on Poverty' remained a topic for social analysis in America well after its 'demise' in the early 1970s, with the left typically complaining that it was a reform measure which did not address fundamental inequality while the right has variously attributed its 'failure' to the creation of a dependency culture or the improvidence of individuals (see Murray, 1984 and Mead, 1986).

6  Originally envisaged as a Pole, this is how the detective's name was spelt in the pilot.

7  It is significant that the dogged champion of the defendant in real life was not a detective but a reporter called Selwyn Raab. His book eventually recounted the full details of the case and it was he who kept the defence lawyer in touch with relevant information. Given the importance of the role of the press in the 1970s – both in the thriller and in the investigative reporting that broke the Pentagon Papers and Watergate stories (*New York Times*, 1971; Ungar, 1989; Woodward and Bernstein, 1974; 1977. See also Cobley, 2000) – this is notable. In a set-up which recalls the anonymous Watergate informant, Deep Throat, Kojack tells Weinhaus that he is taking a risk in leaking information because 'I was expecting somebody else to do it – but nobody is'.

8  Reiss notes that 'The only offenses for which detectives accounted for at least two in every ten arrests were arson and fugitives from justice' (1971: 108).

9  The exception to the rule about Kojak's colleagues is, of course, Sergeant Crocker (Kevin Dobson) who became a sex symbol in his own right. Dan Frazer, who played Captain McNeil, found himself in the similar role of lugubrious and semi-bureaucratic boss of the heroine in blaxploitation classic, *Cleopatra Jones* (1973).

# REFERENCES

Alex, N. (1969) *Black in Blue: A Study of the Negro Policeman*, New York: Appleton Century Crofts.

Althusser, L. (1977) 'Contradiction and Overdetermination', in *For Marx*, trans. B. Brewster, London: New Left Books.

Bennett, T. (1987) 'Texts, Readers, Reading Formations', in D. Attridge *et al.* (eds), *Post-structuralism and the Question of History*, Cambridge: Cambridge University Press.

—— (1990) *Outside Literature*, London: Routledge.

Bennett, T. and Woollacott, J. (1987) *Bond and Beyond: The Political Career of a Popular Hero*, London: Macmillan.

Cobley, P. (1997) 'The Specific Regime of Verisimilitude in the Thriller', in I. Rauch and G. Carr (eds), *Synthesis in Diversity: Proceedings of the 5th Congress of the IASS*, Berlin: Mouton.

—— (2000) *The American Thriller: Generic Innovation and Social Change in the 1970s,* London: Macmillan.

Coles, R. (1971) 'Policeman Complaints', *New York Times Magazine,* 11 June. Reprinted in Potholm and Morgan (1976).

Daly, M. (1975) *Telly Savalas,* London: Sphere.

Denning, M. (1998) *Mechanic Accents: Dime Novels and Working-Class Culture in America* (2nd edn), London: Verso.

Ellroy, J. (1994) 'Without Walls: The American Cop', Channel 4 (broadcast 29 November).

*Evening Standard* (1973) 'BBC and ITV Battle for Telly the US Cop', 10 December.

Farber, D. (1994) *The Age of Great Dreams: America in the 1960s,* New York: Hill and Wang.

Fogelson, R.N. (1977) *Big-City Police.* Cambridge, MA, and London: Harvard University Press.

Gelfand, M.I. (1987) 'The War on Poverty', in R.A. Divine (ed.), *The Johnson Years Vol 1: Foreign Policy, the Great Society and the White House,* Lawrence: University of Kansas Press.

Green, C. (1986) 'The Role of the Media in Shaping Public Policy: the Myth of Power and the Power of Myth', in M. Kaplan and P.L. Cuciti (eds), *The Great Society and Its Legacy: Twenty Years of U.S. Social Policy,* Durham: Duke University Press.

Greenberg, D. (1977) *The Super Cops Play It to a Bust,* London: Futura (orig. publ. 1975).

Handler, J.F. and Hasenfeld, Y. (1991) *The Moral Construction of Poverty: Welfare Reform in America,* Newbury Park and London: Sage.

Harper, R. (1969) *The World of the Thriller,* Cleveland: The Press of Case Western Reserve University.

House, H. (1960) *The Dickens World* (rev. edn), Oxford: Oxford University Press (orig. publ. 1941).

Knight, S. (1980) *Form and Ideology in Crime Fiction,* London: Macmillan.

Livermore, J. (1980) 'Policing', in R.J. Lundman (ed.), *Police Behavior: A Sociological Perspective,* New York and Oxford: Oxford University Press.

Martindale, D. (1991) *Television Detective Shows of the 1970s: Credits, Storylines and Episode Guides for 109 Series,* Jefferson, NC, and London: McFarland.

Mead, L. (1986) *Beyond Entitlement: The Social Obligation of Citizenship,* New York: Free Press.

Menzies, I. (1986) 'Random Observations on the Role of the Media in Covering the War on Poverty', in M. Kaplan and P.L. Cuciti (eds), *The Great Society and Its Legacy: Twenty Years of U.S. Social Policy,* Durham: Duke University Press.

Merry, B. (1977) *Anatomy of the Spy Thriller,* Dublin: Gill and Macmillan.

Messent, P. (1997) 'Introduction: From Private Eye to Police Procedural – the Logic of Contemporary Crime Fiction', in P. Messent (ed.), *Criminal Proceedings: The Contemporary American Crime Novel,* London: Pluto.

Murray, C. (1984) *Losing Ground: American Social Policy, 1950–80,* New York: Basic Books.

*New York Times* (ed.) (1971) *The Pentagon Papers,* New York: Bantam.

O'Reilly, K. (1995) *Nixon's Piano: Presidents and Racial Politics from Washington to Clinton,* New York and London: Free Press.

Palmer, J. (1978) *Thrillers: Genesis and Structure of a Popular Genre,* London: Edward Arnold.

Panek, L.L. (1990) *Probable Cause: Crime Fiction in America,* Bowling Green: Bowling Green State University Popular Press.

Pencak, W. (1998) 'Semiotics and History', in R. Kevelson (ed.), *Hi-Fives: A Trip to Semiotics,* New York: Peter Lang.

Piven, F. and Cloward, R. (1971) *Regulating the Poor: The Functions of Public Welfare*, New York: Pantheon.

Potholm, C.P. and Morgan R.E. (eds) (1976) *Focus on Police: Police in American Society*, New York and London: John Wiley.

President's Commission on Law Enforcement and the Administration of Justice (1967) *The Challenge of Crime in a Free State*, Washington: U.S. Government Printing Office.

Reiss, A.J. (1971) *The Police and the Public*, New Haven and London: Yale University Press.

Richardson, J.F. (1974) *Urban Police in the United States*, Port Washington and London: Kennikit Press.

Roth, M. (1995) *Foul and Fair Play: Reading Genre in Classic Detective Fiction*, Athens and London: University of Georgia Press.

Rubinstein, J. (1980) 'Cop's Rules', in R.J. Lundman (ed.), *Police Behavior: A Sociological Perspective*, New York and Oxford: Oxford University Press.

Sebeok, T.A. (1979) 'Neglected Figures in the History of Semiotic Inquiry: Jakob von Uexküll', in *The Sign and Its Masters*, Austin: University of Texas Press.

Thernstrom, S. and Thernstrom, A. (1997) *America in Black and White: One Nation Divisible*, New York: Simon and Schuster.

Ungar, S.J. (1989) *The Papers and the Papers: An Account of the Legal and Political Battle Over the Pentagon Papers* (rev. edn), New York: Columbia University Press.

Uspenskij, B.A. (1977) '*Historia Sub Specie Semioticae*', in D.P. Lucid (ed.) *Soviet Semiotics: An Anthology*, London and Baltimore: Johns Hopkins University Press.

Wambaugh, J. (1970) *The New Centurions*, New York: Knopf.

Whittlemore, L.H. (1974) *The Super Cops: The True Story of the Cops Known as Batman and Robin*, London: Futura (orig. publ. 1973).

Wiley, M.G. and Hudik, T.L. (1980) 'Police–Citizen Encounters: a Field Test of Exchange Theory', in R.J. Lundman (ed.), *Police Behavior: A Sociological Perspective*, New York and Oxford: Oxford University Press.

Wilson, J. (1975) *Police Report*, Boston and Toronto: Little, Brown.

Woodward, B. and Bernstein, C. (1974) *All the President's Men*, London: Quartet.

——(1977) *The Final Days*, London: Coronet (orig. publ. 1976).

Zarefsky, D. (1996) *President Johnson's War on Poverty: Rhetoric and History*, Birmingham: University of Alabama Press.

# 4

# 'A LONE CRUSADER IN THE DANGEROUS WORLD'

## Heroics of science and technology in *Knight Rider*

*Nickianne Moody*

### 'ZERO DEGREE STYLE'? *KNIGHT RIDER* AND EIGHTIES DISCOURSES OF SCIENCE AND TECHNOLOGY

In September 1982 Universal Television released a new action adventure series, *Knight Rider*, onto American TV screens. *Knight Rider* (1982–86) told the story of Michael Long – an ex-cop, seriously wounded and disfigured whilst undercover. Rescued by a terminally ill industrialist, Wilton Knight, Long regains consciousness after plastic surgery to find that he has been bequeathed not only a new face, but also a new identity – Michael Knight (played by David Hasselhoff) – together with a new vocation as a vigilante crime-fighter. And to help him in his missions he has also been provided with a futuristic, computerized super-car, the Knight Industries Two Thousand – or KITT. A sleek, black Pontiac Trans-Am, KITT was a muscle-car with a difference. With a cruising speed of 300 mph and the ability to leap fifty feet in the air, KITT also came with such optional extras as infrared sensors, flame-guns and smoke bombs. But, more importantly, KITT was equipped with its own – rather peevish – personality. Yet, in spite of its foibles, KITT was devoted to Michael and regularly smashed through brick walls or braved hellish infernos to rescue its imperilled driver. In their fight for justice, Knight and KITT drew upon the vast fortune left by their deceased benefactor and administered by the shadowy Foundation for Law and Government (FLAG – led by Wilton Knight's former associate, Devon Miles). And so, assisted by the financial resources of FLAG and the automotive super-powers of KITT, Michael Knight set out (as the first season's epilogue soberly intoned) as 'a lone crusader in the dangerous world … the world of the Knight Rider'.

Coming at the end of a long line of successful action–adventure TV series for Universal, the four seasons of *Knight Rider* proved immensely popular with audiences.[1] One of the hits of 1982, *Knight Rider* was a particular favourite among both children, wooed partly by the range of toys and merchandise marketed in conjunction with the series, and heterosexual women, perhaps smitten by David Hasselhoff's dark good looks and tight jeans. For television historians and cultural critics, however, *Knight*

*Rider* has proved less interesting than some of its peers. Thornton Caldwell, for example, has damned the stylistic techniques that the show deployed, turning it into a 'systematized film based telefilm production with uniform settings, lighting, looks and cutting' – in effect a competent 'B' movie drama for idealized family viewing (1995:57). For Caldwell, the series is of interest merely as an example of a specific production outlook determined by financial pressures as the TV industry responded both to the growing threat of cable broadcasting and emergent strategies of market research regarding ratings and audience composition. Other critics have sidelined *Knight Rider* in their accounts of 1980s television in favour of the period's other, more celebrated, prime-time successes – for example, *Hart to Hart* (1979–84), *Magnum PI* (1980–86), *Matt Houston* (1982–85), *Remington Steele* (1982–87), *Miami Vice* (1984–89) and *Moonlighting* (1985–91) (Fiske, 1986; Kaplan, 1987). Such shows have been viewed as indicative of a 'postmodern' aesthetic that emerged in 1980s North American TV in which an emphasis on style and 'surface' was coupled with an ideologically 'disruptive' or 'transgressive' obsession with interrogation and self-reflection. For most critics, however, *Knight Rider* demonstrates none of the intriguing qualities of its rivals, displaying instead a 'zero degree style' (Caldwell, 1995: 372) and a premise that appears to derive from a dated and simplistic formula of TV crime-fighting in which a hard-boiled detective fights for justice on behalf of the wider community.

Certainly, *Knight Rider* did not provide the lush, MTV-style, hyper-reality of *Miami Vice*. And, despite its tongue-in-cheek and playful humour, the series lacked the guileful, self-referential irony of *Moonlighting*. Nevertheless, the discourses of science and technology that lie at the heart of *Knight Rider* reveal the programme to be much more deeply engaged with the issues and controversies of 1980s cultural life than critics have hitherto acknowledged. The revamped, TV-movie version of the series, *Knight Rider 2000* (1991), was undoubtedly hackneyed and cliché-riven – Michael Knight being recalled from retirement to fight crime in a lawless, post-industrial Seattle, assisted by KITT (now installed in the 'body' of a '57 Chevy) and a female cop whose brain is implanted with a powerful computer chip. But, in contrast to the dark, dystopic tropes disinterred in *Knight Rider 2000*, the original series presented a more complex vision of the impact of technology on American life. During the 1980s *Knight Rider* emerged on the cusp of a significant transition in perceptions of technology and its impact on the individual which, as Susan Jeffords argues, reverberated through 'the entire decade' (1993: 40) – and it is the way *Knight Rider* engaged with this process of transition that makes the series deserving of closer scrutiny and critical appraisal.

In the realm of film analysis, the term 'action–adventure' has frequently been used to describe the dominant trend in Hollywood output during the 1980s and early 1990s. Many films of this period demonstrated 'a propensity for spectacular physical action, a narrative structure involving fights, chases and explosions, and in addition to the deployment of state-of-the-art special effects, an emphasis in performance on athletic feats and stunts' (Cook and Bernink, 1999: 228–29). Most analyses of films in this genre or cycle (for instance, the trilogies of *Alien* (1979, 1986, 1993) and *Die Hard* (1988, 1990, 1995) or *Point Break* (1991)) have centred upon the ideological significance and scope of such films, arguing that they articulate a set of discourses about the masculine body and national identity pertinent to the cultural politics of the era (Britton, 1986; Kellner and Ryan, 1988; Sartelle, 1996; Traube, 1992; and Wood, 1986). In particular, Douglas Kellner has argued that, in the way such texts deployed particular kinds of identities, role models and ideals, they were implicated in the elaboration of a conservative political hegemony that worked to define situations and agendas in a manner that 'filter[ed] out oppositional ideas' (1990: 18). During Ronald Reagan's first Presidential term, public acceptance of technological warfare was a crucial facet to the establishment of a New Right political hegemony and Kellner points to the ways in which popular narratives figured in the administration's attempt to garner support for hi-tech defence projects such as the Strategic Defence (or 'Star Wars') Initiative. The Reagan administration collaborated with news programmes to produce simplified animated simulations of satellite- and ground-based weapons systems that could supposedly eliminate Soviet missiles, thus employing 'the images and codes of television to bolster the fortunes of the President' (Kellner, 1990: 139). In a similar fashion, in the TV presentation of the American bombing of Libya in 1986, 'combat footage of Libyan planes [was] interspersed with other combat footage to dramatize the event' (Kellner, 1990: 139). According to Kellner, moreover, popular fictions also made an important contribution to the successful impact of such imagery on the American public. Hi-tech combat sequences were habitually featured in blockbuster films of the period (exemplified by *Top Gun* (1986)), these sequences producing images with a resonance that managed 'to marshal emotions around the excitement of dramatic action while mobilizing the patriotic sentiment that often emerges during times of war or national crisis' (Kellner, 1990: 138).

The Reagan administration's 'hard' stance on law and order – articulated through a concern with 'defending the ordinary citizen' – also suggested a new significance for technology in the everyday lives of Americans as the public became more aware of the uses of computerized surveillance technology in combating crime. At the same time, however, highly developed electronic technologies were held up as a beacon of hope for industry and the economy. Yet the beneficent potential of technology was represented in political discourse as precarious and dependent upon the ability of the security forces to 'defend' the nation against criminal 'elites' who – if permitted unregulated access to technological advances – might undermine the United States through either espionage or sabotage.

Appearing at a time of slim public awareness or understanding of computer-based technologies, *Knight Rider* can be seen as one of the first popular texts to visualize and narrativize effectively the potential of these technologies to transform daily life. More significantly, while *Knight Rider*'s representation of technology was, in some respects, broadly congruent with the New Right hegemonic agenda, in other ways it offered a much more complex and ambiguous vision.

## KITT: COMPUTERIZED CREDIBILITY IN THE COMMONPLACE WORLD

The dramatic nature of shifts in public awareness of computer-based technologies and their potential applications can be illustrated by a brief discussion of the rapidity of technological development in post-war America. Up until the late 1970s, the prospect of the entry of computer technology into the ordinary American home must have seemed slight. A flourishing electronics industry had existed since the 1950s in California's Santa Clara County, but it was only in the 1960s that Fairchild Semiconductor managed to develop an integrated circuit in a form that could be mass produced. This 'silicon chip' (as it came to be known) was a microscopically small electronic component, placed on a piece of silicon crystal only a few millimetres square – and it was this that revolutionized the electronics industry through its use in everything from calculators and TV sets to satellites and space vehicles. The rise of the computer was, perhaps, the most significant consequence of these technological developments and, as the 1970s progressed, computer systems were increasingly found installed in business and public utilities. For many observers, however, the computer seemed destined to remain largely the preserve of the industrial realm. By the late 1970s a computerized home-life was already possible – but for many it seemed an unlikely prospect and as late as 1977 Ken Olson, the president of Digital Equipment Group, confidently asserted that he could see 'no reason for any individual to have a computer in their home' (cited in Stoll, 1995: 12). By 1982, however, this climate of opinion was shifting dramatically as the public's access to, and interest in, the potential of computers began to grow.

The popular embrace of the pocket calculator in the 1970s was the key point at which computer technologies entered the everyday lives of many Americans. A consequence of Intel's development of a programmable microprocessor, the success of the calculator testified to public interest in the personal applications of advanced technologies and laid the way for the launch of a marketable desktop computer. Previously dominated by the production of immense 'mainframes' geared to the demands of business and industry, the computer industry was revolutionized in 1981 when IBM launched their first 'personal' computer aimed at the domestic consumer. By 1983 the domestic market for such technology was clearly evident, companies such as Tandy and Radio Shack (and later, of course, Microsoft) increasingly competing against IBM in the market for computer products geared to the home and personal use (Cringely, 1996: 168).

In the era of the mainframe, popular texts had invariably presented computers in scientific or military contexts – housed in sterile rooms full of flashing lights, reel-to-reel tape or punched cards. With the dawn of personal computers geared to the domestic market, this imagery began to change – and it was amid this transformation that *Knight Rider* took to the road. *Knight Rider* was significant for the way it reconfigured popular representations of computer-based technology as excitingly attainable. Crucially, KITT was a *computerized* car – an everyday artefact in which the new, 'futuristic' technologies had been successfully incorporated (see Figure 4.1).[2] The

*Figure 4.1*  The friendly face of futuristic technology – Michael Knight (David Hasselhoff) and KITT in *Knight Rider* (1982–86).

attractiveness of KITT lay in the way it made powerful technology accessible, flexible and portable. Moreover, this 'domesticated' technological power was presented as reliable and secure. KITT is able to be the 'fastest, safest, strongest car in the world', we are told in the series' pilot episode ('Knight of the Phoenix'), because Knight Industries' microprocessors facilitate operation in which it is impossible for the vehicle to be involved in any kind of mishap or collision unless ordered to do so. Michael Knight is, himself, initially amazed, comparing KITT's cockpit to 'Darth Vader's bathroom'. Yet Knight's incredulity (together with that of the audience) is redressed throughout the series. The speed, power and resources that the car affords Knight may be awesome – but it is always made plausible. Whilst the vehicles featured in *Knight Rider*'s contemporary rivals were foregrounded as almost magical agents of justice – for example, Luke and Bo's souped-up Dodge Charger, the 'General Lee', in *The Dukes of Hazzard* (1979–85), or the various machines miraculously assembled from bits of old junk in *The A-Team* (1983–87) – the credibility of KITT is stressed through the visuality of its technology. This is achieved through the overlapping of motivated and iconic signs – for example, the presentation in a single frame of the electronic readout of KITT's attempt to stop a vehicle and the view of the same event through KITT's windscreen. Graphic and numerical readouts are also frequently featured, together with in-car TV screens and other devices which make the audience party to the data KITT supplies its driver.

The credible representation of advanced technology in *Knight Rider* is also emphasized by the 'everyday' locations of its narratives. Contemporaneous film fictions such as *Star Wars* (1977), *Alien* (1979) and *Blade Runner* (1982) portrayed the (often negative) consequences of technology in a version of the far-flung future that Frederic Jameson terms 'inverted millenarianism' (1984: 53) – with images of a futuristic technology that has become depleted and worn. In contrast, *Knight Rider*'s technological iconography is gleaming and fresh – and is firmly located in the worldly and the familiar. The pilot episode is exemplary, offering a tale of archetypal industrial espionage in California's 'Silicon Valley' (then emerging as the centre of America's computer industry). Some of the episode's central sequences take place against the relatively mundane backdrop of a corporate-sponsored family outing to a demolition derby, while the target of the espionage is not an outlandish weapon but a memory chip with the potential to launch a new generation of affordable consumer products. The chief victims of the crime, moreover, are presented not as wealthy computer industrialists, but the ordinary American consumer and the workers whose job security is jeopardized by the theft.

Indeed, it is the 'ordinary' citizen for whom Knight Rider fights. As the show's opening monologue explains, Michael Knight is 'a young loner on a crusade to champion the cause of the innocent, the helpless, the powerless, in a world of criminals who operate above the law'. Invariably, Knight is enlisted in the service of a community and/or workforce threatened by the schemes and conspiracies of the powerful – evil scientific geniuses, double-dealing management or corrupt military officials. This sits in contrast to the heroes of many other American adventure series of the period, for example Thomas Magnum in *Magnum PI* (1980–88), or even – on a more genteel level – Jessica Fletcher in *Murder She Wrote* (1984–96). Whilst Magnum and Fletcher largely solve crimes on behalf of the wealthy, Knight usually gives his support to 'regular Joes' – independent truckers, family firms and single mothers.[3] Occasionally he does indulge the world of the rich and the powerful, but as a rule it is the excesses of corporate capital that he tries to police. Certainly, the Knight Rider's exploits are supported by FLAG, in turn financed by Wilton Knight's legacy. But FLAG is portrayed as robustly independent of government and big business – a champion of the little man and small town values.[4]

The significance of *Knight Rider*, then, lies in the way it presented a 'domesticated' vision of the revolution taking place in computer-based technology. On one level *Knight Rider*'s representation of this technology as 'friendly' and commonplace can be seen as working to legitimate the hegemonic strategies of the New Right – bolstering Reaganite claims to the benign character of hi-tech defence initiatives and reinforcing calls for technological advances to be harnessed in the service of social control. At the same time, however, the portrayal of 'ordinary' communities threatened by high-level corruption and the machinations of big business created contradictions and ambiguities that were less easily reconciled with dominant ideological discourse. The ambiguities inherent to *Knight Rider*'s narrative structure, moreover, became even more pronounced in the show's treatment of the relationship between man and machine.

## MACHISMO AND MACHINERY IN THE 1980s

The fine line between the uses and abuses of new technology is a recurring motif in *Knight Rider*. Throughout the series Knight and KITT are regularly called upon to protect a community or workforce whose well-being has been endangered by the manipulation of advanced technology by malevolent forces. In the pilot episode even KITT is portrayed as a technology that, in the wrong hands, could bring disaster. After FLAG's research secrets are stolen by a villainous agent, Tanya, it is feared that the safeguards intrinsic to KITT's design will be suppressed in favour of commercial profit – so that the whole future of American road safety is imperilled.

*Knight Rider's* first season also introduced KITT's evil alter-ego – the Knight Automated Roving Robot, or KARR. An early prototype, KARR was superficially similar to KITT, though had one crucial difference – rather than the protection of human life, KARR's prime directive was its own survival at all costs. Consigned to the Knight Museum of Technology, KARR quietly gathers dust for several years until it is inadvertently activated by a gang of thieves and begins to wreak havoc. The second season, meanwhile, introduced another of the Knight Rider's arch-enemies – Goliath. Returning from imprisonment in Africa, Garthe Knight (Wilton Knight's estranged son, also played by David Hasselhoff) sets out to destroy Michael using a huge truck – 'Goliath' – manufactured from the same kind of 'molecular bonded shell' used in KITT's design. Another episode from the second season also sees seemingly 'good' technology deployed to evil ends, in this instance a talking teddy bear attempting to lure Michael Knight to his doom.[5]

Because technological advance is not always viewed in the series as 'progress', its use by Knight in the fight against injustice has to be carefully negotiated within the text – hence the spectacle of action usually centres on KITT's ability to withstand, rather than initiate, an attack. *Knight Rider* has plenty of action sequences, but these are invariably focused on pursuit or flight, or the spectacle of KITT smashing through concrete, glass or brick walls. In many episodes driving stunts, skills and expertise also contribute to the spectacle. Despite the presence of gun-fights, therefore, it is not these that make up the bulk of the action but the skilful mastery of technology – demonstrated by Michael Knight in high-speed chases, or in his use of KITT to combat larger and more heavily armed vehicles.

Generally, academic commentators have seen the relationship between 'man' and 'technology' represented by the Knight/KITT partnership as an exploration of the insecurities of 1980s masculinity. John Fiske has argued that *Knight Rider* is ideologically underpinned by the performance of a masculinity in which power and competence are dramatically realized – so that KITT becomes a classic example of car as 'penis-extension'. The use of guns and vehicles in the series is, Fiske states, 'an attempt to close the gap between the penis and the phallus, between the real and the imaginary, or the material and the ideological' (Fiske, 1987a: 210–11). Elsewhere, Fiske argues that the male bonding between Knight and KITT 'allows an interpersonal dependency that is goal-centred, not relationship-centred' and that this works to reinforce 'masculine performance' instead of threatening it with the 'feminine inadequacies' of dependence, love and intimacy (Fiske, 1987b: 263). However, while Fiske's relatively straightforward reading may have its place in the analysis of male relationships in action series such as *The A-Team* or *T.J. Hooker*, a closer analysis of the diegesis of *Knight Rider* suggests that Fiske overlooks the strong emotional emphasis placed on the relationship between hero and car which is central to the programme's narrative.

The conventions of the 'buddy' formula are a recurring feature of action films and TV series during the 1980s. And they certainly feature, as Fiske observes (1987b), in the relationship between Knight and KITT, with the inadequacies of one part of the duo compensated for by the strengths of the other. KITT, for example, is more powerful than its driver, more intelligent through its access to immense data banks, and often more morally responsible. The personality of the car, however, finds it difficult to grasp the intricacies of human social and personal life – and the banter between Knight and KITT is often structured around this naiveté. The relationship, however, is an unusually dependent one and both Knight and KITT are vulnerable without the other. Throughout the series KITT, for example, is increasingly educated in the complexities of human emotion and behaviour by Knight, whilst Knight learns from KITT that technology must be respected and carefully safeguarded. Indeed, in many ways the nature of this dependency is configured as a relationship between a father and young child.

In relation to the action–adventure films of this era, Jeffords (1993) has argued that the presence of such father/son relationships in popular narratives is resonant with the matrix of conservative social and militaristic values promoted within the Reaganite hegemonic project. Jeffords argues that conservative political discourse was articulated in the narratives of action–adventure films through representations of masculinity, the post-Vietnam 'crisis' in national spirit being configured, especially, as a crisis in fatherhood and 'the ability of the son to adequately replace – though not overwhelm – the father' (Jeffords, 1993: 67). For Jeffords, this construction of fatherhood was combined with an increasingly complex representation of the masculine body and:

> ... whereas the Reagan years offered the image of a 'hard body' to contrast directly to the 'soft body' of the Carter years, the late 1980s and early 1990s saw a reevaluation of the hard body, not for a return to the soft body but for a rearticulation of masculine strength and power through internal, personal and family oriented values.
>
> (Jeffords, 1993: 13)

According to Jeffords, then, Hollywood's representations of masculinity during the 1980s can be seen as redolent of Reaganite political initiatives geared to the radical supplanting of the attitudes, public policies and national concerns that characterized the Carter administration (Jeffords, 1993: 15). Using the example of the Rambo trilogy (1988, 1990 and 1995), Jeffords argues that the figure of the 'son' is a key motif in 1980s action–adventure narratives – the 'son' functioning as an agent through which the community values once fought for by the 'father' can be maintained and regenerated. Though not explicitly referred to by Jeffords, the relationship between Knight and KITT can also be read as exemplifying these preoccupations. In the episode 'Knight in Disgrace', for example, Knight embarks on an undercover mission, the details of which are withheld from KITT. As a consequence, KITT becomes increasingly distressed by the prospect of losing Knight and having him replaced by another, 'less worthy', driver. At the conclusion of the narrative KITT appeals to Knight to treat him with more respect – in effect, to treat him 'as a grown up'. KITT, therefore, is externally strong and robust – but within is childlike and vulnerable and in need of 'parenting' by Knight. The importance of the father/son relationship between Knight and KITT is further emphasized in the series through the presence of dysfunctional father/son relationships. As the series develops, the audience discovers that the face Wilton Knight constructed for Michael Long after the detective's near fatal shooting was that of the industrialist's own (but unredeemably evil) son, Garthe. With Garthe's face, Michael becomes Wilton Knight's new, 'ideal' son, ultimately fighting and defeating Garthe on two separate occasions.

The father/son dimension to the relationship between Knight and KITT, therefore, contrasts with Fiske's account of the buddy-pairing in *Knight Rider*. Fiske's analysis is also problematized by the role of women in the series. Fiske (1987b) asserts that in action–adventure texts the power of masculinity is frequently confirmed by the presence of women, whose potential threat to the masculine buddy-pairing is repeatedly played out and resolved in a manner that reasserts the supremacy of white, heterosexual masculinity. Women, according to Fiske, must attract the hero through the possibility of an intimate relationship, but are ultimately rejected at the conclusion of the narrative (Fiske, 1987b: 263). Whilst it is true that Knight aids many 'damsels in distress' in the course of the series, they are seldom configured as a love interest and they are not positioned as a threat to the Knight/KITT partnership. KITT may be frequently exasperated by his driver's attraction to beautiful women, but Knight knows that his status as 'a man who does not exist' precludes the development of any romantic relationship. This is underlined in the 1983 episode 'White Bird', in which Knight meets the woman who was his fiancée prior to his change of identity at the outset of the series. The encounter certainly tests Knight's integrity, his commitment to work and his loyalty to KITT – but ultimately it is the 'lone crusade' to which he pledges himself.

Michael Knight, therefore, is constructed above all as an aspiring parental figure (rather than an established patriarch). Indeed, Knight's role as a caring father is especially emphasized by the organization of the FLAG 'family'. During most of its missions the Foundation operates from the FLAG Mobile Command Center, a mobile 'home' that transports all the resources needed for the maintenance of KITT. Overseeing the Command Center is the 'motherly' Bonnie Barstow, a female technician with responsibility for the care of both KITT and Michael – Bonnie always showing a touch of maternal concern as the pair drive off on a mission.[6]

Knight, however, represents a particularly sensitive and nurturing kind of father. Though David Hasselhoff's physique is conventionally muscular and rugged, the character of Michael Knight has a distinctly unspectacularized – even 'feminised' – masculine persona, allowing him to respond sensitively to the human dilemmas that are the narrative focus for many of the crimes he encounters.[7] And it is Knight's ability to listen and observe the nuances of human emotion, rather than his ability to fight, that is invariably the key to the success of his investigations. In this sense, then, Knight can be read as a manifestation of the 1980s New Man – a set of developing constructions of masculinity that (in the wake of shifts in the terrain of sexual politics and the rise of lifestyle marketing) eschewed traditional, 'armour-plated' machismo in favour of a more emotionally literate masculine ideal.[8] Before his staring role in *Knight Rider* David Hasselhoff had already begun to develop this persona in the soap opera *The Young and the Restless* (1973–79), where he played Dr Snapper Foster – a character who could operate successfully in a narrative dynamic dominated by women and in which action was subordinate to gossip. With the character of Michael Knight, Hasselhoff successfully transplanted the qualities of the New Man into the field of action–adventure TV – a niche he subsequently made his own with the success of *Baywatch* (1989–2000) in which he starred as Mitch Bucannon, the single parent and 'caring Adonis' who headed a team of Californian lifeguards.

## 'ONE MAN CAN MAKE A DIFFERENCE … '

The complexities of the alliance between Michael Knight and KITT, therefore, make *Knight Rider* a more elaborate text than the exemplar of 'zero degree style' it has often been dismissed as. Its portrayal of the partnership between man and car provided audiences with an avenue through which the rapidly shifting relationship between humankind and technology could be understood. On one hand the series visualized the dawn of advanced technology as holding tremendously destructive potential – but, on the other, this sense of foreboding was always held in check by the programme's central axiom of the possibilities of a responsible and productive relationship between man and machine. Moreover, rather than being a hulking and fearsome 'beast', the figure of KITT represents a model of 'domesticated' technology – undoubtedly powerful, but also a 'friendly' and accessible consumer product.

This 'friendly' accessibility can, in some respects, be seen as compatible with dominant ideological discourses of the period – especially the visions of 'beneficent' and propitious technological innovation mobilized in a Reaganite hegemonic strategy that sought to legitimate more confrontational foreign policies and more coercive strategies of social control. *Knight Rider*, however, was hardly a straightforward 'hegemonic' text. The pairing of KITT and Knight was not the simple buddy-ship of Cold War warriors common to many Hollywood texts of the period. Instead, layers of complexity make *Knight Rider* a relatively ambiguous text – the character of Michael Knight, especially, articulating a version of masculinity whose nuances of 'feminine' sensitivity sharply contrasted with the 'tough-guy' machismo of other 1980s action heroes.

## NOTES

1  Universal's earlier TV successes included *Columbo* (1971-78), *The Six Million Dollar Man* (1973-78), *The Bionic Woman* (1976-78) and *Delvecchio* (1976-77).

2  The contemporary setting of *Knight Rider* and its presentation of advanced technology in an 'everyday' context contrasted markedly with producer Glen Larsen's other creations for Universal during the period – most notably the avowedly futuristic *Battlestar Galactica* (1978–79) and *Buck Rogers in the Twenty-Fifth Century* (1980–82).

3  Heroes fighting for the weak and the powerless against bureaucratic corruption and commercial mendacity was a theme common to several other American action–adventure series of the 1980s, most obviously *The A-Team* (1983–87) and *The Equaliser* (1985–89).

4  In contrast, *Airwolf* (1984–87) – an imitator that followed on the heels of *Knight Rider* – saw a computerized, supersonic helicopter carrying out clandestine 'good deeds' on behalf of the CIA.

5  KARR features in the episodes 'Trust Doesn't Rust' and 'KITT vs. KARR', which figure in the series' first and third seasons respectively. Garthe Knight and Goliath appear in 'Goliath' and 'Goliath Returns', both from the second season. The talking teddy bear appears in 'A Good Knight's Work', also part of season two.

6  During *Knight Rider*'s second season, contractual problems meant that Bonnie Barstow was replaced by April Curtis – though Curtis fulfilled the same 'motherly' functions within the narrative. In the fourth season of the show Reginald Cornelius III (or 'RC3') also joined the FLAG team. A streetwise and relatively young African–American, Cornelius is 'rescued' from tough back-alleys by FLAG's patriarch, Devon Miles, and is 'adopted' by the Foundation 'family'. In these terms 'RC3' can be situated within an 'assimilationist' tradition in American action–adventure TV series in which black masculinity is reassuringly and acquiescently incorporated within the liberal establishment. See Elaine Pennicott's contribution to this volume (Chapter 6).

7  Indeed, the 'feminine' dimensions to this articulation of masculinity might go some way towards accounting for the popularity of *Knight Rider* among female audiences.

8  For a discussion of the various permutations of the 1980s New Man see Chapman (1988).

## REFERENCES

Britton, A. (1986) 'Blissing Out: The Politics of Reaganite Entertainment', *Movie*, Vol. 31/32, Winter.

Caldwell, T. (1995) *Televisuality: Style, Crisis and Authority in American Television*, New Brunswick, NJ: Rutgers University Press.

Chapman, R. (1988) 'The Great Pretender: Variations on the New Man Theme', in R. Chapman and J. Rutherford (eds), *Male Order: Unwrapping Masculinity*, London: Lawrence and Wishart.

Cook, P. and Bernink, M. (1999) *The Cinema Book* (2nd edn), London: BFI.

Cringely, R. (1996) *Accidental Empires*, London: Penguin.

Fiske, J. (1986) 'MTV: Post Structural Post Modern', *Journal of Communication Inquiry*, Vol. 10, No. 1, Winter.

—— (1987a) *Television Culture*, London: Methuen.

—— (1987b) 'British Cultural Studies and Television', in R.C. Allen (ed.), *Channels of Discourse*, London: Methuen.

Jameson, F. (1984) 'Postmodernism, or the Cultural Logic of Late Capitalism', *New Left Review*, No. 146, July–August.

Jeffords, S. (1993) *Hard Bodies: Hollywood Masculinity in the Reagan Era*, New Brunswick, NJ: Rutgers University Press.

Kaplan, E.A. (1987) *Rocking Around the Clock*, London: Methuen.

Kellner, D. (1990) *Television and the Crisis of Democracy*, Boulder, CO: Westview Press.

Kellner, D. and Ryan, M. (1988) *Camera Politica: The Politics and Ideology of the Contemporary Hollywood Film*, Bloomington: Indiana University Press.

Sartelle, J. (1996) 'Dreams and Nightmares in the Hollywood Blockbuster', in G. Nowell-Smith (ed.), *The Oxford History of World Cinema*, Oxford: Oxford University Press.

Stoll, C. (1995) *Silicon Snake Oil*, London: Macmillan.

Traube, E.G. (1992) *Dreaming Identities: Class, Gender and Generation in 1980s Hollywood Movies*, Boulder, CO: Westview Press.

Wood, R. (1986) *Hollywood from Vietnam to Reagan*, New York: Columbia University Press.

# PART II

# REPRESENTATION AND CULTURAL POLITICS IN THE ACTION TV SERIES

# 5

# ANGELS IN CHAINS?

## Feminism, femininity and consumer culture in *Charlie's Angels*

*Anna Gough-Yates*

### 'ONCE UPON A TIME, THERE WERE THREE LITTLE GIRLS WHO WENT TO THE POLICE ACADEMY ... '

On a Wednesday night in March 1976, *Charlie's Angels* saw its prime-time premier on America's ABC network. The show featured three glamorous female private detectives – Jill, Kelly and Sabrina – who employed a winning combination of beauty, brains and bravura to solve their undercover assignments. Stymied in their police careers by institutional sexism, they accepted jobs in a detective agency headed by the mysterious 'Charlie' – an unseen employer who relayed the Angels' missions by telephone while his bumbling sidekick, Bosley, was on hand to help the girls out and fret about the expenses.

Running to five series (and surviving a number of cast changes) *Charlie's Angels* was, in its early years, a tremendous success – with an estimated 59 per cent of American TV sets tuning into the programme during its first season (Durkee, 1986: 112). The show's depiction of women drew heavy criticism from those who saw the Angels as little more than 'braless, mindless, walking-talking sex-and-violence fantasies' (Rosen, 1977: 102–9), some critics even labelling the series 'one of the most misogynist shows the networks have produced recently' (Coburn, cited in Condon and Hofstede, 2000: 45). Yet ratings research suggested that *Charlie's Angels* was not only a (predictable) hit with lascivious teenage boys, but also had a significant audience among women aged under fifty and was especially popular among the educated and upwardly mobile – students, college graduates and households with incomes exceeding $10,000 a year all regularly tuning in to the Angels' adventures (*Time*, 22 November 1976).

Of the few academic appraisals of *Charlie's Angels*, most interpret the show as part of a wider 'backlash' against feminism in the American media during the late 1970s (see Bradley, 1998: 161). In these terms the perceived threat to the existing social order from the women's movement is seen as being absorbed by money-hungry television executives – notions of women's 'independence' being recuperated through a sexual objectification of 'liberated' heroines. Cathy Schwichtenberg (1981), Sumiko Higashi (1980) and Lorraine Gamman (1988), for example, have all argued that

*Charlie's Angels* peddled myths and stereotypes that ultimately functioned in the service of patriarchal relations. According to these authors, the joke was on an audience who believed themselves to be watching a 'progressive' representation of femininity, but who were unwittingly consuming a text permeated by patriarchal reaction. More recently, Susan J. Douglas has acknowledged that *Charlie's Angels* offered some pleasures for knowing feminists who (like herself) could enjoy reading the show 'against the grain' of its sexist discourse – though even Douglas insists on the show's underlying conservativism, arguing that it pulled off a 'neat trick' by placing feminism and anti-feminism 'in perfect suspension', espousing female liberation whilst simultaneously promoting the objectification of women (Douglas, 1994: 216).

Whether one sides with the critics or the audiences about the merits (or not) of *Charlie's Angels*, the popularity of the programme during the late 1970s and early 1980s provokes some interesting questions: What was it that made these depictions of women both possible and highly contentious? What does it tell us about the relationship between TV representations of, and cultural discourses about, feminism and femininity? What does it reveal about the institution of network television during this period? And how can we account for the popularity of such a seemingly reactionary text with audiences of both men *and* women – some of whom were presumably (to differing degrees) sympathetic to the aims and ideals of the emergent women's movement?

## THE FALL AND RISE OF THE 'ACTION GIRL'

*Charlie's Angels* sprang from an intensification of competition for audiences among the American TV networks. During the 1960s ABC had already established itself as the market-leader in action–adventure series, a position it sought to further exploit in the 1970s as, along with its bigger rivals CBS and NBC, it sought to gear itself towards a younger audience demographic (d'Acci, 1997: 74).

For the most part ABC's action shows of the 1960s and early 1970s had been dominated by male heroes – though there were one or two exceptions. Based on a series of pulp detective novels and produced by Aaron Spelling, *Honey West* (1965–66) featured Anne Francis as a glamorous yet resourceful female sleuth. Though the 'private eyeful' was, in some respects, inscribed by a male gaze, *Honey West* can also be seen as presenting a powerful and autonomous image of femininity, with a title character who 'might control her own desires as well as the narrative, and might wield power in the public sphere along with cars and weapons' (d'Acci, 1997: 82). In this construction of femininity the influence of the British action series *The Avengers*, is clearly detectable. Though not itself screened on ABC until 1966, the network's executives were impressed by the British show's sexy, yet active and challenging heroines – Cathy Gale (Honor Blackman), followed by Emma Peel (Diana Rigg) – and in *Honey West* sought to develop an American equivalent (Miller, 2000: 54). NBC followed suit with its own show centred around a daring female adventurer, *The Girl From U.N.C.L.E.* (1966–67), though low ratings meant that neither series survived its first season and the networks pulled back from the 'action girl' formula.

The action–adventure series was, once again, left to the men, while more conventional representations of domestic femininity were re-emphasized in situation and fantasy comedies such as *That Girl* (1966–71) and *Bewitched* (1964–72). A process of recuperation was even detectable in *The Avengers*. In 1968 the replacement of Emma Peel by the younger, less assured Tara King (Linda Thorson) marked a move away from a confident, 'liberatory' female identity towards a brand of femininity 'contained, if not in a home, in a role and object defined by the needs and desires of men' (Miller, 2000: 70).

It was only in the mid-1970s that female protagonists returned to centre-stage within an action TV series. In a period of relative experimentation across network programming (see Litman, 1979: 393–409), *Police Woman* (1974–78) proved an unexpected hit for NBC. Starring Angie Dickinson as Sgt. Pepper Anderson, an undercover Los Angeles cop, *Police Woman*'s impressive ratings suggested that action heroines could be effectively used as a device that would attract audiences by putting a new spin on a familiar formula (Spelling, 1996: 105–6). With the success of *The Six Million Dollar Man* (1974–78), therefore, ABC also cautiously launched a spin-off 'sister' series, *The Bionic Woman* (1975–77). With Lindsay Wagner in the role of a beautiful cyborg secret agent, *The Bionic Woman*'s audience appeal underscored a new potential for the 'action girl' genre. Following a number of pilots ABC launched *Wonder Woman* as a regular series in 1976,[1] though it was in *Charlie's Angels* that the 1970s action girl found her most successful manifestation. By mixing 'liberated' action heroines with a liberal dose of glamour and a touch of the tongue-in-cheek camp/pop aesthetic that had worked so well in *The Avengers* (and the earlier ABC series, *Batman* (1966–68)),[2] the network hoped it had come up with a sure-fire hit and that *Charlie's Angels* would appeal to male *and* female audiences alike (Spelling, 1996: 110).

## THE 'SINGLE GIRL' AND 'LIFESTYLE FEMINISM'

*Charlie's Angels*' brand of 'liberated', action–glamour femininity touched a nerve in 1970s America, the show responding to (and itself constituent in) the profound changes in gender relations that had been underway since the 1950s. The kind of representations of femininity central to *Charlie's Angels* – three single, sexy, curvaceous, dedicatedly careerist ex-policewomen turned private eyes – paralleled a dramatic shift in attitudes towards women, and particularly single women, in America during the 1960s and 1970s. Whereas the single woman had traditionally been associated with a pitiable inability to 'get' and 'keep' a man, by the early 1960s the existence of women outside marriage and the domestic sphere was beginning to be reconfigured. Within popular culture there emerged a new archetype of the 'single girl' – a young woman who was independent, confident in her sexuality and who enthusiastically pursued a lifestyle of cosmopolitan consumerism.

Barbara Ehrenreich (1983) shows that during the 1950s and 1960s American men were less constrained by the fetters of domesticity and the traditional ideal of the male breadwinner. Increasingly influential, she argues, was a new model of self-indulgent masculinity that prioritized personal gratification in a sparkling world of endless leisure, luxury and lascivious indulgence – exemplified by the success of *Playboy* maga-zine and its associated enterprises.[3] But men were not the only ones beginning to leave behind the shackles of domestic commitments. During the 1960s the idea that marriage and family life were inevitable for women was also increasingly being chal-lenged – both by the rise of feminism and by the emergence of new popular texts and cultural archetypes.

The popular success of Betty Friedan's *The Feminine Mystique* (1963) testified to the growing impact of feminist ideas in America in the early 1960s. In her book, Friedan urged American housewives, dissatisfied with lives that were stultifying and unfulfilled, to bond with other women, raising one another's consciousness and carving out a more vibrant and meaningful alternative to suburban domesticity. Friedan's work enjoyed a high cultural profile, her publisher ensuring that the author was booked for interviews on radio and television in the hopes of reaching a lucrative market of middle-class women (Bradley 1998: 163). The interest in Friedan's ideas spurred initiatives such as the formation of the National Organization for Women (NOW) in 1966, Friedan using actresses, television producers and female public rela-tions experts to promote the movement as the full force of the media was drawn upon to keep NOW in the national eye (Bradley, 1998: 165).

Although the nascent women's movement was avowedly anti-hierarchical, the media were keen to find 'leaders' or 'stars' on whom they could focus their coverage. Though Friedan was influential, she was perceived by journalists as 'a tough interview' – humourless, aggressive and lacking in 'entertainment value' (Bradley, 1998: 164). A more 'media-friendly' alternative was found in the figure of Gloria Steinem, a women's movement activist, investigative journalist and (in 1972) founder of the popular feminist magazine *Ms*. For the media, Steinem possessed 'star quality' in the way she challenged prevalent stereotypes of feminists as 'ugly, humorless, disorderly man-haters desperately in need of some Nair' (see Douglas, 1994: 227). In 1971, for example, *Newsweek* foregrounded Steinem's appearance above all else, commenting on her 'long, blond-streaked hair falling just so above each breast', and her 'incredible body' (ibid.). Young, successful, attractive, and heterosexual, Steinem was presented by the media as the sexy face of feminism. Wearing fashionable aviator glasses, close-fitting jeans and neat T-shirts, and smiling and laughing in her press interviews, Steinem's 'celebrity' image can be interpreted as signalling 'safety rather than change' – this partly accounting for the eagerness with which she was courted by the media (Bradley, 1998: 167). At the same time, however, Steinem cultivated an aura of confi-dent independence. Reputedly single by choice, Steinem's sexual autonomy, combined with her media depiction as both desirable and glamorous, gave her lifestyle an intrigue and appeal for both men and women.

Steinem's public persona, therefore, articulated a version of feminism more exciting and alluring than the dour stereotypes that had traditionally been associated with the women's movement. Steinem personified a version of feminism in which it became possible to evade the confines of marriage and domesticity while retaining the conventional qualities of sexual attractiveness. Steinem's single lifestyle was promoted by the media as exciting and independent, though the main basis of its attraction lay in the way it combined a commitment to gender equality with the pleasures of consumption. Steinem represented a form of feminism that was comfortable with consumerism and which guiltlessly enjoyed the construction of sexual identity through strategies of commodity consumption. In short, Steinem was 'a feminist who looked like a fashion model', Susan J. Douglas recalling the impact of Steinem's public image and how it seemed to give her permission to:

> continue to shave my legs, wear mascara, covet nice clothes, sleep with men, and still be a feminist … [she] made me feel that women could cobble together elements of the codes of femininity they were unable to expunge with a feminism they were eager to adopt.
>
> (Douglas, 1994: 230–32)

Steinem's 'single woman lifestyle' registered such an impact, at least partly, because it capitalized on existing media representations of the 'swinging single girl'. Images of a femininity that was financially independent, sexually confident and at ease with the pleasures of modern leisure and consumption had become increasingly commonplace in America from the early 1960s. Indicative was the popular success (and cultural resonance) of Helen Gurley Brown's *Sex and the Single Girl* in 1962. This best-selling 'expert' advice manual urged women to use sex as a 'powerful weapon' which would help them to 'squirm, worm, inch and pinch their ways to the Top', though the author also stressed to young women the importance of a career as an avenue to economic independence and the universe of consumer pleasures.

The success of Brown's book (revised and reprinted in 1970) was followed in the early 1970s by a proliferation of books and manuals on sex and sexual technique, often written from a female perspective. Books such as the best-selling *How to Become the Sensuous Woman* by 'J' (1970), Nancy Friday's *My Secret Garden* (1973) and Shere Hite's *The Hite Report* (1976) all sought to proclaim a newly confident and 'liberated' sexual status for American women. Fictional representations of the sexually-liberated woman also had a high profile among 1970s bestsellers with the success of Erica Jong's novel, *Fear of Flying* (1973) – a depiction of a young woman's search for an anonymous 'zipless fuck' – selling over 3.5 million copies within two years of its publication (Boulware, 1997: 87).

It was *Cosmopolitan* magazine, however, that became the self-proclaimed bible of the single girl during the 1960s and early 1970s. In 1965 Gurley Brown had been appointed as *Cosmopolitan*'s editor and, with her at the helm, the magazine increasingly promoted an image of femininity in which the manacles of sexual 'repression' were thrown off and personal fulfilment was sought through a prosperous and independent lifestyle. In the pages of *Cosmopolitan* this freedom was conceived in explicitly consumerist terms, suggesting that sexual autonomy (and implicitly women's liberation) were only available to those who worked at being physically attractive to men. Like publications produced from within the women's movement, *Cosmopolitan* asserted that women could transform their lives, though for the '*Cosmopolitan* Girl' the route to this transformation lay not in campaigning and consciousness-raising, but in image-making and the manipulation of consumer products. For *Cosmopolitan*, the power of the single woman lay in her sexual confidence and her ability to deploy her sexuality as a weapon in a quest for material reward and personal fulfilment. It was a winning formula and, within months of Gurley Brown becoming editor, *Cosmopolitan's* readership had increased 15 per cent and its advertising revenues had soared by half.

Nor was the new 'single girl' a phenomenon confined to media representations. The introduction of the Pill and the greater availability of contraception in the 1960s helped undermine ideologies in which women's sexuality had been subordinated to reproduction within the context of stable monogamy (Brunt, 1982: 152). The growing legitimation of female sexual pleasure was accompanied, moreover, by a trend towards the postponement of marriage as more women entered further education and gave greater priority to their careers as employment opportunities – especially within the expanding retail and service sectors – opened up (D'Emilio and Freedman 1997: 309). Increasingly, therefore, men and marriage were no longer seen as the only possible routes to success in life – both single and married women entering the workforce in growing numbers and experiencing greater economic independence than ever before. And it was these changing discourses around women, sexuality and 'lifestyle' that framed and guided the representations of 'single girl' femininity that were integral to *Charlie's Angels*.

## ANGELS ON THE AIR

As white, attractive, heterosexual and autonomous working women, Charlie's Angels embraced and articulated perfectly the 'single girl' ethos that had taken shape during the 1960s and early 1970s. Without the obvious presence of romantic male partners, Jill, Kelly and Sabrina (and their subsequent colleagues) were configured as modern and excitingly dynamic single women – active, confident and avowedly independent. In *Charlie's Angels*, therefore, the '*Cosmopolitan* Girl' had become a gun-toting glamour-sleuth.

*Charlie's Angels* can be seen as configuring its heroines as 'lifestyle feminists' in several respects. Jill (Farrah Fawcett), Kelly (Jaclyn Smith) and Sabrina (Kate Jackson) are three stunningly attractive ex-policewomen, who have undergone extensive training in the Los Angeles Police Academy. On qualifying, however, they face the institutional sexism of the Police Department and are allocated conventionally 'feminine' duties – typing, filing and supervising school crossing patrols. Yet all three are dedicated to their careers and jump at the chance of leaving behind the chauvinism of the Police Department to work as private eyes for Charles Townsend Investigations. Throughout the series it is regularly underlined that the Angels have chosen to pursue their careers as detectives in preference to marriage and domesticity. None of the Angels are involved in romantic or sexual relationships – or, if they are, it is never for very long. As a rule, the Angels reject the possibilities of romantic liaisons, preferring to live alone and to work together. On the occasions that romance does rear its head, it is usually as part of an undercover assignment – the Angel involved engaging in a romantic role-play, using her powers of sexual allure to gain information. For example, in 'The Mexican Connection', the second episode of the first season, Kelly poses as a bikini-clad schoolteacher holidaying in Mexico to ensnare a notorious drugs baron, while in 'Dirty Business' it is Jill who uses her sexual guile to dupe a corrupt district attorney. A recurring theme in *Charlie's Angels*, therefore, is the idea of sexuality as a performance – a masquerade which, while constructing femininity as a spectacle, also offers women a degree of empowerment and control.

*Charlie's Angels* also frequently alluded to liberal feminist calls for equality of opportunity in the workplace. For example, published in conjunction with the series, the five *Charlie's Angels* novels were all careful to mention the Angels' deliberations as they considered leaving the police force.[4] For each, it is the economic incentive that is decisive in their choice to join the private sector, the novels describing how the women are approached by Bosley, Charlie's avuncular emissary, with 'an identical and unrefusable offer' – jobs that required 'only periodic duty, with more time off than work' and a salary 'which was considerably higher than they could ever expect to earn as policewomen' (Franklin, 1977a: 9–10).

The Angels also often found themselves solving crimes in the sphere of the workplace – invariably in fields renowned for their sexism, exploitation, and/or objectification of women and which were targets of campaigning women's groups during the 1970s (see Davis, 1991). Thus they go undercover as high fashion models, showgirls, car racers, gamblers, soldiers, playmate centrefolds, 'call girls', masseuses, and even actresses in the 'adult' film business. With missions set in health spas, massage parlours and Las Vegas nightclubs, the series ensured the sexual spectacle of the Angels – the detectives frequently appearing either scantily clad or in a variety of sexually provocative costumes. At the same time, however, the characters invariably challenged their configuration as sexual objects and resisted the sexism of the contexts in which they found themselves. In 'To Kill An Angel', for example, they refuse to pose naked for a pornographic magazine in order to gain information, instead scaring off the offending male by vociferously debating the penalty for 'pornographic requisitioning'. In 'Lady Killer', meanwhile, we see the Angels take on an undercover assignment in the Feline Clubs – a thinly-veiled caricature of the, then popular, Playboy clubs. Initially frustrated in their mission to unmask a killer, the Angels beseech the spirit of lifestyle feminism in an attempt to energize their investigation – Kelly resoundingly declaring 'You know, I just had this horrible image of Gloria Steinem drumming us out of the corp for not solving this case!'[5]

Many of the women encountered by the Angels in their missions are not as 'liberated' as the detectives – down-trodden and doleful, they accept their lot with resignation. Frequently the victims of macho, sexist employers, these women are badly paid and are either young and misguided, or old and embittered by their experiences. Either way, they have not been assertive enough to make demands for equality and it is up to the Angels to show them that this is a fundamental right. The episode 'Angels on the Street', for example, sees the team rescue an abused teenager from the clutches of a violent pimp, while in 'Little Angels of the Night' they bring to justice a wife-beater and serial killer.

In their own workplace, the Angels are also adept at parrying sexism. The enigmatic Charlie, their employer, is hardly a reconstructed male. The personification of the 'swinging bachelor', he lounges around his mansion or swimming pool while a bevy of scantily clad women massage him, ply him with cocktails and attend to his 'plumbing' and 'electrics'. The women at Charlie's mansion serve as both domestic labourers and sexual trinkets, but the Angels themselves are trenchant in their refusal to conform to such roles. Indeed, Charlie's less than subtle sexual innuendoes ('I'm going down under for a few days') are usually rebuffed through the Angels' world-weary humour – the detectives exchanging knowing glances and groaning derisively at their boss's juvenile attempt at wolfishness. The blundering Bosley, meanwhile, is a virtually sexless representation of masculinity. His unconvincing sexual banter shows he is not oblivious to the Angels' charms, but he is constructed as fundamentally ineffectual, an ancillary character who exists simply to facilitate the exploits of the show's more capable protagonists – the Angels.

Notions of friendship and collective solidarity among women was also a recurring theme in *Charlie's Angels* – an issue which also figured prominently within the women's movement of the 1970s, with its emphasis on the power of 'sisterhood' and the role of consciousness-raising groups (Davis, 1991: 87–89). The Angels novels are especially explicit in their highlighting of the emotional bonds between the women, emphasizing that at 'Police Academy they had become close friends' with a 'tacit agreement' that 'either they would all accept Charlie's offer, or none of them would' (Franklin, 1977b: 4). The strength of friendship between the Angels is also stressed by the absence of family in the narrative. In the episode 'To Kill An Angel', for example, Kelly (an orphan) is accidentally wounded. On her arrival in hospital, instead of worried parents, we find Jill, Sabrina and Bosley all sitting anxiously in the waiting room. And, when asked by a nurse if they are members of Kelly's family, they all reply emphatically that they are, with little pause for thought.

With such an intensity of friendship between the Angels, the show went to great lengths to ensure their relationship was not interpreted as potentially lesbian. The task of emphasizing the Angels' heterosexuality was largely performed through the use of female villains who clearly *are* coded as lesbians – or, at least, are represented in terms of popular lesbian stereotypes. The episode 'Angels in Chains' offers the most striking example in the form of a 'butch' prison warder, Maxine, who orders the Angels (on an undercover mission in a women's prison) to 'strip down to your birthday suits' in front of her. When the sinister Sheriff Clint suggests to Maxine that the Angels will be 'just right' for their prostitution racket, the predatory warder eyes Jill approvingly, and remarks 'Especially the blonde – I'll try not to bruise her tender skin too hard'. Forcing the Angels into a shower room, Maxine peers over the cubicles' saloon-doors and, looking them up and down, orders each to 'open your towel' as she sprays the naked Angels with disinfectant. By juxtaposing the detectives against such unmistakable lesbian stereotypes, therefore, the show hoped to anchor the characters securely around the norms of heterosexuality.

The bonds of friendship between the Angels were seen as so fundamental to the *Charlie's Angels'* formula that near panic ensued among the production team when the most popular Angel – Jill (Farrah Fawcett) – announced her departure from the show at the end of the first series, tempted by lucrative offers of product promotion from companies such as Fabergé (Durkee, 1986). Fearing that audiences would desert the show, a replacement Angel was cleverly introduced as Jill's younger sister, Kris (Cheryl Ladd), allowing the new character to be readily welcomed as 'family' into the heavenly arms of the Angels (Spelling, 1996: 113).

The fears surrounding Jill/Farrah Fawcett's departure, however, were well-founded as, to a large extent, other female characters had functioned as simple foils to the Angels' glamorous protagonism. Indeed, a comic-strip spoof of *Charlie's Angels* – 'Churlie's Angles' – featured in *Mad* magazine during 1977 had highlighted the marginality of other women in the programme, naming one character 'Miss Zilch' (*Mad*, 1977, No. 187). *Mad's* writers and artists were wise to the *Charlie's Angels* formula, as, compared against the Angels, the show's other female characters are constructed as 'lacking' in some respect – either they are not as 'liberated' as the detectives (as with hapless victims they rescue), or they *are* liberated but fail to conform to dominant conceptions of attractiveness or heterosexuality. The superiority of the Angels is also attested to by their portrayal as women who are successful and fulfilled (though a token presence) in their field of employment. They are successful precisely because they have found the perfect balance between women's liberation and traditional forms of femininity – though in attaining this success the Angels effectively separate themselves from the world of 'ordinary women'. In these terms, therefore, *Charlie's Angels* can be seen as striking a relatively conservative tone, constructing liberation as something to be achieved by women on an individual basis rather than through collective action.

Overall, *Charlie's Angels* was a deeply contradictory text in the way it seized upon a variety of feminist issues central to contemporary political and cultural debates. The aims of the programme producers were to reconcile the 'feminist' with the 'feminine' – developing female characters who conformed to traditional notions of sexual attractiveness, but who could also be read as 'liberated' women. Like Gloria Steinem – the media-friendly face of 1970s feminism – the Angels were glamorous career women who enjoyed the swinging life of the 'single girl'. And, like Steinem, their liberated lifestyles were capable of being reconciled relatively easily with traditional forms of gender relations. Nevertheless, whatever we may think about the ambivalent nature of these representations, in its characters, themes and relationships *Charlie's Angels* undoubtedly contained a degree of 'feminist' resonance – and this may go some way towards accounting for its popularity among female audiences.

## CHICKS, FLICKS AND THE MASQUERADE OF 'COMMODITY FEMINISM'

One of the major appeals of *Charlie's Angels* was its glamour – signified by at least eight costume changes throughout each episode (see Figure 5.1).[6] With fashion designer Nolan Miller hired to provide costumes for the show, each Angel was given her own high-fashion 'look' at a cost of $20,000 per episode (Spelling, 1996: 110). Above all it was Jill/Farrah Fawcett who was a hit with audiences, prompting the press to coin the

*Figure 5.1* Sabrina Duncan (Kate Jackson) and Jill Munroe (Farrah Fawcett) employ intellect, charm and evening gowns to outwit a villain in the first season of *Charlie's Angels* (1976–77).

phrase 'The Farrah Phenomenon' to describe the star's popularity (Higashi, 1978: 54). One famous poster of Jill/Farrah sold eight million copies in 1976 alone (Fawcett herself attributing the sales to the prominent outline of her nipples in a figure-hugging swimsuit) (*People Weekly*, 7 March 1994), the star also appearing as a doll (complete with cosmetic kit and gowns) and on a mountain of mugs, beach blankets, beanbag chairs and wristwatches.

Apart from her nipples, Farrah Fawcett's most popular asset was her feathery, flicked, blonde hairstyle. Created by stylist Allen Edwards, the cut became known as 'The Farrah Flick' and was integral to the Farrah Phenomenon. A key appeal of the 'Girls World' Farrah dolls was (speaking from experience) its blonde tresses which could be shampooed, styled and blow-dried into the characteristic 'Flick'. The cultural significance of 'The Farrah' cannot be underestimated.[7] In a contemporary analysis of the style's appeal, journalist Marjorie Rosen suggested that 'The Farrah' seemed to promise the same kind of confident, sexual allure that was central to *Charlie's Angels* – 'just the right cut' allowing a woman to transform into Farrah's 'spit and image' (Rosen, 1977: 102).

As *Charlie's Angels* moved into its fourth series its links with consumer culture grew both within and beyond the text. Though her television and movie career quickly stalled, ex-Angel Farrah Fawcett remained prominent in her endorsements of an array of products that ranged from cosmetics and jewellery to T-shirts and lunch-boxes. Her manager of the time, Jay Bernstein, even claims that she turned down a lucrative offer from a company wanting to bottle water 'from Farrah's own faucet' (Durkee, 1986: 115). The existing Angels were also highly marketable, particularly in the realm of children's toys where they appeared on the packaging of girls' cosmetics, as well as on 'Magic Slate' and 'Rainy Day' play-sets, walkie-talkies, Halloween costumes and as a range of dolls with increasingly glamorous outfits (the Hasbro versions actually appearing in an episode of the show).

The popularity of the Angel 'look' lay in the notion that, in adopting their fashion accoutrements, it would be possible for women not only to change their appearance but also transform their lifestyle. In these terms, the products of commercial capitalism could be configured not as symbols of women's oppression (as many feminists had argued), but as agents for women's liberation. Within the world of *Charlie's Angels*, therefore, women could be empowered through immersing themselves in the world of consumerism – commodity consumption allowing for a performance of femininity that could deceive and evade the exercise of dominant patterns of gender relations. Here, the Angels can be seen as exemplifying Judith Butler's notion of gender as a 'corporeal style' that is fabricated and sustained through a set of performative acts and 'a ritualized repetition of conventions' (Butler, 1990: 31). The Angels use clothes and makeup to assume a limitless range of identities – as prostitutes, nurses, professional roller-skaters, dancers, air stewardesses, bodyguards and even traffickers in black-market babies! Of course, the audience know the Angels are masquerading, but the (frequently ludicrous) disguises are enough to fool a legion of male criminals. The show's memorable credit sequence also emphasizes the Angels' skills in the arts of masquerade, clips of the Angels in glamorous model-type poses and/or in classically feminine evening wear inter-cut with 'masculine' action sequences – Sabrina shown as a racing driver and Jill a professional roller-skater, while Kelly 'unmasks' herself by lifting off a motorcycle helmet. Even the Angels day-to-day appearances are deceptive. Superficially, Jill, Kelly and Sabrina might be taken as stereotypical 'helpless bimbos', but their traditionally 'feminine' looks conceal three intelligent, gutsy women who are experts in the fields of martial arts, gunplay and stunt driving.

Even Bosley participates in this commodity-driven masquerade – depicted in the credit sequence as both a buffoon (sporting a ridiculous straw hat) and a sober businessman, rising from his office desk to hand the viewer a gift-wrapped present. Schwichtenberg (1981) interprets this as Bosley making a gift of the Angels who, like Charlie, the audience can possess. An alternative reading, however, might be that this gift is a metaphor for the show's narrative. Bosley's function is to provide the Angels with information on the *cover* stories for their assignments, but beneath this 'wrapping' await a few surprises for those who judge the detectives solely on their outward appearance.

The affinity between *Charlie's Angels* and the masquerade of 'commodity feminism' continued into the show's later incarnations (see Figure 5.2). When Kate Jackson – who played 'clever' Angel, Sabrina – announced she was quitting her role in 1979, ostensibly objecting to scripts that were 'so light … [they] … would take a week to get to the floor if dropped from the ceiling' (Durkee, 1986: 112), the series producers set about a widely publicized search for a replacement Angel. In Shelley Hack they found an ideal candidate. A tall, slender and blonde model, Hack was introduced to the show as Tiffany – an Ivy League scholar and (somewhat improbably) also a graduate of the Boston Police Academy. Hack won the role partly through her existing familiarity with television audiences, having appeared as the face of Revlon's 'Charlie' perfume in a series of TV and magazine advertisements in 1979. Like *Charlie's Angels*, Revlon's perfume campaign had conjured with notions of a new generation of young, liberated women consumers. Hack, 'disguised' in a tweed suit, had been shown marching determinedly into bastions of male chauvinism such as the Gentlemen's Club – and getting away with it because she smelt right![8] The producers of *Charlie's Angels* could not resist the intertextual associations and quickly signed Hack up for a tour of duty. Tiffany/Hack did not, however, prove popular with audiences and following a drop in the show's ratings the actress was released from her *Charlie's Angels* contract. But the slide in audience ratings could not be reversed and, despite the introduction of an unknown actress, Tanya Roberts, as model-turned-detective Julie, and a stint featuring the Angels in Hawaii, the show finally came to an end in 1981.

## REDEMPTION FOR FALLEN ANGELS?

*Charlie's Angels* was both constituent in, and a consequence of, attempts by the commercial market to reroute (and thus depoliticize) feminist discourses into the logic of commodity relations and individual consumer 'lifestyles'. For Robert Goldman and his associates, such representations of 'commodity feminism' may, at

*Figure 5.2* Aaron Spelling's priority was to 'bring back the glamour' in season four of *Charlie's Angels* (1979–80). From left to right: Kelly Garrett (Jaclyn Smith), Kris Munroe (Cheryl Ladd) and Tiffany Welles (Shelley Hack).

first glance, seem to be evidence of a 'new era of democratic cultural pluralism', but in fact amount to little more than a 'pastiche' of feminism which is virtually interchangeable with the more traditional commercial signifiers of femininity (Goldman *et al.*, 1991: 348–49). 'Feminism' is co-opted by the market, turned into a simple 'attitude' which can be purchased in a perfume or a fashionable outfit. Indeed, this form of hegemonic negotiation was evident in *Charlie's Angels*. The Angels may have had access to the independence afforded by money, career and power, but this is compromised by the way it can only be achieved through engaging with the dominant forces of the market and its ideals of gender and sexuality. Ultimately, therefore, the potential threat of three gun-wielding, kick-flipping career women is neutralized through the knowledge that independence is, like femininity itself, only a masquerade.

Nevertheless, recognition of these contradictions between feminism and femininity within *Charlie's Angels* should not mean that its audiences – and particularly the female viewers who watched and enjoyed the series – were the simple victims of a pernicious 'false consciousness'. By situating the series within its broader historical context we can see the ways in which it engaged with shifting discourses around feminism and the lifestyles of single women in a meaningful (albeit commercially-oriented) way. Bonnie J. Dow has argued in relation to the *Mary Tyler Moore Show* (1970–77) that, rather than duping its female audience with images of a depoliticized feminism, the programme provided viewers with opportunities to reflect on and 'make sense' of feminism (Dow, 1996: 49). It is possible to see *Charlie's Angels* as offering a similar space for meaningful engagement. Though the series offered a highly selective interpretation of (liberal) feminism to its viewers, that feminism is nonetheless tangible – rather than absent or displaced – within the text. The feminism of *Charlie's Angels*, therefore, functioned not only as a way of differentiating the programme within a competitive TV market, but also as a way of giving 'relevance' to the show – allowing viewers to make a personal connection with its rhetoric.

The declining appeal of *Charlie's Angels* in the late 1970s can be located not in unconvincing characters or poor scripts, but in shifting images of the 'liberated woman' within American culture. By the end of the 1970s, the feisty glamour of the Angels was being out-paced by the power-dressed and business-like assertiveness of characters such as Sue Ellen and Pam from *Dallas* (1978–91) or Krystle and Alexis in *Dynasty* (1981–89). This success reflected a general Zeitgeist for women's self-improvement in the late 1970s, promoted by best-selling advice books such as *The Managerial Woman* (Hemmig and Jardin, 1978) and *Dress for Success* (Molloy, 1980), which encouraged women to assert themselves through 'playing men at their own game'. The same sense of a guileful feminine 'performance' was still there, but the Angels' low-cut tops and bikinis had now given way to Joan Collins' shoulder-pads and big hair.

More recently, however, a resurgence of interest in the Angels has been sparked by a combination of a vogue for 1970s retro-chic and media interest in the marketability of a 'Third Wave' feminism. The latter has been largely prompted by the emergence, from the late 1980s, of concepts of 'post-feminism' exemplified in books such as Naomi Wolf's *Fire with Fire* (1993) and Kate Roiphe's *The Morning After* (1993), together with public and media responses to the gender politics of films such as *Thelma and Louise* (1991), *Basic Instinct* (1992) and *The Last Seduction* (1994). As Bonnie J. Dow notes, notions of 'post-feminism' tend to:

reject difference feminism and claim for women the right to be as sexually aggressive and power seeking as men are presumed to be, and all have a tendency to cite the discourse of academic feminists as evidence of the feminist 'party line' they are critiquing.

(Dow, 1996: 203)

Post-feminism's frequent appeals to 'common sense' have made it a media-friendly discourse. Its emphasis on individual freedoms and choices has been mobilized, for example, in a number of women-oriented 'lifestyle' TV series such as *Murphy Brown* (1988–98), *Grace Under Fire* (1993–98) and *Cybill* (1994–98). Here, gender politics is configured as a matter of 'choices' for individual women rather than being grounded in structural inequalities and power struggles. 'Post-feminist' representations, moreover, are also driven by a commodity logic, equating success as a feminist with a form of femininity achieved through the adept use of both sexual and economic resources – a strategy remarkably similar to that articulated in *Charlie's Angels* during the 1970s.

It is hardly surprising, then, that the Angels – whom many had consigned to the dustbin of political incorrectness – were resurrected in the late 1990s. *Charlie's Angels* appeared again in syndicated re-runs all over the world, while Sony also remade the series as *Angeles* – a Spanish version that offered America's surging Hispanic population the gun-toting, cat-suited trio of Adriana, Elena and Gina. Closely following in their footsteps came BKS/Bates Entertainment's weekend prime-time series *The D.R.E.A.M. Team* (1999). Based on the original *Angels* formula, the show featured four 'supermodels' who shot, kick-boxed and used their sex-appeal in undercover missions under the aegis of the Charlie-esque J.W. Garrison. But it was in the Drew Barrymore co-produced movie *homage* to the original series that the retro-popularity of the Angels reached its peak. *Charlie's Angels* (2000) puzzled some audiences with its abstruse plot, while some critics raised a cynical eyebrow at the film's sexual blatancy, Rita Kempley noting that the movie had 'more bounce than kick' (Kempley, 2000). Writing in the *Washington Post*, however, Desson Howe insightfully observed that the film also articulated other pleasures and that, for some audiences, the movie version of the *Angels* was not about content but 'about form – the way the Angels look, their lifestyle, their three-musketeer partnership' (Howe, 2000).

As with the original series, then, the newer incarnations of *Charlie's Angels* maintain a complex relationship between feminism and femininity. They show that media representations of independent and autonomous women are inevitably selective and partial, yet still engage meaningfully with feminist discourses. These texts are not simply a lucrative source of profit for media producers, but also offer women viewers an entertaining – and satisfying – avenue through which they can make sense of their social and cultural lives. The effectiveness of these responses as a political strategy is obviously limited – and possibly detracts from feminism as a collective form of social action. Nevertheless, for all their contradictions and limitations, popular texts such as *Charlie's Angels* have offered pleasurable glimpses of female solidarity and strength for women audiences as they formulate their cultural identities in the wake of the momentous social and political impact of the women's movement.

## NOTES

1 Variable audience figures saw *Wonder Woman* abandoned by ABC in 1977, though the show was picked up by CBS and ran for a further two seasons (see Higashi, 1980: 27).

2 Leonard Goldberg, one of *Charlie's Angels'* producers, was reputedly a fan of *The Avengers* and had originally conceived the Angels as *The Alley Cats* – 'three Emma Peel-like women in leather jackets' (Condon and Hofstede, 2000: 5).

3 See also Osgerby (2000).

4 Published in 1977, and all written by Max Franklin, the five *Charlie's Angels* novels were *Charlie's Angels; Angels in Chains; Angels on a String; Angels on Ice;* and *The Killing Kind.*

5 As well as invoking the spirit of their 'lifestyle feminist' guru, this was also a reference to Steinem's own 'undercover' exploits – the author having infiltrated the Playboy clubs in 1963 to write a series of exposé articles for *Show* magazine.

6 After the first series Farrah Fawcett had a contractual dispute with the show's producers and agreed to make further guest appearances only on condition she could be seen in twelve costume changes per episode (Durkee 1986).

7 In one Midwestern town, the tabloid press reported, jealous schoolgirls threw tar at a class-mate who had been the lucky recipient of the first 'Farrah Flick' in town (Rosen, 1977: 102).

8 The 'Charlie' campaign was no doubt intended to echo a media event staged by the orga-nizers of NOW in the late 1960s, activists storming the Oak Room of New York's Plaza Hotel from which women had formerly been excluded.

## REFERENCES

Boulware, Jack (1997) *Sex American Style: An Illustrated Romp through the Golden Age of Hetero-sexuality*, Los Angeles, CA: Feral House.

Bradley, Patricia (1998) 'Mass Communication and the Shaping of US Feminism', in Cynthia Carter, Gill Branston and Stuart Allan (eds), *News, Gender and Power*, London: Routledge.

Brown, Helen Gurley (1962) *Sex and the Single Girl*, New York: Bernard Geiss.

Brunt, Rosalind (1982) '"An Immense Verbosity": Permissive Sexual Advice in the 1970s', in Rosalind Brunt and Caroline Rowan (eds), *Feminism, Culture and Politics*, London: Lawrence and Wishart.

Butler, Judith (1990) *Gender Trouble*, London: Routledge.

Condon, Jack and Hofstede, David (2000) *Charlie's Angels Casebook*, Beverly Hills, CA, and London: Pomegranate Press.

D'Acci, Julie (1997) 'Nobody's Woman? *Honey West* and the New Sexuality', in Lynn Spigel and Michael Curtin (eds), *The Revolution Wasn't Televised: Sixties Television and Social Conflict*, London: Routledge.

Davis, Flora (1991) *Moving the Mountain: The Women's Movement in America Since 1960*, New York: Simon and Schuster.

D'Emilio, John and Freedman, Estelle (1997) *Intimate Matters: A History of Sexuality in America*, Chicago and London: University of Chicago Press.

Douglas, Susan J. (1994) *Where the Girls Are: Growing Up Female with the Mass Media*, London: Penguin.

Dow, Bonnie J. (1996) *Prime-Time Feminism: Television, Media Culture and the Women's Movement Since 1970*, Philadelphia: University of Pennsylvania Press.

Durkee, Cutler (1986) 'When Angels Were the Rage', *People Weekly*, Vol. 26, 20 October.

Ehrenreich, Barbara (1983) *The Hearts of Men: American Dreams and the Flight From Commitment*, London: Pluto.

Franklin, Max (1977a) *Charlie's Angels: Angels on Ice*, New York: Ballantine Books.

—— (1977b) *Charlie's Angels: Angels in Chains*, New York: Ballantine Books.

Friday, Nancy (1973) *My Secret Garden: Women's Sexual Fantasies*, London: Quartet.

Friedan, Betty (1963) *The Feminine Mystique*, New York: Dell.

Gamman, Lorraine (1988) 'Watching the Detectives: The Enigma of the Female Gaze', in Lorraine Gamman and Margaret Marshment (eds), *The Female Gaze: Women as Viewers of Popular Culture*, London: The Women's Press.

Goldman, Robert, Heath, Deborah and Smith, Sharon L. (1991) 'Commodity Feminism', *Critical Studies in Mass Communication*, No. 8.

Hemmig, Margaret and Jardin, Anne (1978) *The Managerial Woman*, London: Boyars.

Higashi, Sumiko (1978) '*Charlie's Angels*: Gumshoes in Drag', *Film Criticism*, Vol. 2.

—— (1980) 'Hold It!: Women in Television Adventure Series', *Journal of Popular Television and Film*, Autumn.

Hite, Shere (1976) *The Hite Report*, New York: Macmillan.

Howe, Desson (2000) 'Angel's Play All the Right Angles', *Washington Post*, 3 November.

'J' (1970) *How to Become the Sensuous Woman: The First How-To Book for the Female Who Yearns to be All Woman*, London: W.H. Allen.

Jong, Erica (1973) *Fear of Flying*, London: Martin Secker and Warburg.

Kempley, Rita (2000) '*Charlie's Angels*: Has More Bounce Than Kick', *Washington Post* 3 November.

Litman, B.R. (1979) 'The Television Networks, Competition and Program Diversity', *Journal of Broadcasting*, No. 23, 393–409.

Miller, Jeffrey S. (2000) *Something Completely Different: British Television and American Culture*, Minneapolis: University of Minnesota Press.

Molloy, John T. (1980) *Women: Dress for Success*, London: Foulsham.

Osgerby, Bill (2000) '"Bachelors in Paradise": Masculinity and Leisure in Post-War America', in John Horne (ed.), *Masculinities: Leisure Cultures, Identities and Consumption*, LSA Publication No. 69.

Roiphe, Kate (1993) *The Morning After: Sex, Fear and Feminism on Campus*, New York: Little, Brown.

Rosen, Marjorie (1977) '"Farrah Fawcett-Majors Makes Me Want To Scream!" A Look at TV Sex: *Charlie's Angels, Police Woman* - and Now, *Soap*', *Redbook Magazine*, September.

Schwichtenberg, Cathy (1981) 'A Patriarchal Voice in Heaven', *Jump Cut*, No. 24/25.

Spelling, Aaron (with Jefferson, Graham) (1996) *A Prime-Time Life: An Autobiography*, New York: St. Martin's Press.

*Time* (1976) 'Charlie's Trio of Sexy Angels', 22 November.

Wolf, Naomi (1993) *Fire with Fire: The New Female Power and How It Will Change the 21st Century*, New York: Random House.

# 6

# 'WHO'S THE CAT THAT WON'T COP OUT?'

## Black masculinity in American action series of the sixties and seventies

*Elaine Pennicott*

### 'CAN YOU DIG IT?'

American television action shows of the 1960s and 1970s have been an important, though seldom acknowledged, arena for the construction of notions of black masculinity. Representations of black masculinity in shows such as *I Spy* (1965–68), *Mission: Impossible* (1966–73), *Ironside* (1967–75), *The Mod Squad* (1968–73), *Shaft* (1973–4) and *Starsky and Hutch* (1975–79) have been a significant component in the cultural grammar organizing the way images of black masculinity have become 'known' to the world – these programmes' ambivalent cultural legacy still detected in recent literature, photography, music and an array of film releases.

At first glance American popular television of the late 1960s and early 1970s appears to have included a reasonably wide range of (often positive) representations of black masculinity. The streets were owned by the stylishly tough private eye, John Shaft (played by Richard Roundtree in both a succession of films and a brief TV series). In *I Spy* Alexander Scott (Bill Cosby) travelled the world as the heart-stoppingly handsome trainer to international tennis ace Kelly Robinson (Robert Culp) – an ingenious cover-story for the duo's exploits of daring espionage. Mark Sanger (Don Mitchell) stood as right-hand-man to Chief Inspector Ironside, while in *Starsky and Hutch* even frumpy Captain Dobey had the trappings of power and authority.

As this chapter will show, however, these representations can be situated within a long history of racist stereotypes which have served both to vilify and control black masculinity. At the same time, however, these images also included elements of ambivalence and contradiction that allowed some audiences space for processes of negotiation and reinterpretation.

## THE GREATEST INVENTION OF THE
## TWENTIETH CENTURY ...

Black masculinity, according to Thelma Golden, represents 'one of the greatest inventions of the twentieth century'. As the site for the elaboration of powerful cultural mythologies, Golden argues that black masculinity has been historically constructed by western culture as animalistic, sexually permissive, violent and standing beyond the boundaries of so-called 'civilized' society (Golden, 1994: 19). In a similar vein Kobena Mercer, drawing on the work of Frantz Fanon, notes how representations of black masculinity have been circumscribed by stereotypes which contain the black man as a 'phobic other' – fixed as always dangerous, excessive and animalistic, but ultimately known and contained by the all-powerful white master. Such stereotypes have been fabricated by white, patriarchal culture not only to allay the fears and anxieties of the dominant, but also to justify the brutalization of colonized peoples and absolve the colonizers of any vestige of guilt (Mercer, 1994: 137).

According to Stuart Hall such stereotypes reproduce 'a grammar of representation' which 'construct the image of black people in the white imaginary' (Hall, 1997: 250–51). As such, they have been a recurring feature within mainstream cultural life – from the figure of the docile 'Uncle Tom', through minstrel entertainers and images of 'threatening natives', to 1970s 'Superspade' icons such as Shaft. For Hall, these stereotypes of black masculinity are constituted by a contradictory set of bi-polar representations – the 'good black' and 'bad black' (Hall, 1990: 15–16). This binary stereotyping, moreover, refuses to accept its origins in colonial discourse. Instead, it offers an ahistorical axis of identification around which ambivalent and contradictory binary knowledges and feelings about black masculinity can be secured. It is, as Homi Bhabha notes, just this ambivalence that gives the colonial stereotype its strength and which:

> ... ensures its repeatability in changing historical and discursive conjunctures: informs its strategies of individuation and marginalisation; produces that effect of probabilistic truth and predictability which, for the stereotype, must always be in excess of what can be empirically proved or logically construed.
>
> (Bhabha, 1983: 16)

Images of black masculinity, then, are organized by the enduring logic of colonization – that 'regime of truth' which needed to explain the threatening differences of race, gender and sexuality in terms of fixed and hierarchical truths about the superiority of white men. As Bhabha explains:

> The objective of colonial discourse is to construe the colonised as a population of degenerate types on the basis of racial origins, in order to justify conquest ... despite the 'play' in the colonial system which is crucial to its

exercise of power, colonial discourse produces the colonised as a fixed reality which is at once 'other' and yet entirely knowable and visible.

(Bhabha, 1983: 23)

Within this logic, therefore, black masculinity is always figured in terms of knowable visual difference. To be a black man is to be a visible black body, fixed by the glances of others in a racialized epidermal schema. In *Black Skin, White Masks*, for instance, Frantz Fanon sketches a poignant originating scene of visual recognition in which the black man comes into being:

'Look, a Negro!' It was an external stimulus that flicked over me as I passed by. I made a tight smile. 'Look, a Negro!' It was true. It amused me.

'Look, a Negro!' The circle was drawing a bit tighter. I made no secret of my amusement.

'Mama, see the Negro! I'm frightened'. Frightened! Frightened! Now they were beginning to be afraid of me.

(Fanon, 1991: 111–12) (orig. publ. 1952)

At the moment the Negro is propelled into the 'real world', therefore, he realizes that 'the corporeal schema [has] crumbled, its place taken by a racial epidermal schema' (ibid.). Here, identities, subjectivities, difference and histories are reduced and fixed as a single bodily fact – the black man. To use the language of Michel Foucault, colonial discursive power has produced the black subject who is formed within, and in relationship to, a circuit of colonial power structures. The black man, then, is a sign overloaded with connotative meanings – always fixed by the look of others and always in excess of that which is represented.

American action series of the 1960s and 1970s can be seen as exemplifying the representations of black masculinity germane to the history of colonization. Above all, it is Hall's bi-polar representations that are glaringly apparent. The 'good black' is marked out by his friendly deference and acceptance of the existing social order, while the 'bad black' is a threatening presence – violent and aggressive, an 'animalistic' outsider at odds with the 'civilized' traditions of white society. At the same time, however, these representations were also characterized by elements of conflict and contradiction allowing some black audiences to draw on them as a source of attractive (and potentially empowering) cultural reference points.

## ... GOOD BLACKS

The themes and style of James Bond set the pace for action TV series in America during the late 1960s. The idea of a skilled and resourceful individual hero working within a team that backs him up (Palmer, 1973) resonated with American audiences and the TV networks responded with action shows such as *I Spy*. Launched by NBC in 1965, *I Spy* starred black comedian Bill Cosby in an acting debut for which he was to win no less than three Emmy awards. In some respects *I Spy* was fairly typical of the plethora of spy series produced in America during the late 1960s. Cosby played Alexander Scott, a Rhodes scholar, expert linguist and undercover agent posing as coach and companion to top-seeded tennis player Kelly Robinson (Robert Culp) – whose sporting feats on the world's tennis courts also covered for his escapades in the world of espionage. Set in exotic, foreign locations, episodes such as 'Turnabout for Traitors' and 'A Few Miles West of Nowhere' charted the duo's adventures as they battled a predictable line-up of insidious traitors, renegade Latin American dictators and beautiful, female enemy agents. But what set *I Spy* apart from its contemporaries – for example, series such as *The Man From U.N.C.L.E.* (1964–67) or *Get Smart* (1965–70) – was its pairing of black and white lead characters.

In terms of TV depictions of African–Americans, Cosby's character can (in some respects at least) be seen as a significant breakthrough. Alexander Scott was portrayed as the equal of Kelly Robinson in terms of both his intelligence and his professionalism. *I Spy* created an imagined television community in which black and white men worked together in fraternal harmony. Bill Cosby laughed with, fought alongside and (on several occasions) came to the rescue of Robert Culp. In the context of 1960s America, however, such a pairing was problematic. NBC executives were anxious that the inclusion of Cosby's character might upset Southern white sensibilities, while the programme's producers worried over such questions as whether the two stars should occupy the same hotel room, or even sit together in the front of a car (Lewis and Stempel, 1996: 80).

By setting the show in foreign locations the network neatly side-stepped the issue of segregation, though issues of race and racism did feature as a point of tension in certain episodes. Racism was always dealt with, however, within the hegemonic discourse of moderate liberalism. 'Night Train to Madrid', for example, saw Scott and Robinson assigned as bodyguards to a controversial comedian, Frank Bodie, on his way to entertain U.S. troops in Europe. Bodie's coarse humour and boisterous demeanour threaten to embarrass the American government and the two agents are charged with containing him at any cost. Bodie's credentials of boorish prejudice are quickly established, his loutish treatment of a young dancer prompting censure from Scott: 'The USO thought it would be *nice* if we travelled with you and I think we ought to keep it that way – *nice*'. In response Bodie turns to the agent's white companion and, with all the bile of a red-neck racist, hisses 'He's sensitive. Your *boy* is sensitive'. However, while the racism of the remark was directed at Scott, the camera cuts to a close-up of Robinson and it is the white agent's stinging wit that cuts the racist down to size. Scott, the black man, remains at the margins of the exchange – it is only the white Robinson who has the power to reprimand the comedian's bigotry. The more radical scenario of a black agent challenging white racism in this instance fails to materialize.

In the figure of Alexander Scott, moreover, white audiences were presented with a black character who could be trusted as a friend. At a time when white America was being challenged by an increasingly radical civil rights movement and inner-city ghettos were exploding into violent protest, Scott appeared as a reassuring construction of black acquiescence to the values of the liberal establishment. Scott represented the type of black man white American society didn't mind letting into their homes – polite, unthreatening and supportive of (and deferential to) the existing social order. In these terms, therefore, *I Spy* exemplifies Herman Gray's notion of liberal cultural texts in which 'blackness simply works to reaffirm, shore up, and police the cultural and moral boundaries of the existing racial order' while 'from the privileged angle of their normative race and class positions, whites are portrayed as sympathetic advocates for the elimination of prejudice' (Gray, 1995: 87).

Similar traits were also detectable in *Mission: Impossible*. First aired in 1966, *Mission: Impossible* saw an elite team of secret agents (the Impossible Missions Force – or IMF) handle missions so sensitive they could neither be officially sanctioned nor acknowledged by the American government. Deploying an arsenal of technical wizardry, IMF carried out their meticulously planned missions with cool professionalism. Here, then, was a fantasy of a United States safe in the superiority of its culture and values – the greater intellect, guile and technology of American agents duly thwarting any threat posed to the security of the 'free world'.

Noticeably, such dangers were invariably constructed as emanating from various 'others' existing beyond the civilizing embrace of *Pax Americana*. The 'backward' political systems of Africa and South America regularly featured as the cause of criminal or political disruption that had to be neutralized by an American intervention that was configured as both masterfully proficient and selflessly beneficent.[1] Moreover, the legitimacy of such ventures was underscored by the make-up of the IMF team. As David Buxton (1990: 116) observes, IMF's ability to solve the world's problems relied on its liberal assemblage of trans-class alliances – Jim Phelps, the managerial 'brain'; Willy Armitage, the 'muscles'; Cinnamon Carter, the actress/seductress and Rollin Hand, the master of disguise whose manufacture of faces on demand impressively combined artistic talent and technical skill. Above all, however, the liberal virtues of IMF were underlined by the inclusion of a black team member. Played by black actor Greg Morris, Barney Collier was IMF's technical expert. Like Alexander Scott in *I Spy*, the character of Collier can, in some ways, be read as a positive portrayal of an intelligent and skilful African–American. In other respects, however, Collier can also be seen as a personification of Hall's concept of the 'good black' – unassuming, reliable and compliantly integrated within the dominant social framework (see Figure 6.1). This 'assimilationist' representation of black masculinity developed as a prominent theme within 1960s popular culture and is, for example, conspicuous in many other action TV series of the period.

The same set of constructions, for instance, also appeared in *Ironside*. In many respects *Ironside* represented a quite unique action series. The show was essentially a vehicle for Raymond Burr, the actor having recently finished filming the hugely popular *Perry Mason* (1957–66). In *Ironside* Burr starred as the eponymous hard-nosed, tough-talking San Franciscan Chief of Detectives. Struck down by a sniper's bullet in the first episode, Ironside is left paralysed and wheelchair-bound, yet continues investigating criminal cases as a citizen volunteer with the help of Detectives Ed Brown (Don Galloway) and Eve Whitfield (Barbara Anderson). Ironside's

*Figure 6.1*  Greg Morris as Barney Collier (right) – IMF's 'good black' in *Mission: Impossible* (1966–73).

disability certainly marked the show out from its peers within the action and crime genres, yet its racial politics were from the same liberal-assimilationist mould as *I Spy* and *Mission: Impossible*. *Ironside*, however, was also distinguished by a large dose of white paternalism.

Completing Ironside's team of assistants was a young, black character – Mark Sanger, played by Don Mitchell. In the pilot episode Ironside – like the white hero of a colonialist narrative – 'rescues' the 'ignorant and angry' Sanger from the wrong side of the law and the 'jungle' of the black ghetto. Seeing through the 'jive talk' and the aggressive posturing, Ironside recognizes the potential in the black youth and offers him a job on condition that he returns to school.

More than Alexander Scott or Barney Collier, however, the character of Mark Sanger is an uneasy presence. His clothes mark his otherness. He wears loud shirts and is generally more casually dressed than Ironside and his police colleagues, who always appear respectably be-suited. Moreover, Sanger's wayward youth, the way he explains street slang to his boss, and his familiarity with the criminal (black) underbelly of respectable (white) American life serve to remind the audience of the threatening 'truth' to black masculinity. At the same time, however, Sanger represents the *tamed* threat of difference to the ordered world of Ironside. The character is most clearly distinguished by his role as hired home-help – driving Ironside's customized van and operating its hydraulic lift, as well as acting as the detective's general aide and body-guard. Sanger is seen most often behind the wheel (or behind the wheelchair) or making coffee. Like a naughty schoolchild he is placed firmly beside or behind Ironside, his masculinity thoroughly domesticated and 'feminized' – albeit willingly so. Within the series, then, the character of Sanger functions to demonstrate Ironside's status not only as an agent of justice, but also as a personification of white, liberal benevolence.

Significantly, Sanger also takes the place of Ironside's legs and therefore – symbolically – his masculinity. Through his paralysis Ironside is rendered culturally (and one would assume sexually) immobile/impotent. Sanger is hired not to be his 'boy', but to be his legs. In these terms the black man in the text of *Ironside* – as in Western culture more generally – comes to stand for the absences that threaten the power of white masculinity. Yet the threat is always safely corralled. Sanger is thoroughly contained and incorporated within the structures of Ironside's dominant, white order. Sanger rarely appeared without his boss and was seldom depicted as coming from a wider black community – we do not see him, for example, in the context of a family, a lover or a culture outside the secure fold of 1960s white liberalism. In a notable exception, the episode 'The Last Payment' sees Sanger go undercover (though only with the blessing of the Chief) in an attempt to help an old friend who has got into trouble with loan sharks. Yet, returning to the underworld of black culture, Sanger now appears as an awkward outsider. His clothes are not as loud or extravagant, his language not as 'street' as those around him. And when his work is done he leaves, seemingly without a qualm.

Mark Sanger, therefore, embodies a construction of black masculinity that bell hooks describes as being 'based on an unrequited longing for white male love' (hooks, 1996: 84). Here, the grown black man adores the white master who has the power to confer status and respectability. In the world of *Ironside*, then, Sanger represents a 'good black' – his (black) masculinity tamed and any threat to American white patriarchal hegemony safely contained.

Herman Gray perceptively argues that series such as *I Spy*, *Ironside* and *Mission: Impossible*, by ignoring racial tension and difference and appealing to a notion of racial harmony based on the acceptance of white privilege and hegemony, were firmly moored in the discursive practices of assimilation (Gray, 1995: 84–85). Such shows suppressed any cultural or racial difference in the interests of an imagined national community of shared values. In doing so, the histories of conflict, of slavery, power inequalities and struggles for justice and equality that characterize American society were systematically erased. The racial tensions manifest in America during the 1960s and 1970s rarely intruded into the worlds of Ironside or the IMF, action series reproducing the liberal orthodoxies characteristic of American television during the period. *I Spy*, *Ironside* and *Mission: Impossible* integrated African–Americans into a void where they functioned alone – without love interests, histories or traditions. At best these programmes appealed to colour blindness and a rhetoric of assimilation, and at worst they presented an image of black masculinity as subservient, docile and unquestioning of white authority.

There were, however, a few TV series that more consciously sought to acknowledge the huge social changes taking place in the world around them. *The Mod Squad* (1968–73), for example, was formulated as ABC's attempt to capitalize on the rise of youth-oriented counter-cultures during the late 1960s and early 1970s. *The Mod Squad* retained the conventional narrative structure of police and action shows – establishing an enigma which is then resolved through the agency and ingenuity of the heroes. Yet this time there was a twist. The heroes were a threesome of young hipsters. Recruited while on probation, Pete Cochran (a moneyed Beverly Hills drop-out, arrested for stealing a car), Julie Barnes (a blonde teen on the run from her prostitute mother) and Linc Hayes (a black dude, arrested during the Watts riots) were deployed by the police for their specialist knowledge of the 'happening scene' and their ability to move undetected through the universe of flower power and student radicalism. The characters' disreputable backgrounds, together with their hip clothes and cool slang, served as a benchmark of the show's (supposedly) gritty authenticity. The Mod Squad may have been working for 'The Man', but they were still tuned-in to the groovy world of the counter-cultural underground. And, above all, it was the black Hayes (played by Clarence Williams III) who stood out as the show's badge of street-credibility. Just as the white counter-culture appropriated black styles and culture as a marker of authenticity and radicalism, *The Mod Squad* included a black character – complete with defiant Afro hairstyle – as a way of establishing its street-smart authenticity. Despite sporting some of the trappings of black radicalism, however, the character of Hayes is assimilated almost seamlessly into the essentially white world of the series. Like Sanger in *Ironside*, Hayes is presented as lacking a history, a family or a wider community and his only meaningful relationships are with his two (white) buddies.

## ... AND BAD BLACKS

From the beginnings of American cinema, white supremacist versions of black masculinity have dominated. D.W. Griffith's *Birth of a Nation* (1915) (a film adapted from Thomas Dixon's explicitly racist text, *The Clansmen*) saw the first screen appearance of the menacing, black buck figure. In this film brutal black men, played by blacked-up whites, attack white men and rape white women. Such images were illustrative of the fears and paranoia that attended notions of black masculinity – the black man's skin becoming a marker of moral and genetic degeneracy. Indeed, according to Donald Bogle (1973: 10–18), Griffith's image of the big, black buck was so frightening to white audiences that, in American cinema, blacks were subsequently cast almost exclusively in comedy roles.

It was not until Melvin Van Peebles's 1971 low-budget, independently produced, film *Sweet Sweetback's Baad Aasssss Song* that 'sexually assertive black males [made] their way back on screen' (Wallace, 1993: 260). A film dedicated to 'all the Brothers and Sisters who have had enough of the Man', *Sweetback* marked the beginning of a black film genre consciously aimed at subverting the orthodoxies of mainstream cinema narratives. Hence the street-hustling hero of *Sweetback* was the first black man on screen to meet violence with violence and triumph over white corruption.[2] In an American culture that ensured the symbolic (and sometimes literal) emasculation of black men, Sweetback stood as an embodiment of black authority, power and control. He possessed the typical symbols of white privilege – his economic power signified by his expensive clothes and his strength denoted by both his musculature and his sexual possession of women. Moreover, turning the white supremacist image of the 'rampant black buck' on its head, he showed no concern at breaking the great taboo of American culture – black men fucking white women. For black audiences, then, Sweetback was the epitome of strength and agency at a time when most black men were fundamentally disenfranchised from modern, liberal America and the black community was beginning to reject the ethos of non-violent protest (Reid, 1993:70).

The themes and style of *Sweetback* heralded the arrival of blaxploitation cinema – the blaxploitation canon including such films as *Shaft* (1971) and its sequels, *Superfly* (1972), *Cleopatra Jones* (1973), *Coffy* (1973) and *Foxy Brown* (1974).[3] Though often made by white directors and financed by white studios, the blaxploitation cycle appealed to many black (and some white) audiences by featuring modern soul-funk soundtracks, ghetto settings, lurid violence and sex, extreme fashions and a hero or heroine who fights (and beats) the white establishment. In the wake of these films' success American TV networks tried to cash-in on their popularity. Itself based on a novel by the (white) author Ernest Tidyman, *Shaft* was turned into a TV series by CBS in the early 1970s, Richard Roundtree reprising his big-screen role as black, New York private eye John Shaft (see Figure 6.2). However, the network's traditions of conservativism meant that the TV incarnation of *Shaft* (screened between 1973 and 1974) was very different from the film original. In particular, the signifiers of Shaft's ethnicity were played down – gone were his slick threads, his snappy dialogue and his baad-ass, street-sharp attitude. Shaft's masculinity was also subject to greater measures of control, the TV series steering well clear of his 'wicked way with the ladies'. Like its forerunners in the action TV cycle, therefore, *Shaft*'s racial politics were ones of liberal assimilation – underlined by the way the TV series paired up the black detective with a white friend, Lieutenant Al Rossi, in yet another liberal fantasy of racial accord. In avoiding any hint of social friction and divesting itself of the more intimidating features of black masculinity, however, the TV version of *Shaft* denuded itself of

*Figure 6.2*   Richard Roundtree as baad-ass black detective *Shaft* (1971).

exactly those dangerous elements that had made the original film a success. Through being tamed and assimilated, the TV Shaft lost his audience appeal and the series was dropped by the network after only seven episodes.[4]

Ironically, the TV series that most successfully deployed the codes and conventions of blaxploitation cinema was based around the tyre-squealing exploits of two white cops. Screened on ABC between 1975 and 1979, *Starsky and Hutch* starred Paul Michael Glaser as Dave Starsky and David Soul as Ken Hutchinson – a pair of maverick undercover detectives. In their unconventional methods, disdain for authority and dexterity with cars and firearms, Starsky and Hutch clearly owed a debt to the cycle of 'dirty cop' movies that followed in the wake of *Dirty Harry* (1971). Yet in its fast-paced street scenes, quick-witted humour and sharp sense of style (to contemporary eyes at any rate) *Starsky and Hutch* clearly drew on the themes and iconography of blaxploitation cinema.

*Starsky and Hutch* also included a greater variety of black characters than had appeared in its predecessors. Most obviously, their immediate superior was black – Captain Dobey, played by Bernie Hamilton. However, while Dobey may have been nominally in charge of Starsky and Hutch, he never established any meaningful authority in the show. Certainly, it was unusual to have a black man in a position of power over the white lead characters, yet Dobey was always a marginalized character. His average number of appearances per episode never exceeded three or four scenes, his authority was frequently undermined and he was often ridiculed by his more streetwise subordinates. Dobey, then, was very much a token black in a token position of command. In contrast, the real power was always wielded by the white central characters. Indeed, by the end of each episode Dobey had come to look up to and admire the antics of the duo.

If Captain Dobey was the head eunuch at the court of *Starsky and Hutch*, Huggy Bear was the jester. The detectives' black underworld informer, Huggy Bear was played by Antonio Fargas (a familiar face in blaxploitation films such as *Shaft*, *Cleopatra Jones* and *Across 110th Street*). Huggy Bear inhabited the dangerous world of the black street. He spoke jive talk (which Starsky often asked Hutch to interpret for him [5]), associated with criminals and was often involved in petty crime himself. Yet it was his attire that became his trademark in the show. Echoing the heritage of black minstrelsy, Huggy Bear was almost comical in his outrageous flamboyance. His improbable flares, tartan hats and shirts with the volume defiantly turned up meant he had more in common with Cleopatra Jones than he did with John Shaft. His clothing also struck a marked contrast with that of Starsky and Hutch whose woolly cardigans, leather jackets (in muted browns) and jeans (with the merest hint of a flare) suggested an air of effortless cool. In blaxploitation films such as *Sweetback* and *Shaft* the heroes' expensive clothes – well-cut suits, co-ordinated jumpers and slacks, and well-heeled shoes – were used to signify their usurpation of white economic power and privilege. Huggy Bears' clothes, however, were a TV producer's idea of black style and, rather than denoting prestige and power, they signified the absurd vanities of the hustling pimp. *Starsky and Hutch*, then, was blaxploitation made palatable for white TV audiences. It was, though, the palest of imitations. While *Starsky and Hutch* successfully employed many of blaxploitation's trademark codes and conventions, the TV series carefully avoided the swaggeringly confident representations of black masculinity central to blaxploitation's original appeal.

It would, however, be misleading to celebrate blaxploitation texts as elaborating inherently positive or heroic representations of black masculinity. Blaxploitation's appropriation of white supremacist images of the big, black buck to demonstrate a strong, virulent black masculinity in many ways simply reproduced the violence of the dominant white culture. Just as slavery rendered black subjectivities into objects that could be bought and sold in the market place, blaxploitation portrays women as willing objects to be traded between men. As Michelle Wallace points out in her critique of black political movements of the 1960s:

> … when the black man went as far as the adoration of his own genitals could carry him, his revolution stopped. A big Afro, a rifle and a penis in good working order were not enough to lick the white man's world after all.
>
> (Wallace, 1983: 286)

Angela Davis in her essay 'Black Nationalism: The Sixties and the Nineties' (1992) touches on a similar theme, noting how the dominant image of black masculinity as heterosexually supreme was a recurring theme within black radicalism during the 1960s. Davis observes that, within the rhetoric of Black Nationalism, notions of black empowerment were suffused with stereotypical images of heterosexual, masculine potency – a trait neatly exemplified in Eldridge Cleaver's dictum that 'whom you fuck demonstrates your power … . The most important rule is that nobody fucks you' (quoted in Young, 1996: 179). For Davis, in contrast, her own entry into the Black Nationalist movement was marked by a negotiation with a 'multiracial working class agency' which would give recognition and respect to both her gender and her sexuality. In representations of this historical moment, however, she argues that such dialogues and conflicts have tended to be erased (Davis, 1992: 319–23).

In these terms, the political tracts of black radicals such as Cleaver and blaxploitation texts such as *Shaft* can both be seen as deploying stereotypes of black masculinity that were influenced and informed by those generated within the hegemonic discourses of white culture. Admittedly, in the hands of Cleaver and blaxploitation film-makers these representations were inverted and invested with a sense of black authority and power. At the same time, however, this appropriation of racist discourse also worked to sustain and reinforce power relationships based around gender and sexuality. And partly as a consequence of this kind of racial–sexual dynamic, Cheryl Clarke observes, the attempts of the black revolutionary movement to present a meaningful unity were destined to failure – since it reproduced the sexist and homophobic vision of black masculinity (Clarke, 1983: 197–208). And, challenging the hegemony of the 'black male so-called left', Clarke argues that the continued exclusion of gays from the 'black community cum the black bourgeois intellectual/political establishment' actually serves to perpetuate the very systems of domination that black people should be struggling against (Clarke, 1983: 200; 205).

## 'PAINT ME BLACK AND LET ME WALK OUTTA HERE'

During the 1960s and 1970s action series on American TV were informed by familiar stereotypes of black masculinity – ones circumscribed and fixed by the binary opposition of 'good black' and 'bad black'. Alexander Scott, Barney Collier, Mark Sanger and Linc Hayes were coded as 'good blacks' – their masculinity constructed as submissive to the authority of white hegemonic power. Figures such as Shaft and Huggy Bear were more problematic. In the terms of the TV networks they were potentially 'bad blacks', their characters being derived from the representations of cocksure black masculinity generated in blaxploitation cinema. Yet through processes of incorporation and emasculation the 'danger' of these characters was neutralized and they could be safely assimilated within the 'melting pot' of white liberalism. In the play between 'good' and 'bad' black, therefore, the imagined television community of the United States attempted to contain the perceived threat of black masculinity. It could not, however, control the way that different audiences might read these images.

The narratives and representations of action TV series included spaces that allowed for the elaboration of positive self-images by at least some black audiences – especially, perhaps, those who lived at some remove from the texts' point of origin. The 1960s and 1970s, for example, were a 'creatively sterile' period for British television in terms of its representations of 'race'. Jim Pines points to the proliferation of 'regressive, uninteresting and completely pointless' documentaries and dramas that sought to 'explain' the 'problem' posed by the black presence in Britain (Pines, 1992: 12). Compared to the generally negative, pedestrian and problematic images offered in British TV programmes, American products seemed to offer a set of more positive and exciting representations of black people – and black men in particular. In Britain, American action TV series were screened shortly after their state-side debut[6] and for some black British youngsters texts such as these seemed to offer a set of cultural repertoires more attractive and empowering than anything being generated at home. As Lee Jasper, a black teenager in Britain during the period, remembers:

> [There were figures like] Mohammed Ali. [And] all of a sudden there was Michael Jackson on the TV, *Superfly* in the cinemas and Bruce Lee kicking white arse all over the place. There was an emergence of a brash arrogance, confidence. If a skinhead wanted some action you were going to give it to them bad.
>
> (*Windrush*, BBC TV, 1998)

In these terms, then, it is possible to see representations of black masculinity in action TV series of the 1960s and 1970s as constituent in much wider processes of cultural exchange and interaction. According to Paul Gilroy (1993), black identities cannot be understood in terms of being British, American or West Indian but have to be understood in terms of the black diaspora and the movement and exchange of peoples, ideas and cultural forms back and forth across the Atlantic. Black peoples may be globally dispersed – and their experiences and self-identities have always been plural and divergent – yet they have also been linked by a long history of inter-cultural connections. Blaxploitation cinema and heroes such as Shaft and Sweetback can be seen as elements in these cultural connections and processes of exchange. Their representations of gender and sexuality were inevitably a field of conflict and contradiction. Yet, as they circulated between the various locales of the black diaspora, they were able to provide an important (albeit ambivalent) point of identification in struggles against subordination.

## NOTES

1 After 1969, following the reduction of its budget and the increasing sensitivity regarding American intervention in foreign regimes, *Mission: Impossible* moved its operations back to the United States where IMF were enlisted in the battle against organized crime.
2 For a fuller discussion of the impact of *Sweetback* see Manthia Diawara's title essay in her 1993 edited collection.
3 The full history of blaxploitation cinema can be found in James (1995).
4 A new (2000) incarnation of *Shaft*, saw Samual L. Jackson don the trademark leather trenchcoat in a reworking of the narrative that saw the black private eye (or, more accurately, the nephew of the original gumshoe) wrestling with racist violence in contemporary New York.
5 Interestingly, it was the blond Hutch who interpreted black language and culture for the darker Starsky. To have cast Starsky in such a role would, perhaps, have undermined the security of his whiteness and generated new questions about the power relationship that existed between the two detectives.
6 ITV screened *Mission: Impossible* between 1967 and 1974, *The Mod Squad* between 1970 and 1972 and the short-lived *Shaft* between 1974 and 1975. *Ironside*, meanwhile, figured in BBC1's prime 9:00 p.m. slot on Saturday evenings between 1967 and 1975, succeeded by *Starsky and Hutch* as the high-point to BBC schedules between 1976 and 1981.

## REFERENCES

Bhabha, Homi (1983) 'The Other Question', in *Screen*, Vol. 24, No. 6.

Bogle, Donald (1973) *Toms, Coons, Mulattos, Mammies and Bucks*, New York: Continuum.

Buxton, David (1990) *From The Avengers to Miami Vice: Form and Ideology in Television Series*, Manchester: Manchester University Press.

Clarke, Cheryl (1983) 'The Failure to Transform: Homophobia in the Black Community', in Barbara Smith (ed.), *Home Girls: A Black Feminist Anthology*, New York: Kitchen Table Press.

Davis, Angela (1992) 'Black Nationalism: The Sixties and the Nineties', in Gina Dent (ed.), *Black Popular Culture*, Seattle: Bay Press.

Diawara, Manthia (1993) 'Black American Cinema', in Manthia Diawara (ed.), *Black American Cinema*, New York: Routledge.

Fanon, Frantz (1991) *Black Skin, White Masks*, London: Pluto Press (orig. publ. 1952).

Gilroy, Paul (1993) *The Black Atlantic*, London: Verso.

Golden, Thelma (1994) 'My Brother', in Thelma Golden (ed.), *Black Male: Representations of Black Masculinity*, New York: Whitney Museum of American Art.

Gray, Herman (1995) *Watching Race: Television and the Struggle for Blackness*, Minneapolis: University of Minnesota Press.

Hall, Stuart (1990) 'The Whites of Their Eyes', in M. Alvarado and J. O. Thompson (eds), *The Media Reader*, London: BFI.

—— (1997) 'The Spectacle of the Other', in Stuart Hall (ed.), *Representation: Cultural Representations and Signifying Practices*, Milton Keynes: Oxford University Press.

hooks, bell (1996) *Reel to Real*, London: Routledge.

James, Darius (1995) *That's Blaxploitation: The Roots of the Baadasssss 'Tude (Rated X by an All Whyte Jury)*, New York: St. Martin's Griffin.

Lewis, Jon and Stempel, Penny (1996) *Cult TV: The Essential Critical Guide*, London: Pavilion.

Mercer, Kobena (1994) *Welcome to the Jungle: New Positions in Black Cultural Studies*, London: Routledge.

Palmer, Jerry (1973) 'Thrillers: The Deviant Behind the Consensus', in Ian Taylor and John Taylor (eds), *Politics and Deviance*, Harmondsworth: Penguin.

Pines, Jim (ed.) (1992) *Black and White in Colour*, London: BFI.

Reid, M.A. (1993) *Redefining Black Film*, Berkeley, CA: University of California Press.

Wallace, Michelle (1993) 'Race, Gender, and Psychoanalysis', in Manthia Diawara (ed.), *Black American Cinema*, New York: Routledge.

*Windrush* (1998) BBC TV.

Young, Lola (1996) *Fear of the Dark*, London: Routledge.

# 7

# *KUNG FU*
## Re-orienting the television Western

*Yvonne Tasker*

To contemporary eyes, the series *Kung Fu* feels like high-concept television – 'TV's first Mystical Eastern Western', as the title of a 1993 guide to the Warner Brothers series put it (Pilato, 1993). This popular action hybrid featured David Carradine as Kwai Chang Caine, an exiled Shaolin priest who roams the Old West with a price on his head, encountering spiritual and physical challenges in each episode. *Kung Fu* ran for three successful series before its star departed in 1975 to pursue (depending on which account one reads) either a movie career or a more meditative way of life. Carradine later reprised the role in a second TV movie, also titled *Kung Fu*, in 1986 (with Brandon Lee playing his son) and in a 1993 series, *Kung Fu: The Legend Continues*, in which he plays Caine's grandson in a contemporary urban setting.

The distinctiveness of the original show lay in its martial arts inflection of that peculiar mix of violence and stoicism so characteristic of the Western in its various fictional incarnations. Although *Kung Fu* seemed new and contemporary in its use of martial arts (still a novelty for western audiences in 1972), there was a generic familiarity to the show's male hero: slow to anger but more than capable in combat, a romantic and mysterious wanderer who fights in self-defence, or in defence of others rather than for any personal gain. *Kung Fu*'s Caine was always conceived by the show's creator, Ed Spielman, as a kind of Western hero – a loner, 'rootless, restless, driven by internal and external forces' (Pilato, 1993: 37). Perhaps rather ironically, given the context of a book on action television, the series was marked by a certain reticence around action and violence. There is no one cause for this reticence, which emerged as one of the defining features of the series. Obviously the restrictions faced by prime-time drama played a part, even though *Kung Fu* was clearly an adult Western. So, too, did Carradine's martial arts abilities. But just as important was the explicit desire expressed by many of the creative people involved in the genesis of the show to emphasize philosophy as much as fighting. Both the characteristic use of slow motion within fight sequences and the cross-cutting between China and America (juxtaposing Caine's present with his past) stem from this tension around the place of action in *Kung Fu*, emerging directly from the, in some ways contradictory, conception of a 'pacifist' action series.

Though an attempt to draw on Asian culture for western audiences is clearly central to the series, Spielman drew on several religious and philosophical traditions for the pilot ('Way Of The Tiger, Son Of Death'), saying, 'I employed that which was closest to me, Jewish thought, and a whole lot more' (Pilato, 1993: 7). In keeping with this multi-cultural method, *Kung Fu* glossed the thematic concerns of the TV Western not only with an explicit – if sometimes obscure – mysticism, but with the kind of liberal attention to race and racism in an Old West setting that was also evident in at least some revisionist Westerns on the big screen. Neither its liberalism nor its undoubted innovation extended to the casting of an Asian actor in the central role, although Bruce Lee was apparently seriously considered for the part of Caine. Of course, white actors have regularly played Mexican, Native American and Asian roles in American movies; and films expressly concerned with issues of racial intolerance are no exception to this.[1] Yet the device of a Chinese–American protagonist allows for a fruitful dramatic tension – as Caine himself impassively philosophizes in the 1986 TV movie, 'Those of us with twin roots sometimes become the strongest trees'. Moreover, the series' central character personified an ambivalent heroism with hybrid origins. On the one hand, Caine's soft-spoken, long-haired hero obviously echoed emerging definitions of non-violent masculinity that in turn explicitly drew on non-western cultures. (Here, for example, one thinks of counter-cultural interest in eastern religious systems, fashion and music). On the other hand, Caine's hesitant but inevitable recourse to violence recalls the dilemma of many Western heroes – Shane, most obviously.[2] *Kung Fu*, then, aligns itself with a distinctly counter-cultural version of western heroism – a type of male identity nicely summed up in J. Hoberman's description of Stallone's Rambo as a sort of 'hippie he-man' (Hoberman, 1989: 187).[3] In this chapter I'll attempt to contextualize the genesis, characteristics and success of *Kung Fu* as both an action series/television Western, and as an attempt to harness American perceptions of the east to a revised 1970s masculinity – what I have termed, in my title, a sort of 're-orientation'.

## *KUNG FU* AND THE TELEVISION WESTERN

A staple of 1950s schedules, the television Western thrived up to the mid-1960s. Discussing the 'rise and fall' of the genre, William Boddy provides the following statistics on the heyday of the TV Western:

> In the 1957–8 season, four of television's five most popular programmes were Westerns, and the following season, despite widespread predictions of saturation, Westerns represented nine of TV's top eleven shows; the 570 hours of TV Westerns in the 1958–9 season were estimated to be the equivalent of 400 Hollywood features a year.
>
> (Boddy, 1998: 119)

Boddy locates the success of the television Western within the specific historical and institutional context of the emergent networks, and in relation to developing practices of syndication. But, despite its remarkable success, the TV Western declined as the 1960s wore on as network schedules shifted towards contemporary action series, medical dramas and situation comedies. Like its cinematic counterpart, the TV Western evolved thematically in an attempt to survive. This increasingly took the form of 'genetic mutations and hybrids' – in particular a shift towards 'domestic melodramas' such as *Bonanza* (1959–73) or the 'increasingly domestic-oriented' *Gunsmoke*, introduced by John Wayne ('It's honest; it's adult; it's realistic'[4]), which ran from 1955 to 1975 (Boddy, 1998: 131). Shows such as *The Virginian* (1962–70) also emphasized if not domesticity, then the pleasures of life on the range amongst a group of male friends.

Parody was another weapon in the Western's struggle to survive – a way of distancing new Westerns from the values of the parent culture, whilst the familiarity of generic conventions continued to reassure. Writing in the magazine *Cult TV*, Nick Setchfield has reflected that the 1970s 'saw the death of both the big- and small-screen Western … with its boots on but with its tongue firmly embedded in [its] cheek' (Setchfield, 1998: 40). Exemplifying this tradition of the 'Western spoof' was the spy-themed *The Wild Wild West* (1965–69) – more recently revisited as a big-screen extravaganza starring Will Smith and Kevin Kline (1999). The early 1970s also saw the good-natured outlaws of *Alias Smith and Jones* (1971–73) trading on the success of Paul Newman and Robert Redford's buddy relationship in their 1969 hit, *Butch Cassidy and the Sundance Kid*. With its feature-length pilot first broadcast in 1972, *Kung Fu* also appeared well after the high-point of the television Western – a time when the genre was more often than not either parodic or gimmick-led, or, alternatively, centred on the domestic space rather than the wandering hero. In Setchfield's chronology, *Kung Fu* is positioned as 'mighty strange' – yet perhaps the series was not quite so odd, since it aimed not only to make efficient use of Warner Brothers' existing Western sets and props, but also to cannily offer a version of the West that would appeal to modern American sensibilities and interests.[5]

While Boddy indicates in detail the kinds of complex institutional factors involved in the demise of the television Western, he also draws attention to its flexibility, a facet demonstrated in the sheer range of Western hybrids that have appeared over the years. Moreover, he underlines the continuation of key Western themes within other generic contexts, noting that the 'resonance of the cowboy-hero as the last American individualist, the detached witness of human foibles and dispenser of justice, was clearly evident across the US mass media and survived the decline of the Western genre in the early 1960s'. And, in a similar fashion, the typical narrative structure of the television Western – which followed 'the picaresque adventures of a wandering hero involved with a set of antagonists replenished weekly – was unusually well-equipped to satisfy the balance of novelty and continuity demanded by episodic television'. For Boddy, then, the rise of 'new alienated, rootless heroes' of 1960s TV series like *Route 66* (1960–63) and *The Fugitive* (1963–66) evidences a continuity with the themes and imagery characteristic of the TV Western (Boddy, 1998: 136).

*Kung Fu* also retained precisely the kind of picaresque structure that Boddy identifies. Since Caine has a price on his head, he cannot settle down for long – although he does form relationships with women (for example, with Ellie, a rancher whose land he is working in the episode 'A Small Beheading'). Caine's function as a priest is also expressly described by Master Po in wandering hero terms: ' ... to walk the roads of the land and use what you have learned for the needs and benefits of the people'. Clearly, then, Caine also fulfils two of the other functions that Boddy associates with the Western hero – witness of human frailty and diversity on the one hand, and dispenser of justice on the other. Traversing the Warners backlot, Caine/Carradine encounters a plethora of guest stars (including well-known Asian–American actors such as James Hong), learning from them, defending them and helping to resolve their problems.

Yet the success of the new variants of TV (and cinematic) Western was also indebted to their ability to put distance between themselves and their 'parent' genre – which by the 1960s was increasingly perceived as an obsolete narrative form, part of a conservative 'adult' culture rather than the more vibrant youth culture then on the ascendant.[6] *Kung Fu* used several devices to distance itself from the 'traditional' Western genre. For example, the brush-free desert featured alongside the Chinese temple in the series' credit sequence is not the most familiar Western landscape. Implying Caine's endurance, the desert also functions to signal the empty, rather neutral, space he occupies in generic terms. *Kung Fu* also ensured such a distance by tapping into a developing counter-cultural investment in eastern culture (both mystical and martial), and by touching on both current social issues and alternative lifestyles. (See Figure 7.1.)

Of course, the series also marked its difference through the central importance it accorded to hand-to-hand combat rather than gunplay; martial arts over marksmanship. In his foreword to the *Kung Fu Book of Caine*, David Carradine rather audaciously claims that the series *caused* a 'martial arts explosion' which can still be seen 'running rampant across the big and little screens, not to mention the Dojos and Kung Fu academies' (Pilato, 1993: x). Writing in 1974, Flanigan confirms the timing, if not the trigger: 'In a little more than two years, kung fu (also known as Chinese boxing), the centuries-old martial art, has caught the fancy of the American public and literally become the "fist of fury"' (Flanigan, 1974: 9). As an extremely popular TV series, therefore, *Kung Fu* picked up on and popularized an existing, if restricted, interest in martial arts that was apparent through the late 1960s and early 1970s.[7] Bruce Lee had already attracted attention as a TV martial arts performer through his role as the chauffeur Kato in *The Green Hornet* which, like *Kung Fu*, aired on ABC (though only for the 1966–67 season).[8] Indeed, in discussing the American 'kung fu craze', Flanigan traces a trajectory from the 1960s *Green Hornet* to Carradine in *Kung Fu* – a media history that also takes in the huge success of Tom Laughlin's 1971 movie, *Billy Jack*, the furore that surrounded Bruce Lee's Hong Kong/Hollywood co-production *Enter the Dragon* (1973) and a merchandising boom that included comics, books and training classes, alongside TV movies and a plethora of press and magazine features.

It's worth noting that *Billy Jack* also offered an explicitly counter-cultural – and contemporized – version of the martial arts. This independent action movie, also a Western (of sorts), featured Tom Laughlin in the title role as a former Green Beret – an anti-authority figure and karate expert who turns to his Native American heritage

*Figure 7.1*  David Carradine as Kwai Chang Caine – promotional illustration for
*Kung Fu* (1972–75).

on returning, disillusioned, from Vietnam.[9] The movie is structured around the
misunderstanding and subsequent confrontation between the multi-racial, hippie
'freedom school' and the red-necks of a nearby town. The kind of opposition between
innocence (the child-like, alternative community) and ignorance (the depraved and
fearful straight world) foregrounded in *Billy Jack* is echoed by the recurrent scenes in
*Kung Fu* in which Caine either faces crude passions – greed, ignorance, racial prejudice – or defends others from them. Carradine plays Caine as a naive figure in the face

of all this, his halting delivery a quite distinct inflection of the Western hero's typical economy with words. After *Kung Fu*'s first episode -'King of the Mountain' – was aired, a *Hollywood Reporter* reviewer commented ruefully not only on the 'monoto-nous series of confrontations with distrustful, anti-oriental, brawling louts', but on the 'deadpan expressions and lack of dialogue' that Carradine had to work with (1972: 18). Of course, regular confrontations were necessary to allow the display of martial arts – the kung fu that was so explicitly promised by the series title. Indeed, as I have already suggested, the central contradiction of the series involved the exercise of phys-ical violence by a character who was avowedly passive and submissive.

## ACTION TELEVISION? FIGHTING AND PHILOSOPHY

While Carradine claims credit for the martial arts craze in the US, he is quick to add that '[v]ery little of any of this explosion had much to do with the philosophical points we were trying to make' (Pilato, 1993: x). Such a sense of disjuncture between the aims of the series and popular perceptions of martial arts recurs throughout Pilato's guide to the *Kung Fu* TV series – expressed in both his own commentary and in cita-tions from a range of writers, directors, producers and performers. For example, John Furia, who worked as writer and producer on the show, stresses the importance that he attached to showing the effects of violence and to emphasizing the consequences of human action: 'One thing that I did not want to do was glorify violence and have people revelling in violence in a show that was preaching non-violence. I thought that would be hypocritical' (cited in Pilato, 1993: 11). Thus, although every episode features at least one fight sequence in the Old West (in addition to the regular 'flash-back' sequences of Caine's training in a Shaolin temple), the production team empha-sized the importance of critical reflection on the use of violence. Pilato sums up writer Ed Spielman's perspective on *Kung Fu*: 'the essential lesson of the series [was that] peace is more important than victory, non-violence is to be preferred to violence' (1993: 11).

The distinctive narrative structure that *Kung Fu* evolved can be seen as both antici-pating and responding to an anxiety that 'certain people were tuning in for the fights' (Pilato, 1993: 10). The key feature in this context is the extensive use of flashbacks to Caine's childhood and adolescence in China, where we follow his training as a Shaolin priest. Dubbed 'Grasshopper' by one of his masters, the young Caine (played by Radames Pera) is shown to be naive, but essentially good. Caine's experiences as a child and as a young man in China guide him as an adult in the Old West, breaking up the action and producing a fairly complex narrative structure over the fifty minutes or so of each episode. Individual episodes typically present two stories: one in the present, one in the past, the two stories counterpointing each other, both moving towards a conclusion through the course of the episode.

A closer look at two episodes shows how this narrative structure worked to qualify the action in different ways. 'Alethea', an episode from *Kung Fu*'s first season, cuts between the 12-year-old Caine and the adult character's encounter with a young girl, Alethea, played by Jodie Foster. In the western part of the narrative a stagecoach is held up and Caine is thrown a gun as one of the guards is shot. Although she sees Caine as her friend, Alethea is convinced that he fired the shot and testifies to that effect – but then 'lies' to save him from the gallows. In the section of the narrative set in China, the young Caine is sent on his first errand outside the temple (he is to deliver a precious scroll). En route he is befriended by a stranger who first defends Caine from bandits, but then tricks him and steals the valuable scroll. When the stranger is ulti-mately captured and brought to the temple, the young Caine must choose whether to lie (thus saving the man's life) or to let him be executed. The resolution of the two strands comes through Caine's decision to lie (explicitly presented as a loss of inno-cence) and, in the western setting, by his success in tracking down the stagecoach robbers, defeating them in a fight and thereby demonstrating his innocence to Alethea. The flashback sequences, therefore, frame the episode's contemporary action scenes, working to draw our attention to an analogy between Caine's simplicity and Alethea's childish innocence, rather than to the fights. At one point Caine even calls Alethea 'Grasshopper', indicating the extent to which she stands in for his younger incarnation. Here, then, Caine is literally and metaphorically represented as both child and man – whilst the combat is simultaneously climactic and played down.

In contrast, 'The Passion of Chen Yi' cuts between two versions of the adult Caine in a narrative which revolves around repairing male friendship and misplaced sexual desire. At the outset Caine is mysteriously drawn to seek out Chen Yi (Soon Taik Oh), with whom he had argued when both were growing up at the temple. It is revealed that Chen Yi left the temple due to his failure to control his passion for a woman – in the west he is now in prison, willing to die for another woman, Louise, who has misleadingly claimed to love him. In the Chinese segment, Chen Yi offers an insulting gift which Caine refuses – and in the combat that follows Caine is defeated. In the American west Caine reverses the challenge, defeating Chen Yi and forcing him to confront Louise's treachery – a reconciliation (of sorts) finally being effected between the two men. By inter-cutting images of the fight that Caine lost long ago with his victory as an adult, Caine's victory overrides his defeat. Though this plays out a fairly explicit scenario of vengeance, Caine is still constructed as childlike – both in his simplicity, his ability to see through the desire that blinds Chen Yi, and in his stub-born insistence on seeking Chen Yi's friendship (who hisses with frustration 'I prefer to die without seeing your trusting face staring at me').

The flashback sequences in which Caine is a child and those in which he is a young man function differently, yet the overall effect as the series developed was only superfi-cially contradictory. On the one hand the temple sequences emphasized Caine as contemplative, an individual striving to learn from experience. Equally, however, they suggest a continuity between Caine as child, student and wandering hero. The idea of Caine as 'child–man' is reinforced by his repeated posing of simple questions, requesting explanations of the most basic objects and institutions he encounters – 'What is a railroad?' he asks curiously in the series' pilot. Throughout, Carradine's halting delivery, and the uncertainty it implies, serve to qualify the fight sequences – which are presented in slow motion, as if slowed down to Caine's pace rather than representing an intrusion of western violence into the 'placid' world of the 'orient'.

## *KUNG FU* AS AN EASTERN WESTERN

'As a traditional western hero', writes Herman Miller in his sketch of Caine's character, we 'see him in traditional stories, but with a new dimension' (cited in Pilato, 1993: 28). The combination of violence and spectacle with pacifist philosophizing that characterized *Kung Fu* as a TV Western clearly has generic precedents. To some extent *Kung Fu* shared the structuring dilemma of the classic Western *Shane* (1953), exploring the position of a pacifist hero faced with the need for action. *Shane* had already generated a short-lived television series (1966–67), in which Carradine also played the title role. Indeed, one fan's description of *Shane* as 'the first long-haired TV Western', underlines the ways in which this series anticipated many of the traits later developed in *Kung Fu* – Shane, we are told, 'tried unsuccessfully each week to avoid a gunfight [but] … Every week, at the end of the show, Shane would put on his leather shirt, strap on his fancy gunbelt and ride Candy into town to shoot somebody'.[10] Violence is initially withheld, but always provides a resolution (of sorts) to the narrative.

If the idea of a pacifist, or at least a reluctant, hero was not unprecedented, *Kung Fu* certainly brought something new to the television Western – with its distinctly 1970s spin on mysticism and veneration of nature and the environment. *Kung Fu* offered a caring, 'counter-cultural' articulation of masculinity that was defined primarily in terms of its spirituality rather than its physicality. Although Carradine's body is on display, muscular strength is downplayed in favour of agility and lightness of touch. 'We will find Caine strangely modern in his reverence for life', says Miller, 'in his seeking to be at one with the forces of the Universe' (cited in Pilato, 1993: 28). This dimension of pseudo-mysticism is especially evident in the episode 'Cry of the Night Beast'. Stalked by a team of bounty hunters, Caine experiences a vision that recalls a frightening and confusing childhood dream in which he felt a spiritual affinity with the unborn baby of a woman visiting the temple. As the narrative unfolds, it becomes clear that the dream was a premonition of the scenario that begins to unfold in the new setting of the American west – Caine having to preserve the life of a buffalo calf whose spirit is somehow entwined with that of a woman's unborn child. The baby's father, meanwhile, is a hunter whose future is uncertain following the decimation of the prairie buffalo herds. The episode, therefore, rehearses various different relationships to nature and the environment. On the one hand are the mercenary bounty hunters who search for Caine, on the other the exploitative buffalo hunters and the butchers who depend on them. And on the other stands the itinerant Caine (who survives by trading work for simple food and shelter) and a Native American who collects buffalo bones to grind up for fertilizer, making use of what remains of the environmental resources. In this way, therefore, Caine's mystical connection to birds and animals – with whom he seems able to communicate – is mapped onto contemporary concerns for the environment, the need to provide for a new generation and a nostalgia for the plenitude of the Old West.

A tension between the primitive and the sophisticated – represented in the contrast between the pastoral western landscape and the encroaching modern world of railroads telegraphs, and eastern cities – is a theme central to the Western genre. *Kung Fu*, however, works around an alternative (though in certain respects similar) opposition between East and West, in which the ignorance and materialism of small western communities is contrasted with a construction of China as a sophisticated culture – a nostalgically remembered, candle-lit space associated with spirituality, peace and community. The calm rituals and tranquil atmosphere of the temple are in sharp contrast to the dirt roads, bustling towns and avaricious ethos of the west. *Kung Fu*, therefore, presents a contradictory portrait of America – corrupt and greedy against the peace of the temple, but also offering adventure and opportunities for friendship. The representation of China is equally contradictory, the sense of peaceful spirituality set against an image of tyrannical oppression – Caine unjustly exiled from his homeland after his revenge-killing of the nobleman who murdered his Shaolin mentor, Master Po.

In this way, then, Caine is constructed as American society's spiritual/mystic 'other', as becomes clear in Miller's account of the series:

> [Caine] becomes almost the inadvertent symbol, the unsought-for (on his part) champion of the underdog, with whom he can empathize only too well – the Red Man, the Brown Man, the Yellow Man, and the Black. Though he doesn't seek out this kind of action, he yet attracts it, and, being what he is, a man who cannot endure injustice, he must act on it'.
>
> (cited in Pilato, 1993: 28)

I'm struck here by the similarities between this construction of a western narrative and that which characterizes what Noël Carroll (1998) terms the 'south-of-the-border professional Western'. According to Carroll, this variety of the Western constructs Mexico as a counterpoint to the United States – the heroes, while invariably Americans themselves, are 'motivated by a hatred of tyranny, an attention to the social value of freedom and/or an admiration for the Mexican people' (1998: 60). However, despite *Kung Fu*'s emphasis on themes of racial tolerance, the specificity of marginalized groups is much less in the series, with Carradine's Chinese–American hero somehow standing outside the various communities which he encounters.

## 'WHAT DOES IT MEAN TO BE A MAN?: *KUNG FU* AND COUNTER-CULTURAL MASCULINITY

> ... *Kung Fu* was a story about love overcoming hate, good triumphing over evil. As such, it preached non-violence and thoughtfulness. In each episode, the question of action (versus non-action) was a significant one. Each week, Caine struggled with the oldest of human questions: What does it mean to be a man? What does it mean to be a good man? How should one act?
>
> (Pilato, 1993: 7)

Though Pilato, here, no doubt intends 'man' to stand in for human, the definition of a distinctive version of masculinity – a response to the question 'what does it mean to be a man' – is thematically central to *Kung Fu*, just as it has been intrinsic to the history of the Western genre more generally.

Carradine wasn't cast as Kwai Chang Caine for his martial arts skills. Pilato cites the account of casting offered by series producer Harvey Frand: 'In my eyes and in the eyes of [fellow producer] Jerry Throe, David Carradine was always our first choice to play Caine. But there was some disagreement because the network was interested in a more muscular actor, and the studio was interested in getting Bruce Lee' (1993: 32). Rather than muscularity or martial arts dexterity, it was Carradine's abilities as a dancer that impressed the *Kung Fu* production team. The producers were drawn to Carradine's 'balletic' qualities, seeing them as compatible with the graceful and 'contemplative' feel they were trying to invest in their series. *Kung Fu*'s combination of action and philosophy was in line with stereotypical perceptions of East Asia as a source of not only martial arts skills, but of ancient wisdom and codes of honour. In constructing a pacifist image of Asian culture (that contrasted to the perceived brutality of the west), however, *Kung Fu* loses much of the sense of physical energy displayed in contemporaneous martial arts films and television series – especially those that featured the militant anger of Bruce Lee's performances. Lee's dynamism, however, was quite at odds with the tone of the *Kung Fu* series, with its slow-motion combat and emphasis on mysticism. Elsewhere I have discussed the toughness so central to Lee's star persona as being a response to a history 'of "feminizing" Western representations of Chinese men' (Tasker, 1997: 322). *Kung Fu* sought both to tap into this repertoire of feminized images, whilst also producing a traditional (read, strong) Western hero with the capacity to defend himself and others through his skills in the martial arts.

Though just as committed to notions of right and wrong, David Weir's English adaptation of Nippon Television's 1975 series *The Water Margin* offered less sedate pleasures. *The Water Margin*'s central heroic male protagonist, Lin Chung (Atsuo Nakamura), is resolutely honourable – but the series showed none of *Kung Fu*'s hesitancy around the use of violence. Heralding the addition of *The Water Margin* to the BBC's 1976 autumn schedule, the *Radio Times* contrasted the show to *Kung Fu*, explicitly celebrating the extra action and spectacle on offer in the new series: '*The Water Margin* is Nippon TV's wham-bam answer to David Carradine and his Westernized version of kung fu. And if more is better, why settle for one hero when you can follow the adventures of 108 brave and honourable men and one beautiful and feisty heroine?' (*Radio Times*, 1976: 4) [11] A Japanese production of a Chinese tale, *The Water Margin* – together with Weir's subsequent adaptation, *Monkey* (1979–81) – received enthusiastic responses from western audiences, who were receptive to the spectacular choreography, humour, strong narrative, and to the spirit of friendship these shows evoked. Yet, while *The Water Margin* was less reticent than *Kung Fu* in terms of its violent spectacle, it nonetheless also foregrounded spiritual philosophizing through the use of the 'pearl-of-wisdom aphorisms' in Burt Kwok's narration (Fraser, 1998: 54).

*Kung Fu*, however, was always the master of this particular art. In contrast to the aggressive warriors of *The Water Margin*, Caine was portrayed as a 'child-man' – with the ability to be tough and decisive, but with a disposition that was essentially gentle and contemplative. Carradine's performance emphasized Caine's ability to see through social hierarchies, to set aside prejudice. With its introspection, wistful music and slow-motion action sequences, therefore, *Kung Fu*'s success lay in its ability to invest both the newly popular martial arts and the traditional Western with a counter-cultural flavour. Juxtaposing, even intercutting, scenes of combat with moments of reflection, *Kung Fu* negotiated a prime-time course between the contradictions of pacifism and combat. And in doing so *Kung Fu* occupies a place in a longer tradition of western fascination with, and stereotypical representation of, Asian culture – the themes of which are, themselves, rooted in complex patterns of cultural exchange that stem from conflict, occupation and immigration.

## NOTES

1 See for example, Charlton Heston in *Touch of Evil* (1958), Rock Hudson as *Taza, Son of Cochise* (1954) or Elvis Presley in *Flaming Star* (1960).

2 In many ways this question goes to the heart of the genre itself, touching on the preoccupations of law and order that are central to both heroic outlaws and lawmen: what kind of man is the Western hero? Can he stand alone or must he rely on others? Can his capacity for violence be contained (domesticated, even) or does it represent a threat? The fastest draw repeatedly has to defend his reputation, finding himself drawn into wearying combat, challenged wherever he goes.

3 Hoberman also points out how this image or type involves an appropriation of Native American culture.

4 Wayne's 'extended pre-credit introduction' is cited in Boddy (1998: 122).

5 Warners initially bought the rights to *Kung Fu* in 1970 as a feature film for cinematic release with the use of their existing sets partly in mind. A subsequent deal with ABC generated the television movie and, following its success, the TV series was commissioned (Pilato, 1993: 15–16).

6 The Western had made attempts to acknowledge the rise of new, generationally-based cultures. As early as 1948 Howard Hawks' Western, *Red River*, played off in explicitly generational terms the tough individualism of Thomas Dunson (John Wayne) against the gentler, youthful articulation of masculinity offered by his adopted son, Matt (Montgomery Clift). See the discussion of this film in Cohan (1997: 204–20).

7 Carradine's claim is matched later in the book by Pilato's understated observation that Bruce Lee 'went on to considerable success in the martial arts film world'.

8 Keye Luke, Master Po throughout the *Kung Fu* TV series (and the 1986 TV movie), had played Kato in the 1939 movie version of *The Green Hornet*, together with its sequel released the following year.

9 *Billy Jack* acquired a degree of notoriety when Laughlin successfully sued its distributors, Warner Brothers, for failing to market the film effectively. On its 1974 re-release, however, it was a huge hit generating in excess of $30 million in box-office revenues.

10 For this discussion of *Shane* and *Kung Fu*, see *The David Carradine Home Page*, www.davidcarradine.net (accessed 20.5.01).

11 The 'feisty heroine' in question was swordswoman Hu San-Niang, played by Sanae Tschida.

# REFERENCES

Boddy, W. (1998) 'Sixty Million Viewers Can't Be Wrong: The Rise and Fall of the Television Western', in E. Buscombe and R.E. Pearson (eds), *Back in the Saddle Again: New Essays on the Western*, London: BFI.

Carroll, N. (1998) 'The Professional Western: South of the Border', in E. Buscombe and R.E. Pearson (eds), *Back in the Saddle Again: New Essays on the Western*, London: BFI.

Cohan, S. (1997) *Masked Men: Masculinity and the Movies in the Fifties*, Bloomington: University of Indiana Press.

*Empire* (1996) 'Monkey Business', September: 136.

Flanigan, B.P. (1974) 'Kung Fu Krazy: or the Invasion of the "Chop Suey Easterns"', *Cinéaste*, Vol. 15, No. 3.

Fraser, R. (1998) 'China Crisis', *Cult TV*, January: 53–56.

Hoberman, J. (1989) 'Vietnam: the Remake', in B. Kruger and P. Mariani (eds), *Remaking History*, Seattle: Bay Press.

*Hollywood Reporter* (1972) '*Kung Fu* Series is Offbeat Oater', Vol. 223, No. 23, October: 8.

Pilato, H.J. (1993) *The 'Kung Fu' Book of Caine: The Complete Guide to TV's First Mystical Eastern Western*, Boston, MA: Charles E. Tuttle Co.

*Radio Times* (1976) 18 September: 4–6.

Setchfield, N. (1998) 'How the West was Wild', *Cult TV*, June: 36–41.

Tasker, Y. (1997) 'Fists of Fury: Discourses of Race and Masculinity in the Martial Arts Cinema', in H. Stecopoulos and M. Uebel (eds), *Race and the Subject of Masculinities*, Durham: Duke University Press.

# 8

# 'DROP EVERYTHING ...
# INCLUDING YOUR PANTS!'

## The Professionals and
## 'hard' action TV

*Leon Hunt*

Violent, politically incorrect and fantastically fun, with top clothes, top birds
and skilful cars, this is without doubt the coolest TV show ever.
(Video sleeve for *The Professionals* 1998)

'He's holding a Webley .44 along with a 38 B-cup', observes Bodie (Lewis Collins) to
his partner Doyle (Martin Shaw) as they survey a hostage scene. Moments later, Bodie
is retrieving a live grenade from the bra of hostage Pamela Stephenson – 'You're a
lucky girl, Nurse Bolding', quips Doyle when the excitement has died down, and her
adoring look suggests unequivocal agreement. Here is *The Professionals* in a nutshell.
Hostages. Laddish swagger and in-car banter ('So tell me about that air hostess ... ').
Ford Capris performing handbrake turns. Gratuitous violence and as much titillation
as a just-past-the-watershed slot would allow. No other action show offers quite the
same nostalgic promise of 'guilty pleasure' through the ironic timewarp of 'political
correctness' – horrible fashions, macho posturing, right wing politics. Its virtual disappearance from British terrestrial TV since 1987 has contributed to its forbidden
mystique – a contractual disagreement with Martin Shaw has largely confined it to
video and satellite. But in 1997, it was the highest-rating show on Granada Plus and
was being parodied in an ad for the Nissan Almera ('Go faster!'/'I'm doing nearly 30!'/
'Naughty boy!').

Shut It! A Fan's Guide to 70s Cops on the Box (Day and Topping, 1999) is suggestive
of how retro-cult TV is circulated and celebrated now. Each episode of *The Sweeney*
and *The Professionals* is rated or receives a comment for 'Birds', Booze, Shooters, Cars,
Non-PC moments and the inevitable 1970s fashions. But there are some less predictable pleasures on offer, too – each episode of *The Professionals* gets a 'Slash Fiction
Moment', instances of intense bonding between these two Hard Men. For the unini-
tiated, Slash fiction is fan-generated porno-romance focusing on male pairings from
cult TV shows – the earliest and most prolific body of stories found opportunities for

*Star Trek*'s Kirk and Spock to boldly go where no prime-time buddy relationship had gone before. The narrative payoff is gay sex between ostensibly straight men, but Slash seems to have been traditionally written mainly by straight women, who have been seen as either imagining utopian relationships between equals or more subversively blurring 'straight'/'queer' binaries (Jenkins, 1992; Penley, 1997). Bodie and Doyle loom large in Slash fiction, but it's interesting that the show's homoeroticism has become part of its nostalgic allure – 'pretty boys in leather jackets and cowboy boots playing with lethal toys' (Day and Topping, 1999: 7). *The Professionals*' masculinism never went entirely uncontested – *The Comic Strip*'s parody *The Bullshitters* had outed 'Bonehead' and 'Foyle' as early as 1984.[1] Feminism was catching up with the 'boys' and so were shifts in definitions of masculinity. By late 1979, *The Professionals* was scheduled against the BBC's *Shoestring*, which signalled a shift in TV detectives – kicking in doors was on the way out, sensitivity and quirkiness were in.[2] Doyle may have had New Man trappings – cooking, art classes, an acoustic guitar, *that* bubble perm – but Eddie Shoestring (Trevor Eve) was the real thing. He'd had a nervous breakdown, lived on a barge and wore his pyjama top as a shirt to indicate that he really needed looking after. Bodie would probably have bullied him at school, but Shoestring won the ratings battle.

What do we 'know' about *The Professionals* from its critical and popular reputation? Firstly, that it represents the zenith in the British crime show's collusion with repressive discourses on law and order – a show so right-wing that 'no further escalation was possible' (Whannel, 1994: 185). For the Left, CI5's blurring of the police, the secret service and the military evoked uncomfortable echoes of the use of paramilitary groups like the Special Patrol Group (SPG) in policing demonstrations and the role played by the SAS in the Iranian Embassy Siege (a major TV event) in 1980. Its second reputation is as a show so absurdly and hysterically macho that it inadvertently queers the whole genre. To see Bodie telling leather-clad bikers to 'Drop everything … including your pants' ('Look After Annie') is perhaps to wonder how it was ever taken any other way.

*The Professionals* is a conservative programme – we're never invited to doubt that 'extreme measures' are needed to combat crime – but, like the James Bond films, the 'c' in 'conservative' varies in size, sometimes significantly. This was a populist text transmitted over a 6-year period – a period which includes the Silver Jubilee (referenced on newspaper headlines in early episodes), the Iranian Embassy siege, the Falklands conflict and the IRA's continuing mainland bombing campaign, but also the reverberations of police corruption and brutality, the implication of the SPG in at least one fatality, and the growing visibility of the Far Right in British politics. In *Televising Terrorism* (1983), Schlesinger *et al.* make two useful sets of distinctions in their analysis of TV's representation of 'terrorism' – between *open* and *closed* discourses and *tight* and *loose* formats. A 'closed' (orthodox) discourse, for example, might be tempered by a 'loose' format, which creates a space for ambiguities and contradictions (Schlesinger *et al.*, 1983: 32). Their analysis very much privileges the single play or self-contained serial over the programmed constraints of the series. The British cop show *The Sweeney* (1974–78) would be a good example of this. It originated as a feature-length TV play *Regan* (1974) about the eponymous, rule-bending cop (John Thaw) and his relationship with the new, bureaucratic structure of the Metropolitan police as much as old-style villains. His future is left uncertain at the end of *Regan* – is there still a place for such a maverick? – but these doubts needed to be brushed aside for a continuing series. Subsequently, creator Ian Kennedy Martin's interrogation of policing was replaced by a more conventional cops-versus-villains framework (Donald, 1985: 120–21). But this can conceivably work the other way and I would suggest that *The Professionals* is a case in point. Its format is much more 'closed' and seemingly 'tight' than *The Sweeney*'s – 'Anarchy. Acts of Terror. Crimes Against the Public. To combat it I've got special men ... ' as Cowley (Gordon Jackson) assures all right-thinking citizens in the original title sequence. So far, so New Right. But there are only so many terrorists, anarchists and mad lefties you can find to fill sixty episodes, especially in a show keen to be topical, and so episodes like 'Klansmen' and 'In the Public Interest' look elsewhere for Britain's malaise.[3] Some of this was built in from the start. Doyle was cast to articulate a more reflective and comparatively moderate discourse in contrast to Cowley's New Right rhetoric and Bodie's load-testosterone-and-fire heroics. Moreover, both operatives adhere to a 'permissive' lifestyle when not dealing with the fallout from that permissiveness. To adapt Schlesinger *et al.*'s (1983) distinction into a trouser metaphor, the show is flared rather than straight-leg.

## 'OLD DOG WITH NEW TRICKS': POP, COPS, SOLDIERS AND SPIES

*The Professionals* was the creation of Brian Clemens, joint Executive Producer with Albert Fennell for Avengers Mark 1 Productions. They pitched it to LWT's Brian Tesler in 1977 (Matthews, 1999); filming took place between 1977 and 1981 and the show was broadcast over five seasons between 1977 and 1983. According to Philip Purser, it was Clemens and Fennell who were the 'true professionals':

> the rough tough bunch the programme controller has to call in when all civilised attempts to get ratings has failed. Out come the deadly scissors, the lethal paste, and they go to work, mixing in carefully calculated proportions the cross-talk heroics of *Starsky and Hutch*, the mayhem of *Target*, the above-the-law arrogance of any strong-arm spy thriller and the cultural values of a soft-porn magazine.
>
> (*Sunday Telegraph*, 8 January 1978)

Purser was right about one thing – the programme was a hybrid. *The Professionals* marked the convergence of two generic strands – the 1960s spy–adventure show in which secret agents mediate fashion and consumption while engaging in international espionage, and the 1970s 'Law and Order' show in which hard men do unpopular things to protect the 'national interest'. *The Professionals* positioned itself in between these two strands, 'grittier' than the former but more escapist than the latter. The three central characters also evinced generic hybridity (see Figure 8.1). Head of CI5, Cowley was James Bond's 'M' tailored for the 1970s 'exceptional state'. Bodie represented the world of imperialist adventure mixed in with the mystique of 'Special Services' – a former mercenary (in Angola and Biafra), gun-runner, recruited by the Paras (including a stint in Northern Ireland) and the SAS.[4] Lewis Collins' subsequent film career confirmed his Action Man persona – that rabid hymn to the SAS, *Who Dares Wins* (1982) and a trio of mercenary roles for Italian exploitation director Antonio Margheriti (AKA Anthony M. Dawson), *Codename Wildgeese* (1984), *Commando Leopard* (1985) and *The Commander* (1987). Doyle's backstory seems to locate him within the pre-*Sweeney* British cop show. While he has 'special skills' in the martial arts and marksmanship, he never made it above constable. This has two implications. First, it allies him with the 'community policing' and social conscience of shows like *Z Cars* (1960–78) and explains his more open-minded outlook – 1970s cops like Regan and Hackett (*Target*) tended to be big-city detective inspectors with hard-boiled worldviews. Second, it can be read as a sign of his incorruptibility – with various senior police officers falling from grace in the early 1970s, Doyle's lack of promotion could be taken as a badge of honour – in 'Hunter/Hunted', he's targeted by a corrupt cop he helped put away. In 'The Madness of Mickey Hamilton', a sniper is killing doctors indiscriminately – he blames them for his daughter's brain damage and his wife's death. Doyle manages to convince him that the tragedy was attributable to a *shortage* of doctors, but Mickey is shot by an overzealous marksman before he can surrender. 'Somebody should have helped him sooner', Doyle tells Cowley, whose only concern is that order is restored. Doyle's conscience is particularly central to the introspective 'Discovered in a Graveyard' where his misgivings about 'the job' take on phantasmatic form after a near-fatal shooting – Cowley describes him as an 'idealist – as much as anyone can be doing the job he does ... he's done more, seen more, to make him want to throw it all in than almost anybody his age'.

Clemens' and Fennell's background with *The Avengers* (1961–69) and *The New Avengers* (1976–77) seems to ally the show with what David Buxton has called the 'Pop series', glossy 1960s spy shows in which qualities like 'human nature', 'psychology' and 'depth' were played down in favour of glamorous designs, surfaces and lifestyles (1990: 96, 97–98). In the 'new world of total design' (ibid.: 73) '[c]haracters were no longer social archetypes ... but designed to double as fashion models' (74). John Steed and Emma Peel (*The Avengers*), John Drake (*Danger Man*) and the men from U.N.C.L.E. were agents for conspicuous consumption first and the 'Free World' second. Two developments can be discerned in the early 1970s. In Britain, the 'pop show' transmuted into what I have called the 'Safari Suit show' (Hunt, 1998) in which middle-aged swingers and amateur sleuths like *Jason King* and *The Persuaders!* (both 1971–72) solved crimes as a sideline while sunning themselves and modelling ill-advised outfits in exotic holiday resorts. In the United States, the 'designed' hero/ heroine was absorbed into a new type of crime show in which 'the action is simply *programmed* from the original design' (Buxton, 1990: 118). While the characters were 'prefabricated ... throwaway ideological determinations' (ibid.: 118), *some* limited sense of psychological 'depth' returned. Crime had some impact on 'society' – as

*Figure 8.1* Doyle (Martin Shaw), Cowley (Gordon Jackson) and Bodie (Lewis Collins) – smoothie hard men in *The Professionals* (1977–83).

opposed to *The Avengers'* consequence-free villainy – and characters had some narrative space in which to 'feel' and even to feel something for each other. Which brings us to Bodie and Doyle's cuddlier transatlantic progenitors, *Starsky and Hutch* (1975–9).

Pre-publicity for *The Professionals* sometimes called it 'Britain's answer to *Starsky and Hutch*' (Day and Topping, 1999: 168). Buxton notes how the latter's design hinged on the image of 'two male models' (1990: 130), a blonde and a brunette, suggesting the aesthetics of advertising as much as drama. Like Bodie and Doyle, they were also pin-ups, featured in fold-out fan magazines – David Soul's heart-throb status extended to a pop career, recording just the kind of songs you might expect Hutch to torture his girlfriends with. Similarly, Charlotte Eager relates the story of watching *The Professionals* in a 'Gothic girls' boarding school' in the late 1970s, '50 girls glued to the screen, transported by the first flickerings of adolescent lust' (*Guardian,* 31 March 1997). In both shows' character designs, Opposites Attract – this is where Slash potential commences. Starsky, 'a back-slapping jock whose life revolves around girls, bars, baseball and driving his Ford Torino' and Hutch, 'quiet, serious, college-educated romantic' (Buxton, 1990: 129). Starsky's machismo perhaps has to be taken on trust – those chunky cardigans were sending out other signals. But Bodie was clearly 'rough trade' and proud of it – 'I thought Bodie would throw me over the bonnet of his Ford Capri', reports one of Eager's interviewees. Doyle seemed harder than Starsky and Hutch put together, but was still strikingly more 'sensitive' than his partner. That hairdo said it all – one character refers to his 'pretty curls' – as did the tight jeans and casual jackets. Bodie's look was Squaddie-at-C&A – blazers gave way to an array of 'smart' leather jackets (tan, sky blue, silver) – with cropped hair and fuck-off sideburns. These were both car shows, even if CI5's Escorts and Capris were less spectacular than Starsky's bright red Torino.[5] The car facilitated tyre-screeching chases but also provided an enclosed space for banter and bonding, turning narrative 'dead time' into a source of pleasure.

But *The Professionals* also needs to be located within the British crime show, which was taking a more action-oriented direction in the mid-1970s. This also involved moving away from the cosy world of *Dixon of Dock Green* (1955–76) and social conscience of *Z Cars* to the urban jungle of *The Sweeney* and *Target* (1977–78). *The Sweeney*'s relationship with 1970s discourses on escalating crime and the need for a tough response is well-documented (Dennington and Tulloch; Hurd; Buscombe, all 1976; Donald, 1985). What *The Professionals* picks up on and extends is the need for a 'maintenance man' (or men) with a mandate to 'do what must be done' (Dennington and Tulloch, 1976: 39). CI5's mandate is identified as a 'loophole' in its remit – 'By all means necessary' ('Old Dog With New Tricks').

*Target* was the BBC's answer to *The Sweeney*, and differed in two, largely cosmetic, ways. First, it was even more violent than its inspiration and had the misfortune to coincide with The Belsen Report on TV Violence in 1977. Its transmission was interrupted after growing complaints and it was cancelled after two series, replaced, significantly by *The Professionals*' nemesis, *Shoestring*. Second, Hackett (Patrick Mower) was another hard man – pathological rudeness was by now compulsory for tough TV cops – but marked also by a 'cool urban chic' (Sylvia Clayton, *Daily Telegraph*, 16 September 1978). Mower had the looks of a smoothie, a cad even, but hardened by a boxer's nose. Regan and his sergeant, Carter (Dennis Waterman), favoured shapeless anoraks and flared terylene slacks – real men didn't ponce about with fashion in the Flying Squad. But Hackett is the first sighting of 'Capri Man', a 'hard bastard' who can accommodate fashion into his macho persona.

'Capri Man' (Bodie) – or 'Escort Man' (Doyle) – was another 'Old Dog With New Tricks', a reconfiguration of traditional masculinities.[6] In the 1970s, men were experiencing a Close Encounter with Consumerism as advertising encouraged them to think about products and their bodies in new ways, to contemplate aftershaves and shifting paradigms in underwear. Doyle would have been first in line for Old Spice, the first aftershave to insist that smelling nice could be manly (Simpson, 1994: 124–25). But strictly speaking, by the late 1970s he ought to have been flirting with the sexier Denim, whose ad showed female hands sliding down the shirt of a hairy-chested male. Bodie scorns aftershaves, but he's the epitome of Brut Man – advertised by boxers and footballers, Brut promised to smell of masculinity itself. But it's significant that he now seems the more modern of the two – with his lairy hedonism and insolent charm, he was a *Loaded* icon waiting to happen. 'Blind Run' opens with him performing the 'Sun Exercise', which consists of throwing his arms wide and screaming, an image of wild masculinity which anticipates the forest-bound, anti-feminist men's movement of the early 1990s.

This concerted effort to incorporate men into the world of fashion and cosmetics was one of the factors in the creation of the New Man, a 'hybrid masculinity' which represented 'not so much a rebellion but an adaptation in masculinity' (Chapman, 1988: 235). The idea that New Masculinity was largely (and literally) cosmetic now seems more significant than consciousness-raising initiatives like the Men's Liberation Movement (first sighted in 1973) or books like Andrew Tolson's *The Limits of Masculinity* (1977). Some of Doyle's proto-New Man trappings are purely a matter of acquisitions, objects and details in his ever-changing bachelor pads . But he cries, too – a few sniffles over a dead informer in 'Involvement' but actual tears when Bodie is knifed in 'Klansmen'.

By the early 1980s, the cautious remodelling of masculinity collided with a more aggressive body agenda, namely what Mike Featherstone (1982) has called 'Body Maintenance'. Aerobics, working-out and slimming represented a negotiation of ascetic and hedonistic conceptions of the body, offering a 'calculating hedonism' (Featherstone, 1982: 18). This finds its correlative in *The Professionals'* combination of disciplined bodies and permissive lifestyles. Bodie and Doyle's training is a combination of martial arts' mysticism, military reconstruction and technology – they are combat machines, in contrast to *The Sweeney's* dog-eared protagonists, ravaged by caffeine, nicotine and alcohol. Featherstone observes the 'machine metaphor' in this conception of the body – serviced and upgraded for 'maximum efficiency' (ibid.: 24). Such a body is always partly conceived as an object, and not necessarily one's own – Cowley periodically reminds them of his *ownership* of their bodies – they can be sacrificed at will. Collins' and Shaw's bodies were disciplined and trained for the series – a more tactile extension of the pop series' designed characters – performing many of their own stunts. When Shaw tried to leave the series – as Doyle occasionally tried to leave CI5 ('Involvement') – he was reminded that he, too, was owned.

'Wild Justice' is an episode about what happens when the masculine machine malfunctions. Bodie is performing badly in training – can he be reconditioned, or is it time for a new model? But his performance follows not so much a downward curve as a series of wildly contrasting highs and lows. The 'rationale' offered for this is a gestating death wish carried from his Special Service days – most of his former SAS comrades have died in civilian life, one of them in an altercation with a motorcycle gang. Bodie pursues a vendetta against the gang and only Cowley's gun against his head prevents him from killing its leader. In the course of the episode, Bodie's malaise is diagnosed from a range of perspectives – military, mystical and psycho-technological. For his martial arts master, his 'soul' is divided from and troubled by the actions of his body. But the most interesting voice belongs to Dr Kate Ross, the 'Queen of Cybernetics', one of a series of women in the series less than impressed by the lads' 'simple hairy masculine fun'. She represents two 'threats' – a feminist critique of machismo and a psycho-technological discourse on both the inner and outer body. Earlier, Bodie's girlfriend tells Cowley that 'Bodie doesn't have women problems. It's us women who have Bodie problems'. Dr Ross, on the other hand, mocks Doyle for his 'sexual chauvinism' and 'profound insecurity', before dismissing the pair with a condescending 'Good-bye, *boys*'. But while she is stereotypically humourless, she is

equipped to 'read' Bodie through fluctuations in his voice patterns and the mathe-
matics of Catastrophe theory. Bodie's cycles of elation and depression are about to
reach crisis point, which is precisely what happens. This is one of a pair of 'crisis'
episodes for our heroes – Doyle's occurs in 'Discovered in a Graveyard'. But Bodie's
burden is that of 'real masculinity', and there's a sense in 'Wild Justice' that all this
surveillance and analysis is as much the cause of his imploding machismo as a means
to a diagnostic end.

'Owning' Bodie and Doyle, being able to read and reconfigure them is also one of
the objectives of Slash fiction. 'They don't belong to me. I'm just playing with them',
insists Zoe Rayne at the end of 'A Little Reminder' (1998), in which an incidental
scene from 'Rogue' gives way to Bodie trying out a cock ring bought for him by Doyle.
But she acknowledges 'the satisfaction of watching the lads do as I say'. When Henry
Jenkins describes Slash as 'a genre about the limitations of traditional masculinity and
about reconfiguring male identity' (1992: 191), he could just as easily be describing
*The Professionals* itself, or at least its Slash potential. If *Star Trek* Slash is about imagining Utopian sex – sex between equals, sex in which (Spock's) gender identity is
ambiguous (Penley, 1997) – then *The Professionals'* Slash is about rough sex, picking
up on the tactile qualities of the show, the 'rough'/'sensitive' pairing of Bodie and
Doyle, and, of course, gay culture's appropriation of macho codes. The authors of
*Shut It!* are willing to play along with these 'guerrilla erotics' (Penley, 1997: 101), but
with a caveat – 'it's almost a shame it's impossible to present a same-gender relationship without someone thinking that sex must play a part somewhere' (Day and
Topping, 1999: 7). But if this suggests nostalgia for a time when there was a concep-
tual break in what Eve Kosofsky Sedgwick calls 'the continuum between homosocial
and homosexual' (1985: 1), they do acknowledge that 'if you watch the series with this
in mind, you find a lot of subtle … homoeroticism' (Day and Topping, 1999: 7).
But it's also clear that an ironic knowingness about male bonding can offer a retrospective licence for the series' appalling treatment of women. Bodie and Doyle's
bonds extend to what Sedgwick calls 'traffic in women', the 'use of women as
exchangeable … property for the primary purpose of cementing the binds of men
with men' (Kosovsky Sedgwick, 1985: 26). Bodie's 'birds' are interchangeable and
disposable, but Doyle is periodically compromised by heterosexual romantic ties.
Some turn out to be treacherous ('Hunter/Hunted') or constitute a security breach
('Involvement'). 'Involvement' finds Bodie and Anne (Patricia Hodge) competing for
Doyle – 'You look ravishing, mate', Bodie tells his partner as he prepares for a date and
soon he's spying on his rival. We learn that Cowley has right of approval over his operative's potential spouses, but he observes that he'll never have that problem with
Bodie. Doyle loses Anne and leaves CI5 headquarters in a bit of a state. The final scene
is a high-angle extreme long shot of Bodie going after his partner to cheer him up. We
can't hear what they're saying, but see Doyle shrugging Bodie off before succumbing
to having his friend's arm around him. There *has* to be a Slash version of what comes
next …

## WHERE THE JUNGLE ENDS: POLICING THE LATE SEVENTIES

Bodie and Doyle are very much creations of the 1970s 'Law and Order' society – *Policing the Crisis* provides the most celebrated account of the 'tendency to "criminalise" every threat to a disciplined social order and to "legalise" … every means of containment' (Hall *et al.*, 1978: 288). One manifestation of this was 'violent society syndrome' (Schlesinger *et al.*, 1983: 3), a way of incorporating disparate social phenomena ('mugging', 'terrorism', picket line confrontations) into an almost apocalyptic picture of social breakdown used to justify a 'tough state'. The response took the form of 'extra powers' legislation like the Emergency Powers (Prevention of Terrorism) Act and other initiatives cooked up at the Conservatives' pre-election Selsdon Park conference. CI5 is in many ways a fantasy version of what 'Selsdon Man' might have dreamed up – 'a specialized squad, shadowy and unaccountable, that made its own rules' (Whannel, 1994: 85). If *The Sweeney* imagined society as 'a state of war' and policing a 'war … to defend the law' (Hurd, 1976: 49), *The Professionals* posits 'a jungle with mad beasts crawling through it', a disease-ridden hospital with CI5 as the 'surgeons' ('The Rack'). But 'violent society syndrome' also extended to concerns about television, to publicly criticized programmes like *Dr. Who, Target* and, of course, *The Professionals*. 'Violent society' ('real' problem or, rather, one created within political and media discourse);'Violent TV' (fantasy solution or part of the 'problem') – this is the paradox of *The Professionals*. James Donald has discerned in *The Sweeney* a promise of 'entertaining fear', a 'disenchanted version of myth' (Donald, 1985: 134). That *The Professionals* is less defeated than *The Sweeney* might be because of the way political dystopias can translate into masculinist utopias (Hard Times, Hard Men). If 'the jungle' represents the 'necessary fears' of citizens of the 'ungovernable state', it is also where tough men like Bodie come from. But *The Professionals* is aware of the fascist potential of such a fantasy, keen to distinguish itself from the far right and, in some ways, more sensitive to issues of civil liberty than previous crime shows needed to be.

In 'Old Dog With New Tricks' Cowley makes a speech to some new recruits that is so authoritarian that even Bodie notes the 'fascist overtones':

> Do unto others now what they're still thinking about. Oh, there'll be squeals, and once in a while you'll turn a law-abiding citizen into an authority-hating anarchist. There'll be squeals and letters to MPs, but that's the price they have and we have to pay to keep this island clean and smelling, even if ever so faintly, of roses and lavender.

The episode moves fast to suture the ideological wound left by Bodie's comment. Doyle points out that Cowley still has a bullet in his leg from fighting the fascists in Spain. But if this anti-fascist leg gradually disappears as the series goes on in order to allow Cowley to participate in the action, his concern for civil rights resurfaces in isolated episodes. In any case, the series treads delicately around what was seen as 'new crime' – there are no flying pickets, and while Bodie served in Northern Ireland neither he nor the show will be drawn on the subject. Terrorism is *The Professionals'* main claim to topicality, but the references already belonged to slightly faded headlines – the Angry Brigade (evoked in 'No Stone') and the Baader-Meinhof Gang (the Meyer-Helmut Group in 'Close Quarters'). The Iranian Embassy Siege offered another source of topicality, and is recreated as a training exercise in 'Wild Justice'. Producer Raymond Menmuir noted how the SAS 'became part of the overall "law and order" framework' after the siege (Schlesinger *et al.*, 1983: 73), but Bodie's military past is usually a source of trouble. In 'Wild Justice', the SAS motto 'Who Dares Wins' becomes the nihilistic 'Till Death Do Us Join', while in 'Where the Jungle Ends', Bodie's former mercenary comrades return as a highly trained gang of bank robbers.

The real importance of organized 'terror' in *The Professionals* is in establishing precedents for a broader criminal fraternity through such practices as hostage-taking. In 'Old Dog With New Tricks', the villains are a Kray-like family of gangsters, 'terrors of the East End', the Turkels. Charley Turkel plans to break brother Henry out of prison, but he knows that 'they do things different nowadays' and points to the 'Military Hostage' headline in the *Evening Standard*. His gang knock off an Irish group's weapons haul and hold Cowley hostage. This colludes with the orthodox view that terrorism is criminal (rather than political) violence (Schlesinger *et al.*, 1983: 86), but it also points to *The Professionals'* desire to remain within a populist 'common sense' framework.

Schlesinger *et al.* identify two conservative responses to 'terrorism', which can be extended to *The Professionals'* 'new crime' matrix – 'the new, tough, hard situations all too frequently encountered at the latter end of the Twentieth Century' (Blake, 1978: 17). The 'rule of law' response argues for 'exceptional measures' – new legislation, the use of paramilitary forces (SPG, SAS) – but also wants to hold onto some sense of civil liberty (Schlesinger *et al.*, 1983: 14). The 'populist' authoritarian response acknowledges that 'terrorism' is political but wants to answer in kind with whatever 'extreme measures' will win the 'war' (ibid.: 24–27). *The Professionals* often talks the second discourse – primarily through Cowley – but largely walks the first one. CI5's no-holds-barred mandate seems to vary in potency so that they never quite become legalized vigilantes. In 'The Rack', Doyle appears to kill a suspect in self-defence during interrogation and CI5's existence is threatened by a crusading but implicitly misguided lawyer. This is the extreme end of the series, especially at a time when the Emergency Powers Act was subject to allegations of torture. But if CI5 represents a violent answer to violent crime, then the 'rule of law' must also extend to other threats to the 'Public Order' – to the Far Right and to police brutality. This is a kind of tabloid populism – it wants a no-nonsense response to crime but won't have the police abusing their powers. It values 'democracy' over (Left or Right) totalitarianism, but thinks most politicians are crooked or self-serving hypocrites. It's quite at home with casual racism, but doesn't like organized nationalism.

'Klansmen' has never been shown on terrestrial British TV – a nervous LWT withdrew it. In the episode, Zadie, a black solicitor, defends families facing eviction from seemingly racist property owners and finds himself visited by hooded figures with burning crosses. 'I've seen and fought prejudice of one sort or another all my life', says Cowley and CI5 move in. Doyle investigates The Empire Society, an organization modelled on British far-right groups like the National Front and the British Movement, both more prominent than ever before in the late 1970s. The Empire Society is fond of burning crosses and paint attacks but draws the line at murder. As their leader explains:

> The act of death only engenders sympathy and people leaning towards our cause are suddenly shocked, revolted ... we can weather the assault charges and every time we do, one right-thinking citizen will think 'I see their point', one citizen comes over to our side.

This unnerving pragmatism makes them very hard for CI5 to police, so the episode needs another villain. Two seemingly racist murders are traced back to The Miller Trust, which uses The Empire Movement as a cover for more financially motivated attacks. In a would-be ironic twist, Miller himself turns out to be black and so do some of the men in Klan outfits. In many ways this is as clumsy a treatment of racism as one might expect, but it at least refuses to attribute bigotry only to a pathologized minority. Bodie is rather put out by both Zadie's wealth and his white wife – 'You see his car? More than I could afford ... and he's a spade'. 'Where are you, Bodie?' Doyle responds, 'This is England, now! Don't look behind you because there's no gunboat and Victoria's long gone'. Bodie is knifed by a couple of Miller's men, though he's 'cured' of his xenophobia when a black doctor saves his life. His racism strains against the constraints of the series – it has to be removed (surgically, it seems) but has already been located within CI5. But The Empire Society are a convincingly malign organiza-tion, all the more so for being articulate, pragmatic and patient. While CI5 finally 'bust' them (presumably for assault), it has already been made clear that the problem won't be solved so easily.

'In the Public Interest' is even more striking. In an unnamed metropolitan city, a clean-up campaign by Chief Constable Green has progressed from eliminating porn to driving out a Gay Youth Organisation with threats and violence:

> We don't want your sort in our city ... (The police's) teeth have been drawn when it comes to dealing with filth like you ... Most of us have got wives and kids. We want them to grow up in a clean city.[7]

Homophobia might seem like an even less likely issue than racism for *The Professionals* to tackle, and it *does* tread very carefully. The secretary of the Gay Youth Organisation tells Cowley that 'I'm not homosexual myself, but many of my friends are'. But if actual gay men (or *out* gay men, at least) are conspicuously invisible, this does pave the way for Bodie and Doyle to pose as Gay Youth Organisers in order to investigate. Once again, Cowley dusts off his civil rights hat:

> He's slamming doors on porn and hoodlums and anyone else who doesn't measure up to his particular standards ... Suppose his standards change!

Suppose he suddenly clamps down on those who don't go along with his politics, or ethnic groups or people who grow their hair below the plimsoll line or anyone else who doesn't measure up in his opinion. Unbridled power!

As Green's men, led by the brutal Inspector Chives, close in, Doyle is convinced that there must be 'one good copper' in town, and it turns out he's right. Chives' sergeant stops him from killing the two CI5 men and the dictatorship unravels.

Here, CI5's role anticipates the Internal Affairs series *Between the Lines* (1992–94), produced by Tony Garnett. But the most likely influence on 'In the Public Interest' was another Garnett series broadcast the same year. *Law and Order* (1978) was a four-part drama written by Gordon Newman in which brutalizing suspects and planting evidence were no longer the 'necessary' means to a desirable end – rather, an indictment of 'criminal' abuses of the law by those supposedly upholding it. This was not a populist show and it was savagely attacked by both the police and the right-wing press, but Newman's drama was to create unexpected generic ripples. There *are* differences, of course. Green is clearly both Cowley's double and scapegoat, designed to show us what a *real* fascist looks like (just as the vigilante cops in *Magnum Force* (1973) redeem Clint Eastwood's Dirty Harry by comparison). In addition, these competing models of authority also embody contrasting masculinities. Unlike Cowley, Green never did military service – 'touch of blood pressure' – and has the temerity to offer the CI5 boss decaffeinated coffee. 'Still, you've compensated for it since then', observes Cowley acidly. Chives is another failure – we learn that he applied to CI5 but was turned down. In short, these are not 'real' men, but overcompensating weaklings with too much power. In this sense at least, they embody the same 'playground bully' types encountered in the terrorist episodes. Christopher Booker, writing about 1970s politics, demarcated the Left and the Right as belonging to the respective realms of the 'Mother' and the 'Father'. The 'permissive era' epitomizes for him 'the worst qualities associated with an "age of Mother"'(1980: 139) – 'children who cannot grow up … shrilly rebelling against anyone or anything which can be represented as the brutal tyranny of "Father"' (ibid.: 137). Few texts put quite so much faith in 'Father' as *The Professionals*, the corrective to the 'spoilt children' of the counter-culture or spineless armchair authoritarians. And yet Cowley's role also crosses over into the maternal – his nickname is 'the Cow', and as he reminds Doyle in 'Klansmen', 'a cow protects its young'.

Reading the 'political' through codes of masculinity is an important part of *The Professionals*. And yet it isn't triumphalist enough to be Thatcherite – it's a delayed Heath-era text colliding with some of the more liberalizing agendas of the early 1980s. In any case, we now know that Conservative governments don't hold the copyright on illiberal law-and-order packages. Significantly, CI5 were to return in the Blair–Clinton era.

## POSTSCRIPT: *CI5 – THE NEW PROFESSIONALS*

In some ways, all that needs to be noted about *CI5 – The New Professionals* is the breathtaking indifference with which it has been met. But some of its attempts to tailor CI5 for the 1990s are worth commenting on. If *The Professionals* belongs very much to the imperilled 'island' of the 1970s – an island which must smell 'even if ever so faintly, of roses and lavender' – CI5 has gone global. Operatives Curtis (Colin Wells) and Keel (Kal Weber) do as much travelling as *The Persuaders!* did while dealing with Middle Eastern terrorists, post-Soviet fallout or hydrogen cyanide bombs in Tokyo – a reflection of NATO's new role as 'global police'? But if the narrative (and, by implication, target audience) says 'global', the generic co-ordinates are firmly North American. Bodie's SAS background is replaced by Keel's in the Navy Seals – the American/British pairing, too, speaks volumes. There are no traces here of the original's debt to *The Avengers* and *The Sweeney* – it's as though CI5 only followed the sign marked *Starsky and Hutch*, with stopping-off points at *Miami Vice* (violence in designer suits), *The Equalizer* (Edward Woodward, the epitome of reaction since *The Wicker Man* (1973)) and *The X-Files* (millennial intrigue). Only the product placement for Ford and a guest appearance by Patrick Mower ('Samurai Wind') point to an older tradition. Not only do Curtis and Keel suggest that Capri Man has lost his job to Hugo Boss Man, but their relationship with Bodie and Doyle is not dissimilar to that of Pierce Brosnan's Bond films with Roger Moore's. CI5, like the recent Bond films, have found a way of having their post-feminist cake and eating it, of defusing feminism by giving women 'authority' (Judi Dench's 'M', Charlotte Cornwell's Minister) while largely keeping them out of the action. While producer David Wickes has referred to 'millennium men and women, dealing with millennium problems' (Matthews, 1999), the role of female operative Backus (Lexa Doig) seems to be a kind of secretary-with-a-gun to boss Harry Malone (Woodward). Her bomb defusal in 'Back to Business' contrasts strikingly with Bodie's grenade-in-a-B-cup escapade in 'Old Dog With New Tricks' – she faints immediately afterwards.

The Nissan Almera ads and The Comic Strip's *Bullshitters'* sequel *Detectives on the Verge of a Nervous Breakdown* (1993) confirm that 'Capri Man' can really only be recycled as parody. But irony can be unexpectedly sentimental and betray a longing for the irrecuperable – the words 'politically incorrect' recur on *Professionals* web pages. When 'Bonehead' and 'Foyle' team up with other 1970s 'ten guv a day coppers' in *Detectives*, they are sent up again for their machismo, their closeted sexuality and their inability to drive *past* rather than *through* cardboard boxes. But their 1990s counterparts like 'Dave Spanker' (the BBC's Tyneside detective *Spender*) are represented as a colourless lot, and one scene references such (fictitious) TV creations as *The Dull-as-Dishwater Detective* and *The Whistling Detective Who Lives on a Barge*. Bodie and Doyle, it seems, still have a score to settle with Shoestring.

## NOTES

1   *The Comic Strip* is a group of British 'alternative' comedians who produced a series of TV and theatrical films in the 1980s and 1990s, often with a satirical slant.

2   The shift from film to tape also signalled a move for the British crime series away from action towards character-driven drama.

3   *The Professionals*, interestingly, tackled 'issues' more than *The Sweeney* did, in spite of being ostensibly more formulaic.

4   *The Wild Geese* (1978), about mercenary soldiers in Africa, was a big box-office success in 1978.

5   While early episodes used British Leyland cars, Clemens and Fennell later made a special deal with Ford.

6   These labels depend on 1970s car semiotics – the Ford Capri was a lairy sex-mobile, while the Ford Escort was reliable but a little dull. Significantly, Corgi toys chose the former as *The Professionals'* collectable model.

7   I wouldn't want to imply that Brian Clemens had a particular city or police chief in mind. But as a topical resonance, it is worth mentioning that Manchester's Chief Constable James Anderton had been sending his vice squad on raids since 1977 – although the episode seems to be referencing the broader born-again morality of organizations like The Festival of Light.

## REFERENCES

Blake, K. (1978) *The Professionals: Where the Jungle Ends*, London: Sphere.

Booker, C. (1980) *The Seventies: Portrait of a Decade*, London: Allen Lane.

Buscombe, E. (1976) 'The Sweeney – Better Than Nothing', *Screen Education*, 20: 66–69.

Buxton, D. (1990) *From The Avengers to Miami Vice: Form and Ideology in Television Series*, Manchester and New York: Manchester University Press.

Chapman, R. (1988) 'The Great Pretender: Variations on the New Man Theme', in R. Chapman and J. Rutherford (eds), *Male Order: Unwrapping Masculinity*, London: Lawrence and Wishart.

Day, M. and Topping, K. (1999) *Shut It! A Fan's Guide to 70s Cops on the Box*, London: Virgin.

Dennington, J. and Tulloch, J. (1976) 'Cops, Consensus and Ideology', *Screen Education*, 20: 37–46.

Donald, J. (1985) 'Anxious Moments - The Sweeney in 1975', in M. Alvarado and J. Stewart (eds), *Made for Television: Euston Films Limited*, London: BFI/Thames Methuen: 117–35.

Featherstone, M. (1982) 'The Body in Consumer Culture', *Theory, Culture and Society*, Vol. 1, No. 2: 18–33.

Hall, S., Critcher, C., Jefferson, T., Clarke, J. and Roberts, B. (1978) *Policing the Crisis: Mugging, the State and Law and Order*, London: Macmillan.

Hunt, L. (1998) *British Low Culture: From Safari Suits to Sexploitation*, London and New York: Routledge.

Hurd, G. (1976) 'The Sweeney – Contradiction and Coherence', *Screen Education*, 20: 47–53.

Jenkins, H. (1992) *Textual Poachers: Television Fans and Participatory Culture*, London and New York: Routledge.

Kosofsky Sedgwick, E. (1985) *Between Men: English Literature and Male Homosocial Desire*, New York: Columbia University Press.

Matthews, D. (1999) 'The Authorised Guide to The Professionals', http://www.mark01.co.uk/professionals/profs.html. No longer available online.

Penley, C. (1997) *NASA/TREK: Popular Science and Sex in America*, London and New York: Verso.

Rayne, Z. (1998) 'A Little Reminder', http://www.chisp.net/-zoerayne/stories/remind.html. No longer available online.

Schlesinger, P., Murdock, G. and Elliott, P. (1983) *Televising 'Terrorism': Political Violence in Popular Culture*, London: Comedia.

Simpson, M. (1994) *Male Impersonators*, London: Cassell.

Tolson, A. (1977) *The Limits of Masculinity*, London: Tavistock.

Whannel, G. (1994) 'Boxed In: Television in the 1970s', in Bart Moore-Gilbert (ed.), *The Arts in the 1970s: Cultural Closure?*, London: Routledge.

# PART III

# AUDIENCES READING AND RE-READING THE ACTION TV SERIES

# 9

# THE GAMES WE PLAY(ED)

## TV Westerns, memory and 'masculinity'

*Martin Pumphrey*[1]

This is a piece about TV Westerns, about their history certainly but, more centrally, their survival over time in people's affections and memories. They seldom feature in today's TV schedules and seem unable now to offer the remake possibilities of the other small screen series like *Mission: Impossible* and *Star Trek* that developed along-side them. In the 1950s and early 1960s, however, they were massively popular both in America and Britain. Reflecting this shift, I am interested in how, back then, they became embedded in people's daily lives and then in acts of remembering and re-remembering functioning in what Annette Kuhn has described as that 'never ending process of making, remaking, making sense of, ourselves – now' (Kuhn, 1995 : 16). My particular focus is on how TV Westerns have been remembered by the boys (now men) who grew up with them, and what I have to say bridges three areas of critical writing. For a start, in addressing people's experiences of the genre, I have concen-trated on the processes of TV viewing rather than specific programmes and texts and have drawn on the TV audience research that has followed (perhaps most obviously) from David Morley's arguments in *Family Television* (Morley, 1986). In addition, my consideration of how TV Westerns have been used and reused over time connects recent writing about TV and film memories (Stacey, 1994; Kuhn, 1995) with attempts to understand masculinity in terms of performance and masquerade (Cohan, 1997).

In fact, the TV Western's historical importance is easily obscured by its image as a backward-looking form associated with afternoon reruns, black and white television and embarrassingly outmoded ideas about gender. During the early years of TV, when broadcasters were searching for programming strategies to capture audiences and coincide with consumer desires, the made-for-TV Western was a key favourite (MacDonald, 1987; Boddy, 1998). It was arguably the TV Westerns Warner Brothers produced for ABC that, in the 1950s, began the transformation of that (then ailing) studio into the leisure corporation it is today (Anderson, 1994 : 5). On both sides of the Atlantic, they helped define TV viewing habits and (in the Davy Crocket craze of 1955) provided some of the earliest evidence of the convergence between TV entertainment and consumer behaviour. Arriving in Britain, they carried with them echoes of American concerns about (what would now be called) the dumbing-down many associated with ABC's aggressive commitment to action series in the battle for audience ratings

(Boddy, 1998 : 131). Here, they became associated with the forms of mass culture and Americanization dismissed by Richard Hoggart's polemic in *The Uses of Literacy* (Hoggart, 1957) and his later contributions to the 1962 Pilkington Report on the quality of British television. Historically, in other words, the apparent passing of the TV Western should not obscure that, for a time in the 1950s and early 1960s, it was the most popular of the action TV series formats, that it was a key focus for early attitudes to popular television and that it played a crucial role in establishing what are now familiar structures of TV production, programme scheduling and viewing.

The industry history of the genre is only a starting point, however. The early popularity of Westerns suggests questions about their significance in the memories of those who grew up with them (as I did myself) – the group whose well-being so concerned Hoggart and others at the time. Tim O'Sullivan, in a piece I am indebted to, argues '[TV memories] tend … to function as a point of symbolic, biographical reference, representing some aspects of the difference perceived between identity or circumstances "then" and "now"' (O'Sullivan, 1991: 163). His observation is a starting point for what I have to say, but only seems to account for part of the process. What is interesting, and here I am echoing Kuhn's argument, is the immediacy and presentness as well as the pastness of particular memories. I say this because of the way people responded when I first announced I was interested in the TV Western. I myself was 8 years old in the school year of 1956/7 when my grandfather's death brought us a TV. I instantly discovered the genre and, undeniably, my academic interest here now stems in part from a desire to revisit childhood pleasures. I was taken aback, however, by the spontaneity and energy with which people answered my questions. Complete strangers, I discovered, would launch into Western theme tunes, retrieve names and relive favourite moments from playing Cowboys and Indians, without a moment's hesitation. Not everybody liked the TV Westerns (it is true), but when you talk to children of the 1950s, 1960s and 1970s now about their *general* memories of early television, it is the Westerns that regularly surface first. For Tim O'Sullivan, in the piece just mentioned, it is the whirling wheels of the *Wells Fargo* opening sequence (O'Sullivan, 1991: 163). For others, it is the crack of the *Rawhide* whip, the special elegance of Paladin's quick draw, a quipped line from *Alias Smith and Jones*. As I started this project, the vibrant immediacy in these acts of remembering seemed to me to contradict any notion that they register the past as simply 'the past', something easily shut off from the present. I wondered about the nature of the energy involved in this process of remembering and was prompted to question the relationships we (and I include myself) have had with these memories over time and the significances they have for (some of) us now.

My research began with a modified version of the questionnaire Jackie Stacey used to investigate older women's memories of film stars in her 1994 *Stargazing* (Stacey, 1994: 245–51). I had fifteen full responses. I also instigated a dozen informal interviews to add to, and check, the information the questionnaires threw up. As it turned out, the majority of respondents (eleven) were men between the ages of forty-three and fifty-three – who were part of the first children's audiences for television in the 1950s and early 1960s. The majority (all but two) also worked in Higher Education and, as their responses record, are self-consciously aware that TV Westerns are popularly associated with constructions of gender that are now, at best, unfashionable. It is the group I myself belong to and its particular identity has directed what I have to say in specific ways.

Recent academic interest in film and television audiences has been partly a reaction to the text-based spectatorship debates of the 1970s and 1980s, and is often driven by a desire to give a voice to marginalized audiences. Significant bodies of research and writing have now addressed (for example) children's TV watching, fan culture, and the experiences of black, lesbian and gay audiences. What is notable is that the group identified in the spectatorship debates as the dominant presence in mainstream visual culture (i.e. heterosexual, white men) has tended to remain invisible. This was the group best represented in the responses to my questionnaire – men shaped by allegiance to the demands and benefits of white, heterosexual masculinity. TV Westerns were watched by many differently aligned audiences, but the experiences and memories of that particular group have been the specific focus of my attention. Using the responses of others beyond that focus as a guide, I have tried to look analytically not at general questions about the TV Western and gender but specifically at how memories of the TV Western have been used and recycled over time as part of the lived experience of a particular historical version of white, heterosexual masculinity – a version of masculinity that, of course, has been significantly challenged during the years covered by my questioning.[2]

The idea that 'masculinity' has been challenged and placed 'in crisis' over the past fifty years has become a familiar trope in discussions of gender and sexuality. The social, political, cultural, and economic dimensions of that 'crisis' have been widely debated and it has been a guiding perspective in a number of studies of how popular films have represented masculinity through the period. Steven Cohan's *Masked Men* (1997) particularly singles out the 1950s as characterized by upheavals in men's lives that can be accessed through the films of the decade. Because the majority of the TV memories I am looking at come from the 1950s and 1960s, what I have to say echoes this. I need, however, to make some distinctions. As in my own research, Cohan is interested in gender as performance (one of his starting points is Judith Butler's idea of 'masquerade'), but his perception of 'the post war masculinity crisis' (Cohan, 1997: x) can potentially point misleadingly in a different direction. Understood as the product of a particular history, the sense of a masculine 'crisis' can obscure (by registering it as a historical anomaly) the fact that the process of negotiating cultural differences to sustain lived gender identities *inevitably* involves contradictions. It is that process of negotiation I am interested in. As a starting point, what I have to say begins from the premise I have argued elsewhere (Pumphrey, 1996: 52) that the Western's split allegiance to 'savagery' and 'civilization' has always made it a genre that offers a range of conflicting gender instructions. What follows is a small pilot study that has used that perception as a way of approaching the TV Western, deploying audience research and memory work as tools.

Significantly (because it identifies the specific nature of this study), all but one of the group I have focused on encountered the Western initially through television.

Their experiences of the *film* Western came later. Of course, there are genre overlaps between the two forms, but this group's responses suggest the TV Western's development, programming and involvement in domestic routines made it a different experience to the single narrative (or even serial) film Western. Specifically, that involvement in everyday life highlights how (and how complexly) the genre became involved, both at the time and in memory, in the machinery of identity performance.

## A NOTE ON THE TV WESTERN'S MODES OF ADDRESS

Now the genre has faded, it is tempting to stereotype the TV Western as a series of variations on a simple core narrative and set of themes. In fact, as Yvonne Tasker suggests in her essay on the 1970s series, *Kung Fu* (see Chapter 7 in this volume), its history between the 1950s and 1980s involved constant change. The diversity this produced registers in people's memories not least because of the generational distinctions around which the American networks constructed their programming strategies for early TV broadcasting. A key assumption of American sponsors in the 1950s was that the main target of TV should be families with children. It was an assumption that brought Roy Rogers, Gene Autry and Hopalong Cassidy, along with 'the Lone Ranger' and 'the Cisco Kid' to the small screen at the beginning of the decade. Other children's Westerns, for example (*Rin Tin Tin* (1954–59) and Disney's three-part *Davy Crocket* (1954–55)), followed before Warners and the others entered the field seriously in 1955/56. It quickly became apparent, however, that TV programming had to be strategically developed to recognize age differences and lead viewers through an evening's entertainment from early children's programmes to later adult viewing. As Christopher Anderson argues in his study of 1950s Hollywood, this perception of the audience was crucial in shaping the narrative structures, themes and content of TV Westerns. Picking up on debates flowing around film Westerns like *High Noon* (1952) and *Shane* (1953), the programming schedules developed the concept of the 'adult Western' to market the very different, adult-oriented, TV versions of the genre represented in those early years by *Gunsmoke* (1955–75), *Cheyenne* (1955–63) and *Maverick* (1957–62) (Anderson, 1994: 203).[3]

The distinctions in address and tone between the earlier children's Westerns and the new types of TV Western Warners produced for ABC from the late 1950s highlight the vitality that drove and sustained the genre through to the 1980s. They also provide a key set of co-ordinates around which the memories of the generation that grew up with them are organized. *Cheyenne* and *Maverick* were manifest opposites. *Cheyenne* treated the form seriously and presented a hero whose virtues, outdoor survival skills, combat abilities and commitment to justice and fair play aligned its central character with the traditional Western hero. *Maverick*, by contrast, offered a 'hero' whose cynicism and humour (as its creators themselves announced) were designed to 'puncture the Western genre'. Both, however, were drifting characters and their exploits week by week created an 'anthology style' that permitted a range of wandering adventures (Anderson, 1994: 233). *Gunsmoke*, on the other hand, was set in one place with a permanent group of characters at its centre. These two (drifting and domesticated) narrative structures and two (serious and ironic) modes of address saw many different incarnations between the 1950s and 1970s. Crucially in Britain, as TV Westerns were brought in to play a part in the ratings battles of the late 1950s, the diversity in the genre's address already developed for American audiences spoke to children and adults alike.

The number of Westerns screened on British television did not match that which could be seen in America, but it certainly offered a rich variety of the genre's forms to its audiences. For British viewers this created a particular set of viewing experiences. Notionally, given the much longer history of the Western in literature and film that underpinned the TV Western's popularity in the first place, the TV version of the genre had links with an authoritative and authentic (*serious*) statement of patriarchal masculinity, threatened and contradictory perhaps but ultimately powerful and in control. It constructed that statement in relation to gender, ethnicity, class and sexuality in ways that were readable by British audiences but (safely) distanced and exotic. In other words, far from threatening an Americanization defined by the mean streets of New York or Chicago or the rock 'n' roll hedonism that Richard Hoggart so disliked, it offered (on the surface) traditional gender values and a commitment to social responsibility and community. The interesting thing is that the diversity of address created by the programming history of American television produced something rather more complicated. The TV Western's willingness to shift between seriousness and parody, action and family melodrama, in pursuit of audience attention made it a much more inclusive, flexible and ambiguous form than the film Western it apparently echoed. To be sure, the kinds of self-conscious critique and pastiche I am associating with the TV Western here *are* evident in the film Westerns of the 1950s and early 1960s.[4] They were more evident, however, and more widely available in the TV versions of the genre. Here, the contrasting serious/parodic treatments of the Western ran parallel with each other across a week's TV viewing and this continued from season to season. Consumed domestically in the context of family relationships, the TV Western can be seen retrospectively not as a simple statement of a single (traditional) masculinity, but as a flowing, publicly available, cross-generational debate around the traditional conception of the Western hero. The fact that this 'debate' offered multiple entrances and exits, and narratives that both ironized and confirmed that figure as a role model, seems to have had considerable significance for how British audiences watched, used and have later remembered the form.

## MEMORY, PLAY AND THE TV WESTERN BACK THEN

### *What fun this was ! (SF)*

I noted earlier the delight people obviously had in thinking through their responses to my questionnaire. Comments spread along the margins of pages, are added to and qualified over two or three sittings. Crucially, the memories are not just, or even centrally, about the programmes themselves. Specific images, heroes, actors and events are certainly remembered but so too are the viewing contexts. (*Wells Fargo was on Saturday night and my brother and I would watch it while we dried our hair in front of the adjacent gas fire – because Saturday night was bath night too.* JPC) There are few memories of watching alone. Significantly, where general TV viewing is associated with mixed gender groups, TV Westerns generate memories of male-dominated settings. At first encounter, the comments here seem to confirm that the programmes had a predictable set of attractions. *The whole idea of the West* was *exotic* and exciting. It offered adventure, wandering, moving on, unrestrained existence. The Cowboy heroes are remembered as *self-dependent* individualists and non-conformists. They are loners and outsiders, needed by society but not tied to it. In the mind's eye, they know how to handle themselves, have superior powers of perception and the skills, knowledge and experience to take control and succeed whatever the odds.

The references to watching with fathers and uncles, brothers and friends and the textual memories of favourite TV Western heroes link the experiences to the longer popular history of the Western. They appear to identify the TV version of the genre (whether in its serious or ironic, wandering or domesticated mode) as a traditional, relatively simple form focused around a conventional masculinity that settles conflicts with force, lives by 'the law of the gun' and wants no ties or restraints. Certainly, the memories are regularly described as escapism and their pleasures attributed to their distance from the complexities of the present. (*We are so obsessed with 'now' it is a pleasure to spend a little time in the past.*) On the surface, it seems reasonable to see this as proof of a desire for an unproblematic time before there was need for a conscious verbal awareness of sexuality, class, ethnicity or even gender, though the latter is overtly a focus of the genre's concern. In these terms, the TV Western emerges as a genre tied to an escapist nostalgia for the past with little to offer beyond simple narratives and un-self-critical versions of masculinity.

It is probably important to recognize that this speaks, in part, to what is at stake. Looked at in more detail, however, some rather different perceptions begin to emerge. At the level of the textual memories (of plot events, characters, images), there are interestingly few responses that take pleasure in violence for its own sake. The remembered admiration is for heroes who were stylish, skilful, who used reason rather than strength. (*The 'cowboys' I liked were individualists, nonconformists, weak in ways but with a sense of humour and sharp powers of perception. People who used reason over violence.*) And the repeated refrain throughout is that while the memories retrieve the pleasures and excitement of roaming adventure, they also recall an equally pleasurable sense of security. The character of Hoss from *Bonanza* is noted a number of times as a figure associated with safety (see Figure 9.1). Quite clearly too, when it comes to describing how the TV Westerns were used, what is remembered is *not* slavish imitation or uncritical adulation. The memories are full of references to children actively manipulating and recycling images and scenarios from the genre. The seriousness of the straight Westerns like *Cheyenne*, the cynical undermining of the genre in the figures who followed Maverick, as well as the domestication of a series like *Bonanza*, provide equal possibilities for enjoyment. Clearly too, while the cool Western heroes offered attractive role models, so too did the Indians whose skills and life styles offered inviting alternatives.

*Figure 9.1* Rugged independence meets reassuring security – the cast of *Bonanza* (1959–73).

It is as you make the move out, beyond the textual memories, to the social contexts and settings in which they were/are embedded that significant complexities begin to emerge. In relation to both the original experience of consuming the TV Westerns, and to the processes of recalling those experiences, playing 'Cowboys and Indians' has a central significance. Remembered as a game played by (almost) everyone, endlessly

151

and with endless variations, it illuminates key issues. The memories come in many shapes and sizes but they implicitly confirm the importance the game had in the processes of assimilating and making-over the viewing experience of the TV Western. There are many aspects to this. On one level, playing Cowboys and Indians involved a constant reworking of props, costumes, narratives to fit local conditions. It usually meant 'going out' but it could be played anywhere – in the street, park, school playground, garden – and its structure could be endlessly modified. (*Mark and I would play everyday. Sometimes … I'd lend him my Luger replica and we'd play Cowboys and Germans.* NL) Crucially, playing Cowboys and Indians translated the TV Western into physical performance and bodily experience. This transformation can be seen to have worked in two directions. On one hand the genre itself is translated into the discourses of the everyday. On the other the everyday is transformed. (*That's what we'd do as kids – go out in gangs, usually boys – on journeys of discovery – walking across derelict building sites in B'ham, or further out into the countryside – using sticks as guns.* JPC) What is at stake in this is a process of bodily, performative imagining that magically (with the power of play) translates and merges the worlds of imagination and physical experience, fantasy and the mundane.[5]

The point here is a relatively simple one, but it has implications for how both the original experiences of the TV Western and the later acts of remembering and re-remembering are to be understood. Valerie Walkerdine argued some years ago, in her study of a working class family watching *Rocky III* on video, that we use television viewing to examine, express and control our day-to-day experiences (Walkerdine, 1986). Her point relates directly to the memories of the viewing contexts of the TV Westerns and the games and conversations through which the programmes became part of everyday life. I suggested earlier that the pleasure of these memories might be thought to derive from their association with a time before there was need to acknowledge verbally 'race', ethnicity, class and sexuality. In fact, of course, those forces blew through our lives and we 'knew' them in the shapes of houses, the rub of clothes and the feel of accents. The popularity of the TV Western meant it was watched across gender, class and regional differences – by boys and girls who would become both gay and straight, by those who (with all the implications for those years) would go on to higher education and those who would not. Both at the time of reception and retrospectively, the form gave many different groups images with which to negotiate everyday realities. The fact that (liked or disliked) the genre was inescapably part of the lives of the children who grew up with it, that it spoke obliquely and in a 'foreign' (American) idiom about differences, made it a safe vehicle for negotiating the complexities of British experiences.

The game of Cowboys and Indians is particularly relevant here. One example will be enough to illustrate the point. A number of responses recall (as I myself had forgotten) that it was the art of the dramatic death that was the game's key focus – not the battles. In an extended comment on this, David Lusted talks of a variant he and his friends called 'Custer's Last Stand'. (*One feature of the game that resonates for me even today is its implied award system. To be the Indian was a reward, not a punishment; an odd ideological choice for white boys …. It was the manner of the death and the display of death ... . that was rewarded with the honour of becoming the next killer of white men. This apparently macabre scenario of racial confusion had its more delicate meaning – the reward of aesthetic display .... . This was a game played by working class boys in conditions of otherwise post-war economic depression. We were on the street because poor homes offered few amenities, attractions and pleasures. And we were bound together in a game which rewarded display and beauty.*)[6] That identification with the Indians rather than the Cowboys is referenced regularly in the responses and underscores the point at issue. For some, it clearly became over time the starting point for ethnic and ecological awareness and political commitments that shaped life trajectories. In its context, however, its resistant ironies cannot be seen as a serious engagement with Native American culture or the realities of 'otherness'. It was, rather, a vehicle for articulating a sense of personal identity back then and subsequently (with much more complexity) in repeated acts of re-remembering.

## THE TV WESTERN AND
## THE MACHINERY OF RE-REMEMBERING

*I played Cowboys and Indians most intensely with Gordon – one Summer (c. 1957). His mother used make-up to create us as 'Indian Braves'. It was a wonderfully hot summer. (SF)*

What emerges from this initial set of observations is that, of the two sets of memories (the textual and the contextual), it is the latter that are recalled with most enthusiasm and detail and with repeated references to bodily sensations and pleasures. At the time, and in acts of remembering, it is how the programmes were used in the physical inter-actions of everyday life rather than their textual details that was (and apparently still is) important. I said earlier that the TV Westerns' mix of seriousness, parody and domes-tication over time turned it into something akin to a public 'debate' about the values, themes and heroes associated with the traditional Western. I would add to that now that the translation of the TV programmes into physical play merged the possibilities set in motion by that 'debate' with the everyday social world. This created memories of the TV Western that carry with them the immediacy of the physical sensations and bodily pleasures of the everyday (back then). At the same time, they are also linked to the textual and contextual patterns of playfulness (involving both attachment and distance, irony and commitment) that seem, since then, to have functioned to struc-ture the processes of re-remembering. By re-remembering I mean (to echo Kuhn again) the retrieving (over and over) of memories in repeated acts of reworking and recasting to fit and define the self in the present. The perception echoes closely what David Buckingham has identified in his contemporary investigations into how chil-dren watch TV. In *Moving Images* and elsewhere he has written about the complex ways in which children respond to, and use, the act of watching TV. While he acknowledges that children imitate what they see, he also argues that what is more important is how children perceive and make sense of their TV experiences. Interest-ingly, in *Moving Images* he stresses the need to focus on what he calls 'short term emotional responses' (Buckingham, 1996: 6). What my own brief study seems to demonstrate is that those childhood patterns of critical, playful use are repeated much later in, and throughout, life. Arguably, what the responses of the 43 to 53-year-olds in my survey demonstrate is that their early TV Western viewing provided a playful (essentially contradictory) set of mechanisms for the autobiographical recycling of the experiences with which they were associated.

On one level, I am saying little more here than that the TV Western writers and programmers were doing their job back then. They were successfully finding and speaking to a range of audiences by varying the modes of address of their programmes in line with the programming needs of the period. Equally, my observations identify the strategies 1950s marketing executives were perfecting, that are now the assumed core of contemporary merchandising. Vance Packard in 1957 quotes one such executive talking about the Davy Crocket craze of 1955 as precisely demonstrating the power of linking a TV programme, via a song, a game and an outfit, to consumption (Packard, 1957: 138). What is interesting, however, is the complexity of the ways TV Westerns seem to have worked to provide the generation that grew up with them both landmarks and enduring strategies for the narration of identity over time.

As landmarks, TV Western memories certainly help map out past social relations, register friendships and identify generational agreements and disagreements with parents (*Dad was critical of the things I liked*) and family. They also retrospectively define growing up. There is self-conscious recognition, for example, of the moment when adult Westerns replaced children's Westerns and the shift in viewing is registered as personal growth. Later still, the decline of loyalty to the genre is linked to the growing demands of football or the attractions of teenage life. Even in relation to recent memories, the perception that when they are watched now (as reruns) favourite early TV Westerns seem 'mundane' and 'slow', becomes an excuse for distinguishing a contemporary identity from that which existed 'back then'. All this seems to confirm Tim O'Sullivan's observation that TV memories register 'the difference perceived between identity or circumstances "then" and "now"' (O'Sullivan, 1991: 163). What his suggestion ignores, however, is the distinction between textual and contextual memories. The specific textual memories are certainly thought of as existing in the past. This is far less true of the performance memories relating to the viewing experience and play. Much more complex, those memories are part of an on-going narrative of personal growth away from, *but still in connection with*, a childhood self. They attach importance to continuities as well as to distinctions, and establish the links between 'back then' and 'now' that render identity both visible and coherent.

It is in the acts of remembering and re-remembering ('the making, remaking, making sense of, ourselves – now') that a number of things become obvious. The key issue is the relation between performance and identity (performance and gender) – but the memories of the TV Western I have been looking at seem to have only a limited amount to do with the processes of *identification* that, for so long, have been the focus of attention in the spectatorship debates. It certainly makes sense to talk about identification in relation to the textual memories of favourite figures and heroes who were admired and knowingly imitated. (*I was fond of Hopalong Cassidy ... . I had a Hopalong Cassidy watch.*) What seems to be operating far more powerfully, however, are the implications of the acts of *projection* back then that invested the TV Western with the (extra-textual) meanings of everyday social realities registered in bodily sensations. It is the memories of the physical and imaginative freedom of moving around within the space and time of play that seems to trigger the energy and enthusiasm my questionnaire responses associate with the TV Western. In remembering now, the playfulness of the games merges easily with a conscious awareness of the TV Western's own mix of seriousness and parody to create a fluid negotiation with roles and memories that stretch back over time. (*I played all the roles .... I could be sheriff or badman at will – by cross-cutting the action.* JPC ). For the group of men on whom I have focused, the process of remembering and re-remembering encompasses both serious Western imitation and ironic transformation, being in and out of the game, Cowboy and Indian, goodie and baddie. The mechanisms and rhetoric of memory here allow identity performances that enact both naive, spontaneous involvement and sceptical distance – not least from the forms of masculinity the TV Western is popularly thought to have endorsed.

## THE GAMES WE PLAY

'To be natural is such a very difficult pose to keep up' (Oscar Wilde)[7]

Of course, the TV Western did not exist in isolation and it has to be understood in relation to the much larger picture of contemporary media consumption and socialization. Even in relation to my argument about how it was used as an action series, it has to be acknowledged that there were others (the cop, detective and spy versions, for example) that produced similar kinds of active play and bodily imagining. At the same time, for my focus group, the TV Western manifestly played a central part in the processes of growing up. Popular perception, both at the time and subsequently, has identified the genre with teaching boys 'how to be men' – and that perception clearly inflected the responses I have been discussing. What I have wanted to suggest is that the links between TV Westerns and masculinity are easily oversimplified when understood only in relation to the programme texts. The situation becomes more complex when you take into account the viewing experiences and games that involved them in the processes of everyday life. From the start, TV Westerns were involved in fluid, playful, contradictory forms of performance that seem to have continued to provide mechanisms for 'making sense of the self' much later in life.

What remains is a need to identify a glaring absence in what I have said so far, and to distinguish the particular orientation of the playful strategies I have been discussing – specifically in relationship to the performance of masculinity. Both the viewing contexts of the TV Westerns and the physically liberating play I have associated with them are remembered as involving the bodily pleasures of movement, physical freedom, warmth, security and sensation. They have a latent erotic charge, in other words, that makes it striking that the memories contain few, if any, references to

155

sexuality. Indeed, the dawning of teenage sexual interests is repeatedly cited as a reason for leaving the genre behind in a way that effectively relegates it to a presexual moment. The point is not easily explained in terms of the TV Westerns themselves because, textually, the TV Western heroes are consistently coded as sexually attractive to women and are regularly implicated in romantic situations. The silence here is particularly suggestive because an invisible but inescapable awareness of sexuality and sexual preference clearly determines how the form is remembered and by whom.

The marked enthusiasm in the responses to my questionnaires is expressed by men who locate themselves within heterosexuality. It crosses class, age and region. In contrast, the gay men who responded show little interest in the genre. For them, the forms of masculinity validated by the Western hero (of whatever structure) are regularly identified as alien. Interestingly, lesbian responses speak of the genre with affection – though with a critical sense of possibilities beyond the genre's narrative focus and an astute eye for peripheral characters and narrative sub-plots. Here, it is the complex positioning of a Mexican character or the incongruity of the TV Western's few strong women rather than the more securely (if negatively) centred Indians that attracts attention. (*I loved High Chaparral ... . In one episode Buck Cannon plans to marry an amazing Calamity Jane type woman who could ride and shoot and drink. Everyone said it wouldn't work out because she is too much like a man ... . In the end they realized they were both too independent to settle down!*) The point is that this pattern of response is not expressed in the comments of my core group. The key indicator (it seems) is the unacknowledged but crucial centrality of the heterosexual assumptions around which the plots of the TV Western existed.

It is here, I think, that the fluid strategies of remembering and self-articulation I have tried to talk about cast light on the relationship between the TV Western and the particular group of men of my generation who enthusiastically grew up with and remember it. The Western hero's masculinity straddles, without resolving, the contradictions between (masculine) wilderness/freedom and (feminine) domesticated security. As a role model and set of narrative possibilities, he offers utopian individual liberation encased in the most binding commitment to duty and responsibility. His 'whiteness' masks an essential bond with the Indians; his heterosexuality frames the fact that his most fulfilling (natural) relationships are with other men. These impossible and unresolved contradictions are arguably the target of the playful performance strategies I have been discussing. Evident first within the TV Western's texts, then enacted in the ways they were used back then and finally retrieved in acts of remembering, they offer a mechanism for negotiating a deeply contradictory formation of (white, heterosexual) masculinity. In many ways, they appear to offer the performance possibilities of gay 'camp'. They apparently share, in other words, (to echo Jack Babuscio's specifically gay definition of the term) a similar sense of humour, irony and a playful, almost theatrical, attachment to role-playing and performance (Babuscio, 1977 : 41). In reality, however, there are profound differences.

For gay men, camp is regularly talked about as signalling a critical distance from, and rejection of, social roles and representations. The mechanisms I have been describing have a different significance. They are strategies used by men whose lives

156

have been shaped by loyalty to (despite discomfort with) the rewards and restrictions of white, heterosexual masculinity. Their fluidity makes it possible for the contrasting serious, ironic and domesticated versions of the TV Western hero (and indeed the differently inflected ethnic bodies of the Cowboy and the Indian) to be inhabited and enjoyed all at once. Sourced as they are from a period 'back then', when felt differences could be enacted without need for self-conscious verbal statement, the bodily memories provide a way of 'thinking' (*feeling*) and narrating a coherent identity that reverberates with the contradictions of white, heterosexual masculinity even as it contains and obscures them. With this in mind, it is possible to suggest a number of sources of the enthusiasm sparked by memories of the TV Western. On one level it seems connected to the pleasurable immediacy of the bodily imaginings that (back then) transformed the original programmes. At the same time, in the present, it appears linked to the enjoyment of playfully performing identities that can exist within (not infringe) the conventional frontiers of gender and sexuality. Rather than deploying the subversive ironies of camp, the mechanisms I have been describing offer possibilities for imagining and performing identities that wear contradictions with comfort.

## NOTES

1   My thanks to Phil Dring, Seamus Finnegan, Jason Jacobs, Nick Long, David Lusted, John Pople-Crump and the anonymous respondents who answered my questions so willingly. Thanks also to Erica Carter and Jan Campbell for comments and suggestions.
2   The absence of black and Asian British responses in my brief survey needs to be noted.
3   The dates here relate to American television and are taken from Buscombe (1988: 399–424). For the detailed histories of the TV Western that lie behind this brief summary see Anderson (1994), Boddy (1998), Brauer and Brauer (1975), MacDonald (1987) and Yoggy (1994).
4   For example, in Chapter 7 of this volume Yvonne Tasker notes Steven Cohan's (1997: 204–20) argument about the much wider significance for the period of the generational contrast of masculinities enacted by John Wayne and Montgomery Clift in the 1948 film, *Red River*.
5   In a recent study, Jan Campbell defines and uses the concept of 'the bodily imaginary' in relation to the film spectatorship debates and psychoanalysis. In her words (from an unpublished paper on the subject) 'this imaginary is situated within culture and language and is rooted in an experiential and sensual body that projects and paints a relation to the world through the image' (Campbell, forthcoming: 3).
6   See also David Lusted's (1996) essay, 'Social Class and the Western as Male Melodrama'.
7   Susan Sontag used the Wilde quotation from *An Ideal Husband* in her 'Notes on "Camp"'. In her words, 'to camp … employs flamboyant mannerisms susceptible of a double interpretation' (Sontag, 1967: 282).

## REFERENCES

Anderson, C. (1994) *Hollywood: The Studio System in the Fifties*, Austin: University of Texas Press.
Babuscio, J. (1977) 'Camp and the Gay Sensibility', in R. Dyer (ed.), *Gays and Film*, London: BFI.

Boddy, W. (1998) '"Sixty Million Viewers Can't Be Wrong": The Rise and Fall of the TV Western', in E. Buscombe and R.E. Pearson (eds), *Back in the Saddle Again: New Essays on the Western*, London: BFI.

Brauer, R. and Brauer, D. (1975) *The Horse, The Gun and the Piece of Property: Changing Images of the TV Western*, Bowling Green: Bowling Green University Popular Press.

Buckingham, D. (1996) *Moving Images: Understanding Children's Emotional Responses to Television*, Manchester: Manchester University Press.

Buscombe, E. (ed.) (1988) *The BFI Companion to the Western*, London: BFI.

Campbell, J. (2000) *Arguing with the Phallus: Feminist, Queer and Postcolonial Theory: A Psychoanalytical Contribution*, London: ZED Books.

—— (forthcoming) 'Cultural Rememory: Film Spectatorship and the Bodily Imaginary'.

Cohan, S. (1997) *Masked Men: Masculinity and the Movies in the Fifties*, Bloomington: Indiana University Press.

Hoggart, R. (1957) *The Uses of Literacy*, London: Pelican.

Kuhn, A. (1995) *Family Secrets*, London: Verso.

Lusted, D. (1996) 'Social Class and the Western as Male Melodrama', in I. Cameron and D. Pye (eds), *The Movie Book of the Western*, London: Studio Vista.

MacDonald, J.F. (1987) *Who Shot the Sheriff: The Rise and Fall of the TV Western*, New York: Praeger.

Morley, D. (1986) *Family Television: Cultural Power and Domestic Leisure*, London: Routledge.

O'Sullivan, T. (1991) 'Television Memories and Cultures of Viewing 1950–65', in J. Corner (ed.), *Popular Television in Britain: Studies in Cultural History*, London: BFI.

Packard, V. (1957) *The Hidden Persuaders*, London: Pelican.

Pumphrey, M. (1996) 'Why Do Cowboys Wear Hats in the Bath ?', in I. Cameron and D. Pye (eds), *The Movie Book of the Western*, London: Studio Vista.

Sontag, S. (1967) 'Notes on "Camp"', in *Against Interpretation*, London: Eyre and Spottiswoode.

Stacey, J. (1994) *Stargazing*, London: Routledge.

Walkerdine, V. (1986) 'Video Replay: Families, Films and Fantasy', in V. Burgin, J. Donald and C. Kaplan (eds), *Formations of Fantasy*, London: Methuen.

Yoggy, G.A. (1994) *Riding the Video Range: The Rise and Fall of the Western on Television*, Jefferson, NC: McFarland.

## 10

# THE PERSUADERS!
## A girl's best friends

*Joke Hermes*

A mad car chase, wheels spinning over a deep abyss just off the road, a shoot-out in a scenic abandoned southern-French village, a flippant exchange between the protagonists to underscore that despite the evident danger this was all in a day's fun. Typical scenes from my all-time favourite action series – *The Persuaders!* Originally set to be titled *The Friendly Persuaders*, the series was produced in 1971 at ATV/ITV's Elstree studios (then the most modern in Britain). TV baron Lew Grade's strategy of pre-selling the series to the American network ABC furnished an unprecedentedly high production budget, allowing for breathtaking location shoots throughout Europe, as well as the hiring of two big-name stars – Tony Curtis and Roger Moore – for the lead roles.

Securing such a prestigious duo marked a propitious start to the series. Curtis, of course, was an established Hollywood star (though he had hitherto turned down offers of television work), while Moore's bankability in an action TV series had been proved by his earlier success as *The Saint* (1962–69).[1] *The Persuaders!* saw the duo, themselves sex-symbols in their early forties, cast as Danny Wilde (Curtis) and Brett Sinclair (Moore), both playboys at a bit of a loose end – after all, you can only have so much fun roaming around Europe in your Ferrari (Danny) or Aston Martin (Brett).

The opening episode, 'Overture' established the series' formula. After racing each other to Monte Carlo in their respective sports cars, American self-made millionaire, Danny Wilde, and dandy-esque British aristocrat, Lord Brett Sinclair, continue their rivalry in a restaurant – a fist-fight ensuing as they disagree over the correct way to make a Creole Scream cocktail. Arrested by the gendarmerie, the pair are surprised to find themselves not at the local police station but at the elegant chateau of retired legal eagle turned clandestine crime-fighter, Judge Fulton. Chiding the errant playboys for squandering their wealth, and for their lack of social conscience, the Judge offers them a choice between thirty days' imprisonment or helping him in an investigation involving a beautiful woman. Such a task is, of course, ideally suited to the insouciant talents of the two Lotharios and friendly rivalry develops as they compete for the young woman's attention. The conclusion of the case sees a notorious gangland boss laid by the heels, Wilde and Sinclair subsequently agreeing (though still somewhat reluctantly) to help Judge Fulton in his crusade against high-flying criminals seemingly beyond the reach of the law. And, in the episodes that followed, Wilde and Sinclair ensnared a motley assortment of gangsters, Soviet agents and professional hit-men – always against a background of sumptuous European landscapes and the glitzy world of the rich and famous.

*The Persuaders!* proved a big success in Europe. During the 1970s episodes were spliced together to create no fewer than seven cinema releases for the European market and the series was regularly re-screened on European TV stations throughout the 1980s and 1990s.[2] In America, however, *The Persuaders!* fared less well. ABC pitched the series against CBS's immensely popular *Mission: Impossible* and, in this war of the action series, the British contender came off worst. Its poor ratings prompted ABC to withdraw the show after networking only twenty episodes and – though it was originally projected to run for five seasons of twenty-six programmes each – the lack of an American backer meant *The Persuaders!* had to be cancelled after just twenty-four instalments.[3]

Compared to the heroes of the girls' fiction genres that I love to read and watch, characters such as Wilde and Sinclair are emotionally shallow and immature. Yet on the screen they are irresistible. I have always especially liked the jokes, the clothes and the 'all's well that ends well' resolutions so characteristic of the various permutations of the male 'buddy' TV series. I do not even mind the lack of women in these programmes – or the fact that, when they do appear, women often serve as little more than decoration, or as helpless victims to be rescued by the daring heroes. This chapter, then, will explore (my own) cross-gender identification with these male action TV heroes. Rather than adopting the psychological approaches most usually deployed in such an analysis, I shall draw on a discourse perspective in my argument that action series such as *The Persuaders!* may offer a feminist (lessons in) 'duplicitous masculinity'. Indeed, those of us who assume that constructions of masculinity are prevalently underpinned by notions of activity, rationality and control, should definitely watch *The Persuaders!* In doing so, viewers may well find that they are being offered gendered identities more open-ended than those circumscribed by the usual masculine–feminine dichotomy. As is invariably the case in male 'buddy' narratives, *The Persuaders!* strives to distance itself from any hint of homosexual attraction between its lead characters by emphasizing (sometimes to the point of laboriousness) their heterosexuality. And, indeed, a *faux* homo-erotic desire for Wilde or Sinclair was not what drew me to the series. Instead, for me, the cross-gender allure of *The Persuaders!* lay in the way the series seemed to address my nascent feminist convictions. And it is the potential of the action–adventure genre to serve as a 'feminist project' that I aim to highlight in this chapter, showing that for female audiences feminism may – on some occasions – do quite well without women.

## DUPLICITOUS MASCULINITY

I think I fell for *The Persuaders!* because the series, especially the affable rapport between the two protagonists, offered a sense of light-hearted camaraderie that I much needed as a teenager. To live a life of fun and leisure without being an egotistical hedonist (the duo, after all, are always on hand to help others) is something I still see as a worthwhile goal in life. And to be unfettered by domestic obligations – free to help

Queen, country or damsels in distress – was something I found (and still find) immensely attractive. Indeed, I like to think that this series might have imprinted on my precocious self the need to reflect on the inequalities that underpin the gendering of domestic labour and responsibilities. But, perhaps more importantly, I think the nature of *The Persuaders!'* appeal for me is the fact that, for all its trappings of glamour and material pleasure, it is sentiments of friendship that lie at the heart of the show's narrative. For me, *The Persuaders!* offered the image of having a real friend – a friend who may make fun of me at times, but who would never stop loving me and would always be there to help out.

I was not a feminist at thirteen when I first watched *The Persuaders!* with my mother and sister. But now, as a feminist theorist watching recent re-runs of the series, I am prompted to think about the ways the programme might appeal to female viewers. In fact, while action–adventure series such as *The Persuaders!* are often assumed to have a mode of address that is essentially male, I would argue that in important respects they may be open to mobilization by audiences of women. Indeed, why should a carefree life of jokes, fun and friendship not be for women? Though my feminist consciousness developed later in life – as I studied political science and developed an academic career – on reflection, I think my personal and intellectual questioning of rigid gender boundaries and definitions may well have started with my fondness for *The Persuaders!* and the pleasures it offered in its presentation of life as 'one of the boys'. And today I still enjoy it, partly for those same reasons. Even a mother of two at times likes to reimagine herself as a hip, handsome guy whose affable and easy-going exterior belies his romantic gallantry. I would argue that *The Persuaders!* is a text that lends itself to being used in this way by its female audiences, by virtue of its relatively open coding of masculinity and its presentation of a fairly diffuse and 'ungendered' form of sexual identity.

Throughout the series Wilde and Sinclair habitually hide their true characters and underlying chivalry behind affable smiles and silly jokes – much like their illustrious forebear, the Scarlet Pimpernel – another romantic male hero of my youth. Having discovered my mother's books as a risqué source of delights (I read them in secret, never altogether sure if they were something I was 'old enough' for), I cherished Baroness d'Orcy's creation of a British nobleman who rescues French aristocrats from the guillotine during the 'Terror' of the French Revolution. But the Scarlet Pimpernel was only part action hero. His other half was madly in love with his escaped French wife, Marguerite, who does not return his love until she finds out the truth about his double identity. I know now that a 'real' action hero would never become tied to a single emotional relationship in such a way – but then I cared little about the gendered codes governing the production of popular texts.

In retrospect I also injected my own sense of romance into my reading of *The Persuaders!* But this was not difficult to do. As a textual form, the action TV series may be a genre pre-eminently aimed at men – but it can be reread quite easily as a woman's romantic genre. Perhaps the action–adventure series might even be seen as a romantic genre for men? Like the romance novel, action–adventure series such as *The Persuaders!* thrive on a mixture of humorous exchange, with heroes who do not brag or rely on the indiscriminate use of muscle, but are distinguished by their 'natural authority' and sheer self-effacing courage in the face of injustice. The main difference between these 'feminine' and 'masculine' romantic genres is that, in those aimed at women, the protagonists ultimately 'get' one another. In contrast, the heroes of action series never become 'tied down' to one woman. In these texts the male hero is always kept 'free', independent of any romantic commitment – thus better able to keep the world safe from menacing villains.

My intuitive link between Danny Wilde, Brett Sinclair and the Scarlet Pimpernel is based on how all three men seem to hide their true colours from the world at large. Their strength as champions of justice is enhanced by an outward appearance that conceals their underlying valour and dynamism. The joke is on all those who think they are just silly, foppish aristocrats – idle rich who contribute nothing to merit their lives of indulgent luxury. Romantic novels usually construct more straightforward, traditionally 'masculine' heroes – but even these texts sometimes feature characters whose daredevil gallantry is concealed by a public image of 'feminine' passivity and an obsession with consumption (cf. Modleski, 1986). It is this double-coding that may appeal to many women – the construction of characters who are dashingly attractive and dynamic, but who eschew the swaggering braggadocio associated with conventional representations of 'real men'. 'Duplicitous' hardly begins to describe this kind of male hero.

While early studies of masculinity (for example, that of Tolson, 1978 or Seidler, 1991) contended that men face a tough job in having to contain their emotions and provide for their dependants, many romantic heroes escape from the rigidity of such gender roles. The heroes of some forms of romantic fiction and action TV series, for example, challenge traditional gender stereotypes – offering an enticing glimpse of a heroic identity bound less strictly by the gendered codes operating within many other popular genres. In their presentation of a duplicitous masculinity, therefore, these texts present opportunities for identification by audiences of both men and women. In some senses, however, the heroes of *The Persuaders!* were very different to those in conventional romantic narratives. There were, after all, *two* of them. They were unavailable. They had, in a way, already 'been taken' by one another.

## THE MALE COUPLE

From the outset, the rivalry between Wilde and Sinclair is central to the narrative of *The Persuaders!* – though this is always tempered by the characters' obvious affection for one another. In some ways this played off the relationship between the two actors themselves. During production there was always a degree of friction between Curtis and Moore. Moore was relaxed and friendly with the film crew and would always put in overtime to finish a scene, while Curtis had a volatile temper and insisted on stopping work at five exactly.[4] But, despite their differences, the pair became good friends – developing a close rapport and even sharing a specially constructed sauna during pauses in filming (Richardson, 1999: 14). This friendship was reflected on-screen – the actors regularly bouncing ad-libs and in-jokes off one another as they developed the light-hearted *badinage* that became one of the show's trademarks.

162

The rivalry between the two main characters serves to disavow any suggestion of homo-eroticism. Yet this rivalry is always constructed as taking place within a warm and affectionate friendship – and this is the source of much of the humour in *The Persuaders!* In the episode 'That's Me Over There', for example, Danny Wilde (Curtis) decides to pretend to be Lord Brett Sinclair (Moore) at an auction where he is to receive information that will secure the conviction of a notorious villain ('You know, it's not so tough doing Brett – all you have to do is think "ugly"'). Adopting a ludicrously plummy English accent and fumbling with a monocle, Wilde imperson-ates his friend – buying a hugely expensive Egyptian mummy (delivered to his lord-ship's London flat at the episode's conclusion). And when Sinclair finally arrives on the scene, Wilde brazenly introduces him as 'Danny Wilde', prompting the English Lord to affect a comically exaggerated southern drawl.

Yet the bond between Wilde and Sinclair is meticulously guarded against a sexual (mis)interpretation. A key part of this strategy is the playing-up of the contrasts between the two characters, thereby establishing a 'safe' distance between them. The differences between Wilde and Sinclair are underlined by the contrasting biographical 'scrap-books' that make up the show's opening credits – and, throughout the series, Wilde's 'American-ness' (brash, street-savvy and wise-cracking) and Sinclair's 'British-ness' (sophisticated, urbane and dry-witted) serve as the basis for continual jokes and misunderstandings. It is, moreover, this sense of fundamental 'difference' that serves to secure the two characters' heterosexuality – the cultural gulf separating them helping to displace the possibility of any mutual sexual attraction.

The character of Danny Wilde represents an especially interesting articulation of masculinity. Growing up in the backstreets of Brooklyn, he lacks formal education, but represents the classic American icon of the 'self-made man', making his first million by the time he is thirty. Jokes to Sinclair such as: 'I'm here to see your incestral home', present Wilde both as endearingly naive and as a sharp-witted critic of English aristocratic pretension. His 'Whatever' in answer to Sinclair's correction underscores the possibility of either interpretation. Moreover, though hardly presented as effete, it is possible to see Wilde as being constructed as the 'feminine' counterpart to the more 'masculine' Sinclair. (This is, after all, a British series portraying an Englishman and an American).

In the course of the series the characters' different dress codes accentuate this facet of their relationship. Sinclair's attire befits an English Lord. Of the two characters, he is always dressed more formally, albeit with a heavy dash of dandyism (Roger Moore was allowed to design his own clothes for the show – hence a profusion of wide lapels, flouncy shirts and kipper ties). Wilde, on the other hand, is the non-conformist and affects a more 'hip' sartorial panache – with short, straight, double-breasted jackets and blousons often made of shiny fabrics or supple leather (with gloves to match, of course). This style corresponds with some of the more 'feminine' qualities represented in the character of Wilde. He is the more impulsive of the duo, often acting on instinct, while Brett Sinclair is 'masculine' rationality personified. Therefore, while the cultural differences between the characters serve (on one level) to create a 'safe' sexual distance between them, they also produce a spry romantic *frisson* (see Figure

*Figure 10.1* 'Duplicitous masculinity' – Danny Wilde (Tony Curtis) and Brett Sinclair (Roger Moore) in *The Persuaders!* (1971).

10.1). In classic romances, after all, opposites are said to attract, and love is portrayed as thriving on difference. And *The Persuaders!* can be seen as just such a romance – not in terms of the (fleeting) encounters that Wilde and Sinclair have with the opposite sex, but in respect of their intense and competitive male friendship.

Of course, it could be argued that, rather than being a locus of possible homo-erotic pleasure, the intimacy and closeness of male 'buddy' partnerships simply derives from the co-operative teamwork central to many action–adventure narratives. This interpretation, however, is belied by the amount of sheer effort that action–adventure texts invest in their attempts to dispel any inkling of homo-eroticism. In a discussion of mixed-race male buddy couples in film, Sharon Willis (1998) highlights not only the role of race in foregrounding issues of hierarchic difference, but also the way our pleasure in watching the male body perform (presumably paralleling the male characters' pleasure in watching one another) is legitimated through the characters' endurance of extreme punishment. Bruce Willis, for example, in the *Die Hard* film series (1988; 1990; 1995) withstands extreme bodily abuse which, according to Willis, deflects the homo-erotic pleasure in viewing the spectacle of the male body. Less extreme textual devices can function in the same way. During the 1970s, for example, in many (American) TV comedies that featured two or more men as main characters, word-play and occasional friendly competition over women was enough to ensure that as an audience we engage in the 'correct' reading – the increasingly close relationship between Fonzie and Richie Cunningham in *Happy Days* being a prime example (Spangler, 1992:103). The main characters in *Starsky and Hutch* also obviously cared deeply for one another

– and the occasional appearance of a girlfriend in the script invariably caused friction between the two detectives and mutual accusations of jealousy. This leads John Fiske (1987: 213) to read the series as exhibiting a marked dimension of homo-eroticism – and indeed, it is Starsky and Hutch's partnership that endures, while the women are always a passing interest. Yet Starsky and Hutch are still relatively young – and implicit in the narrative is the likelihood that they will eventually find a 'good woman' and settle down. This is where Danny Wilde and Lord Brett Sinclair are different.

It is not only their debonair countenance and *savoir-vivre* that sets the Persuaders apart from other action–adventure 'buddy' teams. Already in their forties, and enjoying every moment of the luxurious lifestyle that their wealth affords, it seems much less likely that the duo will ultimately settle down to a life of middle-aged heterosexual respectability. I never minded, though, that the Persuaders were, in a way, already married to one another. It was always the *image* I lusted for rather than the men themselves. Their easy camaraderie, especially, appealed to me because it seemed to embody an idyllic marriage. Wilde and Sinclair would do anything for each other and, just as importantly, they thoroughly enjoyed each other's company – they would make jokes, tease one another and have wonderful trips together. In retrospect, I can see that this was something that I coveted in the years before my parents were formally divorced. Obviously, a married couple who always travel in two different cars might signify rather a large degree of personal autonomy – but still, it would have made going on holiday with my parents a lot easier.

For me, though, there was little to be gained in simply reading the Persuaders as a gay couple – and I have always been perfectly happy to go with the text's assurances they were not. The appeal of the series also lay in the idea of expensive cars and the fast life, so clearly beyond the reach of a teenager (or, come to that, a feminist intellectual, teaching cultural studies). I wanted to *be* a Persuader – independent, free to do as I pleased, and always together with my best pal.

Like most girls, I used to read popular fiction intended for both boys and girls. The attraction of boys' fiction lay in the fact that their world of adventure did not seem, to me, to depend on one's gender. It was always easy enough to project myself onto the male characters. Of course, an action genre may be even more compelling when the lead characters actually *are* women. I am thinking, here, of the lesbian detective novel – a great subcultural hit that combines adventure and sex, self-reflexive irony and the thematic exploration of gender, facade and masquerade (issues themselves central to many lesbian subcultures). Just imagine the Persuaders as women! Not a bad idea for a new TV show. But, back when I was a teenager, my mother might not have liked them so much. After all, her wish for me when I was in grammar school was that I should follow in her footsteps and become a secretary.

## WOMEN ...

Roger Moore's cool detachment and Tony Curtis's silly jokes offer a crash course in not taking life too seriously. This was an important part of their appeal – though the fact that they were already a 'couple' militated against one becoming infatuated with them. Here, it is useful to draw a comparison between the heroic duo featured in *The Persuaders!* and a lone action hero such as James Bond (played in the 1970s by Roger Moore, following his stint as Brett Sinclair). In my childhood, I am not sure that I was allowed to go to Bond films – certainly, cinemas never earned much money through my parents. But television was our home cinema – and it seemed that the figure of Bond had informed the style of *The Persuaders!* immensely: the playboy type, the chic entourage, the beautiful women, the mission. Bond, however, is not independently wealthy but is on a payroll and works on orders from 'M'. And Bond (much though I have come to love him) is also much more sexist than Wilde and Sinclair (cf. Bennett and Woollacott, 1987). Bond, especially during the 1970s, was clearly misogynistic in his cynical use of women. And in some respects he was also something of a *noir* hero – insofar as the women he truly cares for stand a good chance of dying before the final credits roll. In contrast, since *The Persuaders!* was made for television, there could be no bedroom scenes – and nor, apparently, was there a necessity for the main characters to develop strong emotions about any women. Femininity, as a result, is a largely unoccupied space in the series. For some, this will count against the programme. And, admittedly, this is something I now feel uncomfortable with, given the dearth of positive representations of women in popular television. But as a teenager it was not something I held against Danny and Brett.

Indeed, the few prominent female characters in *The Persuaders!* never made an especially big impression on me. For instance, Sinclair's niece, an author of detective fiction, I actually mis-remembered as being the villain in 'A Death in the Family' – when her only crime is to be rather large and to wear a pair of floral print trousers that go just *too* far (even for someone as taken with camp and kitsch as me). In fact, the only really memorable 'women' in this particular episode are Curtis and Moore themselves – who don outrageous drag in order to impersonate their elderly aunts. 'The Time and the Place', meanwhile, features a gangster's moll who is won over by the charms of the two heroes and tries to come to their aid. Again, though, the female character fails to make a significant impression (despite having a very nice fur hat). She is, after all, superfluous to the team. There is no need for anyone to take care of our men, they are presented as relying totally on themselves – and on one another. Invariably, then, women in *The Persuaders!* simply appear as relatively incidental plot devices – for example, the glamorous woman who mistakes Wilde for the paymaster of a communist spy-ring in 'Anyone Can Play' (one of my favourite episodes).

Admittedly, *The Persuaders!* featured a handful of female characters who, like the earlier Mrs Peel in *The Avengers* (see Miller, 1997), were active and dextrous – skilled in high-speed car-chases or handy with a gun. And here there would have been spaces created in which female viewers might have imagined themselves. But, as a girl, it was the figures of Wilde and Sinclair themselves that I was drawn to. However incongruous this may sound, the pair seemed to offer a reassuring sense of safety – while, at the same time, I could also project myself into their excitingly fast and luxurious world. In fact, as a teenage girl, *The Persuaders!* seemed to be a television text tailored to fit exactly the needs of my fantasies.

## FRIENDLY PERSUADERS

When I watch an episode of *The Persuaders!* today, it appeals to me in a different way. Part of the attraction is the nostalgic feel of the series. The French Côte d'Azur has changed enormously since episodes of the series were shot there, interior decorating in the early 1970s was something to behold, while the clothes are sometimes wildly funny and sometimes simply beautiful. I am also intrigued by the elements of dressing-up which recur throughout the series. Not only did Danny Wilde wear his wonderful jackets, I also remember many occasions where Curtis's character dresses-up dazzlingly. 'Angie … Angie', for instance, sees the duo in Cannes, on a mission to protect an important witness from a deadly hit-man. Wilde is seen relaxing in his hotel room, wearing a beautiful, champagne-coloured silk kaftan. The softly shimmering robe suggests a world of luxury and endless hedonism – though it can be thrown off in an instant, as Wilde thrusts himself into the mission in hand.

This emphasis on dressing-up – together with the show's silly jokes, its phenomenal clothes and narratives based around artifice and deception – makes me wonder whether *The Persuaders!* might be considered a camp series. The masquerade the two men are engaged in as playboys with a mission, the many occasions on which they disguise themselves, all suggest camp overtones. In 'Greensleeves', for example, the twists of the plot mean that Sinclair actually has to impersonate himself, while Wilde assumes an identity as a Hungarian butler (driving, somewhat incongruously, a red mini). Certainly, like its predecessor *The Avengers,* some of the stylistic elements in *The Persuaders!* might well be considered camp – the elements of masquerade, the playful humour and the irony all suggesting a degree of what Collins terms 'textual hyperconsciousness' (Collins, 1989). And as a teenager I undoubtedly enjoyed the contrived storylines and jokey dialogue ('Are *all* the Sinclairs buried here?' 'No. Only the dead ones'). But, at that time, the 'knowingness' of camp was not accessible to me – I took the series much more seriously.

Back in the 1970s, *The Persuaders!* provided great lessons for a feminist-to-be. The character of Danny Wilde was especially instructive. Superficially, Wilde seemed a composition of the worst aspects of traditional constructions of both masculinity (he's always eager to wade in with his fists) and femininity (his impulsiveness means he acts on intuition rather than logical deduction). But his combination of humour, stylishness and immense loyalty made him seem tremendously appealing. Undoubtedly, it is possible to identify dimensions of sexism – and possibly even misogyny – in *The Persuaders!* While I was a teenager, however, the series' relatively diffuse coding of masculinity offered valuable spaces for a process of cross-gender identification. Though the series struggled hard to establish the masculine, heterosexual credentials of its main characters, what made *The Persuaders!* so very persuasive was the way the gendered identities of Danny Wilde and Brett Sinclair seemed duplicitous and fairly open-ended – allowing them to serve as vehicles for a young woman's fantasies of heroic adventure and carefree happiness. Indeed, on reflection, in my teenage reading of *The Persuaders!,* I think I developed many of the convictions that would later underpin my commitment to feminism – especially the importance of loyalty to one's friends and comrades (not to mention the importance of humour in the face of adversity). Indeed, it is amusing to imagine a world in which women were given a diet of action–adventure series – especially ones like *The Persuaders!* While men, well, what could be better for them than a diet of romantic fiction?

## NOTES

1  In fact, the concept for *The Persuaders!* was originally developed in one of *The Saint's* final episodes - 'The Ex-King of Diamonds' (1968) - in which Simon Templar teamed up with an American playboy to thwart the criminal schemes of a nefarious Egyptian aristocrat. For a thorough-going history of *The Persuaders!* see Richardson (1999).

2  *The Persuaders!* went on to be sold successfully throughout the world – Tony Curtis estimating in his autobiography that, worldwide, audiences of six hundred million people saw the series (Curtis and Pavis, 1994: 238).

3  By this time Roger Moore was already limbering up for his role as the new James Bond in *Live and Let Die* (1973).

4  Curtis would later take full responsibility for the arguments that took place during the production of *The Persuaders!*, explaining that they stemmed from his attempts to strive for perfection (Richardson, 1999: 14).

## REFERENCES

Bennett, T. and Woollacott, J. (1987) *Bond and Beyond: The Political Career of a Popular Hero*, London: Macmillan.

Collins, J. (1989) 'Watching Ourselves Watch Television, Or Who's Your Agent?', in *Cultural Studies*, 3(3): 261–81.

Curtis, T. and Pavis, B. (1994) *Tony Curtis: The Autobiography*, London: Heinemann.

Fiske, J. (1987) *Television Culture*, London: Routledge.

Miller, T. (1997) *The Avengers*, London: BFI.

Modleski, T. (1986) 'Feminism as Mas(s)querade: A Feminist Approach to Mass Culture', in C. MacCabe (ed.), *High Theory/Low Culture: Analysing Popular Television and Film*, Manchester: Manchester University Press: 37–52.

Richardson, M. (1999) 'That's Me Over There', in *Action TV*, 1(1) Winter: 8–17.

Seidler, V. (1991) *Recreating Sexual Politics: Men, Feminism and Politics*, London: Routledge.

Spangler, L. (1992) 'Buddies and Pals: A History of Male Friendships on Prime-Time Television', in S. Craig (ed.), *Men, Masculinity and the Media*, London: Sage: 93–110.

Tolson, A. (1978) *The Limits of Masculinity*, London: Tavistock.

Willis, S. (1998) *High Contrast: Race and Gender in Contemporary Hollywood Film*, Durham: Duke University Press.

# 11

# KING AND QUEEN

## Interpreting sexual identity in *Jason King*

*Andy Medhurst*

'Have you seen his photograph? The man is an affected fop'. That's how Jason King is crisply dismissed in 'Zenia', one episode of the early 1970s series that carried his name, and it identifies economically, if abusively, two key characteristics of this strangest of television action heroes. First, it judges King on the basis of a photograph, but that's wholly appropriate given the way the series centres so unswervingly on the man's appearance. Episode after episode foregrounds King's lavish and meticulous clothing, places him in front of mirrors, features photographs of him on magazine covers and book jackets, and includes dialogue commenting on his looks and style. King was not so much a person as an image, a conglomeration of signs. Second, and consequently, the remark calls into question King's masculinity. He is undeniably a fop, as well as a dandy, an aesthete and (to quote the episode 'Nadine') 'an epicurean peacock', and these are traits that have an ambiguous relationship with conventional codes of masculinity. Those codes customarily see masculinity as natural, non-manu-factured, stemming directly and inevitably from maleness, while foppery (and how satisfying it is to be able to use that word in a collection of academic essays) is very much a performance, a revelling in affectation, a conscious manipulation of artifice. Foppery is never very far away from effeminacy, and effeminacy often blurs into homosexuality. Yet this particular fop is also a stud, with women both on-screen in the episodes and off-screen in the audience finding King a sexual magnet of immense and irresistible proportions.

Jason King, then, is a complex sign, and *Jason King* even more so. This chapter attempts to unravel some of those complexities, especially those concerned with the tensions and parameters of sexual identity, in order to try and understand how this extraordinary series operated. My starting point is the paradox that while King's sexual narratives were entirely heterosexual, his appearance, mannerisms and speech were saturated with elements of camp and queerness. That last phrase needs freeze-framing, however, since to say 'saturated' takes too much for granted. I cannot avoid seeing King as at least partly queer, I can't help reading his exaggerated heterosexual prowess as some sort of extended camp parody of predatory lounge-lizard masculinity, but then I am a gay man (and on ambitious days a queer one) who brings a particular set of preconceptions, sensibilities and paradigms to my understanding of texts. To my queer eyes, King is a queen. Yet the most devoted King fans of the early 1970s were heterosexual women, who made Peter Wyngarde, the actor who played King, a focal point for huge erotic investment. If this looks curious to queer eyes now, it is also seen as odd by a third grouping of King consumers, the kitsch-and-irony lobby who venerate *Jason King* as a key text in those discourses of cult taste which have sought to celebrate the styles, signs and surfaces of the 1970s. For both gay male viewers and kitsch aficionados (and the two do, of course, sometimes overlap), one influential factor in re-readings of King has been the persistent web of rumours and speculations regarding Wyngarde's own sexual identity.

The question of Wyngarde's sexuality raises one further issue in this context, namely the extent to which the camp and queer facets of *King* were enjoyed by gay men (and their clued-in associates) at the time of the original broadcasts. A TV hero given to wearing lavender silk and invoking the name of Oscar Wilde was surely likely to prompt amused recognition, but my use of 'surely' there signifies an acknowledgement that such matters are notoriously hard to pin down on the altar of proof. I have absolutely no doubts that 1970s queers, queens and camp followers, whether they knew directly about Wyngarde's sexual identity or enjoyed inferring it from his image and performance, would have seen Jason King as one of their own – but then I would say that, wouldn't I? Given its focus on such slippery matters as sexual semiotics, subcultural codings and taste hierarchies, this chapter can't hope to offer anything in the way of conclusive evidence, but I offer it as some speculative thoughts about a teasingly complicated knot of issues.

## *JASON KING* AND THE ACTION GENRE

To begin with, let me outline the shape of the series. Jason King had previously been a central character in *Department 'S'* (1969–70), where he was one of a trio of investigators brought in to solve crimes too sensitive or bizarre to be entrusted to conventional law enforcement agencies. He was, in addition, a successful writer of detective novels, featuring a sleuth called Mark Caine. Wyngarde/King became the undoubted star of *Department 'S'*, proving especially popular with female viewers. This popularity generated a spin-off series, and twenty-six episodes of *Jason King* were broadcast between September 1971 and April 1972.

To differentiate *Jason King* from *Department 'S'*, any direct links with organized detection were dropped. King was shown as an international jet-setting playboy, globally famous for his novels and part of a moneyed elite who moved effortlessly between big cities, glamorous beaches, chic ski resorts, exclusive parties, secluded villas and expensive nightclubs. He is constantly seen on aeroplanes, arriving at airports, driving across and between countries, peppering almost every conversation with place names that are simultaneously distant (and desirable) to us and familiar to him. The cosmopolitanism of the series is a defining characteristic. King is based in Paris (he has left Britain to avoid paying heavy income tax), but travels widely in order to research and publicize his books, a plot device enabling episodes to be set in a wide range of

*Figure 11.1*  Crime-fighting was a tiresome interruption in Jason King's world of sex, status and style.

exoticized locations. Africa, South America, Hong Kong, the Caribbean, the Alps, the Balkans, Moscow, Rome, Vienna, Geneva, Athens and Berlin are only some of those featured, each depicted through lamentably, if expectedly, predictable tropes of ethnic and cultural difference. Wherever he goes, King stumbles across or is embroiled in some criminal plot or scheme which he helps to thwart. The overseas settings allow for the copious use of location footage – the neon streets of Hong Kong, the Leaning Tower of Pisa, that helicopter shot of a car speeding along twisting Mediterranean coastal roads which seemed to be obligatory in all action series of this era. Such footage served both to whisk British viewers off to fabulous elsewheres and to assist foreign sales for the series by transcending British parochialism.

If all this sounds familiar, it's because *King* was another in the long line of action series produced by ITC, and it closely follows the template mapped out by *Danger Man*, *The Avengers*, and most of all *The Saint*. It only differs significantly from those precedents in two ways. First, the fact that King writes fiction of the same kind that forms the narratives of *King* allows for some playful self-reflexivity. King's life and identity are repeatedly blurred with those of his hero/alter ego Caine. In 'The Company I Keep', for example, King finds himself investigating a series of murders that match the plot of the Caine novel he is currently writing. Elsewhere he signs autographs with the name of Caine, is constantly muddled up with Caine by those he meets, is seen avidly reading and loudly enjoying his own novels, and greets a policeman who rescues him from one sticky situation with the line '"You're just in time, Inspector", said Mark Caine'.

The second feature that distinguishes *Jason King* from the rest of the ITC stable is the most obvious and the most crucial one: the persona of King himself. King is not a character without antecedents, since the gentleman sleuth is a staple of British detective fiction, but King takes that archetype into new directions, seizing its underlying dandyishness and hedonism and making those traits the dominant ones. He is a man for whom crime-fighting is a tiresome interruption to a life of fame, status, wealth, sex and ultra-fashionable clothes. As Leon Hunt (1998: 65–73) has pointed out in his astute study of 1970s British popular culture, *Jason King* sits alongside *The Persuaders!* as a text where the action series diminished its adventure component in favour of an emphasis on wealthy lifestyles and the trappings of conspicuous consumption (see Figure 11.1). Hence King is an action hero who prefers inaction, who would ideally like no physical exertion beyond tapping his typewriter, lifting a glass of champagne, and draping a louche arm around another grateful female conquest.

The generic determinants of the action series could not be completely shrugged off, so King does get into fights in most episodes. Wyngarde's approach to such encounters, however, is decidedly unusual. King can punch, and sometimes attempts a form of rather effete karate, but as often as not he ends up losing these encounters. There are recurring sights in the series of King falling, winded, prone, flopping, dusting himself down with looks of startled affrontedness. This is one of the many ways in which the action elements required by the genre were scaled down and gently mocked in order to concentrate on the framing, fetishizing and selling of King himself. This places him, throughout the series, in an ambivalent relationship with prevailing masculine norms, and this is apparent nowhere more than in the main love affair of his life, the affair he has with his clothes.

## A MAN IN LAVENDER

In the 1990s, many ITC series were reissued on videotape, each tape beginning with a rapid montage of all the titles currently available. Since there was only space and time for the briefest glimpse of these, it seems reasonable to assume that particularly emblematic images were selected. Jason King appears just once in the montage; he is alone on a bed, reading a Mark Caine novel, dressed in a lavender dressing gown. Solitary, narcissistic and lavender: Jason King encapsulated.

King's clothing is utterly central to the meanings of the series, but those meanings vary for different audiences. For heterosexual women watching the original broadcasts, King's obsessive interest in his own finery marked him out as a daring individualist, brave enough to step out of the masculine rut and express himself. To gay eyes now, his clothes link him to those queers who acted as the often ridiculed but frequently splendid vanguard of male fashion, testing the limits of what a man could wear. For the kitsch-hunters of retro irony, King's outfits offer the deliciousness of excess – nobody was ever quite so extreme in his early-1970s-ness as Jason King.

Shall we wander through his wardrobe? There are sheaves of dressing gowns, usually lavender or purple, mostly silk but with the occasional dash of velvet. Confined to bed at one point in 'If It's Got To Go, It's Got To Go', he wears a purple smoking jacket over lavender pyjamas over a pink cravat. Later in the same episode an elegantly folded silk handkerchief is tucked into the breast pocket of his pyjamas. He had a penchant for kaftans, getting through no less than four in the episode 'Toki' – lavender, pale blue, scarlet and (for entertaining guests) white-and-gold. Sometimes these flowing, dress-like garments had a narrative disguise as nightshirts, inasmuch as he was wearing them just after getting up, but mostly they seemed to be thrown on at any time during the day as a welcome release from the constrictions of trousers. King's trousers, unsurprisingly, were especially constricting, hugging his bottom closely before splaying out into extremely wide flares. Several episodes feature an almost indescribable pale yellow garment, part jerkin part shirt, tightly fastened across his exposed, hairy chest with a series of dangling thongs.

King does wear suits, but King's suits are not like other men's. Extending the look he first tried out, albeit a little mutedly, in *Department 'S'*, the King suit is enlivened by having the shirt cuffs pulled below the jacket cuffs then turned back over them, ensuring that the brighter colour of the shirt takes precedence and the wrists and hands have more room to manoeuvre. In 'Every Picture Tells A Story', set in Hong Kong, he wears a gleamingly white safari suit, tightly waisted and short-sleeved, its imperial adventurer origins turned frivolous and showy. Returning home from the opera in 'The Constance Missal', he is dressed in full Edwardian dandy mode – flowing cape, ruffled lace shirt with clouds of billowing cuff, silver-topped cane. In a few action sequences he dons a skin-tight leather two-piece and tops it off with an extravagant red cravat. King loves cravats, and the programme so loves him wearing them that close-up shots are sometimes crudely inserted with the cravat at *just* the right angle, an angle not seen once a medium or wide shot is resumed. In 'Nadine' he stands at the wind-blown Acropolis for no other reason than to have an unfastened cravat swirl about him while he recites poetry in the voice-over.

King wears most colours during the series, but he has a particular affinity with lavender. It isn't always unequivocally lavender, sometimes emerging as purple or puce, while a roll-neck sweater in 'A Red, Red Rose For Ever' might best be described as pale plum, but the general trend in a lavender direction is clear. King's lavender dressing gown is so essential to *King*'s semiotic armoury that it's visible even when he isn't wearing it, draped over chairs (in one scene it occupies the centre of the frame while the ostensible action occurs at the margins of the image) or wrapped around female companions. Drying off after a dunking in a Venetian canal, King chooses lavender towels, and keeps them swathed around him for far longer than is narratively necessary. Even a relatively restrained grey suit is liable to find itself covering a lavender shirt and tie. It's true that plenty of heterosexual men wore lavender in the early 1970s. As British men tentatively voyaged out from the safe conformity of white shirts under business suits, pastel colours were the first port of call. Yet lavender has resonances not found in pale green, resonances that King and *King* seemed knowingly keen to evoke.

In his exhaustive survey of media representations of homosexuality, Keith Howes (1993:448) estimates that seven out of ten references to or depictions of lavender were signifiers of queerness, while Judy Grahn's study of lesbian and gay subcultural codes begins with a section on the significance of lavender and purple shades for sexual minorities (1984: 3–12). The fact that lavender has become *the* King colour, not just placed at the forefront of episode after episode but emphasized in publicity materials for retro recirculations of the series, thus seems striking. Moreover, King's fondness for lavender sits alongside other codes that exuded subcultural meanings. The wearing of a ring on the little finger was a widely used signal amongst clandestine gay subcultures in the decades before openly gay lifestyles were feasible. King sports one on each hand, a sign of dandyish extravagance to the mainstream audience, but another surreptitious gesture to the few who knew. Cravats emitted comparable vibrations. Although they were at the height of their mainstream male popularity in the early 1970s, they were also used to denote flamboyance and effeminacy in popular comedies and dramas of the era. Antique dealers, shall we say, were immeasurably more likely to be seen decked out in cravats than coal miners, while Clarence, the queeny caricature portrayed by 1970s comic Dick Emery, had a particularly memorable line in excessive neck decor.

Even the dressing gown is an item at odds with certain aspects of hegemonic masculinity. The name itself is intriguing – I think it must be the only garment regularly worn by men to include a word, 'gown', usually associated with women's clothing – while throughout the twentieth century it was linked with a kind of leisured decadence that sits only inches away from fully-fledged homosexuality. Men who spent the day in dressing gowns were suspect, artistic, flouncingly shy of real men's work, too reluctant to climb into unambiguously manly clothes. Noel Coward was often photographed, and even more often conceptualized, as a man in a dressing gown, achieving success and scandal without ever having to get properly, manfully dressed. Jason King, likewise, composes the texts that bring him fame whilst wearing a garment that is separated from a frock by little more than linguistics. In the 1950s, midway between Coward's early impact and King's apotheosis of Gown Man, an excitable American psychiatrist accused the Batman comics of fostering homosexual desires in their readers, and one of his supposed trump cards was the fact that Batman and Robin, when at home off-duty in their shared mansion, lounged about in dressing gowns (see Medhurst, 1991).

The links between King and queer culture are broader than just these semi-secretive deployments of specific codes. For a man in the early 1970s to be deeply interested in fashion was an indication that, at the very least, he was keen to chafe away at traditional demarcations of masculinity. It is only a cliché that male fashion has strong roots in homosexual subcultures because it is so obviously true. The whole 1960s Carnaby Street revolution in menswear which revitalized British men's appearance and redrew the contours of acceptable masculinity had its origins in a small number of shops run by and aimed at queer men. 'Vince', the first of these shops, was owned by photographer Bill Green, whose speciality of near-naked physique photographs kept foundering on the problem that British male underwear was woefully unsexy. Green began selling daringly brief underpants, catalogues of which rapidly achieved almost pornography status amongst British queers, and then extended into a wider range of merchandise. Nik Cohn, in a pioneering history of British male fashion published the year that *Jason King* began, interviewed Green and went on to put his achievement in a wider context:

> 'I always put the emphasis on impact … ', says Green. 'I used materials that had never been used before – lots of velvets and silks … I made everything as colourful and bold as I could. You'd be surprised by our customers, too. Everyone thought we only sold to Chelsea homosexuals but, in actual fact, we catered to … artists and theatricals, muscle boys, and celebrities of every kind … .' Green is quite right – not all his custom was homosexual. But if he'd been in business before the war, it would have been, and that's what made Vince new and important: it sold stuff that could once have been worn by no one but queers, and extremely blatant ones at that; now the same things were bought by heteros as well … within a few years, the same sexual relaxation was to form the basis for Carnaby Street and all its triumphs … .
> To an extent, in fact, all male fashion of the sixties was homosexual-derived. In that, the retired Indian Army majors and lorry drivers were quite correct, yelling 'Fairies' and 'Poufs'. They remembered the signals of their youth and now that the message had been altered and complexified, it was natural that they should be confused.
>
> (Cohn, 1971: 61–2)

This view from the outside (Cohn's viewpoint was that of a heterosexual commentator) is corroborated from an insider, gay perspective by Richard Dyer:

> Carnaby Street was originally a group of very queer little shops or 'boutiques', a word borrowed from female fashion marketing and only one of the many steps taken to incorporate the feminine into male clothing ... Carnaby Street went mad on colour, not only pinks and purples and powder blues and other sissy colours, and not only on ties but on shirts and, most shocking of all, jackets and trousers .... Shirts were waisted, fitting tight to the body; trousers were flared, creating a flowing line at odds with the military precision and control of straight legs.
>
> (Dyer, 1994: 184)

Reaching even further back, Dyer (1994: 182) notes how in the 1893 novel *Teleny* (published anonymously but thought to be the work of Oscar Wilde and some of his circle) a small coterie of metropolitan queer sophisticates measured out their difference from dominant masculinity by wearing suits in unconventional colours, adding an extravagant flower to the lapels of otherwise unexceptional jackets, or favouring large and bright cravats instead of ties. Most of all, this bold band of queens took particular, meticulous pains with the minutiae of appearance: for queers, detail mattered.

King's style, then, undoubtedly had queer credentials if you knew how to read them, but they had to stay half-buried, since no mainstream big-budget TV series in 1971 was likely to centre its narrative on an undisguised homosexual. Oblique degrees of dabbling in queer-influenced looks, however, were very much in keeping with the flavour of the day. The early 1970s were a time when heterosexual men, influenced by the trickling down of queer styles and the androgynous inclinations of hippie garb, were venturing further away from tame, drab masculinity in their clothing than at any other point in the twentieth century. Fashion-conscious straight men had rarely looked less straight, as processes of semiotic osmosis widened the remit of what ordinary males could wear. This was the era that went on to produce Glam Rock, a musical trend that began in 1971, just like *Jason King*, and which encouraged heterosexual men to risk a little glitter and swish.

King, though, was hardly Glam, standing distinctly aloof from its headlong plunge into spangles. He may have been a fop, but you can't imagine him wearing silver lamé. There are three connected reasons for this. First, Glam was a youth cult, and King was no longer young (Wyngarde was nearly forty at the peak of *King*'s success). Second, King's sartorial vocabulary belongs to that precise moment just before Glam really took off, when 1970s fashion represented a final gaudy efflorescence of 1960s trends rather than a new look for the new decade. King never looks remotely like Marc Bolan, let alone David Bowie, but he might (if this comparison isn't too outlandish) pass for a white Jimi Hendrix or a middle-aged member of Love Affair. Third, Glam was a widespread, popular success, not the jealously guarded province of a select elite. It was too mass market for an aesthete like King, a man who stresses in several episodes that he is so committed to stylistic individuality, and has so much disposable income, that he designs his own clothes.

King's wealth is a key factor in both his look and his wider meanings, since it indicates how the sexual ambivalence of his persona needs to be cross-referenced with his class position. Revealingly, in 'Buried In The Cold, Cold Ground', he disdainfully shuns the suggestion of eggs and bacon for breakfast, that being a meal designed to stoke up a working man's body with fuel for the day's labours, opting instead for the sybaritic delights of strawberries and champagne. The term 'idle rich' could have been coined to categorize King. Nik Cohn, once again, is useful here, with his account of how a select group of rich, young Englishmen turned to extravagantly dandyish dressing in the early 1960s:

> Public schoolboys, arriving in London, were no longer faced by clearcut alternatives – politics, the army, the city. They were no longer born to govern, had no inbred function. On the other hand, they had not yet been assimilated into the mainstream … . Stranded, the brighter and more unconventional ones looked around for diversions. Where once they would have been busy building empires, now they gambled and smoked hash, and immersed themselves in Pop … . That was the secret, to keep always on the move, so that tedium and the sense of futility could never catch up. There were nightclubs and journeys, constant treats, novelties of every kind. Above all, there were clothes … . This was not a phenomenon to be confused with Carnaby Street … it sprang from the same sources – ignorance of the war and its aftermath, increased leisure time, a sense of safety, the rise of Pop – but it had a very different atmosphere. Although they may have rejected pre-war moral values and lifestyles, they remained traditionalist in that they cared very much about quality, and style. They were Pop, certainly: but they weren't popular, meaning common, and they had nothing but scorn for Carnaby Street in its tattiness.
>
> (Cohn, 1971: 92–93)

Remarkably, Cohn's sketch of these 1960s dandies seems not just to pinpoint a vital component of Jason King's obsession with appearance, but also to prefigure the narrative basis of the entire series. King was restless, style-obsessed, always hungry for 'nightclubs and journeys, constant treats, novelties of every kind'. (His effeminized safari suit in that Hong Kong episode might even be seen as a deliberate retort to those previous expectations of imperial endeavour that Cohn mentions here.) From this perspective, King's peacock extravagance is not just a sexual signal, but also an indicator of class privilege. It is the richly complex interweaving of those two strands that makes King so fascinating. He dresses as he does to announce that he is not like other men, and this means, simultaneously, a flirtation with sexual subcultures and a distancing of humdrum, everyday paid employment. King's flamboyance is an attempt to nullify drabness, to ward off the ordinary with a flurry of silks and cravats, in a process that draws on signifiers of both sexuality and class. Different audiences will be drawn to different aspects of that fusion, which returns me to the vexed question of King's appeal to multiple constituencies.

## MISTER WORLD: KING AS STUD

Of all the audience positions taken up around *Jason King*, the one that might seem most difficult to understand, especially to those of us who enjoy *King* for its camp or kitsch, is the viewpoint of the heterosexual female fanbase. When arch young irony-mongers ridicule King, part of what their laughter targets is the presumed naiveté of his adoring female public. How can those women, such laughter asks, have been so gullible? How could they not see that King was a queen?

One way of answering those questions, and refuting their implicit misogyny and class condescension, is to place the series in its precise historical context. In the early 1970s, homosexual codings in popular culture were only just beginning to become decipherable to mainstream heterosexual audiences. *King* now looks drenched in camp, but finding such meanings in the series requires a grounding in queer subcultural sensibilities that was not then widely available. Translating *King* into the lexicon of camp also obliges a subtext-hungry audience to look beyond the surface narratives of extravagantly heterosexual romance. The straight female fans of King had no need to seek perverse pleasure through snuffling out truffles of semi-concealed quasi-gay playfulness. What they wanted, what they got and what they loved was all there in front of them: Jason the ladykiller, King the lothario, Wyngarde the embodiment of sophisticated cosmopolitanism with a girl, or more usually a female flotilla, in every spot on the globe.

It should never be underestimated just how impregnable an icon of heterosexual desirability Wyngarde, in his role as King, was in the early 1970s (see Figure 11.2). A few anecdotes may help. While he was making a personal appearance at a London department store in 1970, one hundred and twenty three women offered him pairs of knickers to autograph. In 1971, he chaired the judges' panel at the annual Miss World beauty contest. In the same year, his publicity trip to Australia began with thirty thousand female fans greeting his arrival at Sydney Airport (there had been a mere twenty thousand when he visited Norway). He was awarded the Best-Dressed Man in Britain title in both 1970 and 1971. Advertising campaigns for Tabac aftershave posited him as the epitome of masculine stylishness. Between 1971 and 1973, he was voted 'Most Kissable Man' by the teenage readers of *Petticoat*, 'Mister World' by readers of the *Daily Mail*, 'Man With the Sexiest Voice on Television' by readers of *The Sun*, 'Neck-Tie Man of the Year' in West Germany, 'Most Compulsive Male Character' by the readers of *TV Times*, 'Man We Would Most Like To Be Lost In Space With' in a survey of Texas schoolgirls, and 'Man We Would Most Like To Lose Our Virginity To' by the readers of a leading Australian newspaper. Evidently, King was anything but a queen to most of his viewers.

He was such a byword for potent heterosexuality that the popularity of the name Jason rocketed during the heady years of his greatest success. In Britain at least, many men called Jason share two characteristics: they are of the age to have been so

*Figure 11.2* An icon of heterosexual desirability – Peter Wyngarde as *Jason King* (1971).

christened during the heyday of *Department S* and *Jason King*, and they come from working-class backgrounds. It isn't hard to see the appeal of Wyngarde's King for those men's mothers. King's fantastical adventures in fabulous, fabulized locations offered them brief windows of escape. The series was the polar opposite of kitchen-sink naturalism, and hence exerted a particular appeal to women seeking to shove the ever-present demands of the kitchen sink to the back of their minds. Working-class audiences relish escapism, since there is much in their lives that prompts dreams of escape: it is only middle-class educators, aesthetes and evangelicals who see any beauty or nobility in the cultural representation of repetitive drudgery.

*Jason King* tapped into the same veins of wish-fulfilment fantasy once catered for by escapist film genres. Pam Cook's analysis of the 1940s cycle of Gainsborough melodramas (Cook, 1996) has argued that those films allowed British female working-class audiences to relish a heady melange of romantic narratives, strong men (played by stars like Stewart Granger), international settings and lavish costumes. That's a recipe from which *King* stole several ingredients. Analogously, Joanne Lacey's study of how working-class women in Liverpool enjoyed Hollywood musicals (Lacey, 1999) reveals how the pressures of domesticity are related to the allure of glamour and excess. *King* was not a musical, but its emphasis on utopian lifestyles and its delight in sensuous *mise-en-scène* offered comparable pleasures.

Bearing in mind those traditions of escapist consumption, and remembering the historical context of the very early 1970s, King's magnetism for heterosexual women seems wholly understandable. In their consumption of King, the queer facets of his dandy image were either simply not perceptible or were irrelevant compared to the appeal of his romantic, almost aristocratic, hedonism. His rejection of run-of-the-mill masculinities made him not a fairified fop but a rarefied stylist. He promised to whisk you away from chips in Ipswich to oysters in Antibes. He was the romantic lead in a musical without songs, Heathcliff in cravat and flares, a Byronic hero for the Bond generation, Stewart Granger gone Carnaby crazy.

## MR QUEERLY: KING, *KING* AND HOMOSEXUALITY

Even if some female viewers did detect the wrinkle of queerness in the cut of King's cape, this merely placed him in a long line of might-be-queer icons worshipped by heterosexual fans. As Sheryl Garratt has noted in her account of female pop fandom:

> A touch of homosexuality seems to *enhance* a male star's popularity with women, in fact – especially if it is carefully denied elsewhere … . Perhaps it makes them safer. Or perhaps this hint of deviancy titillates. Maybe even women feel that they would be the one to mother the boy, to love him and set him back on the right path.
>
> (Garratt, 1990: 402–3, emphasis in original)

This is not entirely applicable to King, primarily because Wyngarde's age made the label of 'boy' far from applicable. Similarly, the connections made later by Garratt between the sexual ambiguity of the boy pop star's persona and his androgynous appearance, don't work with King, whose luxuriantly hairy chest is unleashed on the slightest pretext and whose moustache is a visual badge of 'King-ness' that might even outstrip his dressing gown for emblematic centrality. Nevertheless, Garratt's contention that a sprinkling of homosexuality can help to prompt heterosexual female interest seems irrefutable when looking at the history of British popular culture. A line can be traced from covertly homosexual idols such as the writer/actor Ivor Novello, whose greatest successes came in Ruritanian fantasy musicals which drew on iconographies of exotic escape not at all dissimilar to certain Gainsborough melodramas and some *Jason King* episodes (see Harding, 1997), to contemporary gay performers like the partly-out and partly-outed George Michael and Stephen Gateley.

Wyngarde in the persona of King represents an especially interesting point on that graph. In many ways, this was the last time that the majority audience for an iconic television hero would overlook those elements of sexual ambivalence that delighted minorities who were watching more deviously. In fact, it could be argued that Jason King, with his quasi-queer codings so unabashedly on show, marked the precise point at which an 'innocent' reading of such a persona became unsustainable. In the years after *King*, cultural and social shifts ensured that camp, queer and homosexual threads in texts became steadily harder to ignore. Indeed, given the centrality of camp to the Pop Art boom of the 1960s, it's mildly astonishing that King's queenliness didn't register more than it did. I suspect the hirsute look was crucial here. King may have been a symphony of silky swirls, but the 'tache and the chest hair still contradicted prevailing stereotypes of homosexual men as plucked, girlish nancies. A juicy irony here is that from the mid-1970s onwards gay male subcultures strenuously sought to masculinize their visual styles. With the rise of butch, clone and leather looks, body and facial hair were cultivated and eroticized, eventually being parodically packaged in the shape of the Village People. Viewed through this lens, Jason King seems doubly queer – a Village Person before his time, yet still encased in the bouffant hairdo and ruffled frontage of the Carnaby queen.

Wyngarde's own sexuality is clearly pivotal here, although since he has never, to my knowledge, made any public disclosure on this subject, it is not possible to affix any unequivocal label to him. It is both possible and interesting, however, to note that prior to *Jason King* he appeared in several open or coded homosexual roles in television dramas, at a time when to do so was a much more conspicuous and career-risking decision: a TV version of *Rope* as early as 1950; *South* (1959), a play refused a public theatre licence because of its direct treatment of homosexuality; *On Trial* (1960), in which he played the executed Irish politician Roger Casement, whose scandalous diaries revealed his homosexuality; as Garry Essendine in *Present Laughter* (1964), a Noel Coward farce centred on a thinly-disguised self-portrait of a demandingly queeny, dressing-gown-clad writer. Wyngarde then prefaced his stint as King with notably camp guest star slots in both *The Avengers* and *The Saint*. Of course, plenty of heterosexual actors have played queers – but few did so back then, and certainly not quite so often. Once this curriculum vitae is placed alongside the roaring flamboyance of King the character and the queer nuances of *King* the series, all those acres of lavender seem unusually intriguing.

Speculation about Wyngarde's sexuality inevitably orients my understanding and enjoyment of *Jason King* in particular directions. It facilitates a reading of the series as an extended camp jest, with King's hyperheterosexuality the droll centrepiece of the comedy. I watch *King* to enjoy the spectacle of Wyngarde subjecting the super-straight super-stud persona to protracted ridicule. The political potential of camp, for me at least, resides in its capacity to reveal the arbitrariness, the performativity, and hence the mutability, of gender roles. *Jason King* is great camp because of Wyngarde's calculated outrageousness as King, the flagrant theatricality of his acting, his refusal to pretend for one second that the texts he was performing, the genre they inhabited and the framework of gender relations on which that genre depended, were anything other than profoundly foolish. Leon Hunt (1998: 71–72) has expressed concern that earlier comments of mine celebrating *King*'s camp dimensions overlooked the series' misogyny, but Hunt's well-meant anxiety overlooks two important points. First, the gratuitously sexist comments King makes and the pervasive air of insufferable male arrogance he oozes don't strike me as being endorsed in the series: they are instead part of what is held up for mockery. Second, if camp is a queer strategy that seeks to undermine the ideological hegemony of heterosexuality, then heterosexual women who buy into and profit from that regime are legitimate targets as well as heterosexual men. If *King* is, pardon the expression, bent on subverting conventional gender hierarchies through an excessively camp depiction of sexual polarities, it would lose half its effectiveness if it only ridiculed the preposterous struttings of ultra-macho men and spared from attack the ultra-feminine women who flocked twitteringly around them.

A final issue that needs raising in this section is the range of queer and camp codings in the series that extend beyond King himself. Such codings flourish across the whole action TV genre (think of the cravat-heavy male bonding in *The Persuaders!*, note the drag queen femininities of *Charlie's Angels*, and ask yourself whether there has ever been a more perfectly polished example of overground camp than the Diana Rigg years of *The Avengers*) but their closeness in *Jason King* to King himself gives them a special tension. Mostly, these codings cohere around particular villains that King confronts, many of them intriguingly placed in pairings, though the precise contours of the coupledom are left open to interpretation. In 'A Thin Band Of Air', for example, the kidnapper Hewlett has his bedroom walls plastered with bodybuilder beefcake photos (snapped by the proprietor of Vince menswear?), cradles a pet bunny rabbit, plans his life via his horoscope (not exactly a manly preoccupation) and expresses his wish to be revenged on Jason King in droolingly physical detail, while his sidekick, René, displays that brand of all-purpose feline smarminess often allocated to queers in this genre. (Balancing the picture, King is helped out in the case by two male friends, Armand and Gregoire, who seem as fond of each other as they are uninterested in the women who drift through the episode.)

Consider, also, Sandro and Dacre in 'Buried In The Cold, Cold Ground', who not only dabble in queer sartorial codes – Sandro goes for a double whammy at one point with a florid cravat *over* a white roll neck – but also leave their male murder victim noticeably under-dressed. He wears trousers when they arrive at his hotel room, but is found dead later wearing only shirt and underpants. Perhaps a continuity error, perhaps a sly gesture at unrepresentable acts. Then there is the very close relationship between the deceitful English aristocrat and his blindingly blond, Aryan-chic German manservant in 'The Constance Missal'. The latter episode also boasts what might just be a lesbian couple in the shape of the two female thieves, but lesbian imagery is difficult to sustain in a series so committed to displaying narrative heterosexuality while flirting with subtextual male homosexuality. These sexually ambiguous villains parade across the series in an attempt to bolster King's heterosexuality (though to queer eyes it may well have the opposite effect). Similar strategies of displacement – Jason's not queer, but these strange people are – also underpin the programme's rare, regrettable lapses into homophobic humour, exemplified by King's laboured insistence in 'A Deadly Line In Digits' on pronouncing Mr Quirly's name as 'Mr Queerly'. The urge to respond with 'it takes one to know one' is hard to suppress.

## A SHAGMASTER IN CYBERSPACE: *KING* AND KITSCH

The final dimension of *King* consumption to consider is kitsch, the role played by the series in that broad wave of reappropriative irony which is so central to the recent history of popular cultural aesthetics. Under this rubric, *King* is a benchmark text both for its exposition of particularly extreme sexual politics and for its similarly alarming repertoire of style and fashion codes. In both cases, the pleasures of the series for kitsch-seekers lie in its irredeemability: it says things and wears things that are no longer acceptable, giving it the lure of forbidden fruit and the frisson of political incorrectness.

The rediscovery through irony of the popular culture of previous generations – a process encompassing fashion, music, film, television, advertising, even academic texts like the book you are at this moment reading – is both a tempting and a troubling phenomenon. It tempts many, myself included, by opening up a space for critiques of outmoded attitudes. Its troubling dimensions stem from the fact that since irony is a discourse most accessible to privileged groups, those who mock through pastiche the taste codes of earlier eras need to guard against retrospective condescension, snobbery disguised as hindsight, in which the processes of kitsch appropriation mock not only the artefacts and outlooks of another time but the foolishness of those who consumed or espoused them. The retro-irony reading of King, as I suggested earlier, is sometimes fuelled by misogyny and class prejudice towards a ridiculed 'implied other', the female working-class fans of the original series. Even when this is not the case, many kitsch readings stay at the level of superficial taste games, lacking any wider cultural critique.

To see this process in full flow, visit the website 'Jason's Groovy Pad' (website addresses are listed at the end of the chapter). Over a backdrop of eye-popping early 1970s wallpaper, the site invites you to savour photographs of Wyngarde as King, read details of his two television series, and even e-mail 'King' (presumably the heavily fantasizing website author) who will then reply in typical fashion either as 'Jason' or as

'Nicola', his publishing editor in the series who has been demoted on the website to a mere PA. A typical letter begins:

> Dear Mr King,
>     My orange bellbottoms almost exploded with delight to find your website! After pouring a stiff brandy and putting some Mantovani on the hi-fi I sat down by the fireplace on my purple crush velvet sofa, I resolved to send you an e-mail to express my delight …

Here, and throughout the site, *Jason King* is a text worshipped under the kitsch mantra of 'it's-so-bad-it's-good'. TV cable channels which specialize in broadcasting series like *Jason King* join in the game, using continuity announcements and publicity material to fix the parameters of ironic consumption. A Granada Plus trailer for *The Saint* lovingly jibes at the series as coming from a time 'when back projection took you anywhere around Elstree', referring to the programme's tendency to suggest exotic foreign locales with clumsily obvious studio back projection. The kitsch aesthetic, then, is an invitation to wallow in tackiness, to underline the goodness of our good taste by demonstrating our ability to identify and luxuriate in the badness of bad taste. The unforgivable faux pas would be to enjoy the likes of *King* with a genuine, non-ironic enthusiasm.

The reference to Mantovani in the website letter links King with another branch of the kitsch boom, the rediscovery and rebranding through irony of easy listening music. One series of easy listening compilations, The Sound Gallery, both includes the theme music from *Jason King* and reprints in the sleevenotes a tribute poem to its composer Lawrie Johnson, purportedly written by 'King' himself. The Sound Gallery website employs a linguistic register deeply redolent of King's world: 'Jet setter couples … in a velour and glass decorated penthouse suite … . Afternoons by the pool sipping Campari and making millions with a single phone call … .' In the discursive world of the easy listening revival, a subversive delight in taste transgression that playfully refutes established rock music aesthetics can slide into a more questionable nostalgia for the social world that spawned the sounds – in particular, I would argue, the sexual politics of that world. The marketing of this music mobilizes an iconography of bachelor lifestyles, Rat Pack masculinities, debonair playboys who can call on endless streams of compliant, leggy women. This may be couched in terms of irony, but beneath the knowing smirks sit worrying attitudes. The sexual semiotics of bachelor-pad kitsch cloak a nostalgia for life before feminism.

Appropriately, the King text which best exemplifies this syndrome is the record album Peter Wyngarde made in 1970 to cash in on the success of *Department 'S'*. It rapidly sold out its original pressing, but no further copies were released, due to the controversial nature of the track 'Rape'. The scarcity of the record, and the fact that video reissues and cable channel revivals of *Department 'S'* and *Jason King* had placed Wyngarde high in the pantheon of 1970s kitsch, made it a sought-after cult item. Consequently the album was released on CD in 1998, with the title changed from 'Peter Wyngarde' to 'When Sex Leers Its Inquisitive Head', a line from the original sleevenotes written by Wyngarde in the persona of King. Within the discourse of King-kitsch, the aspects of the album which once proved its undoing become its chief attraction, with the publicity, sleevenotes and reviews all pinpointing 'Rape' as the key track. This is understandable, since 'Rape' is an extraordinarily revealing document, but what it reveals to me is that some elements of the King persona need to be vigorously criticized, not indulged under the banner of kitsch.

The album begins with a track called 'Come In', which consists of Wyngarde/King welcoming a female dinner guest into his home. 'Let me take your coat ... . Do go in ... . Here's to a pleasant evening and a few surprises'. 'Rape' follows shortly afterwards, and consists mostly of Wyngarde/King listing different national styles of rape, while the music changes accordingly. In France, he tells us, 'rape is hardly ever necessary' (the mind-boggling implication, therefore, is that in other contexts rape *is* necessary), while the section on Russia features male backing vocals singing 'raaa-aape' to the tune of 'The Song of the Volga Boatmen'. The supposed humour here might just be more tolerable if the track hadn't begun with the sound of animalistic male grunts and a protracted female scream.

Elsewhere, the album veers between the banal and the bizarre. 'Hippie and the Skinhead' begins with Wyngarde reading out a letter written to a newspaper by two skinhead girls about how society misunderstands them. Then, over incongruously twangy country music, he delivers a lyric about a hippie and a skinhead involved in some kind of violent and/or sexual encounter. The exact details are hard to decipher, but the fact that it takes in queerbashing, cross-dressing and cottaging (sex between men in public toilets) suggests a familiarity with gay subcultural slang – 'troll the Dilly' (look for sex at Piccadilly Circus) is one phrase that emerges loud and clear from the indistinct mix. Other tracks feature recitations of poetry, cod-medieval ballads, love songs sung in French and post-Beatles pop. It is, undeniably, a treasure trove of kitsch excess, yet to call 'Rape' kitsch starkly reveals the limitations of that aesthetic.

One review of the album in an on-line magazine (Whited, 1999) commends the record to 'true fans of *Austin Powers*, *The Avengers*, or other campy shagmaster-type characters'. This is the dispiriting voice of depoliticized kitsch, where giggling at a pair of flared trousers takes precedence over questioning an attempt to turn sexual brutalization into comedy, and where there is a palpable nostalgia for a pre-feminist world in which sexual liberation meant the chance for men to earn status by screwing around as much as they liked. Kitsch strategies, as this example shows, can all too easily drift from an attempt at wrong-footing the stuffier, more humourless end of 'political correctness' to an endorsement of those reactionary worldviews which 'PC' set out, quite rightly, to challenge. This is where the fundamental differences between kitsch and camp need to be spelled out, since many who trade in the irony market (note Whited's use of 'campy') mistakenly see them as identical. They are in fact anything but, and what differentiates them is their relationship to politics.

For gay men, as I have argued at length elsewhere (Medhurst, 1997), camp is rooted in the experience of social marginalization. Historically, it utilized one of the few cultural spaces open to queers (the space of the wit) as a launching pad for its attack on the norms and hierarchies of heterosexual privilege. Kitsch is camp without the politics, camp de-fanged, camp reduced to a game about taste, camp stripped of its ability to undermine through mischief, camp shorn of its critical purpose and recast as mere play. Camp, for gay men, can be a life-saver – kitsch, for slumming straights, is little more than a brief holiday from respectability. 'Rape' is the test case here: it may be kitsch, but it has no place in my conception of camp. I may have said above that camp sometimes needed to target heterosexual femininity as much as heterosexual masculinity, but there are limits to this, and 'Rape' shows with graphic exactness precisely where those limits are.

## KINGS AND QUEENS: FINAL THOUGHTS

If it does nothing else, this exploration of *Jason King* establishes the importance of insisting on the multiplicity of meanings that attach themselves to media texts. Furthermore, it shows how that multiplicity is not made up of irreconcilably polarized opposites but consists of overlapping, interwoven threads. It would have been easy to assume, for example, that the kitsch and camp versions of *King* had made the adoring female fan standpoint unsustainable, but that assumption is swiftly detonated by visiting another website. 'The Hellfire Club' is the official Peter Wyngarde fan site, and while it borrows a few words from the dictionary of kitsch, describing Wyngarde as one of 'the righteous, velvet-suited dudes to step out of the Seventies', it ranges far beyond the single role of King. The site surveys Wyngarde's entire career, includes interview material with the man himself rather than a masquerade 'Jason', and lovingly places him as an object of heterosexual female desire. It's worlds away from the kitsch confines of 'Jason's Groovy Pad', proving that King, like any significant media icon, is very much up for grabs. King and queen, fop and stud, misogynistic shagmaster and subversive jester – he remains all these and more.

Indeed, the only people who seem distressed by the diversity of interpretations applicable to King are a few men scribbling on the internet who long to be able to enjoy action series 'innocently', untroubled by the complexities of sexual identity that thirty years of interpretation and reinterpretation have brought into play. Their yearning to regress is frequently characterized by homophobic asides. The Internet Movie Database pages on *Department 'S'* contain the verdict that:

> ... flamboyant hero Jason King was over the top even for those days and now looks like a buffoon. When it became public in the 70s that Wyngarde was something considerably less in real life than the suave ladykiller he portrayed, then the 'campness' of the character took on a whole different meaning. So much so in fact that it is difficult to take this once enthralling show seriously any more. The follow up series *Jason King* ... is too awful to be described (Mount, 1999).

Somewhere out there, clearly, there are men who would still like to take *Department 'S'* seriously, who can't believe in any story in which queers play heterosexuals (a stricture which would wipe out around 90 per cent of Hollywood cinema), and who are so traumatized by the thought of campness that they have to quarantine the word inside inverted commas. I may have spent time in this chapter insisting that all reading positions deserve respect, but some people, frankly, are beyond help.

## REFERENCES

Cohn, Nik (1971) *Today There Are No Gentlemen: The Changes in Englishmen's Clothes Since the War*, London: Weidenfeld and Nicolson.

Cook, Pam (1996) *Fashioning the Nation: Costume and Identity in British Cinema*, London: BFI.

Dyer, Richard (1994) 'Fashioning Change: Gay Men's Style', in Emma Healy and Angela Mason (eds), *Stonewall 25: The Making of the Lesbian and Gay Community in Britain*, London: Virago.

Garratt, Sheryl (1990) 'Teenage Dreams', in Simon Frith and Andrew Goodwin (eds), *On Record: Rock, Pop and the Written Word*, London: Routledge.

Grahn, Judy (1984) *Another Mother Tongue: Gay Words, Gay Worlds*, Boston: Beacon.

Harding, James (1997) *Ivor Novello: A Biography*, Cardiff: Welsh Academic Press.

Howes, Keith (1993) *Broadcasting It: An Encyclopaedia of Homosexuality on Film, Radio and TV in the UK 1923–1993*, London: Cassell.

Hunt, Leon (1998) *British Low Culture: From Safari Suits to Sexploitation*, London: Routledge.

Lacey, Joanne (1999) 'Seeing Through Happiness: Hollywood Musicals and the Construction of the American Dream in Liverpool in the 1950s', *Journal of Popular British Cinema*, No. 2.

Medhurst, Andy (1991) 'Batman, Deviance and Camp', in Roberta Pearson and William Urrichio (eds), *The Many Lives of the Batman*, London: BFI.

—— (1997) 'Camp', in Andy Medhurst and Sally R. Munt (eds), *Lesbian and Gay Studies: A Critical Introduction*, London: Cassell.

Mount, Alan (1999) IMDB user comments for *Department 'S'*, http://us.imdb.com/ CommentsShow?63893. (Accessed 20.5.01.)

Whited, David (1999) Review of Peter Wyngarde CD, http://ink19.com/issues_f/99_09. (Accessed 20.5.01.)

## WEBSITES

The Hellfire Club, http://www.hermes58.freeserve.co.uk (Accessed 20.5.01.)

Jason King's Groovy Pad, http://members.tripod.com/~waynetiki/ (Accessed 20.5.01.)

The Sound Gallery, http://www.scamp-records.com/sound_gallery (Accessed 20.5.01.)

# PART IV

# THE CULTURAL CIRCULATION OF THE ACTION TV SERIES

## 12

# TV GETS JAZZED

## The evolution of
## action TV theme music

*Elizabeth Withey*

Dramatic, swinging jazz writing and improvisation in the modern idiom has
all but taken over the many current TV series concerned with crime. Singu-
larly meaningful, jazz-based tone painting, paralleling action and emotions in
a contemporary way, has appeared and taken hold. The music heard thus far
has been generally impressive, and has stimulated and affected the average TV
viewer to the point where conversation concerning these whodunnits is
equally divided between the plots, characters and the music.

(LP liner notes to Leith Stevens and His Orchestra,
*Jazz Themes for Cops and Robbers*, Coral Records, 1959)

### MUSIC OVER MIND: THE CONNOTATIVE POWER OF
### THE TV THEME

Television theme songs have been absorbed into the individual and communal
consciousness. Themes which originally signified a current television programme
have come to symbolize historic eras. For example, the first four descending notes of
the original *Star Trek* theme instantly call to mind the late 1960s and its characteristic
combination of utopian ideals and conservative colonialism embodied in the moon
walk and the Vietnam war. Likewise, the insistent rhythms and brass of the *Hawaii
Five-O* theme bring to mind collective memories of plunging waterfalls, jiggling hips,
and tough, bouffant-coiffured cops. These instant associations are possible because of
the peculiar ability of sound to fuse memory and emotion, so that when a melody is
heard, the original thought, memory, and/or emotion is triggered and rises in the
mind.[1] We have a kind of Pavlovian response to music. We hear it and we remember,
or we hear it and we feel. Music is a tool which can bypass 'rational' thought – plug-
ging directly into emotions, memories, mind. If we have enjoyed a television show
once, chances are that when we hear its theme playing in the next room, we will put
down what we're doing, walk through, and watch.

In action TV series, music played a crucial role in defining the genre from the
outset. Blake Edwards' creation, *Peter Gunn* (1958–61), with its jazz theme and

191

incidental music composed by Henry Mancini, became the show that set the standard for action series music for years to come.

## SHOOTING WITH THE MUSIC IN MIND: HENRY MANCINI, JAZZ, AND THE *PETER GUNN* PHENOMENON

In retrospect, the marriage of jazz and action TV series seems an obvious match. As a twentieth-century American art form born in New Orleans' brothels and raised in Paris nightclubs, jazz could create a sense of contemporaneity and automatic associations to the nightlife nether-worlds so often inhabited by the characters of action series.

By the time *Peter Gunn* hit TV screens in 1958, jazz was already beginning to be associated with a masculine archetype which would dominate action film and television through the 1960s. The representative of this new masculinity was sophisticated, suave, a connoisseur of fine things – wine, art, food, music – and, of course, beautiful women.[2] He possessed an air of virility and sexual licence. Though he was an independent thinker, in some ways a maverick, this archetypal male almost always worked for and/or reported to an overarching entity. He was a new breed of 'anti-establishment establishmentarian' who, when he went to a jazz club, wore a sharp suit rather than a black turtleneck and matching beret. Jazz (in particular, modern jazz) was becoming associated with an acceptable form of intellectual hedonism – laid-back, yet also intellectual and discerning.[3]

*Playboy* magazine was one of the chief promoters of this link between the new masculinity and jazz. From its launch in 1953 through the 1960s, *Playboy* consistently ran reviews of new jazz albums, together with features and photo-spreads related to the world of jazz and jazz musicians. The early 1950s saw *Playboy* take several steps to further cement its links to jazz. In 1955 the magazine launched an annual *Playboy* Jazz Poll – 'the biggest, most successful popularity poll ever conducted in the field of jazz music' (*Playboy*, February, 1957). By 1957 the poll had generated *The Playboy Jazz Allstars* album, featuring many of the finest jazz artists of the day,[4] followed in 1959 by *Playboy*'s sponsorship of its own Jazz Festival – an instant success which, over thirty years later, remains one of the most prestigious jazz events in the world. By deliberately cultivating these associations, *Playboy* linked both itself and its readership to the stylish and intelligent connotations that surrounded modern jazz. And by continuing, through the 1960s, to show a preference for jazz over rock 'n' roll, the magazine could promote an image that was hip and street-smart, while at the same time sophisticated and clearly set apart from the more rebellious and subversive connotations of the burgeoning youth subculture.

Jazz was also Mancini's natural choice for *Peter Gunn* – Blake Edwards' private eye hero who spent his off-hours in a jazz club ('Mother's') and dated the female singer of the resident band. Mancini's jazz theme neatly encapsulated the character's off-beat panache (Burlingame, 1996: 31).[5] As a creative form, however, jazz did not conform easily to the constraints of television. Rooted in improvisation, jazz was at odds with the restrictions inherent in TV production. Although Mancini handled the synthesis of jazz and television with great success, others had more difficulty. For example, Count Basie's driving brass and piano heard in the theme to the tough police drama, *M Squad* (1957–60), was judged too large a sound to sustain the show's underscore (Burlingame, 1996: 34). Moreover, the problems inherent in merging the artistic processes of jazz and the production methods of TV became glaringly apparent when Duke Ellington was commissioned to compose music for the ABC pilot of *The Asphalt Jungle* (1961). As Harry Lojewski, the MGM music supervisor involved with the Ellington recording session, remembered:

> Frankly, there were a lot of problems with Duke's score. They were very disorganized. They finally had to lock the doors of the scoring stage because every time they'd call a 'ten' the band would go to the bar next door. Finally some of them came in and set up a little bar behind their music stands. Many cues were done, but Duke didn't understand what the timing was all about. So during the final dubbing of the pilot, there had to be a lot of editing.
>
> (see Burlingame, 1996: 43)

Why was it, then, that Mancini had such overwhelming success in using a jazz score for *Peter Gunn* – the thirty-minute show often having as much as fifteen minutes of music per episode? His success was due, in part, to Blake Edwards' enthusiasm for jazz. According to Mancini, Blake Edwards 'has always been a kind of hip guy – he liked jazz, he always played it, and loved it' (see Brown, 1994: 300). Moreover, Mancini was struck by the way Edwards considered music an integral part of the narrative. The jazz score was intrinsic to the creation of slick storylines and enigmatic characters, Mancini remembering how the director 'always used to shoot with the music in mind' (see Smith, 1998: 76).

Blake Edwards' enthusiasm was, however, only one factor in the success of Mancini's score. One of the other most important reasons for the show's musical success was the fact that viewers could actually hear it. Prior to *Peter Gunn*, the sound quality of music accompanying TV programmes was generally poor. Often entire rhythm sections were recorded with only one centralized microphone – which could mean that an acoustic bass would never be clearly heard over a trap set and piano. According to Mancini, before *Peter Gunn* 'People had never heard a walking bass behind a scene before, unless it sounded like it was coming from the toilet or something like that' (see Brown, 1994: 301). Mancini brought the sound out of the toilet by incorporating miking techniques which were innovative for the period. He miked certain instruments (such as acoustic bass and flutes) individually, adjusting the sound in the dubbing room so that high and low pitches (usually lost in the television mix) were equalized to the core of the sound. For the first time every member of a jazz combo – like the thirteen-member group that recorded the *Gunn* score – could play over television and be heard (Brown, 1994: 300–301). Blake Edwards' appreciation of jazz, coupled with Mancini's miking techniques, also allowed the *Gunn* combo to incorporate a degree of improvisation in the theme – an element of jazz never successfully repeated in subsequent TV scores.

Another important reason for the great success of the music from *Peter Gunn* is that each episode featured an original score. This apparently simple concept was actually a major sea-change in television production. Prior to 1958, strictures set by James C. Petrillo (then President of the American Federation of Musicians' Union) meant that most TV shows could not afford to use original scores and were tracked with pre-recorded cues from purchased libraries. Petrillo held that the use of recorded music, whether in film, radio, phonograph records, or television, was detrimental to musicians' chances of being employed for 'live' performances (Burlingame, 1996: 4). And in 1950 his requirement that TV networks pay a 5 per cent levy on the cost of every show using 'live' musicians made the cost of using original music prohibitive for most television productions. Though some programmes – notably *Dragnet* (1951–59) and *Danger* (1950–55) – did use original music, such shows were the exception rather than the rule.[6]

Union policy finally changed in 1958. Pressure in Los Angeles culminated in the formation of a new union and prompted Petrillo's resignation – his successors no longer demanding the prohibitive 5 per cent levy (Burlingame, 1996: 29). The change in union policy cleared the way not only for Mancini's success with *Peter Gunn*, but for a veritable explosion in original music for television – with scores for action series leading the way.

In the late 1950s theme music became increasingly big business.[7] Indeed, the lucrative potential of the *Peter Gunn* score was recognized almost immediately by Alan Livingston, Vice President in charge of television programming at NBC. Livingston had formerly worked in the music business and, after seeing the *Gunn* pilot, he made a call to contacts at RCA records. Just one week after *Peter Gunn* first aired, RCA recorded an album of the show's music – *The Music from 'Peter Gunn'*. Within five months the record was rated number one in the *Billboard* album charts (a position it held for ten weeks) and was not only nominated for an Emmy, but was named 'Album of the Year' at the 1959 Grammy Awards. Inevitably a second album followed: this time *More Music from 'Peter Gunn'* (see Figure 12.1), which received six Grammy nominations and climbed to number seven in the *Billboard* charts (Burlingame, 1996: 32–33). The revenue possibilities of television theme music, therefore, appeared astronomical and, after the success of *Peter Gunn*, recordings were released of scores from almost every action TV series produced.

Another consequence of the action TV music explosion was a cross-pollination between the television industry and composers writing for film. Jazz had been used in film scores prior to *Gunn* (notably, Elmer Bernstein's 1955 score for *The Man with the Golden Arm*), but it was largely non-improvisational in style. Composers working in the film industry were frequently classically trained and most film music was still written in the nineteenth-century style of the late Romantic composers. As film composers began to work in the field of TV, however, their traditional (fully-scored) style began to combine with the tempo and idioms of jazz, creating a style of theme music which would become a defining feature of action TV series for the next decade – a non-improvisational, jazz-based style which we could term 'action jazz'.

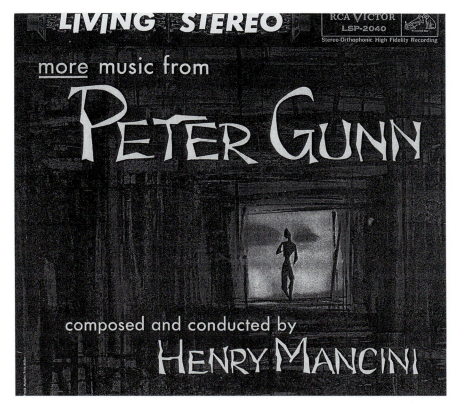

*Figure 12.1* Peter Gunn launches the action jazz phenomenon.

### ACTION JAZZ SCORES A HIT

Action jazz utilized idiomatic jazz sounds – blue notes, mute trumpets, swinging rhythms, screeching saxophones – but did not allow for improvisation. These idiomatic jazz sounds became a way of punctuating TV programmes – fully-scored and timed for specific cues, they might be used to announce the show or lead climactically into a commercial break. Mancini had called this genre 'dramatic jazz' as opposed to 'real jazz' because it lacked improvisation (Smith, 1998: 74). Though other composers termed it 'semi-jazz' or 'jazz-oriented', the action jazz theme came to be a cornerstone of the action TV series. Viewers came to expect trumpet blasts to accompany fight scenes, percussion alongside chase sequences, and a sliding clarinet or saxophone as the hero leaned in to kiss the love interest for that week. And most of all, viewers came to expect jazz sounds in their favourite weekly theme songs.

By the early 1960s the jazz sounds viewers were familiar with were being influenced by events on both sides of the Atlantic. At the same time as English pop musicians became fascinated with American rock 'n' roll, America became increasingly interested in all things British. The coming of the James Bond series to the big screen with *Dr. No* in 1962 popularized the swinging, jet-setting, spy figure – accompanied by musical scores featuring electric guitar.

John Barry is usually credited for the pulsing 'guitar twang' riff synonymous with Bond. Barry had spent some time as a big band arranger, but it was as the leader of the John Barry Seven that he began to make an impact in the music business. Barry thrust the Seven into the exploding rock 'n' roll scene. The band initially imitated various rock 'n' roll standards, but carved out its own niche by developing a unique instrumental sound that fused racy guitar twang with heavy, dramatic brass – a combination that became the quintessential sound of Bond (Fiegel, 1998: 96). Perhaps surprisingly, however, Barry does not receive a writing credit for the 'James Bond Theme'. Bond film producers Harry Saltzman and Albert Broccoli had originally engaged composer Monty Norman to compose the entire score to *Dr. No*, specifically requesting 'a calypso song about the exploits of James Bond' and a 'Scottish theme … to distinguish James Bond throughout the picture' (Smith, 1998: 107). Broccoli and Saltzman got the Calypso they wanted, but were disappointed with Norman's version of the Bond theme – the characteristic guitar riff worked well, but the whole composition seemed to move at a 'funeral pace' (Fiegel, 1998: 95). At practically the last minute, then, John Barry was drafted in to revamp the piece and, using the twang and brass sound he had developed with the John Barry Seven, he crafted the theme which has woven itself through the Bond film series ever since.[8] Barry's amalgamation of 'rock guitar twang' and dramatic brass also inaugurated a new sub-genre of 'action jazz' in film and TV themes. Echoes of Barry's style, for example, can be heard in John Mulendore's theme to *Honey West* (1965–66) and Laurie Johnson's score to the later series of *The Avengers* – both compositions pairing guitar twang with up-tempo jazz and/or utilizing the structural device of the brass-dominated swing break to bring out different moods within the theme.

Barry's style of 'action jazz' adeptly embodied the themes of glamorous sophistication and masculine sexual power that were at the heart of the 1960s spy vogue that followed the success of the Bond films. Indeed, these associations became unmistakable on many of the sleeves to the various compilation albums spawned from the Bond craze (see Figure 12.2). Nor were these associations lost on entrepreneurs in other commercial fields. By the mid-1960s, for example, *Penthouse* magazine was promoting itself as a British contender to the *Playboy* throne and the magazine's attempt to establish a reputation for stylish hip was exemplified in the release of its own 'Bondian' jazz LP – *Penthouse Magazine Presents the Bedside Bond* (Decca, 1965). As *Penthouse* explained in its promotion of the album, the magazine liked to see a clear affinity between itself, the laid-back confidence of jazz and the jet-setting world of 007:

> Bond is basically a lone wolf, a sybarite and a man of action – his sexploits are legend, his tastes incomparable. PENTHOUSE enjoys the same exclusivity of direction, taste and unbending individuality. It seemed only natural that a

*Figure 12.2*   Action jazz and the sixties spy craze.

mixture of Bond and PENTHOUSE with a boudoir beat to bridge the gap
and a bed to set the stage would groove with audiophiles everywhere.
(*Penthouse,* October/November, 1966)

In America, meanwhile, a growing cultural obsession with all things English was
instrumental in prompting the purchase of British action TV shows by the American
networks. These programmes presented a variety of scenarios loosely framed in the
spy genre popularized by the Bond films. Among those most popular in the United
States were *The Avengers, The Saint,* and *Danger Man* (*Secret Agent* in its American
incarnation) – and all had 'action jazz' themes.

*The Avengers* was already in its second incarnation when it reached the American
market in 1966. The earlier, black and white versions of the series which date from
1961 projected an aura of British *film noir* and were scored accordingly. Much like
Mancini's score for *Peter Gunn,* the original jazz score for *The Avengers* (composed by

John Dankworth) used the small combo jazz sound to reflect a 'hard-boiled detective urbanism' (Miller, 1998: 97). Yet Dankworth's score was abandoned in 1965 when the music, along with the show's image, was transformed. This point saw the launch of the title sequence most usually associated with the series – featuring Patrick Macnee, Diana Rigg and a bubbling champagne bottle – together with a new score penned by Laurie Johnson. Johnson's music underlines the wit and sophistication of the show's lead characters. After a bongo-driven teaser, the theme opens with an upbeat ostinato on electric keyboard, over which is layered a sweeping triadic melody in strings. Macnee and Rigg pop champagne corks with pistols and lead viewers through a coy dance of sexual innuendo. In the closing credit sequence, meanwhile, the music opens with the keyboard/strings theme and then the style shifts to a big band brass sound (modelled on John Barry's 'Bondian' swing break) as the pair assume various fighting poses to demonstrate their mettle. Rigg executes a few balletic judo postures; Macnee points his umbrella threateningly. The music and visuals work together to set the slick, sexy and stylishly chic tone of the series.

Composed by Edwin Astley, the theme to *The Saint* (like that to *The Avengers*) uses swinging big band sounds and rhythms to set the tone for the series and its debonair hero. Played after the opening teaser of each episode, the theme presents a seven-note cell in antiphonal call-and-response, introduced by female voice and mute trumpet and answered in succession by guitar, drums, and flute (Burlingame, 1996: 208). With the theme music to *The Saint*, Astley began a dynasty of themes for ATV productions. While these were jazz-based (like the themes of American action series), Astley's style projected a lighter and more ironic tone than American 'action jazz'. Whereas Mancini's *Peter Gunn* score reflected an urban *noir* minimalism, and Count Basie's driving big band theme to *M Squad* projected the image of the larger-than-life American tough-guy, Astley's music swung to a lighter beat. His scores utilized jazz idioms to delineate a Bond-like sophistication, though on the smaller scale of television.

Astley's style is nowhere more evident than in his theme to *Danger Man* (1960–66) starring Patrick McGoohan as the international troubleshooter, John Drake. Notably, Astley's theme for the show – which he entitled 'High Wire' – does not use electric guitar, as might be expected of a British spy programme in the wake of Bond. Astley's choice of electric harpsichord as the primary instrument allows him to create a theme with no automatic associations to Bond's qualities of violence and sexuality – two aspects of the spy genre with which McGoohan had felt uncomfortable. Indeed, the harpsichord's limited potential for volume and depth of colour creates a chilling sound, and Astley's rigid rhythmic treatment (largely in keeping with the 1960s inter- pretation of Baroque music) produces a feeling of inflexibility. Yet Astley countered the rigidity of his harpsichord scoring with the edge and volume of brass and precise syncopation. In effect, Astley created a jazz-Baroque hybrid style – his unrelenting, percussive scoring for the harpsichord being offset by rigidly swinging brass to create a tangible sense of Baroque fugue.[9]

When *Danger Man* was networked in America by CBS during 1965, it was trans- formed into *Secret Agent* and given a new theme. The commission of new theme music no doubt had something to do with the increasing desire of film studios and TV networks to mine the vast amounts of revenue available from the recording industry – and by 1965 this meant tapping into the increasing youth market. The result was the first successful rock 'n' roll-based theme song (Burlingame, 1996: 209). Whereas Astley's 'High Wire' had consciously distanced itself from the electric guitar, 'Secret Agent Man' – composed by Phil Sloan and Steve Barri and sung by Johnny Rivers – is dominated by the instrument. The song's style was heavily influenced both by John Barry's (by that time famous) guitar-based Bond theme, as well as his then highly successful theme to *Goldfinger* (1964), sung by Shirley Bassey. At the time Sloan and Barri were composing 'Secret Agent Man' they had not seen the TV show itself, though Barri remembers: 'Basically, we were thinking that we were writing a James Bond theme. We just wanted to come up with a guitar hook for the beginning since the Bond theme had a guitar hook' (Burlingame, 1996: 209). Reaching number three in the *Billboard* charts, 'Secret Agent Man' proved immensely popular, cementing the associations of masculine power and sexuality developed in the world of Bond – even though, as Patrick McGoohan has observed of his character, 'Drake was the only secret agent who never carried a gun and never went to bed with a girl' (cited in Lewis and Stempel, 1996: 67).

## MARCHING TO A DIFFERENT DRUMMER: MARTIAL JAZZ, MODERN MYTHOLOGY AND MOOG

The American version of the TV spy genre found particular expression in two enormously successful programmes, *The Man from U.N.C.L.E.* (1964–69) and *Mission: Impossible* (1966–73). Working within the non-improvisational action jazz style, the themes to these programmes began a new stylistic era in themes for action TV series. This was marked by the rise of 'martial jazz' – an idiom which incorporated martial musical elements into the pre-existing 'action jazz' style composers were then using in music for action TV series.[10]

Composer Jerry Goldsmith used meter and instrumentation in unique ways to create a sense of off-balance militarism in *The Man from U.N.C.L.E.* theme. Goldsmith wrote the piece in 5/4 meter. This time signature creates a slight sense of musical vertigo in an otherwise march-like theme and accounts for much of the swing inherent in the music. Goldsmith chose to score the theme for brass, woodwinds and percussion, as well as prominently featuring instruments traditionally associated with military marching bands – for example, the piccolo, trumpet and snare drum. This instrumentation adds a militaristic colour to the piece while syncopated rhythms help to create the 'jazz feel' already associated with the action TV genre. The result is a feeling of off-balance militarism – of a world nearly (but not quite) in control.

Lalo Schifrin, composer of the theme to *Mission: Impossible* (perhaps one of the most memorable of all TV scores) worked for a time on *The Man from U.N.C.L.E.* after Goldsmith had left the series. Like the score from *U.N.C.L.E.*, the *Mission: Impossible* theme is composed in 5/4. According to Schifrin, he chose 5/4 because, 'We needed a theme for the main title that had to be a little more tongue-in-cheek. I wanted a little humour, lightness, a theme that wouldn't take itself too seriously … . There is something unpredictable about five/four' (see Burlingame, 1996: 205–6). Schifrin's music – scored for brass, flute and bongos – described a hip, paranoid militarism. Made up of three layers, the theme was structured around repetition. Ostinatos in brass and bongos supported a sequence built on a three-note pattern in flute, with a heavy downbeat at the beginning of each measure to provide the ear with an audible structure. As the theme raced to its conclusion, the flute theme entwined with brass and ended in an unresolved blast. This was a new kind of martial music. Like the show's agents, the theme gave a feeling of militarism with no 'officially sanctioned' military elements.

At the other end of the martial jazz spectrum is the theme to *Hawaii Five-O* (1968–80). In his music for *Five-O*, composer Morton Stevens created a new Hawaiian music and, for many viewers, a new Hawaii. No more the blissful days of gentle breezes and ukuleles. Stevens' music described a paradise where hard cops stepped to the beat of a Wagnerian marching band. Leonard Freeman, the show's creator, insisted on the show's sense of dead-pan grit as he described its central premise to Stevens – 'It's about a guy who's hard as a rock. And he's living on a rock. And he's hard'. Stevens interpreted Freeman's succinct description to mean that he wanted the music to portray a 'macho strength', and the *Five-O* theme was the result – Stevens later recalling that Freeman 'didn't want the typical Hawaiian sound, so I found a new Hawaiian sound that Hawaii didn't know it had' (see Burlingame, 1996: 50).

One show stands out for the way it wove together the conventions of action TV, the enigmas of absurdist theatre and the startling spectacle of the big top. *The Prisoner* had a suitably imaginative theme composed by Ron Grainer. Grainer's theme works together with the programme's dramatic title sequence to generate a tone that could be described as 'pop Teutonic opera' sprinkled with elements of Greek tragedy. Alongside Grainer's music, the opening sequence uses dramatic elements – thunderclaps, mime, and a kind of *Sprechstimme*[11] – to present the programme's back-story. Like everything else about *The Prisoner,* Grainer's theme was influenced to a large degree by the series' producer, director and star, Patrick McGoohan, who reputedly had whistled a version of the tune he wanted to Grainer (Carraze and Oswald, 1995: 220).

Aspects of *The Prisoner*'s score seem to be extensions of Astley's stylistic language in his original music for *Danger Man.* This may be because, like Astley's 'High Wire' theme, *The Prisoner*'s theme was originally conceived as a composition for harpsichord. This harpsichord version, composed by Grainer, was entitled 'The Age of Elegance' but was not deemed powerful enough to match McGoohan's vision for the series. As a result, Grainer reworked the harpsichord arrangement for two electric guitars, percussion, bass and brass. The guitars – scored in a fairly high, bright register – are more dramatic, but not unlike the sound of a harpsichord playing the same material. The use of guitar in this manner, then, gave the theme more power – but also served to underscore the show's associations with its predecessor, *Danger Man.*

Grainer's use of guitar also brought with it other associations. As with the revamped score to *Secret Agent* (which replaced Astley's 'High Wire' theme), the use of an electric guitar worked to summon up connotations of 007. Grainer's theme, therefore, managed to link *The Prisoner* not only to Patrick McGoohan's earlier successful series, but also to the whole spy genre that was then in fashion. Moreover, by sublimating the harpsichord style into guitar and incorporating elements of opera and tragedy, McGoohan's series announced its intention to present viewers with a modern 'classic'.

While McGoohan was creating myth, American action TV was increasingly trying to deal 'realistically' with issues of the day. Two programmes, *Ironside* (1967–75) and *Mod Squad* (1968–73), used innovative plot devices to bring a new sense of realism to the genre. Like their storylines, the scores to these two series utilized musical tools in (for television) new and innovative ways. Quincy Jones was engaged to compose the music for the *Ironside* pilot, and created a jazz-based score that was highly dramatic. Jones used unusual instruments, such as the cymbalum, to reflect what he described as the main character, Robert Ironside's 'metallic' character (Burlingame, 1996: 47).

When the *Ironside* pilot became a series, Jones composed a new, forty-second, title theme. This score retained the cymbalum, but added an instrument which would change the face of film composition. *Ironside* became the first television series to use the moog synthesizer. The synthesizer was the perfect solution to Jones' quest for an instrument which could create the effect of a police siren – though Jones toned down his musical style for the series after an NBC executive reputedly criticized his score for containing too much 'street music' (Burlingame, 1996: 48). Jones' theme for *Ironside* remains one of the most powerful examples of action jazz – one which pushed back the boundaries of television theme music as never before.

For the music of *Mod Squad*, composer Earle Hagen used other compositional techniques to stretch the existing bounds of television's action jazz style. Like *Ironside,* the show's premise and characters had much to do with determining the style of music. *Mod Squad* featured a trio of young hipsters working undercover for the Los Angeles police in violent, drug-ridden city streets – and in dance clubs where rock music could be daringly used in the programme's underscore. Rhythmic motifs in the show's theme matched the speed of the young detectives as they ran through dark, ominous alleyways – while the score's use of electric organ mimicked the prominence of the instrument in the rock music of the period. It was, though, in the programme's underscore that some of the most innovative musical elements existed. According to Hagen, the compositional team used 'rock and roll for open spots: chases, fights and things like that' but actually used serial techniques to create tension under dialogue (see Burlingame, 1996: 57–58).

## THE CHANGING OF THE GUARD: POWER SHIFTS AND THUNDERING GUITARS

If composers Quincy Jones and Earle Hagen pushed back the boundaries of action jazz, Mike Post and Pete Carpenter revolutionized the style with their Grammy award-winning theme to *The Rockford Files* (1974–80). Post was one of the first composers writing for television who had not risen through formal musical training, having been primarily a rock musician with a strong background in guitar. Pete Carpenter, on the other hand, came from a big band background and understood the intricacies of arranging and scoring for television. The pairing was extremely successful. Basing the theme to *Rockford* on Jim Rockford's (played by James Garner) relaxed, 'California-beach-style' persona, Post and Carpenter constructed a swinging, country-rock theme for the show. The Post/Carpenter theme is a sonic characterization of Jim Rockford. Scored for harmonica, synthesizer, electric guitar and driving percussion, the music merges associations of violence and sexuality with Rockford's country charm and straight-shooting character. As Post relates, 'the theme isn't real rock 'n' roll, but it's close ... . What it was, was our turn: guys who were raised on Chuck Berry, Bo Diddley, and the Rolling Stones ... . It isn't five saxophones anymore: it's thundering guitars' (see Burlingame, 1996: 61–62).

Like Mancini's jazz theme for *Peter Gunn,* the Post/Carpenter score for *The Rockford Files* created a sense of both contemporaneity and change. This was appropriate to a show that, itself, embodied the changes taking place in the television industry – away from network-produced television towards independent productions. Indeed, in some respects Mike Post was, himself, a personification of the shifting structures of power – away from traditionally-trained composers, toward those from a pop/rock background. As had the action jazz of *Peter Gunn* in 1958, the new musical style of the *Rockford* theme resonated with the style and tempo of the time, representing in sound the changing world beyond the television screen.

## NOTES

1   The concept of music triggering associative thoughts is central to Richard Wagner's theory and philosophy of composition. See his *Art and Revolution* (1849), *The Artwork of the Future* (1850), *Opera and Drama* (1851), and *Music of the Future* (1861).

2   It is interesting to compare Peter Gunn's minimalist connoisseurship and that of the ultimate filmic connoisseur and spy-spoof hero, Derek Flint (*Our Man Flint*, 1965; *In Like Flint*, 1967). Peter Gunn's penthouse apartment holds an extensive album collection (presumably jazz), while the walls display a variety of Asian prints, small surrealist paintings, and small statuary. In contrast, Derek Flint's penthouse apartment holds wall-sized paintings in the style of Chagal or Jasper Johns which alternate at the flick of a remote control, while life-sized Greek, Roman, and Renaissance statuary mix serene shapes with a Giacometti-like linear 'stick figure' and the very *un*stick-like figures of four (or three, depending on the film) beautiful women who live with Flint and cater to his every whim. The artistic tastes of both Gunn and Flint, therefore, function as a totem of the masculine, playboy–consumer – though Flint represents an exaggerated parody of the original archetype.

3   The Modern Jazz Quartet was largely responsible for creating an intellectual, even 'scientific', image for modern jazz. Classically trained, the ensemble utilized formal musical structures, such as fugues, in their pieces. And, through their serious dress and demeanour when performing, the quartet encouraged audiences to appreciate jazz as a serious art form and make the music a topic of intellectual discussion. See Hamm (1995: 76–77).

4   The 1957 Playboy Jazz Allstars included such luminaries as Louis Armstrong, Chet Baker, Dizzy Gillespie, Benny Goodman and Dave Brubeck.

5   The jazz-oriented themes of *Peter Gunn* were taken even further in the series *Johnny Staccato* (1959–60). Here, the private eye hero was a former jazz musician and worked out of Waldo's jazz club in down-town New York.

6   *Danger*, directed by Yul Brynner, is an example of one of the most interesting uses of

original music in television. Each week, guitarist Tony Mottola attended rehearsals for the show – after which he would compose a score for solo guitar based on the episode's script. Mottola performed his score during the live airing of the show while sitting in a control booth wearing headphones through which he could hear dialogue in one ear and receive instructions from the director in the other. See Burlingame (1996: 13–14).

7   In the same period film studios also increasingly sought to capitalize on the popular appeal of movie themes. For example, Paramount's acquisition of Dot Records in 1957 heralded the major film studio's bid to exploit the lucrative potential of its film scores. United Artists quickly followed suit by creating its own subsidiary, UA Records, and by mid-1958 Warner Brothers, Twentieth Century Fox and Columbia had all created their own recording subsidiaries. See Smith (1998: 33–44).

8   For an excellent discussion of the compositional techniques John Barry used in thematically 'bonding' together the Bond films, see Smith (1998: Chapter 5).

9   This grafting of Baroque elements onto popular musical genres was also deployed in the late 1960s by the Beatles in such pieces as 'All You Need Is Love' (which includes harpsichord) and in the scoring for 'Penny Lane' (which incorporates piccolo, trumpet and strings).

10  During the 1960s martial jazz was the defining style of a wide variety of dramatic TV scores – featuring, for example, in the stirring themes that Barry Gray composed for Century 21 sci-fi puppet shows such as *Thunderbirds* and *Stingray*.

11  *Sprechstimme* is a type of heightened vocal production somewhere between song and speech used primarily in early-twentieth-century opera such as Schoenberg's *Die Glückliche Hand* and Alban Berg's *Wozzeck* and *Lulu*.

## REFERENCES

Bazelon, Irwin (1975) *Knowing the Score: Notes on Film Music*, New York: Arco.

Brown, Royal (1994) *Overtones and Undertones: Reading Film Music*, Los Angeles: University of California Press.

Burlingame, Jon (1996) *TV's Biggest Hits: The Story of Television Themes from 'Dragnet' to 'Friends'*, New York: Schirmer.

Carraze, Alain and Oswald, Helene (1995) *The Prisoner: A Televisionary Masterpiece*, London: Virgin.

Fiegel, Eddi (1998) *John Barry: A Sixties Theme - From James Bond to Midnight Cowboy*, London: Constable.

Hamm, Charles (1995) *Putting Popular Music in its Place*, Cambridge: Cambridge University Press.

Lewis, Jon E. and Stempel, Penny (1996) *Cult TV: The Essential Critical Guide*, London: Pavilion.

Miller, Toby (1998) *The Avengers*, London: BFI.

Smith, Jeff (1998) *The Sounds of Commerce: Marketing Popular Film Music*, New York: Columbia University Press.

## SELECT DISCOGRAPHY

Edwin Astley and His Orchestra (1965) *The Saint*, RCA.

Des Champ (1966) *Penthouse Magazine Presents: The Bedside Bond*, Decca.

Henry Mancini (1958) *The Music of Peter Gunn*, RCA.

—— (1959) *More Music from Peter Gunn*, RCA.

Phase 4 Stereo (1966) *Themes for Secret Agents*, Decca.
Leith Stevens and His Orchestra (1959) *Jazz Themes for Cops and Robbers*, Coral Records.
Various (1957) *The Playboy Jazz Allstars*, Playboy Magazine.
Various (1965) *Music of Mystery, Mayhem and Murder*, MFP.

The themes to the 'classic' action series of the 1960s and 1970s are currently available on numerous CD compilations. Among the best are *Crime Jazz: Music In The First Degree* (together with its sequel, *Crime Jazz: Music In The Second Degree*, both Rhino Records, 1997), *The Cult Files* (Silva Screen, 1996) and *This Is … Cult Fiction Royale* (Virgin, 1998).

# 13

# THE COMICS CONNECTION

## Low culture meets
## even lower culture

*Roger Sabin*[1]

Despite the narrow focus of most TV histories, TV shows do not exist in a void. There is a spillover into all kinds of other art forms (not to mention merchandising and ephemera), and this has been as true historically for action TV as for any other kind. Notwithstanding the spin-off novelizations and movies, the most fertile relationship in this regard has been with comic books. For in the pages of the so-called 'funny books', the action TV genre has made a perfect fit – albeit with a certain amount of tweaking to make sure it suited the predominantly juvenile readership.

Yet, relative to other comics, adaptations of action TV shows were never big news. They were a sub-genre of TV adaptations *per se*, which themselves were rarely, if ever, as popular as the major comics genres (i.e. superheroes and comedy in the United States, and kids' humour in Britain). They came in two basic forms – strips in anthology comics and discrete comics devoted to particular shows – and production-wise were typically not of the best quality, consisting of lowest-common-denominator hackwork done for an audience that was perceived to be uncritical. On top of this, since both comics and TV were widely imagined to be 'bad' for children – not least because they diverted them from such 'improving' pastimes as reading proper books – the cultural standing of such comics was extremely low. We can imagine that many parents were hardly overjoyed at the emergence of this form of surrogate, portable TV.

This cultural positioning had obvious repercussions for the way the comics went about their adaptations – what to retain from shows, what to jettison, and how to re-mould them in an acceptable manner. Many comics were, after all, in the business of making adult TV fare available to kids – a potentially risky undertaking bearing in mind the scrutiny comics found themselves under (at various points in their history) as perceived 'agents of delinquency'. It also affected how they were slotted into publishing strategies, how their creators came to be exploited by a work-for-hire system, how readers negotiated their enjoyment, and how the industry faced up to competition – including from TV itself. It is often assumed that the rise of TV was disastrous for comics, but clearly some sectors of the business were able to make decent profits on the back of it.

The following paper seeks to trace an outline account of this curious by-water of comics history, as seen from a British perspective.

## THE BRITISH TRADITION

In the UK, there has been a tradition of cross-fertilization between comics and other art forms from the genesis of the medium. Indeed, the title some historians consider to be the first ever comic, *Ally Sloper's Half Holiday* (Gilbert Dalziel, 1884), included reworkings of music hall routines.[2] As other forms of entertainment developed, so comics kept pace. Thus, the emergence of the classic *Film Fun* (Amalgamated Press, 1920), followed by *Radio Fun* (Amalgamated Press, 1938), that eventually gave way to the less classic *TV Fun* (Amalgamated Press, 1953), which included adaptations of *The Arthur Askey Show, Family Theatre* and others. These three titles were important for setting standards for adaptations, and for refining comics art. In an attempt to capture the look of movies and TV shows, the artwork was boldly black and white, and the action was visual, often based on the sight-gags of comedians of the period. In the future, as TV comics took off, the adapters of action programmes would learn much from this approach.

Although *TV Fun* was the pioneer television comic, the boom in such publications did not come until several years later, by which time the number of homes in the UK with TV sets had jumped considerably.[3] Chronologically, important titles include *TV Picture Stories* (Pearson, 1959), digest-size comics devoted to individual shows (*Robin Hood, Hawkeye*, etc.), which became *TV Photo Stories* (Pearson, 1960), with photostrips of *William Tell, The Buccaneers* and so on. *TV Express* appeared in 1960 (Express, 1960), with strips that included *Biggles* and *Colonel Pinto* and was closely followed by the launch of *TV Comic* (News of the World, 1961) – which began with *Muffin the Mule* and went on to include sci-fi series such as *Fireball XL5* and *Dr Who*. *TV Century 21* (City, 1965, later *TV21*) took the Gerry Anderson theme further and was almost entirely devoted to *Thunderbirds, Captain Scarlet* and the like, whilst *Lady Penelope* (City, 1966) starred the eponymous Anderson puppet but also included fare such as *Space Family Robinson*. In 1966 *TV Toyland* (Fleetway, 1966) showcased *Champion the Wonder Horse* and *The Magic Roundabout*, while the following year *TV Tornado* (City, 1967) – a mix of text and strip stories – was notable for including American material (mostly reprinted from US comics) such as *Voyage to the Bottom of the Sea, Bonanza* and *The Lone Ranger*. There was even a bogus title that tried to cash in on the boom: *TV Heroes* (Miller, 1958), which was subtitled 'Your Favourite TV Stars and Others in Action' – but which hilariously contained the disclaimer that, 'There is No Connection Between This Magazine and the Transmission of Any Television Programme.'

Most of these titles concentrated on kids' shows and were correspondingly juvenile in tone. The core age-range of the readership was assumed to be 5–12 years of age, with adventure-leaning examples selling mostly to boys. If titles proved to be particularly successful, they were collected into hardback 'annuals', often with added quizzes and photographs (supplied by the TV studios), which sold especially well at

Christmas time. The principle was increasingly extended to specific strips within the comics, which became annuals in their own right (e.g. *Thunderbirds Annual*, *Robin Hood Annual* and so on).

However juvenile the comics may have been, adaptations of more adult cop shows and action shows soon become a staple. Thus, *The Saint* made appearances in *TV Tornado* and *TV21*; *The Man from U.N.C.L.E.* in *TV Tornado* and *Lady Penelope*;[4] *Danger Man* in *TV Express* (as illustrated text stories); *Burke's Law* in *TV Century 21*; *Highway Patrol* in *TV Picture Stories*; and *The Avengers* in *TV Comic*, *TV Tornado* – and, interestingly, in the girls' comics *June* and *Diana* – evidently one action programme thought to be as appealing to girls as to boys.[5]

One title went the whole hog, and became the first comic to be devoted entirely to TV action shows: *TV Crimebusters* (TV Publications, 1962). It included *Danger Man*, *The Avengers*, *Four Just Men*, *77 Sunset Strip*, *Hawaiian Eye*, *Charlie Chan* and … um … *Dixon of Dock Green*. A curiously old-fashioned looking comic (even for its time), with heroes in crisply pressed suits and villains in cloth caps, it was a mix of text and strip material, the latter taking the unusual form of having photos of action scenes from the shows interspersed among the panels. *TV Crimebusters* was an interesting experiment, but, despite being turned into a better-than-average quality annual, only lasted one year (see Figure 13.1).

TV comics generally adapted action shows with the same approach. In one sense, the writers and artists had an advantage in that they knew a lot of the work was 'done for them' – many readers already knew the formats of the shows, their idiosyncrasies, how the characters talked, and how they looked. This meant creators could get straight down to the action without much thought for character development or atmosphere (or indeed, often for the actual likenesses of characters). On the other hand, there were readers who simply did not have access to the original TV shows: it would be fair to assume, for example, that a percentage of readers would not have had a TV set in their home (see figures referenced in footnote 3). For them, the comics would have provided an *entrée* to television culture, and thus presumably a way of 'staying up with the (TV) times'. Similarly, younger readers might not have been allowed by their parents to stay up late to watch these shows (first runs of shows like *The Saint*, *The Avengers* and *The Man from U.N.C.L.E.* were in the evening, usually from 8 p.m. onwards, though later they were repeated at earlier times, occasionally in the afternoons), and for them the strips must have been something new; a window onto a forbidden (adult) world. In this instance, creators had another excuse for poorly executed work, because when it came to likenesses as such, readers would not necessarily have known any better.

Stylistically, most strips stuck to the classic format introduced by *Film Fun*, with an opening panel consisting of a photo of the action star(s) accompanied by the name of the strip, followed by a black and white story lasting, typically, between four and eight pages. The vast majority of plot-lines riffed on the show, but did not copy episodes directly. Often they combined elements from different episodes – though sometimes they took inspiration from elsewhere entirely. For instance, *The Saint* strip 'Blast Off Midnight!' in *TV Tornado Annual* (1966) features two key scenes – a speedboat chase

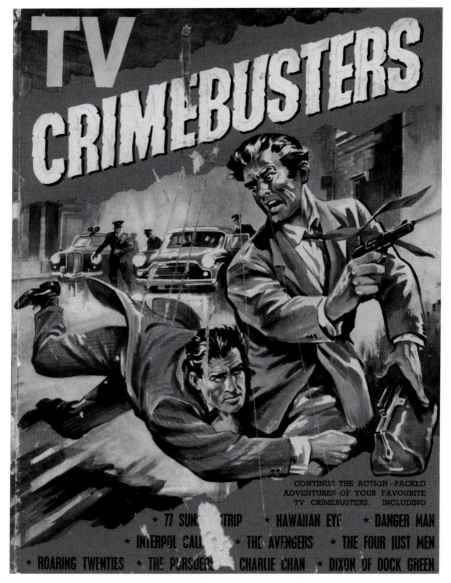

*Figure 13.1* 'Don't crease me suit, Guv'nor!' *TV Crimebusters Annual (1962)* – the first British comic devoted to action TV shows.

in which floating petrol cans are ignited by firing shots at them, and the ramming of a villain's luxury yacht – which were clearly inspired by the James Bond movies *From Russia With Love* (1963) and *Thunderball* (1965) respectively. *TV Crimebusters,*

208

however, was not typical in this regard. By comparing an *Avengers* story entitled 'The Drug Peddler'(*TV Crimebusters Annual,* 1962) with a detailed TV series episode guide, it is possible to conclude that individual scenes in the strip were copied from different episodes and then linked together (in a not altogether coherent fashion), and that in all likelihood the story was 'written around' the photos at hand.[6] (Other strips in the comic look to have been similarly constructed.)

In general, the tone of the strips was dictated by what editors felt it was acceptable to retain. Capturing the essence of an hour-long show in an eight-page strip was no easy feat, and obviously much was going to be lost. Often stories made little sense, and arguably, coherence was not a priority because, as ever, creators assumed they were working for a young and uncritical audience. Particular themes were certainly modified: missing, for example, are the romantic interludes that were so much a part of *The Saint* and *The Man from U.N.C.L.E.* No doubt it was assumed by editors – probably quite rightly – that this would be a turn-off for young boys. The level of violence was also toned down: after the furore over American comics in the 1950s (see below), nobody was taking any chances. Finally, any political or ideological elements in the shows – such as they were – were softened (for example, the Cold War posturing in *The Man from U.N.C.L.E.*).

There were also aspects that were added to the stories. Creators were increasingly allowed to stray from the set formulas of the shows, and to be more imaginative. After all, it was possible to do things in the comics form that it might not have been so easy to achieve on television, not least because in comics there were no budget restrictions save the price of paper and ink. Thus, action set pieces tended to be that bit more extravagant, locations that bit more exotic, and explosions that bit bigger. As more and more liberties were taken, strips could sometimes take off on flights of fancy: for example, *The Saint* story in *TV Tornado Annual* (1966) involves a bizarre invulnerable robot never witnessed in any episode of the TV series.

The strips, therefore, tended to be highly compressed bursts of energy, a sort of 'alternative TV' – but without the 'fat'. The stories were certainly infantilized, but they were also made faster, 'bigger' and more fantastic – and they did not last longer than a kid's presumed attention span. This did not mean they were necessarily any good and, as we have seen, the art was often poor and the writing rudimentary to say the least. Yet they were undoubtedly a powerful form of simulacrum capable of generating their own buzz. The fact that children were making their own choices about buying such comics with their pocket money, often unpoliced by parents, must also have served to heighten the reading experience.

For these very reasons, however, the comics were often held in low regard by cultural commentators. The comics medium was customarily looked down upon (especially by self-appointed, middle-class observers) for being 'lowbrow', and was even considered to be 'a threat to literacy' – the prejudice against comics as a form of entertainment for the working class being a hangover from the days of *Ally Sloper*. The fact that these particular examples were dealing with television – a medium which through the 1950s and 1960s was generating its own kinds of moral panic – made things even worse. If kids absolutely had to read comics, it was argued, far better for them to be buying something like *The Eagle*, with its old-fashioned morality tales.

Such attitudes had a knock-on effect for the circumstances of the comics' production. Conditions in the industry were bad enough: creators worked for an often meagre per-page fee, with no royalties and no control over copyright. Their work was anonymous, and their status in the production process correspondingly low. Added to this, the TV comics were particularly disliked by artists because they entailed sketching from photos ('swipe files' provided by the studios), and sometimes even speed-sketching from the shows themselves (these were the days before videos with freeze-frame functions) – neither of which was considered particularly creative work. Bearing in mind this alienating context, perhaps it is no wonder that creators felt little connection with, or affection for, what they were doing, and that so many of the comics were poorly executed.

## THE AMERICAN BOOM AND
## THE ESCAPE FROM CENSORSHIP

However popular the British TV action strips were becoming by the late 1960s, the most impressive exemplars of the form (from a creative standpoint) were American. Such comics were not easy to find in Britain at first because importation was sporadic, and British reprints were on a small scale (though, as we have seen, individual strips appeared in anthologies like *TV Tornado*). But as the 1960s progressed, so distribution became better organized, and a wider range of material was made available.

There were a number of reasons why the US product was superior. The original titles were in full colour, and came with often stunning photo covers, backed by blocks of bright colour, and with stylish typography borrowed from the show credits. They were mostly published by Dell and Gold Key, and were in a smaller and thicker format than British comics, being monthlies and therefore more expensive (it should be noted, however, that the British reprints, by companies such as Miller and Thorpe and Porter, were not of the same quality, and were in black and white).

It was not just the colour and the covers, however, that attracted British kids. The comics also offered a taste of an exotic and exciting television culture, and the content could sometimes be relatively adult, since in the US a percentage of the readership was assumed to be over sixteen. The TV shows that were adapted in US comics were also commonly slow to make it onto UK screens, and sometimes were not transmitted at all – which made the comics all the more intriguing. *Martin Kane: Private Eye* (Fox, 1950) was the first American comic to be based on a TV detective show. This was followed in sporadic fashion by others, often adapting long-standing programmes that had recently made the transition from radio to TV, such as *Big Town* (National Periodicals, 1951), or starring long-established characters that were making a similar shift. *Dick Tracy*, for example, became a TV show in 1950, spurring Harvey Comics to reprint Chester Gould's newspaper strips, while *Ellery Queen* became a TV series in the same year, and became a comic published by Ziff-Davis in 1952. Other early action shows were quickly adapted, such as *Mike Barnett: Man Against Crime* (Fawcett, 1951), though curiously the biggest of them all, *Dragnet*, never had its own comic. Instead, as historian Mike Benton has observed, there were a number of shameless *Dragnet* rip-offs. *I'm a Cop* (Magazine Enterprises, 1954), for example, borrowed its title from the lead character's opening line – 'My name's Friday: I'm a cop', while *The Informer* (Sterling, 1954) had a tag-line: 'From the files of the police DRAGNET!' (Benton, 1993: 136).

American comics in general, however, had a problem becoming established in the UK. Added to the prejudices that existed against comics in general in Britain, was the fact that anti-Americanism was a very real force through the 1950s. Above all, there were the effects of the backlash against American crime and horror comics in the mid-1950s (see Sabin, 1996: 68). This was predicated on the (mistaken) belief that they caused delinquency in young people, and led to the introduction of a Comics Code (administered by the Comics Code Authority, or CCA) that essentially censored anything but the most anodyne content (and which set limits on the depiction of violence, sex, drug-taking and social commentary). In Britain, an Act of Parliament was introduced – The Children and Young Persons' Harmful Publications Act, 1955 – which banned the importation and publication of horror and crime comics. The results of these measures in the comics industry were instant and dramatic – titles were cancelled, publishers folded, and crime and horror comics became virtually a thing of the past. In America, the business was plunged into the worst recession it had ever seen.

How did this crisis impact on the sales of TV action comics produced in the US? Curiously, it did not – and in fact, it proved to be a fillip for them. By this time, the main publisher of TV adaptations *per se* was Dell who, along with their licence to produce versions of Disney and Warner Brothers' TV and movie cartoons, also published versions of lightweight comedies such as *I Love Lucy*. Dell claimed that such comics were inoffensive ('Dell Comics Are Good Comics' as their publicity ran), and that therefore they should not have to submit them to the Code Authority. This was accepted by the Authority, and Dell promptly began to explore the possibilities of adapting more action-oriented TV fare. This was a cunning strategy because they knew that, if they could get away with it, it was likely that a proportion of the former fans of crime comics would turn here for their fix and that there would not be any other publishers as competitors. This, indeed, is exactly what happened, though there was one competitor – Gold Key – which, because it had once been part of Dell (it split in 1962), also managed to strike a deal whereby it did not submit its comics to the CCA.

There followed a boom in action TV comics, without doubt historically the biggest and most important flowering of the form. Both Dell and Gold Key argued that such comics were different in tone from the old crime comics, and they were right to a point. Certainly the violence was nowhere near as explicit, and by adapting shows from TV they were automatically more 'acceptable'. But it is also interesting to note that many of the writers and artists who had once worked on the crime comics were now employed on the TV action titles, and that Dell itself had, in its earliest incarnation, been a publisher of true crime fiction. From the Dell stable major action TV titles included: *Peter Gunn* (1960), *77 Sunset Strip* (1960), *The Detectives* (1961), *Danger Man* (1961), *Mike Shayne* (1961), *The Untouchables* (1961), *Target: The Corrupters*

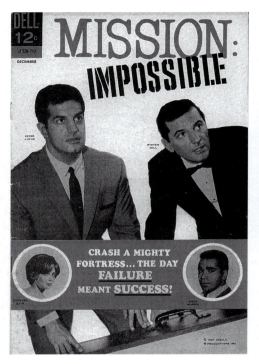

*Figure 13.2* Dell and Gold Key Comics (USA)
– leading the way in the adaptation of sixties'
action TV.

(1962), *Perry Mason Magazine* (1964), *The Defenders* (1962), *Cain's Hundred* (1962), *Espionage* (1964), *Burke's Law* (1964), *87th Precinct* (1962), *Charlie Chan* (1965), *Mission: Impossible* (1967). From the rival Gold Key camp came: *Checkmate* (1962), *Hawaiian Eye* (1963), *The Man From U.N.C.L.E.* (1965), *Secret Agent* (1966), *Honey West* (1966), *I Spy* (1966), *John Steed and Emma Peel* (1967) (so-called in order not to infringe Marvel's copyright on the name of their superhero series *The Avengers*), and *The Girl From U.N.C.L.E.* (1967). All these comics were imported into Britain in increasing numbers, and a few were reprinted (see Figure 13.2). (By the 1960s, American comics were no longer seen as the malignant force they had once been, and besides, the Act of 1955 was always there to fall back on if anything went wrong.)

Like their British counterparts, very few of the American comics were based on actual episodes from the series on which they were predicated – the vast majority spun new stories around the characters. Some were more faithful than others: *77 Sunset Strip* was written by Eric Freiwald, who also wrote for the TV show (hence the same hipster dialogue: 'What's cooking in troublesville, doll?'). The shows were not infantilized to quite the same extent as in British comics because the American titles were designed to appeal to a 'crossover' readership of children and adults (the core US market being teenagers as opposed to kids). However, things were toned down and condensed, and self-censorship applied. For example, the TV show *Peter Gunn* was notoriously risqué in its early days – according to *TV Guide* it featured 'Hot jazz, Hot action, Hot women' – yet the womanizing and nightclub settings were considerably softened in the comics in favour of run-of-the-mill fisticuffs. Similarly, *The Untouchables*, a TV show criticized in the press for its 'gratuitous violence', was limited in the comics to usually one shoot-out per story (Benton, 1993: 157). As with their British peers, US comics also took liberties with the source material, and the Americans arguably went further in this regard. For example, one issue of *Mission: Impossible* from 1968 features massive Bond-style missile silos, while another has the team donning frog-suits in order to do battle with a giant octopus. The approach could sometimes be taken to surreal lengths: e.g. an issue of *John Steed and Emma Peel* from 1967 featured a 'mirage machine' that can conjure up animals, including a charging elephant. Obviously not the kind of scenario to which a TV budget could run.

For all their flash, however, the quality of the comics was often poor. There were the wonderful covers, of course, but too often they promised more than the interiors could offer. The scripts were clichéd, the artwork rushed, and the colouring perfunctory. It is possible to find issues of individual comics by some of the great artists of the period (for example, *Burke's Law* by Gene Colan, and *77 Sunset Strip* by Alex Toth and Russ Manning). These were, however, very much the exceptions, and lightning-speed hackwork was more the order of the day. The lamentable quality of such comics was primarily the result of an economic set-up that was not much better than in Britain. As with their British counterparts, American creators had no rights over their work, were paid a flat page-fee, and did not receive royalties. Even more so than in the UK, they were considered workers on an assembly line – just one step in a production process that included writers, pencillers, inkers, letterers, and colourists. This system guaranteed their anonymity, and militated against collective action (unions were all but impossible to organize). Once again, the quality of the comics was bound to be a low priority.

The Dell and Gold Key boom continued through the 1960s, but then ran out of steam. Their canny manipulation of the Code situation, plus their virtual monopoly on licences, had frustrated other publishers, and forced competitors to think of alternative ways of cashing in on the action TV genre (for example, Marvel's *Nick Fury, Agent of SHIELD* was a superhero take on *The Man From U.N.C.L.E.*). But the heyday of Dell and Gold Key couldn't last – and the days of their TV titles were numbered when the studios started to up their licensing rates. As sales of TV comics went down, and other genres surged in popularity, it was clear that this particular era was at an end. Dell ceased publication of comics in 1973; Gold Key in 1984.

## ACTION GOES MAD

There was one strand of American comics that pursued an alternative take on TV action fare, and which did not have any problems with licensing costs – satirical comics. The genre was dominated by one title, *Mad* (EC Comics, 1952), and it is fair to say that without this particular publication the nature of satire itself would be very different today. *Mad* established the principle that no aspect of American life was beyond parody, be it politics, advertising, movies or television. As it spawned versions of itself (the British edition debuted in 1959) and imitators by the dozen all over the world, so a generation of teenagers was given an education in how 'not to believe the hype'. Just how 'subversive' this education was is still open to debate, but there is no doubt that it had a considerable effect on the 1960s counterculture.

*Mad's* focus on TV parody became increasingly pronounced. In 1953 *Dragnet* was the first-ever action show to be spoofed – rechristened 'Dragged Net!' and given a thorough working-over by editor and writer Harvey Kurtzman and artist Will Elder (the same pairing had a second crack at the show a few issues later). *The Untouchables* was similarly dismembered. Having changed from a comic to a magazine format in 1954, to avoid the strictures of the Code, *Mad's* satire became more pointed, and the 1960s saw some remarkable short strips, such as the occasional series 'TV Scenes We'd Like to See' (one famous take on *Mission: Impossible* was scripted by Chevy Chase). It was clear that *Mad* had some of the greatest caricaturists in the business, and it was no secret that a few moonlighted on covers for publications like *TV Guide*.

It was not until the 1970s and 1980s that large-scale narrative take-offs of action shows became a *Mad* commonplace. These 5–7-page strips had previously been reserved mainly for movies, and were designed to allow creators the space to attack their targets in some detail. Now, very few action shows escaped: *Charlie's Angels, Starsky and Hutch, The Six Million Dollar Man, The Bionic Woman, The A-Team, Miami Vice, Hill Street Blues, The Fall Guy* and many more were mercilessly taken apart. Yet, for all that, the underlying politics of the shows tended to be eschewed in favour of much broader character comedy. To give a fairly typical example, a 1987 version of *The Equalizer* ('The Tranquilizer' by Dick DeBartolo and Angelo Torres, in *Mad* 302) makes little attempt to satirize the essentially right wing 'vigilante' philosophy of the show, and instead focuses on the doddery hero. When he finds his quarry lives on the first floor of an apartment block, he utters in relief, 'Thank God! Car chases and shoot-outs are one thing, but at my age and shape, stairs are killers!'.

Such strips were supplemented by the shorter 'Scenes We'd Like to See', which continued from the 1960s, and which were joined by other variants. These included 'TV Emmy Awards We'd Like to See', featuring a prize for 'Most Innovative Use of a Car Chase Wind-up in an Action–Adventure Series to Cover Up Bad Writing', and 'TV Spin-Offs We'd Like to See', which paired off characters from different action shows and set them in unlikely situations. Other one-offs similarly filled the space, such as 'Upcoming TV Cop Teams', featuring characters with names like 'Dazed and Confused' and 'Bitch and Moan'.

This trend towards the inclusion of more movie and television parodies was influenced by the British version of the magazine. Former editor Dez Skinn (1975–79) recalls that he ' … pushed for more adventurous covers, and specifically covers with movie and TV references – previously *Mad* had mostly featured covers with one-shot gags. We'd keep the mascot, Alfred, of course, but incorporate him into spoofs of the shows'. There were other changes, too, and Skinn began to ' … commission more work from British creators, so that we could parody our own shows – we even did *Coronation Street* – and this was another significant change because previously the role of the British editor had basically been to Anglicise the [American] gags'. The reaction to this general change in direction was, according to Skinn, very positive and '[e]ven the producers of the shows and films were impressed. They took it as a compliment, and often tried to buy the artwork'.[7]

*Mad* reached a peak circulation in 1973, selling more than a staggering 2.5 million copies per issue. By this time, it had spawned numerous imitators, none of which were nearly so popular. These included, in the 1950s, *Eh!*, *Whack*, *Wild*, *Riot*, *Unsane*, *Panic*; and in the 1960s, *Trump*, *Help!*, *Humbug*, *Wacko*, *Trash*, *Nuts*, *Blast*, *Cracked*, *Sick*; and in the 1970s, *Brand Echh* and *Crazy*. Some went in for media parodies, some did not. Today, though its sales figures have drooped, *Mad* is still going strong (unlike its rivals), many historians putting the magazine's longevity down to its relatively enlightened employment policies (*Mad* paid creators roughly double the rates of any other publication in the business and so, despite huge battles over royalties and copyright control, managed to attract the best talent in the field). But at the dawn of the twenty-first century, *Mad* has certainly lost the cutting-edge reputation it had in the 1950s and 1960s – a change underlined by the fact that it has given its name to a sub-*Saturday Night Live* television sketch show – exactly the kind of 'TV product' it once lampooned so mercilessly.

## THE 1970s BRIT REVIVAL

By the 1970s, the excitement surrounding the imported Dell and Gold Key lines and their British reprints had all but died down, and the old-style British TV comics were not faring as well as they once did. A shot in the arm was needed, and this came with the arrival of two British titles launched in the same year – namely, *Countdown*

(Polystyle, 1971), which was pitched as a 'Space Age Comic!' and featured such TV Science fiction shows as *UFO, Dr Who* and *Thunderbirds*, and *Look-In* (Independent Television, 1971), created as a branch of the commercial TV channel and marketed as 'The Junior *TV Times*'. As they evolved, both would take a close interest in the burgeoning new wave of action TV series.

*Countdown* was first off the mark. By the end of 1971, the science fiction motif of the comic was being rethought, and a new strip was brought in to herald a change in direction: *The Persuaders!* It was adapted in full colour and soon became one of the comic's most popular strips, retaining its place as the cover feature for the rest of the title's duration. This move away from Science fiction material was confirmed the following year when the comic was rechristened *Countdown for TV Action*. Now, a whole new range of stories was added to reflect the concurrent revival in action TV series, and *The Persuaders!* was joined by *Hawaii Five–O* and *Mission: Impossible*, then later by *Cannon* and *The Protectors*. Yet by this point the comic was already in financial trouble, and cutbacks were being made, with the result that these strips appeared in black and white – colour tending to be saved for the more 'in-yer-face' kids' shows. Eventually the comic's reformulation became complete, its name being shortened to simply *TV Action*.

*TV Action*'s strips kept to the spirit of the shows as much as they could and, although their quality was variable, they sometimes featured top-notch artists – such as Harry Lindfield on *The Persuaders!* and John Burns on *Mission: Impossible*. Burns' spare, dynamic style was perfect for black and white action fare. 'It was dull to work from photos on the TV comics, so I used to spice things up by being inventive with the action sequences', he explains. 'So, for example, if a character has to fall off a building, I'd work out how to make it look exciting, work out all the angles and so on, so it became interesting for me to do'.[8]

In 1973, *TV Action* itself was merged, this time with the long-running *TV Comic*. This marked a move downwards in terms of the age-range of the readers, and though many of the action shows adapted by *TV Action* were junked, others were added with time – notably, *Kojak* (drawn for a while by another excellent artist, David Lloyd) and *Charlie's Angels*. Once again, the essence of the shows was retained as far as possible. In one *Charlie's Angels* episode from 1979, for example, the girls infiltrate a biker gang to solve their case – a plot-line that closely followed the classic formula for the show. Such strips, however, did tend to look a little odd next to material such as *Basil Brush* and *The Pink Panther*, and *TV Comic* eventually bit the dust in 1984.

*Look-In* was much slower to take the action route, mainly because it saw itself as a cross between a funny paper and a music magazine, with kid strips like *Catweazle* rubbing shoulders with *Please Sir!* and pin-ups of Marc Bolan. Action strips were, however, gradually added. These included *Jason King, Charlie's Angels* and *Kung Fu*, though by the end of the 1970s the big stories focused on the cyborg duo *The Six Million Dollar Man* and *The Bionic Woman* – both strips appearing in full colour. The latter were extraordinary not just because of the quality of the artwork, but also for the liberties the writers sometimes took with the source material. In one *Six Million Dollar Man* episode, for example, it was as if the ghost of H.P. Lovecraft had invaded the comic: 'The evil, devil-driven spirit of Zecatyl, ancient mystic of lower California, is released and takes over the living tissue of Steve Austin's friend! ... ' (*Look-In*, 8 July 1978).

*Look-In* continued into the 1980s, evidently buoyed-up by money from Independent Television, and continued to adapt the hot action shows, which by this time included *Chips, Magnum, Knight Rider* and *The A-Team*. However, the glory days of the 1970s were clearly gone, and these strips appeared mainly in black and white, and were increasingly poorly drawn. As time went on, *Look-In* eschewed strip content almost entirely in favour of the pop material, and by the 1990s it had transformed itself into a glossy magazine, closer to the teen-music title *Smash Hits* than to any comic. It eventually folded in 1994.

It should be noted that, in terms of economics, on both *Countdown/TV Action* and *Look-In*, the old work-for-hire, fee-per-page, system still operated, and as a result the creators were rarely a happy breed. They were not as anonymous as they had been in the 1960s (in all the titles, they were clearly credited), but the fact that they were still only one step in a longer process continued to be a problem. 'The production people didn't necessarily care about the work,' explains John Burns, 'and a "colour slip" or a speech balloon re-positioned in the wrong place could ruin what you'd done'. And there was the additional irritation of who actually owned the artwork: ' ... the publisher would keep it, presumably to syndicate it later and make more profits. Sometimes individuals from the publisher would sell it at auction or through the specialist shops – and again, the artist wouldn't see anything from that'.[9] Burns eventually decided to be pro-active about the situation, and co-founded the Society for Strip Illustration (SSI), which became an important campaigning body for creators' rights.

This is not, however, the end of the story for British TV comics during the 1970s. They had one last burst of energy, which took them into much darker territory in terms of tone. During the period of the ascendancy of *Look-In* and *Countdown/TV Action*, the action shows were adapted in much the same way as they had been in the 1960s. They were juvenilized, expurgated, toned down, spectacularized, and generally made more exciting for an 8-year-old. Such self-censorship meant that there was never any chance that parents would complain about content, even when adapted shows were adult-oriented and aired after bed-time. *Look-In* was particularly careful about this and, as if to indicate which shows it thought were acceptable, included a weekly schedule of television programmes on ITV that stopped abruptly at 8 p.m. As the 1970s progressed, however, this strict delineation of what was acceptable began to change as more violent content made its way into comics. Increasingly, the grittier a comic was, the more the readership liked it – and that went for TV adaptations as well.

One title in particular forced the agenda – *Action* (IPC, 1976). This was not a TV comic as such, but was widely recognized to have been highly influenced by adult shows such as *The Sweeney*, as well as certain violent movies (in particular *Rollerball, Jaws* and the 'Dirty Harry' series). The tabloid newspaper panic that this style of content provoked, and the subsequent withdrawal of the comic by its publishers, has

*Figure 13.3* 'What's the matter with you, Kootchy-Koo?' Kojak gets his man in Target (1978).

been well covered elsewhere (see Barker, 1990). Suffice to say, a signal had been transmitted for other titles to follow.

One such was *Target* (Polystyle, 1978), a 1970s TV comic that was unique in two key respects. The first was its exclusive devotion to action TV series (the first British comic to be so oriented since *TV Crimebusters* in 1963). The second was its darker tone – obviously influenced by *Action*. A short-lived anthology, it was a poor quality product, mostly in black and white but with some limited use of colour, and its emphasis was on the tough-guy shows that were currently popular. Indeed, it was named after the eponymous series starring Patrick Mower (itself criticized at the time for excessive violence). The other main British show featured was *Hazell* (a grim, cockney saga – 'There are some geezers who are very naughty about paying their rent … '), while American-rooted stories included *Kojak* and *Cannon*.

*Target* represented 1970s 'kick-down-the-door' action TV transposed into comics form – and it was not a pretty sight. Yet, after the fuss over *Action*, it had to be very careful about its levels of violence. Even so, it managed to be darker than virtually any other TV comic – in its fourth issue, for example, Detective Inspector Hackett ('Target') arrives at a car wreck to find a victim bleeding in an almost fluorescent red. The language was also grittier, though any swearing was sensibly cut ('Stone the crows!' being a favoured, very British, alternative). *Target* was a bold idea, but perhaps its lack of faithfulness to the 'realism' of the source shows put readers off – times had moved on and, post-*Action*, readers were not so 'innocent' any more (see Figure 13.3). *Target* lasted one year, and then was merged with *TV Comic*. In retrospect it stands as the last gasp of the British action TV comic.

## WHATEVER HAPPENED TO ACTION TV COMICS?

The decline of action TV comics was inextricably linked to the collapse of the comics industry as a whole (see Sabin, 1996, Ch: 6). However, there were factors that were more specific to the genre, including rising licensing costs and the fact that the growth of colour television took away some of the novelty of colour strip-versions of TV shows. Additionally, the reconfiguring of action TV series themselves post-1980 made traditional formula strips less relevant.

   Within the relatively small specialist comics fan-shop market, there continue to be television tie-ins – though these are rarely 'action TV' adaptations in the established sense: recent hits include the more idiosyncratic *The X-Files*, *Buffy the Vampire Slayer* and *Xena: Warrior Princess*. Meanwhile, sporadic attempts in the 1990s to resuscitate comics based on *The Man From U.N.C.L.E.* and *The Avengers* (for example, the Grant Morrison scripted *Steed and Mrs Peel*, Eclipse/Acme, 1990) have fallen flat. The trouble with the specialist market is evidently that it is too specialized – hence sadly its future prospects are debatable. Thus, arguably whether action TV comics can revive is not just a matter of whether the genre itself can make a comeback, but whether the industry will still be there, in any viable form, if it does.

## NOTES

1   Thanks to Paul Gravett, Dez Skinn, John Burns, David Lloyd, Steve Holland, the librarians at the British Newspaper Library, and the many dealers who helped me track things down.

2   Dates given are of the first date a comic appears. For full dating details, see one of the collector guides - e.g. D. McAlpine (ed.), *The Official Comic Book Price Guide for Great Britain*, London: Price Guide Productions (most recent edition: 1996); or R. Overstreet, *The Official Overstreet Comic Book Price Guide*, Cleveland, TN: Overstreet Publications/ House of Collectibles (annually).

3   In 1952, the number of TV licences totalled 1,449. By 1963, the figure was 12,443. The total number of TV sets in British homes would have been much bigger, of course. See Seymour-Ure (1991: 76–77).

4   There was also a cutely feminized homage, 'The Girls From N.O.O.D.L.E.S.', included in *Diana* (1965).

5   *The Avengers* TV show repaid the compliment with an episode focusing around a comic book: 'The Winged Avenger' (air-date: 18 February 1967).

6   The sequence in the strip where Dr Keel (Ian Hendry) bluffs a criminal with a syringe full of water was certainly taken from an episode entitled 'Hot Snow' (1961). Other photos could have come from any number of other episodes (see the website http:// davidksmith.com/avengers/keel.htm) (Accessed 20.5.01.). The comic is also of use to TV

historians since only one of twenty-six episodes of the original series of *The Avengers* survives (seven went out live).

7  Interview with the author, 1 February 2000.
8  Interview with the author, 9 March 2000.
9  Interview with the author, 9 March 2000.

## REFERENCES

Barker, M. (1990) *Action: The Story of a Violent Comic*, London: Titan.
Benton, M. (1993) *Crime Comics: An Illustrated History*, Dallas, TX: Taylor Publishing.
Sabin, R. (1996) *Comics, Comix and Graphic Novels*, London: Phaidon.
Seymour-Ure, C. (1991) *The British Press and Broadcasting Since 1945*, Oxford: Blackwell.

# 14

# OF LEATHER SUITS AND KINKY BOOTS

## *The Avengers*, style and popular culture

*Marc O'Day*

[In 1963] a new craze took over the nation's Saturday nights, on the commercial channel – a black and violent thriller series, *The Avengers*, starring a bowler hatted Old Etonian actor Patrick MacNee [sic] and Miss Honor Blackman as a pair of mysterious secret agents. The show aroused particular excitement through Miss Blackman's 'kinky' black leather costumes. And indeed the London-centred craze for 'kinky' black boots, 'kinky' black raincoats and 'kinky' black leather or plastic garments of all kinds raged throughout the autumn.
(Christopher Booker, *The Neophiliacs*, London: Fontana, 1970: 211)

### *THE AVENGERS* AND THE DURABILITY OF ICON-LED STYLE

It's almost forty years now since the cult action spy series *The Avengers* first aired on British television and currently its classic status seems more assured than ever. *The Avengers* is that rare phenomenon, a show which set out to be self-consciously escapist, topical and trendy, yet managed to change and develop its formula over what, in televisual terms, became a very long shelf-life indeed. Beginning as a tough spy-thriller starring Ian Hendry and Patrick Macnee in 1961, it came to incarnate the 'swinging sixties', evolving through six – increasingly surreal – seasons which partnered Macnee in turn with Honor Blackman, Diana Rigg and Linda Thorson, until its demise in 1969 (a victim of poor US ratings). But the formula refused to die and, revised as *The New Avengers*, returned for a further two seasons in 1976–77, this time with Macnee joined by Joanna Lumley and Gareth Hunt. After this co-production foundered, no sooner had rumours of further series drifted away than fresh ones concerning a Hollywood blockbuster emerged to take their place, until the big screen *The Avengers* (1998), starring Ralph Fiennes and Uma Thurman, returned us once again to the series' 1960s iconography. One hundred and eighty-seven episodes and a movie later,

*The Avengers* is at once a rich series of texts unfolding over time and a highly durable popular cultural phenomenon.

Confirming its canonical status, the series has been well served by both fan and academic writers alike. From the reference guides by Dave Rogers and others (Rogers, 1989; Cornell, Day and Topping, 1998; Carraze and Putheaud, 1998) to the critical monographs by David Buxton and Toby Miller (Buxton, 1990; Miller, 1997), *Avengers'* enthusiasts point out that it has become a cult classic and a pervasive popular cultural presence by virtue of a single, albeit multi-faceted, quality: its style. All agree that the look, sounds and feel of the series – its iconic spy characters, witty repartee, sublime fashions, fabulous cars, picture-postcard England, surreal pop imagery, smooth jazz theme tunes and weird comic-strip plots – which together comprise its distinctive style, are the main reason for its continuing popularity.

How has *The Avengers'* style established its place in popular culture from the 1960s to the present? This essay proposes that by inflecting the codes of the topical spy genre through its witty, surreal and, above all, icon-led style – a style at once 'stylish' and 'stylized' – *The Avengers* was able to respond to and influence developments in various realms of popular culture (notably fashion, pop and the broader image-and-style oriented consumer culture which emerged in the 1960s and 1970s), as well as light-heartedly mediating contemporary social agendas (including gender and class mobility and the relationship between tradition and modernity in an increasingly science- and technology-based society). As the series developed, its style came to distinguish it as Britain's prime TV drama exemplar of what George Melly termed 'the Pop Arts' (Melly, 1972) and predominantly iconic aspects of this style were separated from their televisual source for adaptation into other media and merchandising, furthering its dissemination into popular culture. And when the recycling of styles became the norm in the postmodern era, its status as an icon of style ensured that *The Avengers* has continued its profitable life in contemporary popular culture. Defining style, adapting style and recycling style: let's examine each of these.

## DEFINING *THE AVENGERS'* STYLE: ICONIC SPIES, POP AND FASHION

The foundation of *The Avengers'* style was its sparkling deployment of the spy couple caper formula, with its leads providing television's most enduring representations of the English gentleman in Patrick Macnee's John Steed and the independent action heroine in his leather-clad partners, Honor Blackman's Cathy Gale and Diana Rigg's Emma Peel. As David Buxton explains, *The Avengers* (along with *Danger Man* and their close cousin *The Saint*) was British television drama's prime example of the 'pop' series, a form in which superficial characters without psychological depth but with great wardrobes engage in fantasy adventures which (broadly) promote a hedonistic ideology of pleasure and consumption.[1] Both Buxton (1990: 22) and Todd Gitlin (1994: 64) confirm that attractive casting and character are vital to a series' success in achieving a popular cultural presence. *The Avengers'* producers were among the first working in Britain to learn this from the American-type action series and, after the first season, developed the programmes' principal characters as internationally marketable fashion icons in a period when the importance of individual style was becoming increasingly foregrounded in popular culture, the media and everyday life more generally.

*The Avengers'* initial male couple formula, partnering Ian Hendry's Dr David Keel with Macnee, was developed by ABC's Head of Drama, Sydney Newman, as a light and gimmicky variant on the spy thriller format of Ian Fleming's James Bond novels and Alfred Hitchcock's *North by Northwest* (1959).[2] Bond was already well known through the serialization and cartoon strip which had appeared in the *Daily Express* in 1957 (Bennett and Woollacott, 1987: 24–29) and Steed in the early seasons was certainly partly akin to Fleming's international playboy spy, whose touristic, voyeuristic and consumerist 'licence to look' has been analysed by Michael Denning (1987: 103). In 'Death Dispatch' (December 1962) Steed, ostensibly poolside on a mission in Jamaica, is a roguish sexist leering at bikini-clad girls.

The formula on which the series' popular cultural durability is based, however, and the one which draws more fully on the heterosexual romance codes which distinguish the Hitchcock thriller (Ryall, 1996: 138–39), was dependent on pairing Macnee with a 'proto-feminist' woman partner. Initially, in the second and third seasons (1962–64), with Honor Blackman's Mrs Catherine Gale, a sophisticated, but not upper class, ex-pat widow possessing a PhD in anthropology, whose conscience often leads her to question Steed's unscrupulous methods. Then, in seasons four and five (1965–67), when the series peaked, with Diana Rigg as Mrs Emma Peel, another glamorous twenty-something widow with academic credentials and independent means.[3] And lastly, in the final season (1968–69), with Linda Thorson's Tara King, an altogether more girlish character than the others and in love with Steed as a kind of father figure.[4]

The couple caper formula which *The Avengers* initiated with these pairings was to prove extraordinarily versatile. While working with action genre codes which had previously tended to feature lone males (as in *Danger Man* or *The Saint*), buddy couples (as in *The Avengers'* original season) or male teams with a token woman (as in many of Howard Hawks' movies), the man–woman couple set up could also rework codes from 'feminine' genres such as screwball comedy (the couple sparring, witty sexual tension) and the musical (fights choreographed as dance sequences), not to mention accommodating the recycling of other crime, gothic, sci-fi and fantasy elements and the lifting of various motifs and plots from classic movies. With the formation of the iconic action–adventure couple whose relationship is based on mutual respect, professionalism, humour and not a little innuendo (have they or haven't they?), *The Avengers* developed a format which has inspired numerous copycat shows, including *Adam Adamant Lives!* (1966–67), *Hart to Hart* (1979–84), *Sapphire and Steel* (1979–82), *Dempsey and Makepeace* (1985–86), *Moonlighting* (1985–89) and *The X-Files* (1993– ).

*The Avengers'* plots could be superficially serious and even, at times, frightening but as the series developed, it increasingly came to be characterized by the light-hearted style with which the leads undertook their bizarre adventures. It's not what you do, it's the way that you do it: as pop assemblages, Steed and his partners had lots of fun, demonstrating their superiority through the exercise of good taste and refinement based on a combination of traditional and modern elements – especially in the Peel years, when the leads first clinked glasses in the title sequence, the champagne cork popping and the duo riding off into the distance using quaint modes of transport, all the marks of a consummately professional couple enjoying themselves. The show's designers worked hard – especially after the programme was sold in America and went onto film, first in black and white (1965–66) and then in colour (1967) – to create the characters as highly desirable paradigms of fashion. Well off, good looking, healthy, single, multi-talented, classlessly classy, emblematically English and living for the moment, *The Avengers'* characters were distinguished by a highly distinctive appearance, residence and vehicle and by performance codes which foregrounded manners and (as befits an action series) a range of distinctive fighting styles.

Steed became instantly recognizable through his impeccable manners, his Edwardian-style Savile Row suits and, above all, his iconic props – the bowler hat and the wooden shafted umbrella. But he was also a ruthless professional spy whose performative cover never quite hid his 'end justifies the means' philosophy. Macnee developed his character in the tradition of the dandy epicene, a modern Beau Brummell combining steely masculinity with disarmingly feminine manners.[5] His mid-1960s suits were designed by upcoming French couturier Pierre Cardin; by the sixth season they were created 'by himself' (preceding Roger Moore's sartorial endeavours in the consummately pop *The Persuaders!*). Steed wore expensive cufflinks and tie pins, and the carnation in his buttonhole became a series motif with erotic overtones in the fifth-season title sequence. There was also something distinctly Modish about his Chelsea boots, giving him an air of contemporaneity which set off his otherwise Establishment look.

Steed's iconic bowler and brolley, lifted from Ralph Richardson's Major Hammond in *Q Planes* (1939), proved to be vital props and running gags. In 'The Living Dead' (February 1967), for instance, the bowler was comically augmented by a miner's lamp, while his umbrella could also be used as a swordstick, a conceit which inspires humorous moments in both 'The Charmers' (February 1964) and its later remake 'The Correct Way to Kill' (March 1967), where 'gentlemen' being trained to hail a taxi with their umbrellas are really practicing aggressive swordsmanship. Steed himself was a dirty fighter, using his umbrella to poke or trip opponents, and physically never putting himself out more than he had to. His habitus was that of the perennial clubman: his Westminster Mews combined imperialist trappings with modern gadgets and – with American notions of Englishness in mind – in the Rigg and Thorson seasons he drove iconic classic 1920s cars, a range of green Bentleys and also a Rolls-Royce.

If Steed was a traditional icon with a contemporary slant, Cathy Gale and Emma Peel were, in their respective moments, icons of the avant-garde Now. The introduction of an action woman in the second season was perceived as revolutionary in itself, but to dress her in a 'kinky' leather action suit and 'kinky' leather boots, which accessed sado-masochistic pornographic subcultural codes for a mainstream TV audience, was excitingly outrageous. First worn by Honor Blackman in 'Mr. Teddy Bear' (September 1962), the leather suit was designed by Michael Whittaker to enable her to fight effectively with her indomitable Judo style.[6] Whittaker took the leather motif and used it to design a wardrobe of partly interchangeable items, making Cathy Gale a fetishistically charged heroine whose look was arguably the main reason why *The Avengers* developed into a cult sensation (see Figure 14.1). *The Spectator* reported that '[*The Avengers*] keeps the Bright Young Things of Belgravia and Chelsea at home on Saturday nights' (quoted in Rogers, 1989: 56) and the risqué sexual tendencies which Blackman's costumes connoted attracted the attention of 'serious' commentator Gillian Freeman who, in her study of 1960s pornographic literature, opined: 'The trouble is that adult play, except at the non-participant level of fairy tales, or television shows like *The Avengers*, where it can be as kinky as you like without anxiety, acutely embarrasses us' (1967: 5). The implication being that secretly 'we' all love it. Building on the stars' identification with 'kinkiness', in 1963 Blackman and Macnee recorded the one and only Avengers novelty record, 'Kinky Boots', released in February 1964. A flop in its day, it became a top-ten hit when re-released in 1990.[7]

Diana Rigg's Emma Peel, initially resembling a Jackie Kennedy clone, developed the leather look in her first season and contributed to the dissemination of the leather heroine archetype across pop texts from *Batman*'s Cat Woman to Monica Vitti as *Modesty Blaise* (1966), Jane Fonda as *Barbarella* (1967) and Marianne Faithfull in *Girl on a Motorcycle* (1968). Rigg's wardrobe was designed by John Bates, who popularized 'The Look' of Mary Quant – with its mix-and-match harmonies which epitomized pop fashion – with modish black and white op art outfits taking their theme from the lines of the TV image.[8] Mrs Peel's target beret, worn in her first televised episode, 'The Town of No Return' (October 1965), is a fitting emblem of her op art phase. In this season too, Rigg wore the (in)famous Queen of Sin outfit for the Hellfire Club episode, 'A Touch of Brimstone' (February 1966): a sleek black whalebone corset set off by knee-length black boots, a dog collar with large spikes, Devilish make-up and a whip.

In her second, colour, season Emma went gaudily pop, popularizing the mini skirt before it was available in Britain (one was bought from Courreges), wearing Alun Hughes' designed 'Emmapeelers', stretch Crimplene or jersey action suits with buckles, zips, links and matching boots, and going pre-Summer of Love hippie with a florid flared trouser suit in 'The Joker' (April 1967). This was *The Avengers* at the height of its 'pop camp' (Melly, 1972: 174) phase and Emma Peel/Diana Rigg was already well on the way to becoming a monumental camp fashion icon. Julie Burchill sees her as a tough and disciplined variant of the 'Chelsea Girl' (actually she lived in a modern roof-top penthouse in Hampstead), the swinging middle-class model/actress type exemplified by Jean Shrimpton, Julie Christie, Jane Birkin, Charlotte Rampling, Vanessa Redgrave, Susan George and Susannah York, young women who were sexually independent and voracious for intense new experiences (Burchill, 1986: 86). Her choreographed fighting style (Karate-influenced in her first season and Kung Fu in her second), along with her bullet-like powder blue Lotus Elan sports car, marked her out as the paradigm of the independent action heroine even more than her predecessor Cathy Gale.[9]

*Figure 14.1* Classic Savile Row meets kinky leather – John Steed (Patrick Macnee) and Cathy Gale (Honor Blackman) in *The Avengers* (1962–64).

During their heyday – roughly from 1963 to 1967 – the Avengers were British TV drama's grooviest representatives of the media-hyped 'swinging sixties', an era mythically associated with youth, fashion, modernity, mobility and the novelty of a consumer culture based on the regular turnover of images, fashions and styles. The producers took advantage of the performers' growing celebrity status by promoting and retailing fashions relating to the series. In October 1963 Macnee and Blackman appeared (with

*Figure 14.2*   Avatars of the pop moment – John Steed (Patrick Macnee) and Mrs
Peel (Diana Rigg) as *The Avengers* (1965–67).

a great many mannequins) in the 'Avengerwear' fashion show, with Blackman modelling Frederick Starke's designs for her second season wardrobe (Rogers, 1989: 61).

Things had moved on by 1965, when John Bates' costumes for Diana Rigg formed the basis of the Jean Varon Avengers Collection, the first set of fashion items to derive entirely from a television series. This represented an attempt to disseminate the series' look across popular consumer culture, using a merchandising strategy based on the iconic aura of the show's stars, who took on a mantle as models and fictional arbiters of taste previously reserved for the Hollywood stars of the 1930s and 1940s. In Britain, 1965 saw the naming of the 'New Aristocracy' – the upwardly mobile models, musicians, actors, writers, designers, editors and photographers glamorized by David Bailey in *A Box of Pin Ups* – who represented a new, democratized notion of celebrity in consumer society (Booker, 1970: 15; 19–25). *The Avengers* was pivotal to this pop moment; it was no surprise that its iconicity was transformed into merchandising and that style was reinforced as the primary marker of the series' popular cultural presence (see Figure 14.2).

So what of *The New Avengers'* style? Opinion has it that the 1970s is the 'Decade That Style Forgot', when kitsch reigned and fashions were often very silly (see Hunt, 1998: 1–16). Still attempting to move with, or just ahead of, the times, *The New Avengers* was an international co-production with a revised formula which most people think didn't quite work. Steed remained the suave anchorman but returned to something of his original playboy stance, occupying a country residence, sporting girl-friends (this had never been seen before) and driving, among other vehicles, a Range Rover. This time his contemporary female partner was Joanna Lumley as Purdey, a former ballet dancer with long legs adept at kicking offending villains, who wore a pudding-bowl hairdo and outfits stretching from diaphanous flowing Laura Ashley skirts to Annie Hall-like preppie boywear.

The real Joker in *The New Avengers* pack, however, was Gareth Hunt's Mike Gambit, a character who disturbed the couple formula and introduced a boorish, upwardly mobile ethos into what was previously an apparently (upper?) classless Fantasyland. Gambit seemed to have blundered in from *The Sweeney* or a car chase sequence in *Starsky and Hutch*, bringing with him a brashly jingoistic tone and a new 1970s toughness (again in some ways a return to the early days). *The New Avengers* were still fashion icons but they did not capture the popular imagination in the manner of their predecessors. As time has passed, nostalgia has welcomed the last two seasons into memories of *The Avengers* cycle and Joanna Lumley has certainly achieved a cult iconic status (Gareth Hunt less so). But overall *The New Avengers* increasingly lacked that quality which distinguished the original series: charm.

## ADAPTING *THE AVENGERS'* STYLE: MEDIA AND MERCHANDISE

The retailing of *Avengers'* fashions is but one example of a broader set of processes through which the series was promoted and its image disseminated for sale in other forms. These could draw on narrative codes, for example, in adaptations for print media, radio or theatre, or sound codes, such as excerpted theme tunes for recorded media forms. For our purposes, however, those that utilized trademarked iconic visual codes of style, most notably relating to the characters and their props, are of primary interest. Stuart Ewen explains that there are three requirements for the appropriation of an image into the style market of popular consumer culture: '[it] must be able to *be disembodied, separated from its source* ... capable of being *"economically" mass produced* [and] be able to *become merchandise,* to be promoted and sold' (Ewen, 1988: 247). Thus the original cultural commodity's representational aura furbishes these other marketable forms with much of their value.

From the various incarnations of Tarzan and Batman, to *Avengers'* contemporaries such as *The Man From U.N.C.L.E.* and (the cinematic) James Bond, such marketing strategies have long been practised to generate income and nurture the cult status of iconic popular heroes.[10] Learning perhaps from *U.N.C.L.E.*'s commercial example, in true pop style from around 1966 there was a real surge to recommodify *The Avengers* and to disseminate it into other popular media and merchandise.[11] A dozen *Avengers* novels were published in the 1960s, each with character-based iconic packaging and an original storyline, while six comparably packaged *New Avengers* novelizations came out between 1976 and 1977. A range of comics was produced, including the colour two-page serial strip which ran for twenty-six weeks in *Diana*, pitting Steed and Mrs. Peel against a range of zany criminals – among them the infamous Madame Zingara, whose trance-inducing dress temporarily turned Emma into a zombie. There were three 1960s annuals (one Emma, two Tara) and two more in the 1970s, each including significant iconic adaptations in their own right, as well as a short-lived 1971 stage play, a 1972 South African radio play series and several repackagings of the series' theme tunes (a trend which was to continue).

Alongside these media adaptations, in the realm of (allegedly) children's toys and related merchandise, *The Avengers'* visual style iconicity really came into its own. Top of the list in 1966 was the Corgi Gift Set No. 40, comprising replicas of Steed's 1929 Bentley (oddly red rather than the series' green), with the bowler-hatted one at the wheel, and Mrs Peel's Lotus Elan (err ... white rather than pale blue), with a separate standing Emma figure. The set came in a presentation box featuring Steed and Emma in medium close-up, the cars in question (stationary and in action on the road), a pop art Avengers logo depicting a hand (Emma's?) holding a carnation in front of a circular target and the trademark corgi dog. Eleven years later, Dinky issued two, differently customized, versions of Purdey's TR7. There were also Emma and Purdey dolls, *Avengers* and *New Avengers* jigsaw puzzle sets and, of course, the miniature John Steed Swordstick and bowler hat.[12] In line with Ewen's dicta, each of these acquired its aura of desirability by re-presenting aspects of the series' iconic visual style in a separate, saleable material form.[13]

As with all merchandise relating to popular cultural fads, most of the 'original' *Avengers* and *New Avengers* products were well used before being lost or discarded. With cult status gradually attaching to the series, however, the value cycle model invented by maverick theorist Michael Thompson in the 1960s (see Thompson, 1979) has become particularly pertinent. Thompson argues that at any given moment objects (including buildings, people, ideas and values) can be defined as either durable (value rising), transient (value falling) or rubbish (invisible or negative value). Things which have fallen into the rubbish category can, under propitious conditions, transfer into the durable category and rise in value again. Once upon a time *Avengers* bric-à-brac found at car boot sales was transient and heading for the rubbish category. Nowadays you are likely to find that a dealer has got there before you and is selling the Steed Swordstick or 'Kinky Boots' single in a retro shop at a durable price, as it is now defined as collectable. Those Corgi cars 'lost' in the attic, indeed, are currently worth at least £200.

## RECYCLING *THE AVENGERS'* STYLE: FROM THE SEVENTIES TO THE MOVIE

Postmodern times: as early as 1978 (just after *The New Avengers* finished its run) style guru Peter York observed that we were moving into a culture where media recycling of the recent past was becoming the norm of everyday life (York, 1980: 178–92).[14] In postmodern culture, the trademark stylistic elements which distinguish an 'original' cultural commodity are crucial to its potential for successful recycling. Having gained its aura primarily through iconic style, *The Avengers* has been a prime candidate for multiple recycling – through being shown again, and being re-articulated and recommodified – in 'retro' culture since the 1970s.

In terms of domestic technologies, the rescreening of *The Avengers* has mushroomed with the growth of cable and satellite television – but the strategy arguably began in 1964 when, in the lengthy gap between the Blackman and Rigg seasons, selected episodes from the early years were shown as *The Best of the Avengers*. With the spread of video, for the completist collectors among us, the combination of reference guides and the release of the series on video by Lumiere Pictures Ltd in the early 1990s (and subsequently in a variety of other formats) enabled a comprehensive scrutiny both of individual episodes and of changes over time. Since the mid-1990s, also, growing use of the web has opened up new opportunities for further home-based fan activities. Not surprisingly, Miller notes that one of the earliest *Avengers* web sites was mainly devoted to pictures of Diana Rigg in leathers (1997: 156).

Other recommodifications have brought people out of the home for novel Avenger experiences. For those preferring an actual (as opposed to a virtual) community, there have been regular *Avengers* weekends, including treasure hunts somewhat modelled on the cross-country antics of the 1967 episode 'Dead Man's Treasure'. In the early 1990s, meanwhile, Anthony and Annette McKay compiled a tourist guide to locations used in classic British TV dramas, with *The Avengers* given privileged attention. The title of their work, *A Guide to Avengerland* (McKay and McKay, 1993), typifies the Heritage repackaging of place under the prestige of a branded name (see Hewison, 1987). You too could visit the miniature railway at Stapleford Park, Melton Mowbray, Leicestershire, where Emma experienced her Perils of Pauline in 'The Grave-Diggers' in April 1965.

Following the 1978 American copycat pilot *Escapade: Avengers USA* (never picked up for series production), actual remakes of *The Avengers* were thin on the ground, though at various times announcements were made of a new *New Avengers*, with

*Figure 14.3* 'Saving the world in style' – Ralph Fiennes' and Uma Thurman's big screen re-interpretation of Steed and Mrs Peel in *The Avengers* (1998).

mooted reworkings of the formula for *The Avengers – International* and *The Avenging Angel.* In 1998, however, after endless on-off rumours, *The Avengers* movie finally arrived on a wave of action series remakes and postmodern spy spoofs. With its $40 million budget and the promotional hookline 'Saving the World in Style', the movie returned us to the Steed and Peel era, when the series was at its most hip and happening. Thus Ralph Fiennes' Steed sports a dapper Edwardian pinstripe while all Uma Thurman's costumes were designed to lead up to her donning the mythical leather catsuit (Rogers, 1998: 50) (see Figure 14.3). Thurman also plays a Bad Emma double: her suit is scaly, buckled and super-perverse and her boots are impossibly, fetishistically high heeled. (Sex would definitely equal Death with Bad Em.) Steed drives a classic Bentley, while Emma is upgraded to a monstrously phallic E-type Jaguar, which is then ritually destroyed by computer-generated giant bees. The expensive sets, such as Emma's gorgeous sixties pad, complete with mock Warhol screenprint, invoke the mid-1960s *Avengers* on a vastly grander scale, while at every level, as Kim Newman points out (Newman, 1998: 39), the movie lifts bits and pieces from the old shows, including the idea of the invisible spy – Patrick Macnee appearing in a cameo role as Invisible Jones – originally a plot device in 'The See-Through Man' (February 1967). But the film flopped – both critically and commercially.

So what is wrong with this triumphant recycling of iconic style? In a word, its emptiness. The movie has no clearly-developed revisionist stance to offer on its origins or the 1960s more generally. The calculated sets and computer generated images empty out the more makeshift and 'found' resonances of the original series, made at pace and ragged round the edges. And the repartee between the leads lacks any wit or sparkle. *The Avengers'* characters may have been cardboard cut-outs but the performances of Macnee and the leading actresses were filled with humour and *joie de vivre.* Yet the film reminds us that, as style icons, Steed and Emma still look great.

## REMEMBERING *THE AVENGERS*

No doubt by the time you read this, *The Avengers'* fortieth anniversary celebrations will have spawned a TV retrospective night, a fresh round of merchandise and new appreciative tributes to the series and its style. Stuart Ewen argues that, in our commodified popular culture, perception and memory are increasingly shaped by iconic, media-based representations of ephemeral trends, fads and fashions. The complexity of history in any particular era is simplified into a set of visual images which come to define the meaning of an age (Ewen, 1988: 248).[15] This observation chimes well with the findings of Lynn Spigel and Henry Jenkins in their work on *Batman* audiences (Spigel and Jenkins, 1991). When, in 1989, at the height of Bat fever, they interviewed adults about their memories of the 1960s pop camp TV series, they found that these concerned not the specifics of individual plots or episodes but rather prototypical 'repisodic' elements, 'isolated but recurring images' (ibid., 1991: 35) such as the heroes sliding down the batpole, zany graphics and exotic death traps; in other words, mainly iconic visual stylistic traits of the kind discussed throughout this essay.

This, too, is how we remember *The Avengers*. Steed with his bowler and brolley gallivanting through Forever England country lanes in his vintage Bentley (cue Corgi packaging). Em in her catsuit and kinky boots despatching some hapless mad villain in a startling p/op art environment (cue web downloads). And the witty rapport between the leads as they exercised discrimination and domination in the series' surreal world (cue images of champagne or perilous action situations). *The Avengers* is not alone in evoking such vivid memories. Nevertheless, by virtue of its distinctive style it has achieved a 'cult' style status unmatched by any comparable British TV series. *Dr Who* and *Blake's 7* may have bigger fan followings (see Jenkins, 1992) but their sense of style is not associated with that unique aura of period stylishness which underpins *The Avengers'* enduring reputation.

## NOTES

1   On the pop series, see Buxton (1990: 70-76; 96-107; 117-19) and note also that Emma Peel, icon, adorns the distinctly pop arty cover of his monograph. On pop in *The Avengers*, see Miller (1997: 25-40) and on pop more generally, Melly (1972) and Hebdige (1988: 116-43).

2   As well as *The Avengers*, Newman not only brought contemporary drama to ABC's *Armchair Theatre* but also, after moving to the BBC, launched the *Wednesday Play* and *Dr Who* (see Ridgman, 1992: 150; Tulloch and Alvarado, 1983: 38–43).

3   Emma's racing-driver husband Peter returned from the dead in Rigg's final episode 'The Forget-Me-Knot'. In true surreal *Avengers'* fashion, he was an exact double of Steed.

4   Joanna Lumley's Purdey also appears to be in love with Steed. In 'Angels of Death' (September 1977) she seems to be about to reveal her feelings as they are squeezed together by the walls of a shrinking room. But Gambit rescues them before she completes her revelation.

5   See Paglia (1992: 531–72), whose observations on nineteenth-century salon life are often applicable to Steed and Mrs Gale/Mrs Peel, for instance: 'The androgyne of manners – the male feminine in his careless, lounging passivity, the female masculine in her brilliant, aggressive wit – has the profane sleekness of chic' (ibid.: 532).

6   Cathy Gale's most legendary fight is with wrestler Jackie Pallo in January 1964's 'Mandrake'. As Cornell, Day and Topping (1998: 114) remark: 'If your bag is seeing a big strapping man being knocked senseless by a woman dressed in black leather then *this* is the episode for you!'.

7   Gale/Blackman's leather icon status is identified in Freeman (1967:150 and 151), Lurie (1983: 232), Polhemus and Proctor (1984: 14) and Thorne (1993: 135).

8   On Rigg's op art Quant 'Look', see Quant (1967), Bernard (1978: 16; 30–33) and Rogers (1989: 89).

9   Peel/Rigg's iconic status reverberates throughout popular culture: see Miller (1997: 62–63), Cawthorne *et al.* (1998: 59), Rocha (1999: 34–35) and Paton (2000: 33).

10   On Tarzan, Batman and *The Man From U.N.C.L.E.* respectively, see Morton (1993: 106), Uricchio and Pearson (eds) (1991), and Heitland (1988: 159–66).

11   This paragraph is indebted to the detailed summary of *Avengers* and *New Avengers* merchandise in Rogers (1989: 270–85).

12   Setchfield (1997) offers an 'exclusive' Emma Peel Doll, 'a cut-out-and-keep dolly of TV's coolest heroine, complete with fuss-free Spy Chick wardrobe!' (64).

13   Rogers (1989: 272; 278) lists other items of *Avengers* merchandise which were licensed but never issued, including Avengers men's toiletries and a cosmetic gun with lipstick in the barrel and a compact in the butt.

14  For York on postmodernism see his 'Post Modern' (1978, repr. in York, 1980: 210–18). On the passage of pop into everyday postmodern recycling see also Buxton (1990: 117) and Ridgman (1992: 157).
15  For entertaining books on the 1960s which offer such a 'style' model of history, see Cawthorne (1989) and Edelstein (1985). Both refer to *The Avengers*.

## REFERENCES

Bennett, Tony and Woollacott, Janet (1987) *Bond and Beyond: The Political Career of a Popular Hero*, London: MacMillan.

Bernard, Barbara (1978) *Fashion in the 60s*, London: Academy Editions.

Booker, Christopher (1970) *The Neophiliacs: A Study of the Revolution in English Life in the Fifties and the Sixties*, London: Fontana.

Burchill, Julie (1986) *Girls on Film*, New York: Pantheon Books.

Buxton, David (1990) *From The Avengers to Miami Vice: Form and Ideology in Television Series*, Manchester: Manchester University Press.

Carraze, Alain and Putheaud, Jean-Luc with Geairns, Alex J. (1998) *The Avengers Companion*, trans. Paul Buck, San Francisco: Bay Books (orig. publ. 1990).

Cawthorne, Nigel (1989) *Sixties Source Book: A Visual Reference to the Style of a New Generation*, London: Virgin.

Cawthorne, Nigel, Evans, Emily, Kitchen-Smith, Marc, Mulvey, Kate and Richards, Melissa (1998) *Key Moments in Fashion*, London: Hamlyn.

Cornell, Paul, Day, Martin and Topping, Keith (1998) *The Avengers Dossier*, London: Virago.

Denning, Michael (1987) *Cover Stories: Narrative and Ideology in the British Spy Thriller*, London: Routledge & Kegan Paul.

Edelstein, Andrew J. (1985) *The Pop Sixties: A Personal and Irreverent Guide*, New York: World Almanac Publications.

Ewen, Stuart (1988) *All Consuming Images: The Politics of Style in Contemporary Culture*, New York: Basic Books.

Freeman, Gillian (1967) *The Undergrowth of Literature*, London: Nelson.

Gitlin, Todd (1994) *Inside Prime Time*, London: Routledge (orig. publ. 1983).

Hebdige, Dick (1988) *Hiding in the Light: On Images and Things*, London: Comedia/ Routledge.

Heitland, Jon (1988) *The Man from U.N.C.L.E. Book: The Behind-the-Scenes Story of a Television Classic*, London: Titan.

Hewison, Robert (1987) *The Heritage Industry: Britain in a Climate of Decline*, London: Methuen.

Hunt, Leon (1998) *British Low Culture: From Safari Suits to Sexploitation*, London: Routledge.

Jenkins, Henry (1992) *Textual Poachers: Television Fans and Participatory Culture*, London: Routledge.

Lurie, Alison (1983) *The Language of Clothes*, London: Hamlyn.

McKay, Anthony and McKay, Annette (1993) *A Guide to Avengerland: A Listing of Over 250 Locations Used in the Filming of Classic British TV Series*, Doncaster: Time Screen.

Melly, George (1972) *Revolt Into Style: The Pop Arts in Britain*, Harmondsworth: Penguin (orig. publ. 1970).

Miller, Toby (1997) *The Avengers*, London: BFI.

Morton, Walt (1993) 'Tracking the Signs of Tarzan: Trans-Media Representation of a Pop-culture Icon', in Pat Kirkham and Janet Thumin (eds), *You Tarzan: Masculinity, Movies and Men*, London: Lawrence & Wishart: 106–25.

Newman, Kim (1998) Review of *The Avengers, Sight and Sound,* Vol. 8, No. 10, October: 38–9.

Paglia, Camille (1992) *Sexual Personae: Art and Decadence from Nefertiti to Emily Dickinson*, London: Penguin (orig. publ. 1990).

Paton, Maureen (2000) 'The Rachael Capers', *Evening Standard,* 7 March: 33.

Pearson, Roberta E. and Uricchio, William (eds) (1991) *The Many Lives of the Batman: Critical Approaches to a Superhero and His Media*, New York and London: Routledge/BFI.

Polhemus, Ted and Procter, Lynn (1984) *Pop Styles*, London: Vermilion.

Quant, Mary (1967) *Quant by Quant*, London: Pan.

Ridgman, Jeremy (1992) 'Inside the Liberal Heartland: Television and the Popular Imagination in the 1960s', in Bart Moore-Gilbert and John Seed (eds), *Cultural Revolution?: The Challenge of the Arts in the 1960s*, London: Routledge: 137–59.

Rocha, John (1999) *20th Century Icons: Fashion*, Bath: Absolute Press.

Rogers, Dave (1989) *The Complete Avengers: Everything You Ever Wanted to Know About The Avengers and The New Avengers*, London: Boxtree.

—— (1998) *The Avengers: The Making of the Movie*, London: Titan Books.

Ryall, Tom (1996) *Alfred Hitchcock and the British Cinema*, Athlone Press: London.

Setchfield, Nick (1997) 'Imperial Leather', *Cult TV*, Issue 3, October: 61,62,63.

Spigel, Lynn and Jenkins, H. (1991) 'Same Bat Channel, Different Bat Times: Mass Culture and Popular Memory' in William Uricchio, and Roberta Pearson (eds.), *The Many Lives of the Batman,* London: BFI: 117–148.

Thompson, Michael (1979) *Rubbish Theory*, Oxford: Oxford University Press.

Thorne, Tony (1993) *Fads, Fashions & Cults: From Acid House to Zoot Suit*, London: Bloomsbury.

Tulloch, John and Alvarado, M. (1983) *Doctor Who – The Unfolding Text*, London, Macmillan.

York, Peter (1980) *Style Wars*, London: Sidgwick and Jackson.

# 15

# THE SIXTIES IN
# THE NINETIES

## Pastiche or hyperconsciousness?

*John Storey*

### THE SIXTIES REVISITED

Like Austin Powers, John Steed travelled successfully from the sixties to the nineties. He made a double return. Not only did the character make his reappearance in a new, big-screen version of *The Avengers* (1998), but Patrick Macnee, who had captivated 1960s television audiences with a 'camp'[1] mixture of city-gent traditionalism and swinging pop style, reaffirmed his status as a popular cultural icon, as he reprised his role in the video for the 1996 Oasis single *Don't Look Back in Anger*.

Steed was not alone in his return to action for contemporary audiences. The 1990s also witnessed the release of movie versions of *The Untouchables* (1987), *The Fugitive* (1993), *Mission: Impossible* (1996), *The Saint* (1997) and *The Mod Squad* (1999) – a trend which continued into the new century, with the release of *Mission: Impossible 2* (2000), *Charlie's Angels* (2000) and a projected (at the time of writing) movie version of *Hawaii Five–O*.

Similarly, television has been more than happy to recycle its own past. The late 1990s saw the launch of revamped versions of *Kung Fu*, *The Professionals*, and two new incarnations of *Charlie's Angels*.[2] Channel 4 (UK) has even hosted entire evenings dedicated to the 'action classics' *Starsky and Hutch* and (again) *Charlie's Angels*. Contemporary interest in action series of the 1960s and 1970s has also prompted a proliferation in video releases of vintage action programmes, together with numerous re-runs on cable and satellite channels – TNT, for example, resurrecting *Charlie's Angels*, *C.H.I.P.S.* and *Kung Fu*, while other stations have followed this fashion with *The Bionic Woman*, *Jason King*, *Kojak*, *The Professionals* and so on. While the eagerness of cable and satellite channels to recycle television texts from the recent past can be partly explained in terms of an economic need for cheap programming, it is also undoubtedly the case that such scheduling is driven by a desire to exploit a perceived wave of popular interest in these television series.[3]

In fact, contemporary predilections for vintage action TV series have registered across a wide field of cultural texts and practices. The 1990s, for example, saw the release of an array of popular CD compilations such as *Cult Fiction*, *The Son of Cult*

*Fiction* and *The Cult Files*, while TVT Records released four highly successful volumes of general television themes from the 1960s and 1970s.[4] Many contemporary pop artists, exploring a 'sixties-in-the-nineties' theme, have also played with 'action' motifs. For example, Robbie Williams' single *Millennium* (1998) not only sampled John Barry's theme to *On Her Majesty's Secret Service* (1969), but the accompanying video featured a playful recreation of a 1960s Bond-style epic – with a dinner-jacketed Williams surrounded by luxurious sports cars, well-shaken martinis, and a bevy of beautiful women. More generally, there have been many examples of bands, Oasis being perhaps the most visible, who have projected a look and a sound which is clearly that of the 1960s from the perspective of the 1990s.[5] 'Retro' music nights have now become a feature of most major nightclubs, with some – for example 'Carwash' in London and '*Charlie's Angels* Flaming Disco' in Brighton – consciously playing with the themes and imagery of vintage action series. Recent years have also seen the appearance of magazines targeted at the twenty- to forty-something age group, for example, *Cult TV* and *Retro Generation*, focused on the world of retro-television and fashion. Finally, T-shirts, posters and postcards featuring slogans, logos and pictures associated with the 'classic' action canon can be purchased in every high street.[6]

Sooner rather than later in discussions of the contemporary fondness for 'retro'-style and the recycling of the themes and imagery of the recent past, someone always introduces postmodernism as a way of supposedly explaining what is happening.

## POSTMODERNISM: INSIDE THE IMAGINARY MUSEUM

Of all the critics who have engaged in the debate over what is (or which is) postmodernism, the American Marxist cultural critic Fredric Jameson is perhaps the most relevant to a discussion of the 'sixties in the nineties'. For Jameson postmodernism is more than just a particular cultural style, it is 'the cultural dominant of the logic of late capitalism' (1984: 85). His argument is informed by Ernest Mandel's model of capitalism's three-stage development: 'market capitalism', 'monopoly capitalism' and 'late or multinational capitalism' (Jameson, 1984: 78). According to Jameson, capitalism's third stage 'constitutes . . . the purest form of capital yet to have emerged, a prodigious expansion of capital into hitherto uncommodified areas' (ibid.).

Postmodernism is, therefore, so the argument goes, a hopelessly commodified culture. Unlike modernism, which taunted the commercial culture of capitalism from a safe critical distance, postmodern culture, rather than resisting, 'replicates and reproduces . . . the logic of consumer capitalism' (Jameson, 1983: 125); moreover, 'it reinforces and intensifies it' (1984: 85). As a result, 'aesthetic production . . . has become integrated into commodity production generally' (56). Culture is no longer ideological, disguising the economic activities of capitalist society, it is itself an economic activity, perhaps the most important economic activity of all.

Jameson claims that postmodernism is a 'schizophrenic' culture. He uses the term in the sense developed by Jacques Lacan to signify a language disorder, a failure of the temporal relationship between signifiers. The schizophrenic experiences time not as a continuum (past–present–future), but as a perpetual present, which is only occasionally marked by the intrusion of the past, or the possibility of a future. The 'reward' for the loss of conventional selfhood (the sense of self as always located within a temporal continuum) is an intensified sense of the present – what Dick Hebdige (1998) calls 'acid perspectivism' (suggesting that the experience Jameson describes is similar to 'tripping' – being under the influence of the hallucinogenic drug LSD). To call postmodern culture 'schizophrenic' is to claim that it has lost its sense of history (and its sense of a future different from the present). It is a culture suffering from 'historical amnesia', locked into the discontinuous flow of perpetual presents. The temporal culture of modernism has given way to the spatial culture of postmodernism.

Jameson relates this development to the claim that postmodernism marks the 'death of the subject' (1984: 63). He argues that 'the disappearance of the individual subject, along with its formal consequences, the increasing unavailability of the personal style, engender the well nigh universal practice today of what may be called pastiche' (64). According to Jameson, this means the end of the private and unique vision which is said to have informed the aesthetic thinking and cultural practices of high modernism. As he points out, there are two ways to think this. On the one hand, we can agree that the moment of individual style has passed. On the other, we can say with post-structuralism that such 'individualism' was a myth, a construct. It does not really matter on which we decide (he chooses the former), because, according to Jameson, both lead us to the world of pastiche:[7] a world in which stylistic invention and innovation is no longer possible. Given this, 'the producers of [postmodern] culture have nowhere to turn but to the past: the imitation of dead styles, speech through all the masks and voices stored up in the imaginary museum of a now global culture' (65). Therefore, rather than a culture of pristine creativity, postmodern culture is said to be a culture of quotations, a culture of 'intertextuality'. Instead of original cultural production, there is said to be only cultural production born out of other cultural production. In short, according to Jameson, it is a culture which 'involve[s] the necessary failure of art and the aesthetic, the failure of the new, the imprisonment in the past' (1983: 116). It is therefore a culture 'of flatness or depthlessness, a new kind of superficiality in the most literal sense' (1984: 60). A culture of images and surfaces, without 'latent' possibilities, it derives its hermeneutic force from other images, other surfaces; the interplay of intertextuality. What Jameson refers to as the 'complacent play of historical allusion' (1988: 105).

Jameson's best known example of the practice of pastiche in postmodern culture is what he calls the 'nostalgia film'. The category could include a number of films from the 1980s and 1990s: *Back to the Future I, II,* and *III* (1985, 1989, 1990), *Peggy Sue Got Married* (1986), *Rumble Fish* (1983), *Angel Heart* (1987), *Blue Velvet* (1986). He argues that the nostalgia film sets out to recapture the atmosphere and stylistic peculiarities of the past – especially the 1950s. He claims that:

for Americans at least, the 1950s remain the privileged lost object of desire – not merely the stability and prosperity of a pax Americana, but also the first naive innocence of the countercultural impulses of early rock and roll and youth gangs.

(Jameson, 1984: 67)

As he insists, the nostalgia film is not just another name for the historical film. This is clearly demonstrated by the fact that his own list includes the *Star Wars* trilogy. Now it might seem strange to suggest that a film about the future can be nostalgic for the past, but as Jameson explains:

[Star Wars] is metonymically a ... nostalgia film ... it does not reinvent a picture of the past in its lived totality; rather, by reinventing the feel and shape of [a] characteristic art object of an older period.

(Jameson, 1983: 116)

Films such as *Raiders of the Lost Ark* (1981) and *Robin Hood, Prince of Thieves* (1991), *Judge Dredd* (1995), *Independence Day* (1996), *The Phantom Menace* (1999), operate in a similar way to evoke metonymically a sense of the narrative certainties of the past. Therefore, according to Jameson, the nostalgia film works in one and/or two ways: it recaptures and represents the atmosphere and stylistic features of the past; and it recaptures and represents certain styles of viewing of the past. What is of crucial significance for Jameson is that such films do not attempt to recapture or represent the 'real' past, but always make do instead with certain cultural myths and stereotypes about the past. They offer what he calls 'false realism', films about other films, representations of other representations. History is effaced by 'historicism ... the random cannibalisation of all the styles of the past, the play of random stylistic allusion' (1984: 65–66). Moreover, he insists that our awareness of the play of stylistic allusion:

is now a constitutive and essential part of a film's structure: we are now in 'intertextuality' as a deliberate, built-in feature of the aesthetic effect, and as the operator of a new connotation of 'pastness' and pseudo-historical depth, in which the history of aesthetic styles displaces 'real' history.

(Jameson, 1984: 67)

*Austin Powers: The Spy Who Shagged Me* (1999) could be cited as a very profitable example of the random cannibalization of the past. (see Figure 15.1). The movie is said to have grossed almost $55 million within a week of its release in the USA (Floyd, 1999: 77), increasing to $100 million in two weeks (Palmer, 1999:78).[8] As Mike Myers (the film's writer, producer and principal star) himself explains:

I'm a police composite of every comedian I've ever liked, Peter Sellars, Alec Guinness, Dan Aykroyd, John Belushi, Woody Allen, Monty Python, The Goodies, the British TV show Some Mothers Do Ave 'Em, On the Buses, the Carry On films.

(Floyd, 1999: 78)

*Figure 15.1* 'Yeah, baby! Yeah!' – Mike Myers and Elizabeth Hurley in *Austin Powers: The Spy Who Shagged Me* (1999).

Moreover, Myers' account of the origins of Austin Powers could also be cited as evidence of Jameson's argument about the random cannibalization of the past:

> I just love the conventions of James Bond and sixties movies. Wayne's World is everything I was, growing up in the suburbs of Toronto in the mid-seventies, Austin Powers is everything I watched [on TV in the late sixties]. My parents were from Liverpool, and there's no one more English than an Englishman who no longer lives there. Every molecule of British culture that came across the Atlantic was tasted and worshipped.
>
> (Duncan, 1999:18)

> Around 1994, I was driving and listening to Burt Bacharach's The Look of Love, which is so sixties. And it made me think of all those cult TV shows. I went back home and I wrote the original Austin Powers script in just three weeks ... . I mean, this stuff is coming direct from my childhood.
>
> (Palmer, 1999)

Indeed, the very character of Austin Powers can himself be seen as symptomatic of the process Jameson describes: cryogenically frozen in 1967 (the summer of love) and unfrozen in 1997. Even this plot could be seen as a Jameson-esque 'quotation' from the past – Myers' story-line almost certainly being indebted to the BBC action series *Adam Adamant Lives!* (1966–67) in which an Edwardian adventurer entombed in a block of ice since 1902 is defrosted amid the coffee bars and fashion boutiques of the 1960s, battling with assorted fiendish master criminals as he acclimatizes to the racy culture and argot of 'Swinging London' (' "Piece of the action"? Yes, I like that!').

I think there are two responses that can be made to Jameson's position. The first is to point to the fact that most of the despair and 'cultural pessimism' generated by the supposed postmodern condition is an attitude and a perspective which has run concomitant with the development, since the nineteenth century, of what is usually described pejoratively as mass culture. If we situate Jameson's critique of postmodernism in this tradition, it can easily be shown to repeat points that can be found in earlier work by Matthew Arnold, the Leavisites, the Frankfurt School, positions taken in the debate about mass culture in the USA in the 1950s.[9] According to Jameson, when compared to 'the Utopian "high seriousness" of the great modernisms', postmodern culture is marked by an 'essential triviality' (1984: 85), the erosion of the older distinction between high culture and so-called mass or popular culture. This is perhaps the most distressing development of all from an academic standpoint, which has traditionally had a vested interest in preserving a realm of high or elite culture against the surrounding environment of philistinism, of schlock and kitsch, of TV series and *Reader's Digest* culture, and in transmitting difficult and complex skills of reading, listening and seeing to its initiates (1983: 112). Again, in a piece of classic Frankfurt School rhetoric, he writes of:

> 'the older kinds of folk and genuinely "popular" culture which flourished when the older social classes of a peasantry and an urban artisanat still existed

and which, from the mid-nineteenth century on, have gradually been colonized and extinguished by commodification and the market system.'

(Jameson, 1988: 112).

The supposed extinction of a genuine culture of the people, together with the claim
that high culture has been sucked into the degraded domain of commodified mass
culture, produces again what sounds remarkably like the standard Frankfurt School/
Leavisite dismissal of popular culture. Lawrence Grossberg describes Jameson's position with economy:

> For Jameson ... [t]he masses ... remain mute and passive, cultural dopes
> who are deceived by the dominant ideologies.... Hopeless they are and shall
> remain, presumably until someone else provides them with the necessary
> maps of intelligibility and critical models of resistance.
>
> (Grossberg, 1988: 174)

In spite of his rejection of a moral critique as inappropriate ('a category mistake'), and
regardless of his citing of Marx's insistence on a dialectical approach (Jameson, 1984:
86), which would see postmodern culture as both a positive and a negative development, his argument drifts inexorably to the standard Frankfurt School/Leavisite
critique of popular culture. As Iain Chambers has observed, the debate over the
postmodern condition can in part be understood as:

> the symptom of the disruptive ingression of popular culture, its aesthetics
> and intimate possibilities, into a previously privileged domain. Theory and
> academic discourses are confronted by the wider, unsystemized, popular
> networks of cultural production and knowledge. The intellectual's privilege
> to explain and distribute knowledge is threatened.[10]
>
> (Chambers, 1988: 216)

There can be little doubt that 'the disruptive ingression of popular culture' which Chambers refers to has its origins in the 1960s. It is in the 1960s that we see the beginnings of the
connection between popular culture and what is now understood as postmodernism (a
more positive, optimistic version of postmodernism than presented by Jameson). In the
work of the American cultural critic, Susan Sontag, we encounter the celebration of what
she calls a 'new sensibility'. As she explains, 'One important consequence of the new sensibility [is] that the distinction between "high" and "low" culture seems less and less meaningful' (1966: 302). We might think, for example, of the cultural valorization of the music
of popular performers like Bob Dylan or the Beatles. Another obvious example is the Pop
Art movement of the 1960s, with its rejection of the distinction between popular and high
culture: as Pop Art's first theorist, Lawrence Alloway explains:

> The area of contact was mass produced urban culture: movies, advertising,
> science fiction, pop music. We felt none of the dislike of commercial culture

standard among most intellectuals, but accepted it as a fact, discussed it in detail, and consumed it enthusiastically. One result of our discussions was to take Pop culture out of the realm of 'escapism', 'sheer entertainment', 'relaxation', and to treat it with the seriousness of art.

(see Storey, 2001: 49)

The postmodern 'new sensibility' rejected the cultural elitism of modernism. Although it often 'quoted' popular culture, modernism was marked by a deep suspicion of all things popular. Its entry into the museum and the academy as official culture was undoubtedly made easier (despite its declared antagonism to 'bourgeois philistinism') by its appeal to, and homologous relationship with, the elitism of class society. The response of the postmodern 'new sensibility' to modernism's canonization was a re-evaluation of popular culture. The postmodernism of the 1960s was therefore in part a populist attack on the elitism of modernism. It signalled a refusal of what Andreas Huyssen calls 'the great divide . . . [a] discourse which insists on the categorical distinction between high art and mass culture' (1986: viii). Moreover, according to Huyssen, 'To a large extent, it is by the distance we have travelled from this "great divide" between mass culture and modernism that we can measure our own cultural postmodernity' (57). It is clearly the case that Jameson has not himself travelled very far beyond the great divide. John Docker even claims to detect in his approach 'a near automised distaste for mass culture' (1994:127). Bryan Turner's general point about intellectuals and popular culture may have particular relevance to Jameson's position:

> Intellectuals find it difficult to come to terms with the egalitarian implications of mass consumption, since intellectual culture is based upon the assumption that knowledge can only be achieved through the asceticism of disciplined education. Mass education, mass culture, modern systems of transport and contemporary forms of consumerism are generally criticised as a falsification of genuine standards, individual freedom and the autonomy of educated tastes.
>
> (Turner, 1987:153)

The second response that can be made to Jameson's position is to point to the fact that what is being claimed as new is really only an acceleration and intensification of what has been happening in the traditions of popular entertainment since at least the nineteenth century. In other words, what Jameson (and others like him) identify as postmodern culture has always been a feature of modern popular culture. As David Chaney observes:

> the privileged qualities of postmodernism – parody/pastiche, depthlessness, allegory, spectacular show, and an ironic celebration of artifice – have all been central to the submerged traditions of popular culture. One has only to think of the traditions of music and vaudeville, the fair-ground, the circus

and pantomime, the melodramatic theatre and the literatures of crime and
romance to find all these qualities clearly displayed.

(Chaney, 1994: 204)

Elizabeth Wilson makes a similar point with regard to fashion, 'some of the themes
and hallmarks of what is today termed postmodernism have been around for a long,
long time' (1998: 399). She maintains that 'Fashion [which she describes 'as the most
popular aesthetic practice of all' (400)] . . . has relied on pastiche and the recycling of
styles throughout the industrial period' (393). More generally, she contends:

> This evidence [especially Hollywood film from the 1920s onwards] from the
> past that pastiche and nostalgia have been pervasive in popular culture
> throughout the twentieth century and indeed earlier appears to contradict
> Jameson's belief that 'nostalgia mode' is peculiarly a feature of his
> postmodern era.[11]
>
> (Wilson, 1998: 395)

Another feature shared by the texts of the postmodern and the traditions of popular
entertainment, is the play of, and playing with, intertextuality. But this is not something which can be understood using only the concepts of pastiche or nostalgic recycling. As Chaney observes:

> Popular entertainment may be structured by the reiteration of certain
> formulas and genres which provide staple narrative forms, and there may be
> endless nostalgic regression in re-cycling previous eras and styles, but even so
> there will be an overwhelming need for novelty in performance, styles and
> manners. The history of popular music since the development of cheap
> recordings as a medium of mass entertainment specifically targeted at youth
> audiences has shown this clearly.
>
> (Chaney, 1994: 210).

The intertextual, understood as a form of borrowing from what already exists, is
always also (at least potentially) a making new from combinations of what is old. In
this way, popular culture is and has always been about more than a pastiche or a
nostalgic recycling of what has been before. I quoted earlier, in a discussion of
Jameson's notion of pastiche, Mike Myers' account of the origins of *Austin Powers*.
Other things he has to say about how he came to write the two films point to something more complex than pastiche – a certain kind of parody, not of the 1960s but of a
particular way of understanding the 1960s. As Myers explains:

> The movie isn't about the 60s. If anything it's about straight culture's view
> of the 60s. It's like Matt Helm [secret agent played by Dean Martin in *The
> Silencers* (1965), *Murderer's Row* (1966), *The Ambushers* (1967), and *The
> Wrecking Crew* (1969)]. Dean Martin was a man of the 40s and 50s thrust

into the context of the 60s and having to deal with all these liberated young people. That was his response to it, it wasn't pot it was booze. It's something I noticed with my dad. He had mutton chops and dyed hair and he put in a bar downstairs at our house. He was like, 'Hey, I'm still a swinger.' It's the whole world of straight culture going, 'I'm with it. Like the kids, you know?' That's what the whole Austin Powers thing is about…. Austin Powers is like a huge in-joke that I never thought anyone else would get.

(Braund, 1999: 92)

There may therefore be a certain (postmodern) irony in Jameson's complaint about nostalgia effacing history, given that his own critique is structured by a profound nostalgia for modernist 'certainty', promoted, as it is, at the expense of detailed historical understanding of the traditions of popular entertainment.[12]

## POSTMODERN HYPERCONSCIOUSNESS

If neither Jameson's complaint, nor the object of his complaint, is new, does this mean that postmodernism does not itself provide an explanation for the emergence of the sixties in the nineties? I will now discuss work on postmodern culture which in my view (particularly because, unlike Jameson, it keeps in play both 'structure' and 'agency' (Storey 1999) [13] does present a way of thinking critically about 'nostalgia', 'intertextuality', 'recycling', 'pastiche, and 'pleasure'.

Jim Collins has identified what he calls an 'emergent type of genericity' (1993: 248): popular films which 'quote' other films, self-consciously making reference to and borrowing from different genres of film. What makes Collins' position more convincing than Jameson's, is his insistence that such films appeal to (and help constitute) an audience of knowing bricoleurs, who take pleasure from this and other forms of bricolage. Moreover, whereas Jameson argues that such forms of cinema are characterized by a failure to be truly historical, Brooker and Brooker (1997), following Collins, see instead 'a new historical sense … the shared pleasure of intertextual recognition, the critical effect of play with narrative conventions, character and cultural stereotypes, and the power rather than passivity of nostalgia' (7). Brooker and Brooker argue that Quentin Tarantino's films:

can be seen as reactivating jaded conventions and audience alike, enabling a more active nostalgia and intertextual exploration than a term such as 'pastiche', which has nowhere to go but deeper into the recycling factory, implies. Instead of 'pastiche', we might think of 're-writing' or 're-viewing' and, in terms of the spectator's experience, of the 're-activation' and 're-configuration' of a given generational 'structure of feeling' within a more dynamic and varied set of histories'.

(Brooker and Brooker, 1997: 7)

They point to the ways in which Tarantino's work presents an 'aesthetic of recycling ... an affirmative 'bringing back to life', a 'making new' (1997: 56).

Popular culture (television, pop music, cinema, fashion, etc.) has always recycled its own history (remakes, revivals, cover versions, comebacks, etc.). Rapid advances in technology (for example, the technologies of 'sampling', the introduction of cable, satellite and digital television, the film-on-video/DVD market, etc.) have in recent years rapidly expanded and accelerated this process. But are the textual results of this process (which include the materials for the making of the sixties in the nineties) best understood using the term pastiche? 'Sampling' is a favourite example of what Jameson (and those who share his perspective) understand as postmodern pastiche. But, as Andrew Goodwin points out, what is often missed in such claims is the way in which sampling is used:

> these critical strategies miss both the historicizing function of sampling tech-
> nologies in contemporary pop and the ways in which textual incorporation
> cannot be adequately understood as 'blank parody'. We need categories to
> add to pastiche, which demonstrate how contemporary pop opposes, cele-
> brates and promotes the texts it steals from.
>
> (Goodwin, 1991: 173)

Goodwin insists that sampling is often 'used to invoke history and authenticity' and that 'it has often been overlooked that the "quoting" of sounds and styles acts to historicize contemporary culture' (175). In the main, pop music still tends to operate with an aesthetic which drifts between romanticism's tortured genius and modernism's avant-garde artist. Because of this, sampling is rarely, if ever, done as a form of pastiche (or even parody); samples are incorporated into the 'organic whole' in much the same way as occurs in T.S. Eliot's classic monument to modernist poetic practice, *The Waste Land* (1922).

According to Collins, part of what is postmodern about western societies is the fact that the old is not simply replaced by the new, but is recycled for circulation together with the new. As he explains, 'The ever-expanding number of texts and technologies is both a reflection of and a significant contribution to the 'array' – the perpetual circulation and recirculation of signs that forms the fabric of postmodern cultural life' (Collins 1993: 246). He argues that '[t]his foregrounded, hyperconscious intertextuality reflects changes in terms of audience competence and narrative technique, as well as a fundamental shift in what constitutes both entertainment and cultural literacy in [postmodern culture]' (250). As a consequence of this, Collins argues, 'Narrative action now operates at two levels simultaneously – in reference to character adventure and in reference to a text's adventures in the array of contemporary cultural production' (254). The widespread eclecticism of postmodern culture is encouraging and helping to produce what Collins calls the 'sophisticated bricoleur' (337) of postmodern culture. For example, a television series like *Twin Peaks* both constitutes an audience as bricoleurs and in turn is watched by an audience who celebrate its bricolage.

Postmodernist eclecticism might only occasionally be a preconceived design choice in individual programmes, but it is built into the technologies of media-sophisticated societies. Thus television, like the postmodern subject, must be conceived as a site – an intersection of multiple, conflicting cultural messages. Only by recognizing this interdependency of bricolage and eclecticism can we come to appreciate the profound changes in the relationship of reception and production in postmodern cultures. Not only has reception become another form of meaning production, but production has increasingly become a form of reception as it rearticulates antecedent and competing forms of representation.

(Collins, 1993: 338)

In a similar way, Umberto Eco, drawing on Charles Jencks' notion of 'double coding', identifies a postmodern sensibility exhibited in an awareness of what he calls the 'already said'. He gives the example of a man who cannot tell his lover 'I love you madly', out of fear that it might produce only ridicule, and so says instead: 'As Barbara Cartland would put it, I love you madly' (see Collins, 1992: 333). Given that we now live in an increasingly media-saturated world, the 'already said' is, as Collins observes, 'still being said'; for example, in the way television (in a effort to fill the space opened up by the growth in satellite and cable channels) recycles its own accumulated past, and that of cinema, and broadcasts these alongside what is new in both media. This does not mean that we must despair in the face of Jameson's postmodern 'structure'; rather we should think in terms of both 'agency' and 'structure' – which ultimately is always a question of 'articulation' (Hall, 1996; Storey, 1999). Collins provides this example of different strategies of articulation:

The Christian Broadcasting Network and Nickelodeon both broadcast series from the late fifties and early sixties, but whereas the former presents these series as a model for family entertainment the way it used to be, the latter offers them as fun for the contemporary family, 'camped up' with parodic voice-overs, super-graphics, reediting designed to deride their quaint vision of American family life, which we all know never really existed even 'back then'.

(Collins, 1992: 334)

There can be little doubt that similar things are happening in, for example, music, television, advertising, fashion, and in the different lived cultures of everyday life. It is not a sign that there has been a general collapse of the distinctions people make between, say, high culture/low culture, past/present, history/nostalgia, fiction/reality; but it is a sign that such distinctions (first noticed in the 1960s, and gradually more so ever since) are becoming increasingly less important, less obvious, less taken for granted. But this does not of course mean that such distinctions cannot be, and are not being, articulated and mobilized for particular strategies of social distinction. The presence of the sixties in the nineties is the result of many different articulations, and as Mike Myers warns us, we should not take any of these at face value; we must always be alert to the what, why, and for whom something is being articulated, and how it can always be articulated differently, in other contexts.

As I said at the beginning of this chapter, the sixties have made an impressive come-back in the nineties. But if we are to truly understand this comeback, we must not confuse or collapse together the repertoire of texts and practices recycled by the culture industries with what people actually take and make from this repertoire in the lived cultures of everyday life.

## NOTES

1  For an excellent collection of essays on camp see Cleto (1999).
2  In 1999 *Angeles*, a Spanish remake of the original *Charlie's Angels* series, debuted on the Spanish TV channel Telemundo. In the same year *The D.R.E.A.M. Team* premiered in America. Since the rights to the original series were owned by Drew Barrymore (the prime-mover behind the feature film version of *Charlie's Angels*), American television producers had to devise an alternative title. Yet there was no doubting the genealogical origins of *The D.R.E.A.M. Team*, the series being based around the exploits of a glam-orous, all-female squad working under the patronage of an affluent, male supervisor (played, in a telling piece of action series intertextuality, by Roger Moore).
3  Media industry comment on the growing market for 'retro' television can be found in *Broadcasting and Cable* (10 July 1995: 33) and *Newsweek* (12 April 1999: 57).
4  See *Billboard* (8 February 1997: 49).
5  Oasis seem to have made a conscious effort to look like the Beatles, especially as they appear on the covers of *Help* and *Rubber Soul*. Their sound, however, is rather more complex: a circular mix of the Beatles overlayed with the Sex Pistols, and 1990s indie pop as it has sought to sample the music of the 1960s (especially the Beatles). It is, perhaps, also worth noting (and no doubt Jameson would) that whereas Bob Dylan in the 1960s said 'Don't Look Back', Oasis say – in what some would regard as very 1990s postmodern-speak – 'Don't Look Back in Anger'.
6  For a survey of the rise of 'retro' magazines see *Folio: the Magazine for Magazine Manage-ment* (1 January 1997: 36). For commentary on the prominence of 'retro' styling in 1990s popular culture see *The New Republic* (30 January 1995: 11) and Valerie Steele, 'Head to Toe', in *Artforum* (December 1990: 24).
7  Pastiche should not be confused with parody; although both involve imitation and mimicry, parody always has an 'ulterior motive', to mock a divergence from convention or a norm. Pastiche, according to Jameson, is a 'blank parody' or 'empty copy', which has no sense of the very possibility of there being a norm or a convention from which to diverge.
8  In comparison, its immediate predecessor, *Austin Powers: International Man of Mystery*, made less than $10 million in its opening weekend in May 1997. Yet the film was still a major success, yielding $54 million on a budget of $16 million, while its American video release in April 1998 was an instant hit – the film staying in the Video Top 20 for sixty-two consecutive weeks, earning $47 million (Goldstein 1999).
9  For a more detailed discussion of this tradition, see Storey (2001).
10 Mike Featherstone detects a certain nostalgia in Jameson's position: 'he is nostalgically bemoaning the loss of authority of the intellectual aristocracy over the population' (Featherstone, 1991: 9). In similar fashion, John Docker poses the question, 'Is Frederic Jameson the F.R. Leavis of the postmodern world? Is "Postmodernism, or the Cultural Logic of Late Capitalism" yet another rewriting, in the modernist palimpsest, of Mass Civilisation and Minority Culture?' (Docker, 1994: 128).
11 The two Austin Powers films certainly have their predecessors. *SFX Magazine* (Floyd, 1999: 80) lists fourteen films it calls 'true sixties spoof spies': *The Silencers* (1965), *Our Man Flint* (1965), *Dr Goldfoot and the Bikini Machine* (1965), *Murderer's Row* (1966), *Secret Agent Super Dragon* (1966), *Deadlier than the Male* (1966), *Dr Goldfoot and the Girl*

*Bombs* (1966), *The Ambushers* (1967), *In Like Flint* (1965), *Modesty Blaise* (1966), *The Second Best Secret Agent in the Whole Wide World* (1966), *Operation Kid Brother* (1967), *The Wrecking Crew* (1969), and *Some Girls Do* (1971). Xan Brooks, who notes the fact that *Austin Powers: The Spy Who Shagged Me* opens with Powers in bed relaxing watching the spy spoof *In Like Flint* (1967), describes *Austin Powers: The Spy Who Shagged Me* as 'not so much a send-up of James Bond as a send up of the send-ups; a nineties re-branding of a bygone fad' (Brooks 1999: 12), and adds another three spy spoofs to the list: *The Pink Panther* (1963), *Carry On Spying* (1966), *Casino Royale* (1967).

12  We could add that there is also another form of nostalgia in Jameson's argument, a nostalgia for 'real' history, uncontaminated by representations. Unfortunately, as Linda Hutcheon points out, 'there is no directly and naturally accessible past "real" for us today: we can only know – and construct – the past through its traces, its representations ... they are our only means of access to the past. Jameson laments the loss of a sense of his particular definition of history, then, while dismissing as nostalgia the only kind of history we may be able to acknowledge: a contingent and inescapably intertextual history' (Hutcheon, 1997: 39).

13  Jameson's argument is all about structure; the only sign of agency is his own. His mode of analysis leaves little room for consideration of how other people, from other backgrounds, might appropriate, make sense of, and use in lived cultures of everyday life the cultural texts and practices that he identifies as postmodern (see Storey, 1999). Mike Featherstone is surely correct to suggest that we cannot simply rely on 'the readings of intellectuals. In effect we should focus upon the actual practices and changing power balances of those groups engaged in the production, classification, circulation and consumption of postmodern cultural goods' (1991: 5). Docker notes how 'he [Jameson] tells us that when he was in the Bonaventure he didn't actually see the hotel's residential rooms, but "one understands" that they "are in the worst of taste" (Jameson, 1984: 83). The modern ethnographer ... can understand without seeing. And there also apparently exist absolute standards of aesthetic "taste" which the magisterial modernist ever understands. I love that phrase: "One understands that the rooms are in the worst of taste". Is this Modernist Prim?' (Docker, 1994: 121). With a regret that perhaps goes beyond modernist prim, Jameson (1984: 81) also complains about the failure of the hotel's entrances to compare with 'the sumptuous buildings of yesteryear [which] were wont to stage *your* passage from city street to the older interior' (my italics).

## REFERENCES

Braund, Simon (1999) 'Check Out the Figure Baby', *Empire Movie Magazine*, September.

Brooker, Peter and Brooker, Will (eds) (1997) *Postmodern After-Images*, London: Edward Arnold.

Brooks, Xan (1999) 'Spy Spoofs: Why Austin's Not So Dumb', *The Big Issue*, No. 342, 5-11 July.

Chambers, Iain (1988) *Popular Culture: the Metropolitan Experience*, London: Routledge.

Chaney, David (1994) *The Cultural Turn*, London: Routledge.

Cleto, Fabio (ed.) (1999) *Camp: Queer Aesthetics and the Performing Subject: A Reader*, Edinburgh: Edinburgh University Press.

Collins, Jim (1992) 'Postmodernism and Television', in Robert C. Allen (ed.), *Channels of Discourse: Reassembled*, London: Routledge.

—— (1993) 'Genericity in the Nineties: Eclectic Irony and the New Sincerity', in J. Collins, H. Radner and A. Preacher Collins (eds), *Film Theory Goes to the Movies*, London: Routledge.

Docker, John (1994) *Postmodernism and Popular Culture*, Cambridge: Cambridge University Press.

Duncan, Andrew (1999) 'The Andrew Duncan Interview: Mike Myers', *Radio Times*, 31 July–6 August.

Featherstone, Mike (1991) *Consumer Culture and Postmodernism*, London: Sage.

Floyd, Nigel (1999) 'Shagadelic Sequel', *SFX Magazine*, September.

Goldstein, Patrick (1999) 'Austin's Powering His Way to Forefront', *Los Angeles Times*, 16 June.

Goodwin, Andrew (1991) 'Popular Music and Postmodern Theory', *Cultural Studies*, Vol. 5, No. 2.

Grossberg, Lawrence (1988) *It's a Sin: Essays on Postmodernism, Politics and Culture*, Sydney: Power Publications.

Hall, Stuart (1996) 'On Postmodernism and Articulation', in David Morley and Kuan-Hsing Chen (eds), *Stuart Hall: Critical Dialogues in Cultural Studies*, London: Routledge.

Hebdige, Dick (1998) 'Postmodernism and "The Other Side"', in John Storey (ed.), *Cultural Theory and Popular Culture: A Reader*, Hemel Hempstead: Harvester Wheatsheaf/Prentice Hall.

Hutcheon, Linda (1997) 'Postmodern Film?', in P. Brooker and W. Brooker (eds), *Postmodern After-Images*, London: Edward Arnold.

Huyssen, Andreas (1986) *After the Great Divide: Modernism, Mass Culture and Postmodernism*, London: Macmillan.

Jameson, Frederic (1983) 'Postmodernism and Consumer Society', in Hal Foster (ed.), *Post-Modern Culture*, London: Pluto Press.

—— (1984) 'Postmodernism, or the Cultural Logic of Late Capitalism', in *New Left Review*, No. 146.

—— (1988) 'The Politics of Theory: Ideological Positions in the Postmodernism Debate', in Frederic Jameson, *The Ideologies of Theory Essays, Volume 2*, London: Routledge.

Palmer, Martyn (1999) 'Oooh ... Eye Say', in *Inside Film: Austin Powers: The Spy Who Shagged Me*, blackstar.co.uk.

Sontag, Susan (1966) *Against Interpretation*, New York: Deli.

Storey, John (2001) *Cultural Theory and Popular Culture*, (2nd edn), Harlow: Pearson Education.

—— (1999) *Cultural Consumption and Everyday Life*, London: Edward Arnold.

Turner, Bryan S. (1987) 'A Note on Nostalgia', in *Theory, Culture and Society*, No. 4.

Wilson, Elizabeth (1998) 'Fashion and Postmodernism', in John Storey (ed.), *Cultural Theory and Popular Culture: A Reader*, Hemel Hempstead: Harvester Wheatsheaf/Prentice Hall.

# INDEX